1995

CASES FOR
TECHNICAL AND
PROFESSIONAL WRITING

*to
Bernadine —

Jane Ryan Hewett*

CASES FOR TECHNICAL AND PROFESSIONAL WRITING

Barbara Couture

Department of English
Wayne State University

Jone Rymer Goldstein

School of Business Administration
Wayne State University

LITTLE, BROWN AND COMPANY
Boston   Toronto

Library of Congress Cataloging in Publication Data

Couture, Barbara.
    Cases for technical and professional writing.

    1. Technical writing—Case studies.   2. Communication
of technical information—Case studies.   I. Goldstein,
Jone Rymer.   II. Title.
T11.C685   1984   808'.0666021   84-20150
ISBN 0-316-15830-5

Library of Congress Catalog Card Number 84-20150

ISBN 0-316-15830-5

9 8 7 6 5 4 3 2 1

HAL

Published simultaneously in Canada
by Little, Brown & Company (Canada) Limited

Printed in the United States of America

Case 20, "Cashing in a Bright Idea: The Government Employee Suggestion
Case," and Case 24, "Evaluating a Cost Proposal for EMI Suppression: A
Government Contract Case," © 1985 by Elizabeth L. Malone, Barbara Cou-
ture, and Jone Rymer Goldstein. Used by permission.

Preface

Cases for Technical and Professional Writing bridges the gap between the classroom and the professional world by giving students a realistic arena in which to apply their knowledge and skills in communication. The cases give students problems in real-world communication set in organizational contexts that replicate in detail their technical and professional roles, the audiences who need their writing, and the necessary technical information. Each case traces the problem-solving experiences of an actual professional in a business, industrial, or government setting and has students write reports, memos, letters, and other documents required in the particular situation.

For many years cases have been a proven teaching tool for helping students apply what they have learned in the classroom to practical problems they will face on the job in such fields as business and engineering. Cases help students integrate knowledge acquired in school and apply it under conditions of uncertainty—mirroring real situations in which problems are imperfectly formulated, information is often incomplete, and constraints such as personalities, organizational culture, and politics intrude on textbook solutions.

Cases in communication give students the unique opportunity to participate actively in the whole process of analyzing on-the-job problems in communication, and then of planning, preparing, writing, and editing documents that respond to them. Cases let students test their rhetorical skills without the risks associated with on-the-job reporting (such as losing an account or failing to secure approval for a project). At the same time, they introduce students to the typical kinds of communication problems and contexts they will face on the job, helping them to determine the writing strategies that will be effective and appropriate in different situations.

Cases *can* provide all these advantages for students *if* they are realistic and *if* they focus on problem solving in communication. The cases in this text *are* realistic narratives simulating detailed work situations, often explained in dialogue among people solving the technical and managerial problems. We have researched all the cases care-

15-2, 929

v

fully with the cooperation of many technical professionals in diverse workplaces. The cases *seem* real to technical students because they are derived from *real* situations.

The cases in this text are focused on solving problems in communication; they do not demand additional technical knowledge. They provide details on all the critical elements in a rhetorical situation: the writer's professional role, the audience, the technical and managerial problem, the information, and the communication assignments. But they do not tell students how to proceed. The students themselves must form purposes, analyze audiences, and define, plan, and execute their written assignments. Writing a case assignment from this book, like writing on the job, remains a complex task—a problem of "making meaning" in a particular situation; it is not a classroom exercise in applying rules and cookbook formulas.[1]

The cases in this text are designed to reflect problems and assignments in communication typically faced by entry-level professionals in many technical fields. The assignments are focused on basic, generic issues of communication such as developing purpose and interpreting, selecting, and shaping information for multiple, heterogeneous readers. Most assignments require students to produce memos, letters, and informal reports; empirical research shows that professionals in many, diverse occupations write these documents, together with procedures, far more often than any other type of communication.[2] Each case features one of several professions and technical subjects, some of which may differ from your students' career goals. Instructors teaching hundreds of students with these cases have found, however, that most students enrolled in technical and profes-

---

[1] We describe our criteria for a "holistic" case (the kind of cases in this text) and present our methods for researching and preparing one in "Procedures for Developing a Technical Communication Case," in R. John Brockmann et al., eds., *The Case Method in Technical Communication: Theory and Models* (The Association of Teachers of Technical Writing, 1985), 33–46.

[2] Paul V. Anderson, "Learning about Writing at Work Through Survey Research: Methodology and Findings," *Writing in Non-Academic Settings*, ed. Lee Odell and Dixie Goswami (New York: Guilford Press, 1985); C. Gilbert Storms, "What Business School Graduates Say about the Writing They Do at Work: Implications for the Business Communication Course," *The ABCA Bulletin* 46, 4 (1983), 13–18; and Barbara Couture and Jone Rymer Goldstein, "The Writers' Survey: A Comparative Profile of Writing on the Job," paper delivered at the Conference on College Composition and Communication, New York, March 29–31, 1984.

sional writing classes can profitably write the assignments from any of these.

Teaching with cases in communication offers distinct advantages over other methods of instruction in technical and professional writing. Because our cases provide full information on technical topics in organizational settings for students to write about, instructors need not develop appropriate assignments for students who have insufficient technical knowledge or work experience. Cases also encourage students to compare their analyses of a situation, their strategies for solving the problems in communication, and their written documents. By discussing and reading varied responses to the same case, students readily see that several approaches to one task can be functionally effective (though not all equally successful, of course). Students can learn most by discussing issues from each case both before and after writing their assignments. They also benefit, however, from being assigned some cases for impromptu writing without prior discussion. Furthermore, when students are given some cases for reading and discussion only, they can practice planning solutions to many kinds of problems in communication without doing more assigned writing.

Part One of *Cases for Technical and Professional Writing* is organized to help students systematically confront the whole writing process as they work with cases. In it we present a method for analyzing contexts for writing, including a short model case and sample student responses. We describe procedures that students should consider when analyzing any writing context (whether in cases or on the job), and we suggest topics for discussing the cases.

Part Two contains more than thirty cases arranged roughly by length and complexity. This arrangement does not necessarily reflect the rhetorical or technical difficulty of the cases. Real-world writing problems may be simple in some respects yet complex in others, and they rarely fall into the discrete textbook patterns of organization (such as comparison, description, and narration). Our cases thus are not arranged to represent any progression of skills in handling rhetorical or technical information, or to emphasize specific categories of assignments. The "Instructor's Guide to the Cases" (at the back of this book) and the *Instructor's Manual* (available separately) can help you decide on a sequence for assigning the cases to match your instructional objectives.

The responses by teachers and students who have used our cases are the most convincing support for using this text in your classroom. Both experienced and inexperienced instructors (most of whom had never used cases previously) have taught technical and professional communication with the cases in this book. Most used the cases with no guidance from us, and almost all found them a good tool for teaching. In fact, most of the instructors who have tried these cases now have chosen to teach their technical and professional writing courses by the case method. Students also have responded positively to our cases. They find reading cases interesting ("I had to stay up late to finish the case so that I could find out what happened!"); and they find analyzing cases and sharing their views with their peers stimulating. Cases can make learning about rhetorical principles and strategies both relevant and challenging because, as one of our students wrote, cases give you a "real feeling of what it will be like when you are out on the job and you have to write a report."

We hope your experiences will be as professionally satisfying as ours and those of our colleagues when you introduce *Cases for Technical and Professional Writing* to your students.

In closing, we wish to acknowledge the numerous professionals, scholars, relatives, and friends who helped us with this project. We thank all the professionals in business, industry, government, and non-profit organizations who helped us prepare cases—both the persons listed here and all those who must remain anonymous; the instructors who tested cases in their classrooms; and our colleagues who critiqued our plans and manuscripts. They are: Richard W. Bailey, Judith A. Bernhardt, Ellen Brengle, Claire Crabtree, Charles J. Dvorak, Richard W. Force, Richard C. Greve, Dean G. Hall, Jayme Hannay, William L. Henning, Constance Jenkins, Delores Kryszak, Mark Legnini, Valdemar R. Losse, Richard Lutes, Elizabeth L. Malone, B. Omega Moore, Edward Morin, Katherine H. Mull, Barbara Nelson, Susan Kehoe Nicholas, Andrew J. Parker, Paul Pica, Marion Prince, Sharon L. Quiroz, Linda Rayle, Roger Rayle, Renee C. Rymer, James Schulte, Ken A. Thompson, Gerald VanDusen, Susan Wells, Rebecca Wyatt, Mary E. Yvon, James P. Zappen, Bette Zawacki, and Gay Zieger.

We give special thanks to those very close to us, Paul M. Couture, Irwin J. Goldstein, and Chester W. Zawacki, who helped us develop cases and who supported us throughout this project.

Many students at Wayne State University and elsewhere wrote case assignments and offered suggestions for revising cases. We thank especially Jennifer A. Harris, Michael Houghton, Kim Stringfield, and John Tursell.

We are grateful, too, for the comments of those who reviewed our manuscript: Virginia A. Book, University of Nebraska; R. John Brockmann, University of Delaware; Donald H. Cunningham, Texas Tech University; Susan G. Feinberg, Illinois Institute of Technology; Mark Haselkorn, Louisiana State University; Deborah Holdstein, Illinois Institute of Technology; John M. Lannon, Southeastern Massachusetts University; Carol S. Lipson, Syracuse University; John H. Mitchell, University of Massachusetts; Philip Rubens, Rensselaer Polytechnic Institute; John Woodcock, Indiana University; and Gene Young, Texas A & M University.

Finally we give warm thanks to Robin Fosheim, Joyce Buchanan, and Brandt and Garth Goldstein, who helped us prepare the manuscript, and to the Little, Brown editorial staff, especially Joseph A. Opiela, Molly Faulkner, and Julia Winston, and to Peggy and Doug Gordon of P. M. Gordon Associates.

Barbara Couture
Jone Rymer Goldstein

Contents

CASES FOR TECHNICAL AND PROFESSIONAL WRITING

Part One

WRITING FROM CASES AND WRITING ON THE JOB

Learning about Technical and Professional Writing from Cases

WHAT IS A CASE FOR TECHNICAL AND PROFESSIONAL WRITING?

A case is a written description of a situation that presents a problem for you to solve. In many college classes students use cases to practice problem solving. In an engineering or business class, you may have used cases that give information about a technical or managerial problem and then ask you to suggest a solution. For example, a case dealing with a computer firm in the "Silicon Valley" presents you with a problem the company faced in the late 1970s: Should we or should we not produce microcomputers for home and business use? To solve this problem, you study information that was available to the various departments in the computer company, make a decision for or against producing microcomputers, and then defend it.

The cases in this book are different. They are designed to give you specific practice in solving writing problems. Each case presents the process of solving a technical/organizational problem, including the solutions, and then asks you to actually produce the necessary memos, reports, and other documents that communicate solutions or other relevant information to those involved.

The cases in this text are based on the real-world work experiences of professionals who wrote documents similar to those the case assignments ask you to produce. Each case presents in narrative form a complete context for writing, assigning you a role as a technical professional who writes and describing both the people for whom you will write and the problems your writing will address. The cases give you all the information you will use for your writing, and much more, in roughly the same ways the actual professionals learned it on the job. Most important, they present you with typical on-the-job writing assignments, tasks that challenge your analytic and verbal skills and engage all stages of your writing process, from analyzing readers and determining purpose to selecting information, drafting, and revising documents.

WHY USE CASES TO LEARN HOW TO WRITE ON THE JOB?

Cases can give you practical experience, without risk, in the kind of writing you will do in real-world settings. Each case simulates a "field experience" in on-the-job communications and, at the same time, lets you play a game, testing your communication skills within realistic constraints but without obliging you to face the same consequences you would in the workplace. Unlike games, the skills you practice in writing from cases are not divorced from reality. Cases help you discover how communication problem solving complements both technical and organizational problem solving.

Cases Give You Field Experience

Cases can bridge the gap between writing in class and writing on the job by offering many of the advantages of working for a particular company in a specific occupation—without the commitment of time and energy required by a part-time job, a co-op assignment, or an internship. Because each case in *Cases for Technical and Professional Writing* represents a real organization, real technical and communication problems, and the actions of real technical professionals, these "histories" can illustrate the complexities of on-the-job communication problems. [1]

Cases incorporate many of the constraints inherent in on-the-job writing that are not present in the classroom: political pressures that influence projects, company policies that dictate what you can write,

---

[1] The cases in this text are based on extensive research in many organizations, but we have changed proper names and other identifiable data to protect both individuals and employers.

or deadlines for reporting that are imposed by managers before you have finished your investigation. Cases give you a sense of what it is like to write in this kind of messy world and allow you to deal with it inductively, like an apprentice, fashioning your own generalizations on the basis of the nitty-gritty details of a particular situation.

Cases also increase your flexibility and readiness to handle new writing tasks. Many students now in technical programs will spend their working future in a variety of firms, positions, and even fields. To prepare yourself for such a diverse future, you should learn how to apply your technical writing skills to any job, not just the career you are planning today. By completing the assignments from several cases, you will gain "field experience" with many types of organizations, in various positions of responsibility, and in a range of technical fields.

However, preparation for career writing requires more than mere exposure to various contexts for writing in the field. You must learn to analyze these contexts and adopt strategies for solving communication problems in work settings. You must learn to play the communication game, by the rules, as a professional does, in whatever job you may take.

Cases Give You Simulation Gaming Experience

Cases are communication "games" in which you "play" the role of a professional whose goal is to respond effectively to a writing assignment. Your "rules" are company policies, managerial decisions, audience attitudes, deadlines, and a host of other constraints that limit and define your communication assignments. You "play the game" by trying out your reporting skills, testing and sharpening them in complicated environments. Cases invite you to develop a "game plan" for your communication, to explore various approaches, and to anticipate strategies for the next "round" of communications which will follow your "move."

The cases in this text present you with roles and rules for communication games to be played in many different professions (for example, forestry, engineering, science, banking) and many kinds of organizations (manufacturing firms, consulting firms, hospitals, government agencies). They also depict a variety of organizational structures that affect communications in these workplaces. Some cases show highly bureaucratic units with extensive procedures for decision making, narrowly defined job roles, and strict reporting systems (defining exactly who can talk to whom). Other cases show loosely structured units with few rules or regulations, loose job descriptions, frequent decision making at low levels, and very informal communication systems (anyone talking to anyone).

Learning to recognize and adapt to different rules of the game is central to your becoming an effective communicator as a professional. But to write successfully on a real job, you need to know more than how to follow the rules; you need to practice using all the information you have in a particular writing situation to solve a communication problem and to create a solution in writing.

Cases Give You Practice Solving Communication Problems

When you read a case, you experience problem solving on the job from the perspective of a single jobholder. The separate pieces of information in a case, therefore, are not "facts" that you can simply organize and put together in writing. Rather, they are "experiences" that you must absorb and interpret for yourself. In each case, you watch a technical professional from the inside—see him or her responding, analyzing, making decisions, acting, and interacting with others. You observe this person solving technical, managerial, or organizational problems—and sometimes solving all of them at once. For instance, you may witness professionals testing how well a product functions so that they can improve its design and compete with similar products produced by other firms, or modifying a manufacturing process so that they can increase its efficiency and reduce product costs, or facilitating departmental cooperation so that they can serve clients more effectively and humanely.

The cases in this book present the solutions to technical and organizational problems as they were known to the actual professionals who solved them. They do not, however, present solutions to communication problems or solve your problem of deciding to whom, what, when, how, and perhaps even whether you should report. In reading a case, you must decide what the experiences you read about mean, what to say, and how to say it. The job of determining a purpose, stating a message, satisfying audiences, conforming to a format, selecting information to communicate, and writing the document—the whole process of inventing a solution for communication problems—is up to you.

The communication problems in cases have no single solutions, only a range of more-or-less effective options, depending a great deal on the circumstances that suggest the best alternatives and depending in part on the individual professional person you are and will become: your style, your personality, your standards, and the image you want to project. All of these factors demand your involvement in the whole communication act, including fashioning a way to present yourself as a technical professional in writing. Your individual solutions to case problems can start you on the path toward integrating the way you write, speak, and act on the job—toward defining yourself as a professional.

HOW DO CASES PREPARE YOU TO WRITE ON THE JOB?

In completing a memo or report as a professional, you must assess your professional and organizational role in a company, unit, or department, determine how that role affects you as a communicator, and decide how you wish your documents to shape the decisions and actions of the people with whom you work. At the same time you must employ technical or managerial expertise to help you use information to support your message and purpose. And, of course, you must use communication skills to analyze audiences, develop a message, and draft a coherent, readable document. Cases help you learn to use these abilities by assigning you a specific professional identity as a communicator in an organization, by giving you a technical/organizational problem-solving role, and by presenting you with realistic on-the-job communication problems to solve.

Cases Assign You a Specific Professional Identity as a Communicator Within an Organization

Each case in this book puts you in the role of a professional in an organization who must communicate to others in the organization or outside of it. You may take on the role, for example, of a mechanical engineer, or a facilities planner, or a registered nurse. In addition to this professional role, the case assigns you a position within an organization; for instance, you may be a central office executive, a department manager, a project leader, or a technical staff member. Both your professional field and your organizational role will affect the stance you must take as a writer.

In assuming a professional and organizational role in a case, you will "interact" with other professionals who are your superiors, your peers, and your subordinates. You will learn how personnel work together—how managers communicate to supervisors, supervisors to staff, and staff to such external personnel as clients and suppliers. You will learn how the writing from your assigned role functions, how various audiences—supervisors, clients, managers, professional staff, consultants—use your documents, and how different organizations have different procedures for communicating in phone calls, in meetings, or in written reports. In short, you will discover how the communication of a professional depends upon the organizational context, and you will experience a greater variety of these contexts than you could through most other writing experiences.

Cases Put You in a Technical/Organizational Problem-Solving Role

Professionals in all work settings must integrate communication with their technical and organizational problem solving. Through studying cases, you will discover how to plan communications to various audiences to reveal relevant aspects of the technical or organizational problem-solving process. You will discover that the road to solving such problems is not always straight or paved. Professionals often discover the best way to solve a problem *while* trying to solve it. They may take wrong turns and sometimes pursue an investigation which leads to a dead end. Sometimes they expect to use information from sources that never come through, and they have to reach solutions using the information that is available. You will discern how this process of investigation influences report writing and discover for yourself the importance of integrating it into an efficient and effective whole with your process of solving communication problems.

Cases Present You with a Variety of Typical Communication Problems

In writing the assignments from cases, you will experience the difficulties and successes professionals experience in writing typical communications. You will meet deadlines that come up before you are ready to write a report; cope with missing data, contradictory data, or overwhelming amounts of data. You will translate into writing information received orally from other professionals and respond to real-world memos, reports, and letters reproduced in the case. Some of these documents may be reliable, clear, and efficient and some may be fuzzy, contradictory, or lacking in needed information. You will practice writing typical organizational documents—reports, memos, procedures, proposals—and handle a variety of communication assignments. Some may be straightforward and allow you a lot of latitude. Others may be very particular and demand a specific format, length, and purpose. Still others may be vague and not even indicate whether you should write a report or hold a meeting to solve the communication problem. In short, when you assume the role of the professional who is the main problem solver in each of these cases, you will prepare yourself while you are a student to respond to realistic conditions surrounding communications in the world of work.

2

Reading a Sample Case— The Blood Bank Reagent Case

This chapter presents a short sample case which concludes with an assignment to write a report. The Blood Bank Reagent Case describes a simple technical problem, but you may find the technical material to be unfamiliar to you. As in all of the cases in this book, everything that you need to know to handle the technical material is explained in the case itself. Most students can write the assigned report in less than an hour. Nevertheless, the case raises some fairly complex communication problems frequently encountered by technical professionals. Read it carefully. We will use it in the remaining introductory chapters to illustrate guidelines for analyzing communication problems, particularly as those problems are presented in cases.

THE BLOOD BANK REAGENT CASE

You are a technician in the Serological Testing Laboratory of A–1 Hospital Products, Inc., a serological and immunological products manufacturer supplying hospitals and blood banks. Today Marilyn Katkin, your supervisor, calls you in because she has just received a call from Henry Bailey, the supervisor of the Lectin[1] Group in R&D. It seems that John Borg, a young researcher in the group who is fairly new with the firm, has made a big discovery about which Bailey is

---

[1] A lectin is a carbohydrate-binding protein.

very excited—so excited that he has already told the director of R&D, Bob Cranston, about it. Borg has isolated a new lectin from the avocado pit that shows an unusual specificity for type Lewis b red blood cells.[2] Bailey, of course, wants someone in your lab to drop everything and begin testing the avocado lectin against a full panel of human red blood cells.

"If Borg is right," Katkin says, "if the avocado lectin does specifically agglutinate[3] Lewis b cells, he will have hit the big money. It would mean an invaluable new blood bank reagent for routine testing of blood group types. It'd be available in large volume, so it would be much cheaper than the current reagents—either the one they get from human sera or the one obtained by immunizing animals. So, just in case," she concludes, "you'd better get to this testing right away."

Remembering Borg's previous rush job which came to nothing, you begin to open your mouth to protest, but Katkin interrupts. "Look," she says, "Bob Cranston and the folks upstairs would be very happy if this works. They sure wouldn't like to hear we held it up. So despite my doubts, and despite all we have to finish up this week on the Patman Project, you will have to test the lectin immediately."

So you put aside your Patman work and get busy testing the avocado lectin for its blood typing specificity, using standard procedures throughout the study. You dilute the lectin to an initial concentration of 1 mg/ml in pH 7.3 PBS.[4] You line up donors of blood groups O, A_1, and A_2 of each Lewis phenotype[5] and collect their blood into saline containing acid-citrate dextrose (an anticoagulant). Then you treat the red cells with ficin (an enzyme from the fig)[6] by incubating 0.1 ml of washed, packed red cells with 0.1 ml of 0.1% ficin in pH 7.3 PBS for 15 minutes at 37°C. Then you wash the cells three times in saline. For the titration experiments, you add the red cells to various dilutions of the lectin in pH 7.3 PBS. You test for agglutination by incubating two volumes of lectin with one volume of 5% red cells in pH 7.3 PBS for 30 minutes at room temperature. You centrifuge the samples at

---

[2] Written nomenclature for Lewis b is Le(a−b+). The Lewis factor is a biological marker carried on human red blood cells. It has no known function.

[3] Agglutinate means to clump or stick together.

[4] PBS is phosphate-buffered saline.

[5] There are three phenotypes: Lewis b, Lewis a, and Lewis null. Conventional written nomenclature is, respectively, Le(a−b+), Le(a+b−), and Le(a−b−).

[6] Treatment with ficin increases the sensitivity of the agglutination test.

1,000 × g for 15 seconds and examine the cells macroscopically[7] for agglutination.

Finally you tally up the titration values[8] for the avocado lectin against the O, A_1, and A_2 blood types (Table 1). Ah, you think to yourself. Those are very interesting numbers: The titration values are exactly the same for all Lewis phenotypes within each blood group! Specificity for Lewis b? These results certainly don't confirm that idea. Of course you *do* note the small differences among the titration values for the blood groups (32, 8, 16). But these differences are too small to be significant in any way, and they certainly have nothing to do with specificity for Lewis b. Though the avocado lectin may be of academic interest, it certainly does not look like it will be of any use as a blood bank reagent. Upon reflection you begin to wonder about Borg's own testing and what his results looked like.

Taking the figures with you, you walk down to Katkin's office to report your findings. She shakes her head as she looks over the results, saying, "Of course, this is only one set of experiments, but it sure doesn't look good, does it. I wish Bailey would review Borg's work a

TABLE 1.   Titration Values for the Avocado Lectin

O	Le(a−b+)	32
O	Le(a+b−)	32
O	Le(a−b−)	32
A_1	Le(a−b+)	8
A_1	Le(a+b−)	8
A_1	Le(a−b−)	8
A_2	Le(a−b+)	16
A_2	Le(a+b−)	16
A_2	Le(a−b−)	16

---

[7] To examine macroscopically means to examine visually.

[8] The titration value is the reciprocal of the highest dilution at which agglutination still occurs. (The "reciprocal" of ⅛ is 8, for example.) The higher the titration value, the greater the reactivity of the lectin toward the cells. Although there are slight differences in reactivity among the blood groups (32, 8, 16), they are too insignificant to mean anything. In any case, the only values of interest here are differences among the phenotypes of a blood group, for example, between O Le(a−b+) and O Le(a+b−).

little more closely before he asks us to jump. Write up these results immediately. Bailey is eager for the good news, and we mustn't keep him waiting."

"Right," you answer, "and then I'll get back to the Patman Project."

ASSIGNMENT
Write a report to Henry Bailey, Supervisor, Lectin Research, R&D. The report is from Marilyn Katkin, Supervisor, Serological Testing Laboratory, and you should be designated as the writer.[9]

---

[9] Although you must write for your supervisor's signature, you will be recognized as the writer and are expected to speak from your own position. Katkin's signature is really a sign-off system by which everything going out of your department must gain her approval.

3

Exploring Contexts for Writing in Cases and on the Job

The Blood Bank Reagent Case presents a full communication context containing variables that affect the whole process of report writing. The case defines a role for you as a technical professional who must write on the job. It describes technical and organizational problems and explains how your solutions will affect personnel within your organization. The case develops communication problems with situational factors that will, in turn, influence how you design your assigned report. All these elements—a professional role, technical/organizational problems, communication problems, and a writing assignment—work together to define a context for your report. You cannot consider any one of them in isolation when studying a case. Your definition of your role, for example, will influence your analysis of the communication problems and vice versa. In fact, when you read and analyze a case for yourself, you will frequently refine and redefine your views of the whole as you develop your perspective on individual aspects of the context.

This chapter focuses on the four perspectives named above and presents guidelines for analyzing writing contexts both on the job and as they are presented in cases. You can use these guidelines for exploring writing contexts as a supplement to your basic technical communications text and the advice of your instructor. The guidelines provide suggestions for working with cases and explain how writing from these contexts differs from actual writing on the job. Sample analyses of the Blood Bank Reagent Case are offered throughout.

DEFINING YOUR ROLE AS TECHNICAL PROFESSIONAL AND WRITER

All writing on the job requires that you understand the relationships among your tasks as a professional in a technical or managerial field, as an employee in an organization, and as a writer of professional communications. To integrate all these tasks successfully when writing in each new situation, you must define your role, develop an individual perspective, and finally clarify the authority under which you should communicate.

Assess Your Role as Technical Professional and Writer

Your role as a technical professional who writes on the job is defined in many ways: by your profession, by your position in an organization, by your responsibilities in your job, and by your working relationships with co-workers, supervisors, managers, and representatives of external organizations (for example, suppliers or government agents).

A case assigns you just such a complex role. To be fully prepared to address communication problems in the case, you must step into the role of the professional whose story the case tells, viewing that person's problem solving as it relates to subsequent communication. Analyzing the roles you assume in cases can help you prepare for your future as a professional and writer in actual organizations.

As you explore the actions of the professionals whose roles you assume in different cases, you will discover that these people receive some information that you are left to sift through and figure out for yourself and some information that they have already screened extensively. Often they have responded to events selectively, determining what they saw as significant, interpreting and analyzing the details according to their knowledge and experience. These observations limit your perspective, but they also allow you to share in the technical expertise of professionals in fields which you may know little about.

By assuming the role of a technical professional, you get to know other persons in the organization, finding out about their working relationships and political alliances, discovering how their organization works and what its many expectations are for you. You accomplish all this by reading carefully and by using your imagination, filling in the whole context from your brief glimpses of it in your assumed role. If you see a supervisor act in a penny-pinching way when purchasing a piece of equipment, you can conclude that doing things cheaply is a top priority with this person. If a manager compliments you on the brevity of your report, you can conclude that this person's reporting standards include conciseness. In your assigned role, you should draw conclusions from persons' actions within the case and include them in your analysis of the writing assignments.

ANALYZING YOUR ASSIGNED ROLE IN THE BLOOD BANK
REAGENT CASE

In the Blood Bank Reagent Case you must assume the role of a technician in a chemistry laboratory which does service testing for other units in a high-tech manufacturing firm with a large Research and Development (R&D) component. Technical assignments come to you through your supervisor, Marilyn Katkin, the chief of the Serological Testing Laboratory, who also approves the reports you write after you conduct your tests. In this instance, you've been asked to perform tests on the avocado lectin.

The technician whose role you assume in this case gives you a narrow "window" on the world of A-1 Hospital Products, Inc., one based on "your" past experience with assignments to test the results of John Borg's research in the Lectin Group of R&D. You learn in this role that Borg has cried "wolf" before, interrupting other projects for something that comes to nothing. In short, you are asked to live this experience at the A-1 lab, sharing something of the technician's judgment of the Lectin Group, and inferring from Katkin's negative remarks about Bailey how your boss views the whole situation and the information you must communicate.

Develop Your Perspective on the Situation

In approaching any writing assignment, you must develop your own perspective and decide how to interpret the information in the particular context. All your own life and work experiences, as well as your perceptions of your potential readers, will affect how you choose to interpret the case events. Although a case assigns you a well-defined role, you still have the opportunity to synthesize all that you know, both from the case itself and from your own experience, and to decide what it means for you and your audiences. In fact, this is part of your responsibility to your readers: to try to discover new answers and to create a communication that will bring your audience to a fresh understanding of the problem and possible solutions to it.

Closely connected with developing your perspective on the "meaning" of the case events is your choice of how you want to represent yourself in your written response. Your values, beliefs, and ideas about yourself as a technical professional should influence your decision, as well as your professional role in the case, your assessment of the information's meaning in this context, your relationship with the audiences, and your responsibilities in the organization. Taking all of this into account will help you make choices for selecting, arranging, and presenting information in ways appropriate to your professional role.

ASSUMING YOUR PERSPECTIVE IN THE BLOOD BANK REAGENT CASE ASSIGNMENT

As the technician-writer in the Blood Bank Reagent Case, you have a variety of options in representing yourself in the assigned report. For instance, you may wish to sound scrupulously scientific: objective and impersonal. You might select this approach if you interpret the lectin testing as highly questionable, a situation in which both Borg's and your work should be reviewed and compared to determine why the results were so different. Using neutral language, you could focus the report on those aspects of the events that raise questions about concluding anything at this point (for example, the single set of tests which you produced in the Serological Testing Laboratory). Or you may wish to sound like a problem solver: direct and to the point. Your aim here is to show clearly that the R&D lectin project does not seem to work. Using evaluative terms, you could focus the report on the negative results and your conclusion that the avocado lectin cannot differentiate Lewis b blood cells.

Clarify Whom You Represent

A critical aspect of writing on the job is determining what level of authority you should assume in communicating. Some on-the-job writing (and a few cases in this text) present instances where you must respond to a problem by writing a document on your own initiative, speaking only for yourself (or perhaps for some group of subordinates). In more typical situations (depicted by most of the cases in this book), a supervisor assigns you a communication task and later forwards your document to its audiences. Here you, as the professional in the case, speak for a whole unit or department, and you must represent your views, the unit's views, and frequently those of your supervisor as well. For still other assigned tasks, you must secure approval for your writing, usually from a superior who will "sign off" the document. You may also write documents for the signature of another person, typically a supervisor or manager, and in those instances assume the authority and perspective of the higher position.[1]

The cases in this book present many different writers' roles; in each instance you should define what authority is delegated to you. Are you supposed to assume your supervisor's authority, represent a group, or simply speak for yourself—but with your supervisor listening in? After determining the appropriate stance, check how the case assignment tells you to designate the preparers and senders of the communication.

IDENTIFYING WHOM YOU REPRESENT IN THE BLOOD BANK REAGENT CASE ASSIGNMENT

In preparing the assigned report in the Blood Bank Reagent Case, you are expected to write for Katkin's signature. However, the conventions of this organization dictate that your name appear after "Writer" or "Written by," so that all readers will know that you, and not Marilyn Katkin, have written the report. Although you

---

[1] When you speak for a whole unit or department, your supervisor's name might be listed on the "From" line of your report, with your name listed under "Prepared by." Under an approval system, you as the actual writer might be designated on the "From" line, with the supervisor appearing on an "Approved by" line. Your name may not appear at all on documents where you assume the authority of someone above you.

may use the pronoun "we," and speak with some of the authority lent by Katkin's signature, you are expected to write from your own position, not from your supervisor's. In effect, you cannot speak *for* her.

Katkin figures prominently in what you will say, however, because she must sign the report, an indication that she approves it as representing her unit and herself. Thus, in constructing the document, you must not only take into account how you perceive the situation—what you want to say and how you want to say it— but how your supervisor judges it and what she would like your communication to accomplish.

EXAMINING THE TECHNICAL/ORGANIZATIONAL INFORMATION

On the job, you will be expected to solve both technical and organizational problems; sometimes you may even have the opportunity to carry out all the stages of solving these problems—from defining them, to exploring alternative solutions, to selecting, designing, and implementing a solution. In working from cases in this book, you will not solve technical and organizational problems yourself, but rather you will study the problem-solving procedures of the professional whose role you assume in preparing communications.

Study the Technical/Organizational Problems and Their Solutions

The story of the professional's technical/organizational problem solving in the case reflects the way that this person actually went about doing the assigned task. Information comes to you in reading the case much as it came to this worker on the job, often in disorganized bits and pieces. As a result, professionals in some cases may appear to take two steps backward for each step forward. Problem solving frequently happens this way; consequently, to understand it, you should reorganize the information and events that lead to solutions.

To clarify the technical and organizational information in these cases, you should plot the stages of the investigation and the activities of personnel involved, analyzing how each new stage or event refines and redefines the information, even the nature of the problem itself. In plotting a case scenario, you should account for the fact that some data may be filtered by co-workers presenting it to you, and some may be screened and analyzed by the professional whose role you have adopted. (If you require further explanations, additional information is presented in footnotes.) After analyzing the problem solving carefully, you can be confident that you are prepared to present accurate, precise information to your audiences.

PLOTTING THE PROBLEM SOLVING IN THE BLOOD BANK REAGENT CASE

The organizational problem in the Blood Bank Reagent Case provides the framework for your technical problem. The mission of A–1 Hospital Products is to manufacture high-tech medical products. The Lectin Group's work with the avocado lectin affects the organizational problem of trying to develop a new product for blood banks. The technical problem in the Blood Bank Reagent Case is not difficult for "you" in the role of lab technician, of course, but it may seem somewhat complex to you, the student in a technical/professional writing class—especially if you do not have a strong background in chemistry. In fact, however, the problem is fairly simple, and the case explains it quite thoroughly.

What is the technical problem? You, as the technician, must test to see if the avocado lectin will pick out, or identify, one Lewis phenotype against another among the three phenotypes in the same blood group. Your technical results reveal that the lectin does *not* identify one Lewis phenotype over another. Within each blood group tested (O, A_1, and A_2) it "clumps" all the Lewis phenotypes equally. You evaluate the significance of these results, concluding that though the lectin might be of some scholarly interest, it appears to have no potential as a blood bank reagent. Hence, the Lectin Group has not solved A–1's larger organizational problem of developing a new product. Furthermore, this group's strained relationship with your department threatens to affect how both units will cooperate to develop and test new products in the future.

ANALYZING THE COMMUNICATION PROBLEMS

To write effectively on the job, you should identify the most significant components of the context and determine how these factors should shape your documents. Exploring the communication problems includes selecting the appropriate mode for the situation, analyzing the audience's needs, and developing your purposes.

Select Written and/or Oral Modes

Although a primary decision often faced on the job is whether to communicate at all, typically in the technical writing classroom you will have to respond through language. Another choice is whether to report orally, in writing, or in a combination of the two. Many professional communications are handled by telephone, in discussions, or through oral presentations. Sometimes speaking suffices, but more frequently it is accompanied by writing that complements the oral communication in very specific ways (for example, by documenting a discussion or elaborating a briefing). Often, of course, writing stands alone, to be read by others when the author is not present to amplify points or to answer questions.

Many cases in this text represent communication problems that might best be solved by a combination of speech and writing. Sometimes the listed assignments reflect these options; other times they do not. The variety of options to speak and write in this text reflects the ways assignments are given in the real world. You can learn to produce more effective communications in your future job by experiencing, through cases, the ways spoken and written communications typically function.

PLANNING HOW TO COMMUNICATE IN THE BLOOD BANK REAGENT CASE ASSIGNMENT

The assignment in the Blood Bank Reagent Case asks you simply to write up your results. However, your "results" will not cover all the issues raised in the case. Many of these issues might be handled better orally than in writing. You might feel, for example, that the wisest solution to improving working relations with the Lectin Group would be for Katkin and Bailey to discuss privately

R&D's frequent interruptions of your lab's work. You also might believe that the comparison of discrepant results could be explored better in a group discussion than in your written report. Such potential solutions can be raised in class discussions, possibly resulting in suggestions for a modified assignment, combining both writing and oral communication.

Analyze Your Audience Needs and Expectations

All writers and speakers—whether they be novelists, newspaper reporters, politicians, financial managers, or engineers—must consider their audiences. For writers of professional communications, identifying and analyzing all readers can be a very complex task, particularly because a single document in the workplace is often addressed to many audiences both inside and outside the organization. Furthermore, such writing may serve a variety of purposes. In analyzing readers or listeners, therefore, you should consider multiple factors. Perhaps the most significant issue is each reader's specific need for the communication. Other important points are audience expectations for the document, how they will read and use it, and the kind of action they will take as a result of receiving the writing. Furthermore, you should consider audience roles, responsibilities, and interactions with you and with one another, as well as the education and background of the members of the audience, their understanding and working familiarity with the problems addressed in your communication, their attitudes toward your unit and personnel, and their vested interests in any aspect of your topic or solution. Your analysis of these factors should guide your determination of both what to say and how to say it.

ANALYZING AUDIENCE NEEDS FOR THE BLOOD BANK REAGENT CASE ASSIGNMENT

For the Blood Bank Reagent Case assignment there are, as far as you know, four people who constitute the audience: your supervisor, Marilyn Katkin (whom you must also represent); the head of the Lectin Group who requested the test, Henry Bailey; the researcher who discovered the specificity of avocado lectin for Lewis b red blood cells, John Borg; and the supervisor of the R&D Department who hopes for the lectin's development as a blood bank reagent, Bob Cranston. Your supervisor and the supervisor of the

Lectin Group, of course, will both be interested in your solution to the technical problem of whether or not avocado lectin demonstrates specificity for Lewis b cells. However, Katkin and Bailey will each have a different sense of the organizational problem which needs resolution. Katkin is concerned that your negative results be made clear to everyone, but she is also interested in the pattern of the Lectin Group's behavior—hastily jumping to conclusions and unnecessarily demanding rush service from your department. The supervisor of the Lectin Group, on the other hand, hopes to see that your results prove that the avocado lectin specifically agglutinates Lewis b so he can signal the beginning of a new project and eventually a new product. Of course, John Borg will be eager to know if his idea works, exactly what your results were, and how you got them. And the manager of the R&D department will be concerned about the possible development of a new product, the deployment of personnel and resources, and incidentally the effectiveness of his research staff. In this case, as in all professional writing situations, you must question how known and potential readers' involvement in the various problems you are addressing should influence your writing.

Develop Your Purpose

Essential to producing effective professional communication is a clear definition of your multiple purposes before you begin to write. Though your ideas may change substantially during planning, drafting, and even revising, predetermined purposes can help guide your decisions throughout the writing process. Using your perspective on the situation, your analysis of your readers' needs, and your own goals for your writing, you should determine all the purposes for writing which reflect what you hope to achieve by communicating to others.

DETERMINING YOUR PURPOSE IN THE BLOOD BANK REAGENT CASE ASSIGNMENT

You as the professional in the Blood Bank Reagent Case are assigned by your supervisor to report the results of your testing, which should answer the question about the lectin's specificity for Lewis b cells. That is your "official" purpose for writing. This official purpose and others that the communication situation suggests to you will guide your strategy for writing. Is your aim to report the results directly with minimal elaboration, so that management can act quickly to ensure that no more time is wasted on this lectin project? To provide all the details of your investigation, so that you and others can get to the bottom of these discrepant results? To emphasize the negative results and embarrass the Lectin Group with their sloppy science, so that they won't bother the Serological Lab (and Marilyn Katkin) with their ill-conceived projects again? All of these purposes, and still others, of course, are possible. Determining what stance is appropriate for you depends on what you—the writer—bring to the assignment, as well as your responsibilities to the various members of your audience.

DESIGNING THE ASSIGNED COMMUNICATION

After you have selected your mode of communication (oral or written), analyzed your audience, and determined your purposes, you are ready to design your communication. To design a response to an assignment on the job or from a case, you must assess the constraints on your response, choose a format, select and interpret information, plan for any graphic displays, and, finally, organize the whole.

Assess the Constraints on Your Response

Frequently, communication assignments in the workplace come with constraints for planning and shaping a response. Sometimes a supervisor or perhaps a committee will dictate your purpose very explicitly, analyze an audience member at great length, and even determine the language you should use by prescribing specific word choices that they think will best convince a reader. Sometimes a government agency will dictate selection, order, and length of a document. Obviously, you must observe these requirements very carefully in your writing.

On the other hand, sometimes no one will give you explicit direction for assessing a situation or planning a document. Nevertheless, other factors will influence what you say—budgets, available personnel, retrieval systems, production technology, schedules, and a host of other concerns. You must observe these constraints as well.

The case-writing assignments come ready-made with a variety of constraints for planning and shaping documents. Some cases leave much of the decision making up to you; in fact, they may give you almost no guidance. Other case assignments require you to follow your supervisor's dictates, the suggestions of some manager, or the written procedures or criteria established by some agency. Still others ask you to meet deadlines—often before you have all the necessary results. Such tasks reflect typical real-world assignments, many of which occur under less than ideal conditions.

MEETING THE CONSTRAINTS OF THE BLOOD BANK REAGENT CASE ASSIGNMENT

The Blood Bank Reagent Case requires you to report your results in writing for your supervisor's approval, and it requires that you do so immediately. Beyond those constraints, it leaves most choices up to you. Your supervisor does not tell you how to handle the fact that your experiment concluded in negative results—results unexpected by your primary audience. She does, however, suggest how she feels about it. You must then make many choices about what to say, not least of which is whether or not to include any reference to the Lectin Group's now familiar "emergency" projects that interrupt the Serological Lab's work.

Choose a Format

The organization employing you or the one receiving your writing often will dictate the format of your communications; many of these cases do the same. Some assignments define the kind of document, perhaps even furnishing a report form to use in completing the task. Other assignments are open-ended, however, just as they would be on the job. It is up to you to design the most effective format for your readers, while accounting for any special requirements presented in the case. When you are employed, you will learn much about formats for your reports from previous communications written by peers, subordinates, and superiors in your organization. Your employer may even provide a style sheet to guide your reporting. In writing from these cases, however, you do not have a variety of previous documents from the same organization or a company style sheet to work from. When specific guidelines are not given in the case, consider formats provided by your instructor and basic writing texts for technical professionals.

DEFINING THE FORMAT FOR THE BLOOD BANK REAGENT CASE ASSIGNMENT

In the Blood Bank Reagent Case you are asked to write a "report." Conventions in business and industry suggest that you would write this document in *memo* format, but the case does not tell you that, nor does it tell you how to set up such a "memo report." You are left to apply general principles and conventions to this specific context. In short, your goal in planning formats for this case or any other should be to practice applying your knowledge of technical/professional writing conventions in a variety of different contexts. Once on the job, your experience with cases should help you to adapt to format specifications easily and to provide your own formats when necessary.

Select and Interpret the Technical/Organizational Information

In the process of solving problems on the job, you will gather a lot of information, much of which will never appear in any documents you write about your investigations. Furthermore, you will learn much about people, things, and events which you must first interpret for yourself and then present to someone else. Cases, in representing real-world investigations, reveal large amounts of information about problems and their solutions, the people working on these problems, and the organizations that employ them. As in real situations, the meaning of all this information is not all *there* in the case, ready and waiting for you to pick up and insert into your documents. Rather you must create your message from this information, shape an argument, and develop effective supporting reasons by carefully selecting and interpreting the relevant information for your particular readers.

Because a case contains so much detail, you may feel that the documents you write should also be detailed, covering all or much of the case information. You should remember, however, that a case attempts to represent the real world, where some information is pertinent to your problem, some is necessary for you to understand the situation, and some is peripheral or even irrelevant. Your job is to determine what is significant to analyzing the situation at hand, and then—just as in writing on the job—to select carefully only the relevant, necessary details to support your message. At the same time you must take care that you do not overlook information or record it inaccurately. What you hear a supervisor say about a problem in a case, for instance, may not be the whole story. Make sure you have studied all data presented about an issue in a case before you draw conclusions. Once you have analyzed everything, stick to what you know; that is, do not fabricate information that is not in the case itself. As in completing an on-the-job assignment, you must deal with the situation as it exists; you cannot pretend things happened differently, however convenient that might be for composing an elegant document.

SELECTING INFORMATION FOR THE BLOOD BANK REAGENT CASE ASSIGNMENT

The Blood Bank Reagent Case presents several significant options for selecting supporting detail. Almost certainly, you will choose to include the test results, since reporting your findings is your assigned communication task. Whether you choose to include your test procedures, however, is a matter of your reader analysis and your own objectives. If you decide, for example, that your readers are primarily interested in the "bottom line" (that the lectin does not identify Lewis b), you may wish to refer to the procedures as "standard," expecting readers to contact you if they wish to check on any details. If you decide that your readers should carefully examine the discrepancy between your and Borg's results, however, you may wish to include the procedures in full in your report (probably as an attachment). Just as in the real world, your writing job here involves selecting what is relevant for your purposes from a mass of information. As in the real world, your writing will deal with events as they actually happened, not as you may have wished them to happen.

Plan for Graphic and Tabular Presentation

As in selecting and organizing information, your audience analysis and the message of your writing should guide your decision to present information in graphs or in tables. When preparing assignments from cases, decisions to include and design graphics take on a slightly different character from the decisions you make when you are writing in response to actual situations. Some information in cases is already arrayed in graphic and tabular form. Seeing information already arranged in charts, tables, and lists may tempt you to simply reproduce these aids in your documents. This could be a mistake. The cases usually arrange information graphically only when that is how professionals first encountered or recorded the information for themselves. These displays, therefore, do not necessarily show the most effective way to present the data for others. In most instances, rather than reproducing the case graphics or tables in your documents, you should design truly "visual" displays and tables specifically supporting your message for your readers.

DESIGNING A TABLE FOR THE BLOOD BANK REAGENT CASE ASSIGNMENT

The Blood Bank Reagent Case contains a table showing the titration results of "your" experiment testing the avocado lectin's specificity for Lewis b. Although this table could be improved, it adequately displays the differences for the target audiences of your report. Thus you might choose to duplicate it in your own writing rather than designing a new table. Unlike most cases in this text, the Blood Bank Reagent Case does not demand that you design graphs and tables as part of your writing task.

Organize the Document

When addressing technical/organizational problems in writing, you should reorganize your experience in solving these problems so that you focus on your message and your readers' needs. In writing on the job, technical professionals sometimes make the mistake of retelling the history of their own problem solving instead of rearranging information to meet audience needs. Reports that retell problem solving force the readers to wait until the very end to find out the answers, just as the technical professional had to wait for the results until the end of the investigation. This same narrative trap can easily ensnare student writers working from cases as well.

In writing from cases, remember, you are working from a written narrative of a problem-solving event. Because this is so, you may be tempted to repeat the narrative pattern of the case when you write an assignment in response to it, and even to copy passages directly from the case and to incorporate them in your documents. Repeating the case chronology of problem solving in your reports will rarely be an effective arrangement of the information (unless the assignment demands a step-by-step narrative of what happened). Repeating the case language[2] is even less likely to be an effective way to write your assignments because this language usually reflects professionals' casual conversations and their thinking aloud. Hence, neither the organization nor the language of a case will usually be appropriate for the readers of your documents. Instead you should organize the information and select your language according to your readers' needs, your purposes, and your message.

ORGANIZING INFORMATION FOR THE BLOOD BANK REAGENT CASE ASSIGNMENT

In the Blood Bank Reagent Case, as in most on-the-job writing, the message you choose to communicate and your analysis of the audience will strongly influence your organization of the report. If you decide to emphasize the test results and the negative conclusions for the company, you might begin with the overall point that the lectin does not agglutinate Lewis b cells. Following this "bottom line first," you could present the supporting data from your tests. Any details of your investigation would appear in final paragraphs or perhaps in an attachment. On the other hand, if you decide to emphasize the procedures so that audiences could examine how you got the negative results, you might follow a traditional laboratory report structure which would place the results and conclusions last.

---

[2] Even the professional documents reproduced in the cases may not best express the ideas that you need to communicate. Though typical of many of the communications you will see on the job, they are not *models* to be imitated.

A CHECKLIST FOR EXPLORING THE CONTEXT

This chapter has provided some guidelines for exploring the context for professional communications; these guidelines supplement the information that you will find in your basic technical/professional communications text and receive from your teacher. Just as in writing on the job, writing from cases focuses on applying sound communication principles and problem-solving skills to specific contexts. As we have shown, cases demand exploring your writing situation fully, analyzing all relevant detail, and planning documents according to design principles and strategies pertinent to the context.

The checklist below reviews activities you should undertake in exploring the context for writing assignments on the job and from cases. Remember that these activities need not be done sequentially; in fact, you may find yourself going back and repeating many procedures as you prepare to write. In addition, you should also consult your instructor and your basic text for principles of effective written reporting.

WRITER'S CHECKLIST

DEFINING YOUR ROLE OF TECHNICAL PROFESSIONAL AS WRITER

_____ Assess your role of technical professional as writer.

_____ Develop your perspective on the situation.

_____ Clarify whom you represent.

EXAMINING THE TECHNICAL/ORGANIZATIONAL INFORMATION

_____ Study the technical/organizational problems and their solutions.

ANALYZING THE COMMUNICATION PROBLEMS

_____ Select written and/or oral modes.

_____ Analyze your audience needs and expectations.

_____ Develop your purpose.

DESIGNING THE ASSIGNED COMMUNICATION

_____ Assess the constraints on your response.

_____ Choose a format.

_____ Select and interpret the technical/organizational information.

_____ Plan for graphic and tabular presentation.

_____ Organize the document.

4

Evaluating Written Communications

DERIVING CRITERIA FOR EVALUATING WRITING

The criteria for evaluating any writing ultimately derive from the context. Who is the writer? What does the writer want to accomplish? How does the writer regard the subject? Who are the readers? Why are they reading this writing? What attitudes do they have toward the subject? How will they use it now? In the future?

Your standards for effective on-the-job writing will come from answers to questions like these, specifically oriented to the situation at hand. When you have fully analyzed the context which surrounds a writing task, you are prepared to ask the major question which tests the success of your written response: Does the writing fulfill your intended purposes? If it does, it is effective. If it does not, it fails.

Determining whether your writing accomplishes its purpose may not always be easy. This chapter will help you understand how readers evaluate writing and help you evaluate your own writing. The next few pages discuss problems of getting feedback from others, deriving clear standards for effective writing, improving your writing assessment abilities, and comparing your writing to that of others. The chapter concludes with evaluations of four written responses to the Blood Bank Reagent Case assignment.

Seek Feedback, but Know Its Limitations

Feedback on your writing from others at work can be very helpful; good writers seek feedback from many readers. However, what others tell you about your writing may not always help you to improve it to achieve *your* purposes. Your supervisor may tell you that your report was first-rate because *his* boss approved it. With that evidence, you could conclude that your writing is effective. But approval does not give you specific feedback about your writing, and one boss's view tells you nothing about the other people who received your report. Perhaps Jane Smith in the next department did not like the report at all because it ignored her interests. If Smith says nothing, you may never realize that your writing did not answer her questions or solve her specific problem.

Not only may you lack helpful feedback on your writing at work, but you may also find few opportunities to test different versions of a document to see which is the most effective. Unless you design a document for large numbers of users (say a computer manual or an insurance application form), you are not likely to test your writing with a sample group of readers beforehand so that you can evaluate how effectively it accomplishes your purposes with the target audiences.

Evaluating your documents written from cases presents the same problems as assessing documents at work. Although feedback from other readers can be helpful, their reactions may be incomplete or vaguely impressionistic, based on their personal preferences. Although some readers (a few of your peers, your instructor) may judge your writing according to well-established criteria for readability and a thorough analysis of the context, their evaluation still may not match the designated readers' views. This is because the acts of writing and reading are both subjective. Writing is dependent on the individual writer's perspective and self, and reading is dependent on the readers' various views and selves. Since you cannot test most documents with actual readers, you must recognize a possible gap between what your evaluators tell you and the responses of your intended readers.

As in the workplace, you may have limited opportunities in the classroom to test the effectiveness of a document with target readers. Although you may participate in group critiques—a very valuable activity—your peers may not represent your audience well, and they may not be able to identify the critical problems in your texts. Without complete feedback, then, how can you be reasonably sure that your writing will accomplish your intentions? The best way to evaluate your own writing is to derive criteria for the effectiveness of your communication from the context.

Develop Your Own Standards for Effective Writing

There are several ways you can develop standards for your own writing. After asking yourself questions about all the audiences, their interactions, and the potential implications of a communication, you can read your report or memo quickly, as it would be read on the job, to see if it accomplishes its purpose. Or you can assess it more carefully considering each of the different readers it addresses. If you wish to be even more systematic, you can review the context carefully and then establish a prioritized list of questions to serve as analytical criteria for evaluating your writing.

Such a systematic procedure for evaluation depends on *your* interpretation of the context based on your own experience, knowledge, and sensitivity—and your own ideas about yourself as a professional. Thus there may not be total agreement among you, your peers, and even your instructor on a list of criteria. As writers, we all must choose goals and then see how the strategies we use in our writing achieve those goals—well, less well, or not at all. But we must admit from the start that evaluating on-the-job writing or writing from cases, in fact *any* piece of writing, depends upon the perspectives of the evaluators—upon their views of the writing context and how the communication problem should be solved.

So how can you know before sending out your writing whether it will be effective? You cannot know for sure. But you can improve your chances of succeeding by practicing your skills in analyzing and responding to writing situations and by seeking feedback when you can. The key is first to develop criteria for effectiveness based on your own purposes and projections of your target audience's responses, and then to evaluate how your writing fulfills your goals.

Match Your Writing to Your Purposes and Situational Requirements

As we have said before, the key to writing a document that will function well is your thorough analysis of the communication situation. To assess how well your writing will achieve its purposes, you must examine your document to see if it meets readers' needs, presents relevant information, adapts to special constraints of form, and presents your message clearly. When you write at work, you will often have to make these assessments yourself with no opportunity to compare your response with someone else's. However, when you write from cases in the classroom, your instructor may give you samples of effective responses to a case so that you can see various strategies. You must remember, however, that other writers' responses may not match your own goals and purposes for writing in a given context, so their documents may look quite different from yours. Acknowledging this divergence does not mean that you have license to do whatever you wish in responding to a case or that one response is as good as another; rather, it means that you must look at case solutions in light of the writer's objectives, as well as the overall demands of the case situation. You must not assume that there is only one correct response.

Likewise you may believe that if you could compare your documents with the writing of the real professional on the job, the person whose story the case tells, you could know for certain what is a perfect solution to a case assignment. What the actual professional wrote, however, would not be a good measure for you: first, because the case cannot possibly duplicate all the relevant aspects of the organizational environment; and second, because your experience can only approximate the on-the-job experience of the technical professional who actually lived in the world described by the case. For instance, you cannot know the supervisor in the case as the actual professional did because you do not see this person day after day. More significantly, cases give you minimal exposure to the kinds of writing done and the language used in each organization depicted. Although some cases include sample documents written for the very organizations in which you assume a role, your reading of a few memos or even a report will not give you the experience of the real-world professional who has seen hundreds of this organization's documents and has even written many of them.

Clearly, then, the memos and reports you will write from cases cannot be compared with the actual documents written by the professional on the job. However, the point of writing from cases is not for you to duplicate the documents that actually functioned in the real-world situations presented here. The purpose of working from cases, rather, is to raise issues for you and to help you develop strategies for dealing with communication problems. Judging the effectiveness of sample responses against the case context is a reasonable way to learn about becoming an effective writer of professional communications.

COMPARING DIFFERENT SOLUTIONS TO THE
SAME PROBLEM

In this concluding section we present four student memos written from the Blood Bank Reagent Case. These samples represent four typical but very different approaches that student writers took when responding to the situation at A–1 Hospital Products, Inc. The writers' primary purposes for writing appear to be different; certainly the messages they construct and the strategies they use with their readers differ radically. At the same time, each memo reflects in some way a valid response to the case context. This is not surprising. As we have mentioned all along, writers' responses to a case situation will be dictated by their personal and professional experience, as well as by the situational constraints of the case.

Our commentary accompanying each sample is to help you assess the student writing by relating it to its context. In the final analysis, however, you, as reader, must determine from your own perspective how well each sample addresses the communication problems in the case.

Comments on Sample 1

This writer organizes the memo according to the format of a lab report with a brief introduction, statement of materials and methods, presentation of results, and concluding interpretation. The emphasis of her write-up thus falls on the procedures—an aspect of importance to Bailey and Borg, because the writer's results are so radically different from theirs.

Following the lab report format allows this writer to appear very scientific while still considering the readers' expectations for good news. It allows her to soften the bad news by putting it last. The writer further downplays the negative message by drawing a tentative conclusion: The lectin "does not appear to exhibit specificity for any Lewis phenotype."

Other strategies underscore her overall effort to be as objective as possible: the use of scientific nomenclature, a table for the results, the formal formatting using labels that are standard in lab reports, and the omission of personal pronouns. She also emphasizes the tests rather than her own actions by stating most of the procedures in the passive

A-1 HOSPITAL PRODUCTS, INC.

MEMORANDUM

To: Henry Bailey, Supervisor
       Lectin Research — R&D

From: Marilyn Katkin, Supervisor
       Serological Testing Laboratory
       Nancy P.   , Writer

Subject: Procedures and Results for Testing the Avocado
         Lectin

    R&D recently isolated a new lectin from the avocado pit with an unusual specificity for $Le(a-b+)$ erythrocytes. The Lectin Group has asked the Serological Testing Laboratory to test this avocado for its blood-typing specificity, using standard procedures.

PROCEDURE

Preparation   1. Diluted avocado lectin to a
                 concentration of 1.0 mg/ml in pH 7.3
                 PBS.
              2. Collected a range of Lewis
                 phenotypes for blood groups O, A_1,
                 and A_2 in saline containing acid-
                 citrate dextrose.
              3. The red cells were treated with
                 ficin by incubating 0.1 ml of 0.1%
                 ficin in pH 7.3 PBS for 15 min @
                 37°C.
              4. The cells were then washed 3 times
                 in saline.

Titration   1. The ficin-treated red cells were
                 added to various dilutions of lectin
                 (0.2 mg/ml) in pH 7.3 PBS.

Sample 1

-2-

2. Agglutination testing was done by incubating two volumes of lectin with one volume of 5% red cells in pH 7.3 PBS for 30 min @ ambient temperature.
3. Samples were then centrifuged at 1000 × g for 15 seconds and examined macroscopically for cell agglutination.

RESULTS

The titration values for the avocado lectin against 0, A_1, and A_2 blood types are as follows:

0 Le(a−b+) 32	A_1 Le(a−b+) 8	A_2 Le(a−b+) 16
0 Le(a+b−) 32	A_1 Le(a+b−) 8	A_2 Le(a+b−) 16
0 Le(a−b−) 32	A_1 Le(a−b−) 8	A_2 Le(a−b−) 16

The avocado lectin does not appear to exhibit specificity for any Lewis phenotype.

Sample 1, *continued*

(for example, "The red cells were treated," rather than, "I treated the red cells").

The question is, are these strategies effective? Some of them will work for some readers, but some may not work for others. For instance, management readers (like Bob Cranston) may not wish to look over all the details of the procedures before getting the message that the lectin is *not* such a promising discovery after all. Even Borg and Bailey are likely to want to know the "bottom line" first, although, as this is a one-page memo, all readers will easily find the message. The tone of the report implies a formal relationship among the personnel of A–1 Hospital Products, perhaps more formal than the situation suggests. Furthermore, the passive voice and limited personal pronouns might make the report sound stilted to some readers. The situation does not dictate this impersonal approach, and the memo, in fact, could be shorter and more readable if the writer used the first person.

Comments on Sample 2

This writer's focus is on the big picture, the "bottom line" that the lectin—"John Borg's lectin," that is—does not specifically agglutinate Lewis b cells. This message concerns the writer, not the results, much less alone the procedures. He states the message immediately and in terms that emphasize that John Borg's data are questionable. His strategy to expose the failure of the Lectin Group's project even extends to his treatment of the results (which he relegates to an attachment) and to his blunt assertion of the lectin's lack of specificity for Lewis b. This focus, of course, reflects Katkin's private views of the Lectin Group, as well as the writer's own irritation at the pattern of interruptions of his laboratory's other work, so perhaps it is justified.

The writer attacks the Lectin Group by immediately drawing negative conclusions on the use of avocado lectin as a blood bank reagent. He also suggests reviewing Borg's work. The question here is, are these assertions appropriate? Certainly his assignment was not to determine if the lectin would be useful as a blood bank reagent; that possibility only comes informally from Katkin. Although management might like to see a clear statement of the implications of the work, they might find a conclusion that the lectin will not work as a blood bank reagent to be inappropriate. Even with Katkin's support for the writer's views, he has perhaps gone too far in suggesting a review of Borg's work, and instead he might have left the more direct statements about this issue to be handled in informal communication between the two supervisors.

A-1 HOSPITAL PRODUCTS, INC.

MEMORANDUM

To: Henry Bailey, Supervisor
        Lectin Research — R&D

From: Marilyn Katkin, Supervisor
        Serological Testing Laboratory
        Allen F. _____ , Writer

Subject: Avocado Lectin Agglutination of Lewis b Pheno-
          types

    We have tested John Borg's Avocado Lectin for
specificity of agglutination. Our results do not show,
as John Borg's data did, that Avocado Lectin has a
specificity for Lewis b cells. For this reason, it could
not be used as a blood bank reagent for routine testing
of blood group types.

    Titrations were done with Avocado Lectin and the
following blood groups: O Lewis b, O Lewis a, O Lewis
null, A_1 Lewis b, A_1 Lewis a, A_1 Lewis null, A_2 Lewis b,
A_2 Lewis a, and A_2 Lewis null. We found absolutely no
difference between Lewis b and Lewis a or null cells.
See data below. (Standard procedures were used
throughout our study.)

    Since our data show no agglutination specificity, we
suggest that John Borg's work be reviewed.

                    Titration Results

                    O Le(a−b+)   32
                    O Le(a+b−)   32
                    O Le(a−b−)   32

                    A_1 Le(a−b+)   8
                    A_1 Le(a+b−)   8
                    A_1 Le(a−b−)   8

                    A_2 Le(a−b+)   16
                    A_2 Le(a+b−)   16
                    A_2 Le(a−b−)   16

Sample 2

A-1 HOSPITAL PRODUCTS, INC.

MEMORANDUM

To: Henry Bailey, Supervisor
Lectin Research — R&D

From: Marilyn Katkin, Supervisor
Serological Testing Laboratory
Mark A. _____ , Writer

Subject: Blood—Typing Specificity of Avocado Lectin

We regret to inform you that our tests do not indicate any use for avocado lectin as a blood bank reagent. Although we have run only one set of experiments, the results do not confirm Borg's study; in fact, they directly contradict it.

We tested blood groups 0, A_1, and A_2 of each Lewis phenotype. The titration values for the avocado lectin against the three blood types indicate absolutely no difference between Lewis b and Lewis a cells. (See the table below.)

0	Le(a−b+)	32
0	Le(a+b−)	32
0	Le(a−b−)	32
A_1	Le(a−b+)	8
A_1	Le(a+b−)	8
A_1	Le(a−b−)	8
A_2	Le(a−b+)	16
A_2	Le(a+b−)	16
A_2	Le(a−b−)	16

Thus, according to our experiments, the avocado lectin shows no specificity for Lewis b and will not serve as a blood bank reagent.

I am puzzled by the discrepancy between John Borg's test results and ours. I believe it would be beneficial to meet and compare notes on the testing, so that we can resolve the differences that have occurred in this particular case and in the past. Please let me know your thoughts on this.

Sample 3

Comments on Sample 3

The writer of Sample 3 also criticizes Borg by strongly emphasizing the big answer, right at the beginning. But unlike the writer of Sample 2, he softens the bad news, partly through the relationship he establishes with his readers ("regret to inform"), but principally by his suggestion that there might be a procedural reason for the great discrepancy between his results and Borg's.

This writer begins with the larger implication of the lectin's lack of value as a blood bank reagent, supporting this conclusion with the results (prominently displayed) and their interpretation. The major focus of this memo, however, is on the possible difference in test procedures, indirectly suggested in the phrase "it would be beneficial to meet and compare notes on the testing." Although he implies his own and Katkin's dissatisfaction with R&D, he emphasizes a positive suggestion: Let's get together and figure out why our results are so radically different. This memo does not pretend to solve the problem, then; rather it opens the door for future communication.

In the suggestion to get to the bottom of the problem between the two units, the writer is almost assuming Katkin's role, speaking more for her than for himself. The question again is, how appropriate is this approach for the context? Katkin might not like the suggestion that both departments get together to "resolve differences," or she might support such a position. As long as the student writer cannot consult with Katkin before writing, however, this matter is only conjecture, a matter of individual opinion. The case does not warrant a writer assuming that Katkin would support either view.

Comments on Sample 4

Unlike the writers of Samples 2 and 3, the author of Sample 4 never refers to the blood bank reagent issue, but limits her assignment to determining specificity for Lewis b. After mentioning the request for tests, she immediately states the results—and those results are the focus of the entire memo. She briefly condenses her lab activity, summarizes the procedures, provides the results and their interpretation, and restates her conclusion.

This writer senses the limits of her role and leaves the question of determining the lectin's potential as a blood bank reagent to management. In fact, her identification with the technician's position may be too strong, as she refers to "my" results, and "my test." Although she does not furnish the procedural details that Bailey and Borg might

A-1 HOSPITAL PRODUCTS, INC.

MEMORANDUM

To: Henry Bailey, Supervisor
          Lectin Research — R&D

From: Marilyn Katkin, Supervisor
          Serological Testing Laboratory
          Jill P._____, Writer

Subject: Avocado Pit Lectin: Testing for Blood–Typing
          Specificity

At your request of April 26, we have tested the avocado pit lectin recently isolated in R&D. My test results indicate that there is no specificity for any one Lewis phenotype.

In doing my test, I followed standard procedures for blood–typing specificity. (See Company Standard Procedures.) Cells were obtained from Group 0, A_1, and A_2 donors of each Lewis phenotype, treated with ficin, and then washed with saline. Ficin–treated cells of each type were then reacted with various amounts of lectin and examined for macroscopic agglutination. Results are presented in the following table:

	Group 0	Group A_1	Group A_2
Lewis b	32	8	16
Lewis a	32	8	16
Lewis null	32	8	16

Figures in the table show that at three different dilutions of avocado lectin, there is no difference in agglutination among the three phenotypes. Thus the avocado lectin shows no specificity for Lewis b red blood cells.

If you have any questions concerning my results, please feel free to contact me.

Sample 4

want, she states that standard procedures were used and concludes with an offer to answer questions if they have any. The question is whether the Lectin Group will be satisfied with this approach, whether they will find the memo complete for their needs, and ultimately, whether all the other readers, known and unknown, will find their expectations and needs fulfilled.

JUDGING YOUR RESPONSE

Our comments on these responses to the Blood Bank Reagent Case identify those components of the case context we saw reflected in the four student samples. You may have noted other aspects which influenced your evaluation of them. In fact, you may have formed your own view on how to respond to this case, a view that will influence your evaluation of other writers' responses.

As you write your own memos, letters, and reports in response to the cases in this book, you will apply similar procedures in judging the adequacy of your writing. Depending on the complexity of the assignments, your own criteria for effectiveness, and the standards you have learned for professional communication, you will derive criteria for judging your own writing. In approaching this task, you must do the following:

1. Compare your document against the constraints of the assignment and situation presented in the case.
2. Judge your document against the goals you set based on your own experience, values, and interpretation.

Only by seeing yourself as *the* person who must take full responsibility for the effect of your communications will you learn how to cope with the complexities of writing as a professional in the world of work.

Part Two

CASES FOR REAL-WORLD WRITING

Customer Complaint at Beta Corporation: The Copy Machine Case

Hired as a sales trainee by the Beta Corporation, a manufacturer of copy machines and other office products, you are currently working in the Chicago office as a sales assistant to a marketing representative. The sales representatives on the big corporate accounts are so busy that they are each assigned a trainee assistant to help them look after their clients.

Your marketing rep is Carl Hughes. One of your tasks in helping him is to go out once a month to visit each of his accounts, making what Beta calls a "customer satisfaction call." These visits are supposed to discover any problems the customer has with the copy machines or their servicing and to help keep the customer as happy with Beta as possible. (Most big accounts lease their equipment from Beta, and many will readily substitute a competitor's product at lease renewal time. Therefore, ensuring customer satisfaction is a significant issue for marketing reps and their sales assistants.)

During each monthly visit, you, together with the customer's "key operator,"[1] fill out an evaluation form which you turn in to your account representative when you return to the Beta office. You also write a brief summary report for the rep which describes each "customer satisfaction" visit for the month, with a note of any action you took. (You can, for example, provide on-the-spot training, arrange for Customer Service to make a call, or promise a follow-up call by the rep.)

---

[1] The key operator is the employee designated by the customer to be responsible for the copier. He/she supervises its use, teaches new users, makes simple repairs, and interacts with the service personnel from Beta.

You suspect that your rep, Carl Hughes, just files the evaluation form and merely glances over the summaries. To call his attention to problem accounts, you orally brief him at the end of each of your visiting days, pointing out pertinent evaluation forms and summaries. That way Hughes can easily keep on top of all accounts and take action quickly—action that occasionally includes sending copies of the evaluation form and the summary to the branch manager.

However, most customer satisfaction calls do not require much attention from the marketing rep. Either they are rather humdrum events in which the key operator reports minor complaints or reasonable satisfaction (and sometimes nothing at all), or they turn into gripe sessions to which you must bring all your sales skills, "stroking" the customers sufficiently so that they will be favorably disposed toward Beta when it comes to lease time.

During your May visits, you get the usual array of so-so responses until you call on Premium Products, Inc., a potato chip manufacturer. The key operator, Nina Boynton, has never liked the copier much and has complained each month about the quality of the copies. This time, however, she is very quiet, and you sense something brewing. When you ask Boynton for her replies so you can fill out the "Customer Evaluation Form," she glances with disdain at the familiar sheet and then ticks off her answers. (See Appendix A.) To question number 2 asking if the copier has performed to her expectations, she glares at you, and instead of writing anything, shoves the paper back at you, saying, "Definitely not."

"Look here," she charges while opening up the copier and pointing to large accumulations of toner dust. "I have told you about this toner dust problem repeatedly, and though your service people have been out several times, they haven't fixed it so that it lasts. The dust builds up so fast that almost right after the optics are cleaned, dust is all over the place, messing up the copies. See how wonderful they look," she says with a sneer. "We can't even use them for management reports anymore."

You start assuring her that the problem will be corrected and that Carl Hughes, the marketing rep, will be out to see her right away, but Boynton will not let you finish.

"I am totally out of patience. I have talked to my management about this problem, and if it isn't fixed immediately, the machine will be pulled."

You nod, express agreement on the poor copy quality, and tell her that Carl Hughes will be in touch tomorrow and that Service will be out as soon as possible. Then you stuff the incomplete Customer Evaluation Form into your attaché case and beat a hasty retreat.

Out on the street, you find a pay phone and put through a call to Hughes. No luck, and later tries are also unsuccessful. You will just have to wait until you can see him in the office at the end of the day.

At about 4 P.M. you get back to the Beta office and head straight for your rep's desk. Unfortunately, he is in a meeting, so you put through a service request for the Premium Products account, and then finish the evaluation forms of your day's visits and write up a brief summary of each one. The first entries are easy. (See Figure 1.)

The fourth summary, the one on Premium Products, is not so simple, however. As you note the high volume (65,000), you wonder how strong you should make your statement. After thinking it through, you write up the summary, and then walk down the hall to brief Carl Hughes about the situation. Unfortunately, Hughes has left unexpectedly because of some trouble with the Basic Foods account. Recalling that you will be out all day tomorrow at a training session

Borg Pharmaceuticals   Visit 5/25 (Monthly Volume 15,000)
Key operator satisfied. Judges copier quality superior to all competition. Only complaint: jamming is too common when machine warms up.

Mason's Department Store   Visit 5/25 (Monthly Volume 45,000)
Problems with feed rollers. Key operator called 3 times in 3 days before Service came out. Problem only partially fixed. Action: Customer Service called.

Bubble Bottlers   Visit 5/25 (Monthly Volume 9,000)
Everything is fine. Key operator is satisfied, both with performance and service response.

Figure 1.   Summaries of Visits to Customers

downtown, you feel that you cannot risk just leaving the summary and your completed forms for Carl; from past experience you know he may not look at them all day. So you decide to write him a brief memo calling his attention to the Premium account and leave it right on his desk.

ASSIGNMENT 1
Complete the Beta Copier Evaluation Form for Premium Products (Appendix A). (Write it *for* Nina Boynton. Most contacts expect you to fill out the form for them.)

ASSIGNMENT 2
Write the entry on Premium Products for the summary report.

Complete either Assignment 3 or 4:

ASSIGNMENT 3
Write the memo to Carl Hughes, Marketing Representative. Your job title is Sales Assistant.

ASSIGNMENT 4
Upon reflection about Carl Hughes and his habits, you decide that he would prefer to get all the necessary information from your memo alone, without bothering to look for the Premium entry in the summary report. So you write him a complete memo on the Premium problem, a memo that does not assume that he will look at the summary report before acting.

APPENDIX A

Beta Copier Customer Evaluation Form

COMPANY *Premium Products* DATE _____

NAME OF CONTACT *Nina Boynton* POSITION ___*"KO"*___

1. Please evaluate the Beta Copier for the following criteria:

	Poor	Satis-factory	Good	Excel-lent
Copy quality	X			
Consistency	X			
Reliability		X		
Simplicity of use		X		
Effective speed		X		
Service response	X			
Operator intervention				
Other				

2. Has the Beta Copier performed to your expectations?

3. Has Beta sales and service support been adequate? (If not, please explain.)

4. Additional comments: (Use second sheet if necessary.)

Poor Service at Big-1 Car Rental: Blowing the Whistle on the Franchise Operator

As the assistant director for human resources at the Pleasanton assembly plant of the Continental Car Corporation (CCC), you are responsible for helping the plant manager, Frank Page, in a variety of tasks. Today he calls you in to take care of a problem that has him visibly annoyed—probably more annoyed than you have ever seen him.

"The Big-1 Car Rental Agency at the airport has really done it this time," Page says. "Yesterday we had a couple of VPs from a Japanese firm in here, along with an American who represents them out of San Francisco. After lunch, McConkey, the American fellow, and I were walking together out of the restaurant when suddenly he starts telling me about the terrible problems they'd had with the CCC rental car we'd reserved for them at the airport.[1] Seems the heating system didn't work after the first five minutes, so they were freezing during the whole of the 45-minute ride from the Minneapolis–St. Paul airport. But that wasn't all. The car made some funny noises and just wasn't running well. Naturally, the polite Japanese didn't say a word, but McConkey didn't hesitate to say how unhappy and embarrassed he was about the heater not working. Well, if he was embarrassed, can you imagine how embarrassed I was? I didn't know what to say to the

---

[1] Standard procedure at Continental Car Corporation is to rent CCC model cars for visitors from the Big-1 Rental Corporation. Big-1 is the major rental firm for CCC products across the United States. Like most automobile manufacturers, CCC views renting its own brand of cars for visitors as a public relations effort, and so naturally expects the vehicles will be in top operating condition.

Japanese. What a fine way to advertise our products. Yes, sir. Let them see for themselves how wonderful CCC automobiles really are!"

You shake your head. "They must have been miserable riding without a heater all the way back from the airport in this 10-degree weather . . . really impressed with CCC's quality!"

Frank Page nods. "And it isn't as if this is the first time that the Big-1 Agency at the Twin Cities airport has given our visitors lousy service. Several vendors have had problems lately, and have let people in the plant know about it. Why, Manuel Lopez was just complaining to me last week about the poor maintenance on the cars from the airport outlet. Some incident with the reps from the Zorelco Company who got a car that had ten things wrong with it. Lopez finally called in and had the agency come out with another car."

"Actually, the complaints have been coming in for several months at least," you reply. "I remember Joe Bomarito telling me some horror story about a high-mileage car from the Big-1 Agency about the time the addition was being put on the front reception area."

"That's a full seven months ago," Page says tersely. "Enough. We have a sufficient history of complaints on the airport franchise. Now we're going to do something about it."

"So what do you want me to do?" you ask. "Go see the manager at the airport agency?"

"No. There's no point in dealing with him. I believe he's proved his incompetence beyond a doubt. Any outfit that consistently rents poorly maintained cars is running a sloppy operation. I want something to happen. The best-made car in the world won't run well if it's not serviced properly. This Big-1 Agency is causing us an image problem."

"And of course we can't take our airport business anywhere else," you note.

"We have no choice," replies Page. "We can only rent CCC products at the Twin Cities airport by dealing with this outfit. That's why I want to blow the whistle on them—make sure that they get their act cleaned up—NOW."

"So we go to the top, to corporate headquarters?"

"Right," Frank Page says firmly. "I want you to write a letter to the general manager of the Rental Division of Big-1 in New York City."

"You don't want to start giving him chapter and verse on our problems, do you?" you wonder.

"No, I sure don't. We haven't kept any records anyway. Look, Continental Car Corporation and the Big-1 Car Rental Company do a lot of business together. I just want to let the corporate people at Big-1 know that this is an intolerable situation and they'd better do something about it. Get their guys out here to look at this airport franchise. See how the place is being run."

"Got it," you reply as you head back to your desk to draft the letter for Page's signature.

ASSIGNMENT
Write a letter for the signature of Frank Page, Manager, Pleasanton Assembly Plant, Continental Car Corporation, Pleasanton, Minnesota 00000, to Mr. M. R. Young, General Manager, Rental Car Division, The Big-1 Rental Company, Inc., 534 Monroe Avenue, New York, New York 00000. (Write your name on the upper-right corner of this paper to identify it for your instructor.)

The Agricultural Institute Mystery: The Case of the Broken Electrode

The State University Agricultural Institute is an organization composed of numerous specialized laboratories that conduct research and also do service testing for various agencies. One function of the "Ag Institute" is to carry out routine testing for all the county extension services around the state. Citizens bring such items as soil samples or twigs from diseased trees to their local extension office for analysis. Each County Extension Service charges the public a nominal fee which it remits to the Ag Institute for analytical work.

For the past two months you have been working in the Insect Control Division, a new and as yet poorly equipped operation. To complete some of your tasks as a laboratory technician, you must frequently borrow various instruments from other units, particularly from the Soil Science Center and from the Plant Diseases Department, both located in your building. Luckily, you have a couple of pieces of new equipment (such as a spectrophotometer and a fluorimeter) that you are able to let them use in return. Overall, however, you borrow more than you lend, and from what you have heard thus far, this situation will probably continue indefinitely. Your unit is newer than most of the labs, so it has some catching up to do on equipment purchases. Beyond that, however, borrowing seems to be a way of life for all the labs in the Ag Institute. All the departments want state-of-the-art equipment for their research, so they often let the routine service work limp along on borrowed equipment.

On Monday morning you find you must borrow once again. You call up the soils lab and speak to Martha Jones, the principal assistant to the Soil Science Center director, Dr. Al Sampson. You are making up a buffer solution and would like to use their pH meter[1] right away if they are not using it. Jones says, "Fine, nobody is using it now; come on up."

Upstairs in the soils lab, you set to work, turning the knob on the meter from "standby" to "pH." Unfortunately, the meter registers no change. After checking out the battery, you take a look at the electrode;[2] it appears to be all right. You try again, but the meter still does not work. This time you carefully look over the electrode. The fluid level is all right,[3] but then you discover a hairline crack. The electrode is broken, so of course the meter will not work. As you leave the lab, you remark to Martha that the pH meter is not functioning because the electrode is broken. Her only response is, "Oh, really?"

About an hour later you get a telephone call from a rather curt Dr. Sampson. Although he does not accuse you directly, you soon realize that he believes you broke the meter, because nobody else reported it. You begin to protest, explaining that the instrument never worked from the moment you set foot in the soils lab, but Sampson will not listen.

"Look, Martha Jones reports that you use this pH meter a lot, and we didn't know it was broken until *you* used it. I don't mind you people borrowing things, but I expect your group to share in the maintenance of the equipment you use regularly, especially if you break it. A new electrode will cost about a hundred bucks, and I think your lab should pay for it." Sampson rings off, saying that Martha Jones will let you know exactly what to order.

You are almost positive that you did not break the electrode, but you cannot prove it. And you certainly do not want Dr. Sampson to become uncooperative with his equipment; getting your work done would become very difficult, if not impossible. Even though you know that your lab is getting a pH meter soon, there are other pieces of equipment Soil Science owns that you need. But the chief of your own lab, Dr. Hassan Bazzi (who also heads two other small units), is tight with his money, partly because the budget for new equipment

---

[1] A pH meter measures acidity (hydrogen-ion concentration) in a solution.

[2] An electrode comes with the meter, but electrodes break periodically over the life of the instrument and must be replaced. Sometimes a cracked electrode is easily visible, but occasionally it is very hard to see. If the electrode is cracked, the pH meter will give no reading or an erratic one.

[3] The electrode's fluid is a salt solution which must be replaced occasionally.

is so limited and partly because he is eager "to produce as much as possible for as little as possible." Moreover, he is a very "distant" administrator. Rarely does he come around to your quarters in the basement of the Agricultural Science Building, preferring to leave the daily supervision to Jim Beal, a research associate,[4] while Bazzi himself works out of a suite of labs on the 14th floor of the new research quarters in Hadley Hall, one block away.

You have a feeling that Beal is not going to want to get involved in your problem, but you decide to seek his advice anyway. After hearing about the broken electrode, Beal shakes his head. "Looks like you're in a jam! Bazzi hates to spend money. More than that, he gets irritated by sloppy work, and for him that includes breaking things. On the other hand, Sampson will expect the new electrode right away."

Feeling trapped, you ask Beal, "Well, what do you think I should do? Should I try to see Bazzi about it? Talk it over?"

Beal laughs nervously. "Boy, I sure wouldn't do that. Bazzi doesn't like being bothered by what he sees as trivia."

"Trivia?" you say incredulously. "This is hardly 'trivia'! Sharing in maintenance regularly isn't going to be a trivial matter to Bazzi, is it?"

"Oh," Beal replies, "I think all Al meant is that we must help out now and then, especially on items we use a lot."

"Okay," you say, "but Bazzi's the one who must decide whether to okay the purchase."

Beal pauses. "True, but if you go in to see him, he'll probably growl at you to 'put it in writing.' So if I were you, I would write him a memo explaining the situation so that he understands your position and can decide what's best to do."

"Either buy the electrode or fight with Sampson," you quip.

"Well, it's true that he and Sampson aren't friendly, but I should think they'd both want to keep the borrowing system going." Another Beal pause. "It's up to you whether you want to suggest that Bazzi should pay for the electrode," Beal says evasively. "Just make sure

---

[4] The organizational structure of the institute puts all of the power in the individual laboratory directors and leaves the positions under them in a fluid and open state. The lines of supervision in your lab are not strictly defined. According to your job description, you are Bazzi's technician and report to him. However, Bazzi informally works through Beal much of the time, though Beal does not seem to like to run anything.

that you don't leave out anything so that he must call either you or me for more information."

"And also make sure," you mimic Beal, "that it's so short he can read it in two minutes."

"Of course," grins Beal. "Anything you can't say in a page isn't worth saying, you know!"

It's obvious to you that Beal is going to stay very clear of this whole thing. If he does not want to express his opinion on whether you should recommend payment for the electrode, he surely is not going to help you out in any way with Bazzi. So, you call up Martha Jones to get the catalog information and costs on the electrode.[5] Then you think over your options before sitting down to write.

ASSIGNMENT

Write a memo to Dr. Hassan Bazzi, Director of Special Laboratories, State University Agricultural Research Institute, Hadley Hall, Room 1408. Send a copy to Jim Beal, Research Associate, Insect Diagnostic Laboratory, Agricultural Science Building, Room 3. (Beal would prepare the paperwork if Bazzi decides to pay for the electrode.) Dr. Al Sampson is the Director of the Soil Science Center, Agricultural Science Building, Room 106.[6] Your job title is Laboratory Technician, Insect Diagnostic Laboratory.

---

[5] The catalog information on the electrode Martha Jones gives you is as follows: the instrument is a Holtzmann pH meter; the electrode is a "combination glass microelectrode, Catalog No. 2071581," available at $93.00 from Holtzmann Instruments, Inc., Rockbury, New Jersey 00000.

[6] Sampson and Bazzi are equals, each heading a separate unit. Although they are both under the chief of the Agricultural Institute, they would not appeal to him for any interlaboratory operations. The institute has no established procedures on borrowing and would probably not even formally recognize it.

Muddy Waters at Mariners Museum: Clarifying an Architectural Contract

Little did you think that your training in business administration would take you to a resort community, but here you are in Sausalito, California, just miles away from San Francisco and all that beach! Your new job is attractive too—administrative assistant to the curator for the future Sausalito Mariners Museum, which is now under design. Your boss, Michael McCaffrey, seems more like an old salt than a museum curator to you, but he knows museum work and has a natural talent for creating eye-catching, informative displays. His exhibits and the attractive building design by architects Clark, Clark, and Anderson (CCA) of San Francisco promise to make the museum venture a tourist success.

At present, the Mariners Museum personnel are few; they include McCaffrey, yourself, and two exhibit builders. The museum staff members are working in rented space in a new shopping center until the museum is built. Your operation is governed by a board of directors that includes Harold Van Kloss, owner of All-American Bank; Jack Gordon, owner of Gordon's Marina; and Mrs. Amanda Curtis. Mrs. Curtis has donated a considerable part of her fortune from the Fremont Shipping Lines for the museum building.

You and McCaffrey handle multiple tasks. You do public relations work and bookkeeping, and you assist in the management of the construction contracts for the museum. Mike McCaffrey not only plans exhibits and directs the acquisition of materials for the museum, but also manages the construction contracts. This morning Mike stops by your desk with a memo in his hand. He looks a bit puzzled and you ask him what the problem is.

"The minutes of the February 15th meeting of the board, our staff, and CCA have an error," Mike begins. "It appears our architects have misinterpreted their role in interior design. Clark, Clark, and Anderson think they have responsibility for interiors."

"Well, I thought the architects were under contract to handle the interior design," you say, remembering the discussion about this point at the meeting.

"They're supposed to handle interior design all right, with one exception—Louise Smallwood is doing the design of the gift shop."

"Amanda Curtis's personal interior designer," you say, immediately recalling a discussion of this issue at the meeting. Amanda Curtis, as chief donor for the museum enterprise, has stipulated several aspects of the building design and operation which she would like to see carried out. The design of the gift shop by her personal designer is just one of her little demands.

"Smallwood definitely was awarded the contract for the gift shop interior design," McCaffrey repeats. "In fact, it was made quite clear at our meeting that Smallwood would provide sketches, elevations, layouts, and any millwork[1] details for the gift shop. Clark, Clark, and Anderson would then solicit bids and prepare contracts for gift shop construction. However, CCA and Smallwood jointly will recommend to the board which companies submitting bids should receive contracts.[2] None of those details are in the meeting minutes. In fact, here's what the minutes say." McCaffrey reads a portion of the minutes to you. " 'CCA will be responsible for gift shop planning and millwork design.' "

"Hmmmm," you say. "Who took the minutes?"

"Jay Zack, the project architect from CCA. He was the only rep from CCA at the meeting. And he's already sent the minutes to Curtis, Van Kloss, Gordon, *and* Smallwood."

"Ouch!" you say. "What can we do?"

"Well, I think we've got to send a letter to Jay and clarify CCA's responsibilities as we understand them."

---

[1] Millwork refers to custom-made cabinets, counters, and other non-structural furnishings which are permanently installed.

[2] Smallwood has the contract to design gift shop interiors only. CCA will solicit bids for contracts to construct the gift shop interior from companies that build cabinets, hang wallpaper, lay carpeting, and do other work in constructing interior surfaces and furnishings. A bid is a cost estimate based on a description of the work to be done and materials to be used.

"You mean tell them they won't be designing the gift shop, just arranging the bids and contracts? And that Smallwood will review the bids jointly with them?"

"That's it," McCaffrey says.

"Don't you think that will be a little touchy? There's been a lot of tension between Amanda Curtis and CCA. I can understand why Jay Zack got a little aggressive about his firm's interests in the minutes. Curtis has been pretty insistent about getting her way. Remember the argument she had with Zack about the canopy designed for the entrance?"

"Right," says McCaffrey. "On the other hand, CCA is very protective about their design decisions. They're an award-winning firm and feel the client should put complete trust in them. They weren't too happy about the board's decision to let Smallwood handle the gift shop. She's had very little experience designing for commercial spaces. I bet Zack is worried she'll come up with something that detracts from the building."

"You're probably right there, but nevertheless Smallwood *has* been awarded that gift shop interiors contract, and she and Amanda Curtis certainly aren't going to like the looks of these minutes," you say, "no matter what Zack may have meant about CCA being responsible for gift shop planning and millwork design."

"That's true, but in a way CCA is responsible," Mike points out. "Smallwood can't work in a vacuum here. After all, CCA will still arrange the contracts for her work. And she'll review bids for that work. She'll need to cooperate with Zack to get the job done right."

"In fact, we want CCA to offer helpful input to the gift shop design," you say. "They should furnish Smallwood with specs for window details, exterior masonry, floor construction—anything that may affect what she will design."

"I agree," McCaffrey says, "and we've got to make that clear to them." He then continues, "That letter to Zack must go out today. I've got three meetings scheduled this afternoon, so I'm sure I'll never get to it. Will you write the letter for me?"

"Sure," you reply.

"Copies should go to everyone who got the minutes of the February 15th meeting, of course." McCaffrey leans toward you a bit. "You'll have to watch what you say. Got to clear up the issue without making things worse. We want to make sure everyone works cooperatively."

"I'll try."

"Fine," Mike says. "Just leave the letter on my desk for my signature when you've got it done."

Before he's left the office, you've slipped a piece of paper in the typewriter and have started drafting the letter.

ASSIGNMENT

Write a letter to Jay Zack, Project Architect, of Clark, Clark, and Anderson, clarifying the architects' responsibilities in gift shop design. The letter is from Michael McCaffrey, Museum Curator, and copies will go to yourself, Amanda Curtis, Harold Van Kloss, Jack Gordon, and Louise Smallwood. Addresses are: Sausalito Mariners Museum, Sausalito, California 00000; Clark, Clark, and Anderson, 207 Market Street, San Francisco, California 00000. (Write your name on the upper-right corner of this paper to identify it for your instructor.)

Enzyme Testing for Morton-Hayes Drug Corporation: The Keratan Sulfate Case

You work as a research associate in the Biological Laboratory of the Morton-Hayes Drug Corporation. Early one morning, your supervisor, Dr. Bert Pulaski, hands you a rush assignment from Dr. H. K. Harris, head of the Clinical Research Laboratory. Harris's people have just discovered a new enzyme in a fungus. Both Harris and Dr. Kate Wiley in Product Development are highly interested in the enzyme[1] as a possible diagnostic tool for rheumatoid arthritis. They are already anticipating patenting the method and then putting together a diagnostic test kit for clinical sale. Before they can pursue these big plans, however, the clinical staff must test the enzyme's activity with several specific substrates.[2]

That's where you come in. Although most of the required substrates are commercially available, a key substrate—desulfated keratan sulfate—must be specially prepared. Under pressure from Harris (who has some notion that the competition is onto this enzyme too), Pulaski has promised that the Biological Lab can complete the job by one week from today—a very tight deadline, he notes, but one he is confident you can meet.

To save time waiting for the messenger service, you drive over to the local slaughterhouse to pick up some bovine cornea.[3] Over the next

---

[1] Enzymes are proteins produced by living cells that cause chemical reactions to occur without being consumed themselves in the reaction.

[2] A substrate is the substance acted upon by a specific enzyme.

[3] Keratan sulfate is a large complex carbohydrate found in cornea and cartilage. ("Keratan" is the correct spelling.)

three days, you prepare some keratan sulfate according to the standard procedure[4] and set aside a portion of the material. Then, following another standard procedure, you convert the remainder to its pyridinium salt (pyridinium keratan sulfate). Next you desulfate[5] a sample of the pyridinium salt by heating a suspension of the salt in dimethyl sulfoxide-pyridine at 100°C for 9 hours.

Because your objective is to remove all the sulfate, you now analyze the extent of desulfation by performing a sulfate determination on the desulfated keratan sample.[6] You carry out this sulfate determination by subjecting the samples of both the original keratan sulfate preparation and the desulfated keratan sulfate to hydrolysis.[7] (This is done by heating the solutions in 9.5 N hydrochloric acid in sealed ampules in a boiling water bath for 4 hours.)

To prepare a standard curve, you transfer aliquots[8] of a standard sulfate solution (0 to 1.0 ml by 0.1-ml increments) by pipet into test tubes, making up the volume to 1.5 ml with deionized water.[9] To analyze the hydrolysates[10] for sulfate, you take 0.5-ml aliquots of the solutions of both the starting material and the desulfated keratan sulfate, and then adjust the volume in each tube to 1.5 ml with deionized water. Then you add trichloroacetic acid[11] solution (0.9 ml) to the standard sulfate solution and the hydrolysates and mix the contents thoroughly. Next you add 0.6 ml of a barium-gelatin solution to each tube and again mix thoroughly.[12] You allow the tubes to stand for 20 minutes at 20–25°C. Then you measure the absorbance at 360 nm[13] against a reagent blank.

The results are very disappointing. On the starting material of keratan sulfate you get a sulfate determination of 2.33 moles per mil-

---

[4] For this report, assume the adequacy of this procedure and its results, as well as the subsequent procedure for converting the keratan sulfate to its pyridinium salt.

[5] Desulfation is the chemical removal of sulfate from a substance.

[6] Sulfate is estimated turbidimetrically (the amount of cloudiness produced when barium is added to sulfate).

[7] Hydrolysis is the chemical decomposition of a substance in the presence of water.

[8] An aliquot is a measured portion of a given liquid volume.

[9] Deionized water has all its charged metals removed.

[10] Hydrolysates are products of hydrolysis.

[11] Trichloroacetic acid is chlorinated acetic acid.

[12] Gelatin is added to stabilize the barium sulfate suspension.

[13] A nanometer (nm) is 1 billionth of a meter.

ligram. On the final product you get 0.5 moles per milligram. This means that only about 75% of the sulfate was removed. To test the enzyme, the Clinical researchers need a completely desulfated product (0 moles of sulfate per milligram of keratan); it is obvious they cannot use this material.

You go over the procedures but come up with no answers. You simply do not know why the sulfate was not completely removed. Reviewing the results with your boss, Dr. Pulaski, does not clarify matters. The facts are that you do not have enough starting material left to repeat the procedure. (The slaughterhouse had insufficient bovine corneas available when you stopped in, so you could not make any additional keratan sulfate.)

"Look here," says Pulaski kindly, "I know this is a really tricky procedure. It depends on many things—the temperature, the time, the acid concentration. And the reagents must be absolutely dry. With all the humidity we've been having lately, it's just possible that some moisture got into the reagents through no fault of yours. Nevertheless," he shakes his head, "I did promise Harris the desulfated material by today. Since there's no way we can deliver on that, you'll have to write this up for him right away. Find out whether he wants us to try again or what. We could follow one of the other procedures next time around; but I really don't think there's anything questionable about the one you used."[14]

You nod.

"Get the report done immediately and we'll have the co-op student run it over to Harris. I would guess we'll get a phone call from him in short order."

ASSIGNMENT

Write a report to Dr. H. K. Harris, Director of the Clinical Research Laboratory. A copy goes to Dr. K. O. Wiley, Director of Product Development. Dr. B. Pulaski, Manager of the Biological Laboratory, must approve the report, so add his name after "Approved by."

---

[14] There are several standard procedures for desulfating keratan sulfate.

Treadwell Developers, Inc., Gets Caught in the Middle: The Bad Prints Case

It is not often that you smile on your way to work, but this Tuesday morning while reading the *Westwood News* on the bus you do find something to smile about. Dead center on the front page is a picture of your employer, George Treadwell of Treadwell Developers, Inc., shaking the hand of Francis Gauthier, Westwood's mayor. The article below the picture announces the City Planning Commission's decision to approve Treadwell's preliminary plans to construct a Conference Center on the banks of Plum River. The center will include restaurants, boutiques, movie theaters, and two 30-story towers, one for offices and the other to house Great Places Hotel. Best of all, you are assistant project manager for this development, and you are happy to see it get some press coverage.

You fold the paper under your arm and get off the bus at your stop. You are still smiling as you make your way through the corridors of Treadwell Developers, Inc. Of course, you knew a week ago that the City Planning Commission's decision would be announced Monday night, but it sure looks good to see it in writing. Treadwell Developers has subcontracted the Conference Center project to Alspaugh, Jordan, and Vineski (AJV) Associates, an architectural firm regularly employed by Treadwell Developers. Though the official announcement came last night, preliminary designs for the Conference Center actually were approved by the City Planning Commission last month. The Planning Commission is now in the process of doing a second review. They are looking over drawings which respond to comments they made in their first review.

You stop at the front office to pick up your mail and head to your own office. Thinking about the City Planning Commission's second review has affected your good mood somewhat. You wonder whether AJV sent the new drawings for review to the Planning Commission *on time* as promised. AJV is a first-rate design firm, but they are just not willing to go that extra mile necessary to please local government offices that must review and approve designs.

You had one heck of a time getting the firm to submit initial drawings of the Conference Center on time. Randy McNamara, who is your boss and the project manager for the development, was pretty miffed last month when he got his copies of the preliminary drawings 30 minutes before he walked out the door to attend his first meeting with the City Planning Commission. Fortunately, the Planning Commission had received their copies.[1] You have tried your best to make AJV move faster, but you have had trouble dealing with John Alspaugh, who handles their commercial projects. Alspaugh is a talented fellow, but often plays the part of the artist who can't be bothered with mundane details, like submitting documents for review on time. You had to make several calls and do lots of double-checking to get him to act. His behavior annoys you, frankly. Still you have to admit that Alspaugh's got a terrific talent. Real ability for designing commercial spaces that are both beautiful and functional.

When you reach your office, you still have John Alspaugh on your mind. You decide to check out a tube of drawings from AJV that arrived COD late yesterday. You expect that these drawings show the changes made in response to the city's first review last month. Alspaugh was supposed to send copies of these same drawings to the city by overnight mail last Tuesday so the Planning Commission could conduct their second review. You hope they got there all right. The second review meeting is scheduled for Wednesday of next week. At least you have the copies for your boss, Randy McNamara.

Just as you finish laying the drawings out on your drafting board, Randy drops by your office. He does not look happy.

"I just got a call from Elizabeth Beauchamp of the City Planning Commission."

"Oh? Didn't they receive the drawings from AJV?"

"Oh, yes," Randy answers, "but they're having trouble reading them. They claim the changes aren't clearly marked. Either that or the architect didn't make the corrections we agreed to on the drawings."

"Well, I've got the drawings right here," you tell Randy. "They arrived late yesterday COD. I've finally got those guys to send stuff

---

[1] AJV sends duplicate copies of all drawings to be reviewed by the City Planning Commission to Treadwell and the Planning Commission.

to the city by express mail at their expense, but they still send our copies when they get around to it—and COD to boot!"

"Let's take a look at them," Randy says. "There's a couple of things I'm really concerned about. Liz Beauchamp says she can't find 'tenant use' functions marked clearly on the drawings;[2] plus she can't find that change in a fire corridor location which we agreed to make at the last review."

You quickly scan the drawings, with Randy peering over your shoulder.

"Why did they send such a low-quality print?" Randy asks. "Looks like these are prints produced from poor quality transparencies, probably from sepias.[3] They should have made copies from original tracings."

"You bet they should have," you agree. "And look at this; the outlining[4] they used to point out a change in tenant use function from 'retail shop' to 'restaurant' in the Northeast Wing blocks out the lettering naming the function. No wonder Liz was confused about the marking of the functions."

"Here's that fire corridor change," Randy says, looking at another drawing now. "Liz couldn't find it because they didn't outline it. They're supposed to outline *all* the changes we've made since the last review."

You nod and sort through the stack of drawings to find one which shows the remainder of the Northeast Wing. While struggling to figure out which drawing goes with which you note, "They also didn't draw any match lines;[5] you know I . . ."

---

[2] Architects mark "tenant use" functions on drawings by adding lettering which names the type of business to be conducted in a space. The words "theater," "restaurant," and "department store" all describe tenant use functions.

[3] Sepia transparencies are created by placing a drawing or tracing over the light-sensitive side of image paper and exposing the paper to bright light. The lines of the original drawing are translated as opaque lines onto the image paper and fixed using ammonia or another chemical. The term "sepia transparency" refers to the brownish appearance of the developed image paper which becomes largely transparent in processing. Often architects mark design changes on a sepia transparency to avoid marking up the original tracing. Then they will use this transparency as an "original" from which to make copies. Sepia transparencies have less definition than original tracings; hence, a print made from a sepia transparency will be less clear than a print made from an original tracing.

[4] Outlining refers to the circles which an architect draws around portions of the drawing where changes have been made to highlight these changes.

[5] A match line is added to a drawing to indicate at what point a second drawing should be matched to the first to show the rest of the area depicted in the first drawing.

"Wait a minute," Randy interrupts, thumbing again through the prints and this time checking the dates and ID numbers in the corners. "I don't think this is AJV's latest set of prints. Didn't we meet with them on the 14th? These prints are dated the 10th. We reviewed this set and made one additional change at our meeting on the 14th."

"That's right—it was that outside fire stair for the theater," you recall, while looking through the prints to find the change. "Sure enough, it's not here," you add, scanning the drawing which shows the theater complex.

McNamara thumbs through the drawings one more time, shaking his head. "Listen, I want you to get on the phone to John Alspaugh right away and discuss this with him. Have him send a new set of drawings to us by messenger this afternoon. I want you to review the set tomorrow and then get Alspaugh to have someone bring a duplicate set to Liz Beauchamp. If Beauchamp gets good prints by the day after tomorrow at the latest, the commission will be ready to meet with us next week. If not, we may have to reschedule our meeting with them for next month. We can't afford to lose that time. Follow up your call to Alspaugh with a letter stipulating what you want them to do about prints from now on." Randy stops to reflect a moment. "This is pretty embarrassing."

You nod your head in agreement and tell Randy you will get on it right away. He is satisfied that you have the situation under control and leaves your office. You immediately plan a strategy for dealing with Alspaugh, Jordan, and Vineski Associates.

ASSIGNMENT 1

Prepare some notes that you will use while you make a phone call to John Alspaugh requesting a new set of drawings.

ASSIGNMENT 2

Write a letter that documents your phone call and stipulates what you want AJV to do about prints from now on. Write to John Alspaugh, Principal for Commercial Facilities, Alspaugh, Jordan, and Vineski Associates, 201 Greenwood, Westwood, Pennsylvania 00000. Your title is Assistant Project Manager. Your firm's address is Treadwell Developers, Inc., 3400 Arborview Drive, Westwood, Pennsylvania 00000.

The Telemarketing Campaign: A Co-op Trainee Case

Part 1

As part of your cooperative work program in the Capital Corporation, an office equipment manufacturing company, you have recently been assigned to work as a marketing assistant in the typewriter division. You and two other co-op trainees (one of whom is a college friend)[1] are handed a project in "telemarketing" by Lee Ann O'Sullivan, the marketing representative who is supervising your work.

"As you know, sales are way down," O'Sullivan begins in her typical drill-sergeant manner. "So we're going to try some telephone contacts of customers who have a significant number of machines and see if we can get replacement orders. Here's a letter I've written, signed by Mr. Kay[2] and me. [See Appendix A.] Send it out to all accounts with from 5 to 30 machines. Then ten days later, telephone to invite them to an open house showing our new Futura machine. While you have them on the phone, find out if they're interested in any new machines. For each call you make, you should keep track of exactly how much interest they show, and precisely what kind of follow-up will be required. Like, do they want to know prices? Do they want their old equipment evaluated? Do they want to know more about Futura? And if they do, what do they want to know?"

You glance at your two cohorts and try to swallow your apprehensions about getting many people out to this open house. O'Sullivan

---

[1] You and your college friend are roles for you and a classmate, so neither of you has a name in this case.

[2] Richard Kay is the marketing manager, the chief of your unit.

does not notice, however, and continues to run down the telemarketing procedure.

"If they aren't interested in new machines, find out as much as you can about their situation. Are they sitting tight? And why? Or have they decided to buy elsewhere?"

You all nod, madly taking notes as O'Sullivan blasts away.

"You'll have a few jobs to do after you finish sending out the letters," she goes on. "You need to plan a way to keep track of the telephone interviews so that all the data will be clear. Each of you should follow the same system for putting all the information together. So, design a table for keeping records. Also, you'll need to develop a short script of what you're all going to say on the phone. Remember you're Capital Corporation reps and you must sound suitably professional. Make sure you all review the information on the machines, so you'll sound well informed and be able to answer questions. Oh, and let me see the script before you start calling," she closes.

After the meeting with O'Sullivan is over, you and your two fellow trainees grumble a bit about the "old drill sergeant," and then set down to work getting out the letter to the 118 accounts with from 5 to 30 machines, constructing a form to collect the telephone data, and preparing a telephone script.

ASSIGNMENT 1
Construct a form to record the data from the telephone interviews. Format and type it. (Write your name on the upper-right corner of this paper to identify it for your instructor.)

ASSIGNMENT 2
Write a script outline to guide your "telemarketing" conversations. *Note*: The script need not contain any technical information on the machine because each telephone interviewer would refer to company brochures to answer technical questions. (Write your name on the upper-right corner of this paper to identify it for your instructor.)

Part 2

Ten days after sending the letters, preparing the data sheet, and writing the script (which old O'Sullivan did approve), you and your two fellow co-ops start making telephone calls. After spending hours on the phone, the three of you become quite discouraged. Absolutely nobody wants to come to the open house, and it is now only two weeks away. Lee Ann O'Sullivan is not going to like this news. She will probably think that the three of you were not persuasive enough. Worse than the negative response on the open house, however, is the fact that a large number of companies—37 to be exact—have expressed no interest at all in replacing their machines. These firms are hard up and are cutting back, certainly not buying new equipment. A few people simply said that their inventory did not need replacement yet. (Five calls fit into that category.) Then there were six places that could not make any decisions about equipment purchases because their home offices have that responsibility. Another ten accounts you were unable to reach, but you are still trying. Four letters were returned to your office, undelivered. That leaves the terrific total of eight customers who showed some slight interest in Futura. Three of those wanted price information, a couple wanted trade-in values, and the rest just vaguely wanted "some literature." So, after 70 telephone calls things do not look promising.

At lunch in the canteen, you and the other two co-op trainees (Bill Matuzak and your good friend from college) huddle on the matter. It sure is discouraging, you all agree. Bill suggests completing the rest of the calls as fast as possible. "It's not our fault that nobody wants a Futura," he says. "Let's just get the job done."

"We've got 48 left, plus the 10 we couldn't reach," you say with a grimace. "Besides, we're accomplishing nothing. Why continue? After all, O'Sullivan has no idea that things are so awful, especially on the response to the open house. Perhaps the whole campaign should be reevaluated."

Your friend agrees and suggests writing O'Sullivan a progress report with a table summarizing the calls to date to show how things are going. That would at least give her a chance to make adjustments, if she wants.

That seems like a good idea to you, since the open house seems ill-advised, to say the least. "If we can't get one out of almost 70 customers even to show interest in it, what do we expect from the remaining 48?" you wonder aloud.

After some more exchange, all three of you finally agree: the progress report should be written before you make any more calls. However, Bill Matuzak expresses willingness to *sign* the memo only *if* he agrees with what the other two of you write. Apparently he is concerned that O'Sullivan will blame the three of you if you sound as if you are criticizing her campaign. In any case, he is not going to help write the report. That is up to the two of you.

Complete one of the following assignments:

ASSIGNMENT 3
Collaborate with another student ("your good friend from college") and on your own initiative write a progress report speaking for all three of the co-op trainees, you two plus Bill Matuzak. Write the report to Lee Ann O'Sullivan, the marketing representative. Sign the report from W. P. Matuzak and the two of you. (You each have the title Cooperative Work Program Trainee.)

ASSIGNMENT 4
Write the report alone, but sign all your names. (Assume you have their permission, though not their aid.)

ASSIGNMENT 5
Assume your "college friend" and Matuzak both decided not to cooperate on the report and will not sign it. Write it from yourself alone.

APPENDIX A

Letter for Telemarketing Campaign

CAPITAL CORPORATION
24000 West 33rd Street, New York, New York 00000

Dear _____ :

Capital recently announced product enhancements, price
reductions, and quantity discounts for the Capital
Electric "Futura" Typewriter and the Capital Electronic
Typewriters. These changes combine to make these
typewriters more productive and affordable than ever
before.

In addition, Capital customers ordering 1 or 2
typewriters can now save 5 percent by calling a direct
toll-free number (1-800-444-0000).

Capital also has a liberal trade-in allowance on older
model Capital Electric "Futura" Typewriters, and there
are significant tax savings when older, fully-
depreciated machines are replaced by new models.

Within the next two weeks, a Capital Representative will
be calling you to discuss your typewriter needs and to
explain how the Capital Electric "Futura" and the
Capital Electronic Typewriters can satisfy those needs.

If I can be of further assistance to you, please do not
hesitate to contact me at 394-0000.

Sincerely,

Lee Ann O'Sullivan   Richard Kay
Marketing Representative   Marketing Manager

Information and Communications Systems Planning at Pure-Pac: Resolving Who Does What

"That's very, very good news," you think, smiling to yourself as you put down this morning's edition of the *Wall Street Journal*. You just read an article announcing that Pure-Pac will be paying high dividends this quarter because of increased profits. That news promises to make your job as a communications systems planner[1] for the Forever-Seal Division expansion project a lot easier. Pure-Pac management will be more eager to buy communications equipment to accommodate future growth when they are confident that the company will show a profit.

At Pure-Pac, your most important task is to convince Harvey Hamburgh (Forever-Seal Division manager) and James Schreiber (president of Pure-Pac) that the communications systems you plan for the new Forever-Seal Division offices will grow with the company. (See Organizational Chart, Appendix A.) To plan for growth means designing a system which integrates all communications equipment that

---

[1] A communications systems planner directs the selection of equipment that is used to transmit all kinds of information throughout an organization, including telephones, computers, paging systems, security systems, and other devices. In order to recommend adequate communications systems, the communications planner works closely with an information systems planner who determines what kind of information must be transmitted and what systems will manage the sorting, processing, and delivery of information. For example, in planning and implementing a company payroll system, an information systems planner determines what data are needed by the payroll officers (for example, withholding tax, wage rates, information from the corporate financial system) and specifies how this data will come together in the payroll. A communications systems planner analyzes what kind of equipment is needed to store this data, make changes, transfer data, and produce the ultimate output.

may be needed for the foreseeable future by the various Forever-Seal Division offices. The list includes telephone service; video display service for security and employee training; a network of data communications services, such as computer-to-computer, terminal-to-computer, and word-processing systems; and specialty communications services, such as radio paging, intercom systems, and teleconferencing capabilities—not to mention all building management systems, such as fire and security alarms and temperature control systems.

The job of assessing all these needs seems overwhelming at times, but you are working with a team of dedicated and competent people who are managing the entire Forever-Seal expansion project. You have nothing but respect for your boss, Dennis Jaynes, the director of the Division Expansion Office. Jaynes coordinates the work of an internal team of architects, engineers, planners, and interior designers who are working with outside engineering and architectural firms on the expansion.

The planning and designing of the Forever-Seal expansion has gone quite well, particularly because Jaynes has the full support of Division Manager Hamburgh. Also, Jaynes gets along famously with the Forever-Seal director of operations, Jason Firebaugh, to whom your office reports. Jaynes's work would be a lot easier, though, if Adam Updike, the division's director of finance, would trust the leadership of those under Hamburgh. Updike sits at Hamburgh's right hand, and, since he watches the purse strings, he feels that he ought to control every part of the Forever-Seal operation in some way. When he does not succeed, he becomes standoffish. Jaynes believes that Updike would like to totally revamp the Division Expansion Office. In fact, your boss has said that Updike would reorganize every office in the whole division given the chance. That is one of Updike's problems as an administrator; he always has his fingers in too many pies. The irony is that you were hired because of this very behavior.

Adam Updike is responsible for planning the information systems for the expansion project. He recommended that the Division Expansion Office hire a separate communications systems planner; moreover, he supported *your* candidacy wholeheartedly because you convinced him of your commitment to designing a communications system that will accommodate any expansion of the information systems and procedures. Since you have been with the company, however, Updike has given you the cold shoulder. Jaynes has suggested that this is because you took hold of the job so thoroughly, certainly with more gusto than Updike had expected. During the two months you have been at Forever-Seal, you have already established a Communications Systems (CS) Planning Team[2] and have held regular meetings to assess state-of-the-art communications equipment and to assess how new products are being used by other companies. By all rights, Updike should be pleased by that. But for some reason he is not, and he has made no move to work with you. That has seemed strange to you, given his tendency to want to run everything. But Jaynes explained why that might be.

"You see," Jaynes said, taking you aside after a cool reception by Updike at a meeting of central management and the Division Expansion Office, "since Adam is planning the information systems for the new Forever-Seal plant, I think he's afraid you may make him look bad. He hasn't been half as organized as you've been in getting his plans together. That CS Planning Team you put together really got the jump on him."

You asked Jaynes what to do about the situation. He suggested that you "do nothing" at the moment and wait for Adam to approach you instead. You accepted his advice but were a little concerned about the lack of communication (can you believe it!) between the communications and information systems people. The problem could have severe consequences if not resolved soon. Inevitably, your state-of-the-art research has kept you busy enough. But you do tend to mull over what to do about Adam Updike whenever you have nothing specific scheduled—right now, for instance.

You are making a few notes on how to approach Updike when the phone rings. For a moment, you think you are psychic, for it is none other than Updike on the line. He is unusually friendly, so you wonder what is going on. He starts telling you about some meeting of the top officers of Pure-Pac. Apparently last weekend the president, all division managers, and the vice-president and chief financial officer for the corporation were away at a management retreat. Hamburgh could not attend, and he sent Updike in his place. Following a presentation, President Schreiber got especially interested in communications sys-

---

[2] Members of the Communications Systems Planning Team include user representatives from each of the 12 departments in the Forever-Seal Division. The user representatives discuss their future needs for communications equipment in the light of what you have found will be available to purchase.

tems planning for the Forever-Seal Division expansion and wanted to know how short-range and long-range planning for both information systems and communications systems would be carried out. Sure enough, he cornered Updike at the meeting to ask him about it. At this point in his tale about last weekend's powwow, Updike hesitates a bit.

"So what did you tell him?" you ask, anxiously.

"Well, that's why I called you," Adam says, getting to the point. "I told him that I planned to hire a consultant to assist me with information systems planning for the new division offices, and that you were handling communications systems planning."

"And what did you tell him about the communications plans?" you ask.

"Well, I thought it would be best not to speak for you," Updike continues. There is a brief silence on his end of the line. "Perhaps you ought to drop him a line and explain how your office is handling things. Just to let him know you have everything under control."

Cutting short his conversation with you, Adam does not give you time to ask questions. You are totally puzzled and not sure what to do about this situation, so you decide to drop in on Jaynes and discuss it with him.

"Looks like Adam got nailed," Jaynes tells you. "And so now he's trying to get back at us. We've got to do something about this right away. You better write a memo to Schreiber telling him about our plans before he asks us himself."

"Well, what should I tell him?" you ask. "We haven't done much planning because we haven't gotten together with Updike."

"I know that. First, we've got to let Schreiber know that we will design a totally flexible facility to accommodate any future needs for communications equipment. Then we'll tell him you've got research on needed communications equipment in progress—you know—mention the CS Planning Team. Whatever else we say, we can't let him think we have our heads in the sand over here," Jaynes adds with emphasis.

"What do you mean by that?"

"I mean that we must let him think we are working well with other corporate offices," Jaynes explains. "We should mention that you are cooperating with the corporation-wide Telecommunications Planning Committee . . ."

"Of course," you break in, "I meet with that group once a month.

Every Pure-Pac division is represented there.[3] Communications people in all the divisions raise questions about how to use and purchase computers, televideo display systems, the whole bit. My contact with that group has helped me do equipment research faster and more efficiently."

"That's right," Jaynes says. "And it could be important to bring that up now. We know Updike has not gone out of his way to communicate with us, but he may feel that we're the ones who don't want to cooperate. What I fear is that he might give Schreiber that impression. Your work with the Telecommunications Committee should show Schreiber we're team workers." Jaynes steps toward you. "But in that memo to Schreiber, you better mention Updike's 'good works.' Tell Schreiber that Updike's office is in fact planning information systems now, with the help of an outside consultant as he says. Say that we are gathering as much data as we can about communications systems to handle everything from word processing to printing payroll checks, so we'll be ready to suggest alternatives when Updike tells us what he needs."

"So, you want me to emphasize cooperation, but not to say anything too explicit? I see," you say. "But what can I use as a premise for writing this memo in the first place?"

"Be straightforward," Jaynes answers. "Tell Schreiber we're aware of the retreat and heard he's curious about the communications systems planning for the new plant."

Still somewhat uncertain about the situation, you nevertheless say, "Okay," and start out toward your own office.

"Wait a minute," Jaynes stops you. "Before you start that memo, I'm going to give a call to Harvey Hamburgh." Jaynes takes a deep breath. "It just occurred to me, this communication should come from him. If we go straight to Schreiber, it might look like Hamburgh isn't in control of our operation."

---

[3] The Telecommunications Planning Committee was charged by Vice-President Lindstrom eight months ago, before you joined the company. You were appointed to the committee when you were hired. Lindstrom established the group to encourage research in telecommunications at Pure-Pac so that computers and other equipment could be purchased and used efficiently and effectively throughout the company. At committee meetings, company representatives from each division pose problems on the use of telecommunications equipment in their divisions. Vendors are sometimes called in to explain products.

So, you wait while Jaynes phones Hamburgh. After Jaynes reaches him, he soon learns that Updike never told Hamburgh of his conversation with Schreiber. However, Hamburgh gives your office the go-ahead to write the memo to Schreiber for him. When Jaynes hangs up, he asks you to draft the memo to Schreiber immediately, reminding you that it must represent the division as united in its efforts. "We must keep any hint of our feelings about Updike's lack of cooperation out of this," Jaynes emphasizes. "Actually, it probably wasn't so bad that this whole event happened. Now, we'll have to deal directly with the problem of coordinating Updike's efforts with ours. A good way to make it all get off on the right foot is to assure Schreiber we're one big happy family."

Feeling satisfied that everything will be resolved satisfactorily, Jaynes shows you out of his office. Now you must take everything into account and make an effort to solve the problem.

Complete either Assignment 1 or 2:

ASSIGNMENT 1

Draft the memo which Dennis Jaynes asks you to write to James Schreiber, President of Pure-Pac Packing Company. The memo will be from Harvey Hamburgh, Manager, Forever-Seal Division. Steven Lindstrom, Adam Updike, and Dennis Jaynes will be on the distribution list. (Write your name on the upper-right corner of this paper to identify it for your instructor.)

ASSIGNMENT 2

In mulling over what Jaynes has asked you to write to Schreiber, you become uncomfortable with what you have been asked to do. You think you have a better strategy for dealing with the problem. Write a memo to Jaynes which briefly explains your alternative plan and requests him to discuss it with you. Append a draft of any document required by your new strategy (for example, a memo to Schreiber which reflects your approach to the problem).

ASSIGNMENT 3

Assume that you have completed Assignment 1. Harvey Hamburgh has approved your memo to Schreiber, but he is not happy about the mishap which prompted it. He wants Jaynes to provide written documentation of the events that led to your memo to Schreiber. Write a memo from Jaynes to Hamburgh explaining background events. List your own name after "Written by" on your memo.

ASSIGNMENT 4
Write a memo inviting Updike to attend the next meeting of your Communications Systems Planning Team. (You indicate a date.) You will want Updike to brief the team on his plans for gathering data on needed information systems. The memo will come from you, and Jaynes will be on the distribution list.

APPENDIX A

Organizational Chart for Pure-Pac Packing

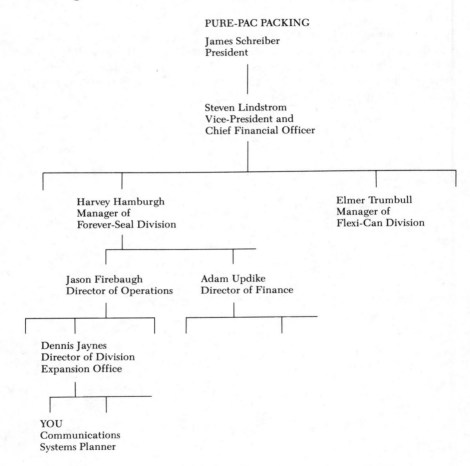

PURE-PAC PACKING

James Schreiber
President

Steven Lindstrom
Vice-President and
Chief Financial Officer

Harvey Hamburgh
Manager of
Forever-Seal Division

Elmer Trumbull
Manager of
Flexi-Can Division

Jason Firebaugh
Director of Operations

Adam Updike
Director of Finance

Dennis Jaynes
Director of Division
Expansion Office

YOU
Communications
Systems Planner

The Stockroom Case: Summarizing the Attendant's Job Description

As the administrative assistant for the Department of Chemistry at Southwest State University, your responsibilities include most of the business functions of the department, as well as its daily operations. One of your minor tasks is to help run the departmental stockroom, a unit nominally supervised by the Stockroom Committee and its chair, Dr. William McIntyre. For quite some time the committee has not met, and you have done little or nothing to help manage the stockroom. However, faculty and staff complaints about stockroom procedures and about the service rendered by the attendant have been growing over the past few months until you can no longer ignore the grumbling. Often staff members have reported that the stockroom attendant does not complete important jobs on time. Most frequently, they charge that the stockman is either "nowhere to be found" or is engaged with other tasks he claims he cannot leave. Several times tempers have flared, and twice professors have called you, irate over the attendant's "poor service"; one claimed the stockman was busy all day on the copy machine, and the other charged a foul-up in his delivery of an important item.

Clearly you will have to do something. First, you call in the stockroom attendant himself, Milton Krim. Under your questioning about the procedures he follows in running the stockroom and the charges of some of the faculty, Krim first defends himself, but then he bitterly attacks his critics for putting him in an impossible position. "The 25 faculty members mean I have 25 supervisors," he says. "I sure can't satisfy all of them all of the time, especially since they all expect me to drop whatever I'm doing to wait on them."

You are beginning to see that the structure of the stockroom attendant's job, together with the unrealistic expectations of the faculty, may be the crux of the problem. So you talk to Professor McIntyre and get him to call a meeting of the Stockroom Committee to review the procedures and the attendant's job. After examining the problems, especially the conflicts over task priorities, the group decides to redefine the stockroom attendant's job and the services the stockroom offers. The five committee members hammer out rules to cover most situations and spell out the attendant's job for the employee himself, as well as for all the faculty and staff members with whom or for whom he must work. The group also establishes new guidelines for supervising the stockroom attendant, sets clear priorities for his duties, and appoints one of its members, Professor Robert Riley, to be the attendant's immediate supervisor.

After a final review meeting with the committee, you are asked by the chairman to write up a "Job Description of the Supervisor of Equipment and Supplies" (the formal title for the stockroom attendant). You produce a ten-part document which details the stockroom attendant's duties in all the service areas set up by the committee and which describes the rules governing the stockroom procedures. (See Appendix A.) The committee unanimously endorses your report at their next meeting. Chairman McIntyre expresses his satisfaction that the committee has dealt so well with this unpleasant situation, but Bob Riley does not think things are so rosy yet.

"Everyone in this department from the faculty down to the dishwashers has to know how to treat Milt in the future," Riley asserts. "There must be close to 150 people[1] who have some contact with the stockroom. They've all got to know what they can and cannot expect from Krim and from the stockroom. If we just send out this job description with a typical, 'Here are the new rules, folks,' very few people will bother to read them through."

"In short," chimes in Nancy Diaz, the youngest professor on the committee, "most people will continue to behave as they did before, ordering Milton around, expecting him to drop everything to wait on them."

---

[1] The approximately 140 employees of the Chemistry Department are faculty members, researchers, research assistants, and graduate students.

"Right," echoes Riley.

McIntyre glances around the room and then rather abruptly changes his tune. Nodding in agreement with what he judges to be the committee consensus, he directs you to draft some guidelines to accompany the job description so that all the staff members will get the point and realize how their actions and expectations will have to change.

"That sounds fine," Riley says. "But we must make sure that everyone will see them. Why not ask the faculty to post the introductory guidelines and the job description itself on their bulletin boards. That way, most staff members will just glance over the first page, but they can look at the full report if they want to."

Again the committee agrees with Riley, so McIntyre advises you to write the introduction to the job description in the form of a one-page cover memo "so that faculty members can post the whole report on their bulletin boards, but with just the introduction showing on top."

"Remember," Riley concludes looking at you sharply, "you must change the actions of everybody from the faculty down to the technicians."

ASSIGNMENT 1

Write an introduction to the Job Description of the Supervisor of Equipment and Supplies (Appendix A) in the form of a cover memo addressed to "All Faculty Members, Department of Chemistry." The memo is from Professor William McIntyre; your name will appear after the heading "Prepared by."

ASSIGNMENT 2

Edit and format the Job Description of the Supervisor of Equipment and Supplies (Appendix A). *Note*: This manuscript contains many errors in style, including grammatical errors, sexist language, and inconsistent number style.

APPENDIX A

Job Description of the Supervisor of Equipment and Supplies

DEPARTMENT OF CHEMISTRY

JOB DESCRIPTION

I. **Position**—Supervisor: Equipment and Supplies

Supervision of employee—delegated by the Chairman to the Stockroom Committee, one member of which will maintain frequent contact with employee and will mediate any problems or complaints of employee or others concerning employee's area of responsibility. Any complaints or suggestions by others for improvements in services should be discussed with that member rather than with employee directly.

Policies concerning area of responsibility are made by the Stockroom Committee, usually after discussion with employee and affected faculty and staff. Modifications of policies and procedures, as described below, may be made only after written approval of the Stockroom Committee.

II. **Capsule Descriptions of Duties**

Most of the duties of the employee are concerned with receiving, storing, dispensing, maintaining, transferring, and disposing of equipment and supplies used in the department. Individual duties are listed below with approximations of their frequency, time requirements, and schedules. They are listed in order of priority. Duties of high priority should not be interrupted or superseded by those of lower priority unless clear evidence of overriding urgency exists.

1. Maintain departmental copier in optimal functioning condition (occasional—$\frac{1}{4}$ to $\frac{1}{2}$ hr per day).
2. Distribute mail (twice daily, at 11:00 A.M. and 3:00 P.M.—$\frac{1}{2}$ hr/day).
3. Prepare student laboratories for use (twice yearly, several hours) and maintain and distribute glassware, supplies, and equipment needed for laboratory classes (Sept. 1 through Dec. 15 and Jan. 2 through April 15. 1–4 hr/day).

4. Receive and distribute materials ordered by department members (daily $\frac{1}{2}$–$1\frac{1}{2}$ hr/day).
5. Maintain and repair equipment under the instruction and direction of departmental electronic specialist (0–3 hr per day, more during summer).
6. Order, receive, stock, and dispense supplies listed in the stockroom inventory (order, receive, stock—occasionally; dispense—daily, at infrequent intervals).
7. Collect soiled laundry (lab coats, mostly); sort and shelve clean coats (weekly—approx. $\frac{1}{2}$ hr/wk).
8. Assist faculty members and staff in tasks and errands that are not appropriately handled by other University employees (occasional).
9. Receive and arrange disposal of waste chemicals (occasional).
10. Maintain orderliness in departmental library and in Conference Room A (Library—approx. $\frac{1}{2}$ hr daily; Conf. Rm.—$\frac{1}{2}$ hr weekly, more occasionally).

III. Requirements of Availability

As with other departmental staff members, employee provides service to many people and is similarly expected to be readily located when needed. The normal 8:00–12:00 A.M., 1:00–5:00 P.M. schedule must be worked Monday through Friday unless an alternate schedule is approved by the committee. Absences and other deviations from schedule should be reported to Stockroom Committee. Scheduling of vacation must be arranged well in advance so that arrangements can be made to minimize disruption of services.

In accord with university policy, employee may take a 15-minute break in the mid-morning and mid-afternoon at an agreed upon time.

Unless on break or on duties that must be performed elsewhere, employee must remain in stockroom (Rm 4713) during working hours. Aside from employee, only the Chairman, Associate Chairman, and members of the Stockroom Committee will be issued keys and authorized to enter that room. The door must remain closed and locked when not in use for entry or exit. Both dispensary windows must remain open when employee is present and closed when he must go where he cannot see them for more than 2 or 3 minutes. When leaving the room for a break or to perform duties elsewhere, an appropriate sign must be posted to indicate the break or the new location.

IV. Policies and Procedures Concerning the Listed Duties

1. *Maintain departmental copier in optimal functioning condition*

The employee will be assigned responsibility as "key operator" of the departmental copier and will be instructed in minor service operations. When the copier malfunctions or needs supplies, it is the employee's responsibility to get it back into optimal service as soon as possible. If expert service is needed, he must make arrangements for it immediately.

2. *Distribute mail*

When notified by intercom that mail has arrived, employee must sort and distribute mail in the mailroom boxes.

3. *Prepare student laboratories for use and maintain and distribute glassware, supplies, and equipment needed for laboratory classes*

a. *Prepare laboratories*

Early in January and September, before the 1st meeting of laboratory classes, employee must clean surfaces of workbenches, equipment and shelving of accumulated dust and materials left from the preceding classes. Such surfaces should be washed at that time. Sink drains and plumbing should be inspected at that time and arrangement made for repairs or service as needed. Refrigerator interiors must be cleaned each summer.

b. *Maintain and distribute glassware, supplies, and equipment needed for laboratory classes*

Between terms, the condition of equipment must be determined and appropriate adjustments and repairs made as needed. When equipment is not to be used for several weeks it must be stored in designated shelves in the student labs or in locked cabinets under the workbenches.

Student equipment may be loaned on request to faculty members for research purposes on an emergency basis, BUT ONLY WHEN NOT NEEDED BY A CLASS. Accurate records must be kept of all loans, showing date of loan, signature of borrower, and date of return. Similar records must be kept for equipment issued from the stockroom to teaching assistants and faculty of laboratory classes. Equipment not returned when needed must be retrieved from borrower by employee.

Student equipment which malfunctions during classes may be brought to the stockroom window. Employee must attempt to repair it or get it repaired as soon as possible.

Student laboratories are scheduled in the Fall and Winter terms only. Most meet from 9:00 to 12:00 A.M. on Tuesday and Thursday. Lab teachers will provide employee with a list of glassware and supplies needed each day. Employee must distribute these from stocks from the Preparations Room (Room 4824) at the time and place and in the numbers requested. After the lab period, he must collect them and remove them to appropriate containers in the prep room to soak. When his schedule allows, the employee must wash the glassware in the 5th room dishwasher, and store it in the preparations room.

Glassware and supplies stored in the preparations room will be used to a small extent by teaching assistants who use that room for making reagents for laboratory classes. Employee must clean such glassware along with that distributed to the laboratories. In preparation for the beginning of classes, employee is responsible for the initial cleanliness and orderliness of the preparations room and should work with teaching assistants to maintain it.

4. *Receive and distribute materials ordered by department members*

Materials delivered to the department are handled by many people, who must account for them by appropriate signatures showing receipt and delivery. Care must be taken to continue such accountability until materials are in the hands of the orderers. When ordered materials arrive, employee must sign to acknowledge receipt of each package. Packages must be delivered as soon as possible after receipt. An appropriate signature must be obtained by employee for each package delivered, including blanket orders delivered to Room 5318. When contained items from the blanket order packages are returned from that office to employee for delivery, employee must sign again to acknowledge receipt.

Items that must be kept cold, according to package instruction, must either be delivered soon after receipt or placed in a refrigerator or freezer, as required, until delivery is possible. Employee should use notes or other reminders to avoid forgetting the location of such packages.

5. *Maintain and repair equipment under the instruction and direction of Mr. Al Bok*, College Instrumentation Supervisor

Employee will be taught simple repair and maintenance methods. He must report daily to Mr. Bok to discuss any needed work. To the extent that it is practical, assigned work should be taken to the 4th floor stockroom so that employee will be available there for the occasional other requests for his services.

6. *Order, receive, stock, and dispense supplies listed in the stockroom inventory (Only items so listed may be ordered)*

Stocks are maintained primarily in two locations—one on the 4th floor under rigid security as described under section III, above, and the other on the 5th floor under less security, as described below.

The 5th floor stockroom will be kept locked but keyed by the key used for entry to the mailroom. That room will contain stocks in small amounts (to allow quick inventory) or frequently used items. Items in this room will be readily accessible on weekends and evenings and at other times when employee is absent or not immediately accessible. To allow charges to be made to the appropriate accounts, users are requested to sign out all materials on the individual order books provided. Employee must check stocks frequently and replace any that have been taken.

Records must be kept of all items placed in stock in the 4th floor stockroom and of all stocks dispensed, either to individuals or by transfer to the 5th floor stockroom or preparations room by employee. An inventory must be made every summer by July 31 to determine whether stocks have been adequately accounted for.

7. *Collect soiled laundry (lab coats mostly) and sort and shelve clean laundry*

Clean laundry will be received from the Dock in a canvas hamper on Thursday. It must be sorted when received and placed on appropriate shelves in the mailroom. The hamper must be retained near the mailroom to receive soiled laundry, which employee must deliver to the dock the following Thursday.

8. *Assist faculty and staff members in tasks and errands that are not appropriately handled by other university employees*

Faculty and staff requesting services other than those listed must do so in writing in a record book kept by employee. This requirement may be waived at employee's discretion for tasks that are relatively simple and brief and to be carried out immediately on request. Usually these assignments will be of low priority in comparison to those listed above but occasionally may be urgent. In the event of a schedule conflict, tasks concerned with general departmental functions should be given priority over services to a specific research laboratory.

Some tasks or errands may occur repetitively. These include the occasional updating of the faculty directory located in the elevator hallway and occasional cleaning of projection transparencies and rolls used in class lectures.

9. *Receive and arrange for disposal of waste chemicals*

Chemicals and wastes that should not be disposed of in the drain or trash containers must be collected centrally for pick-up and disposal by employees of the Department of Industrial Health. Our department stores such collected materials in the hood of the 5th floor stockroom. Employee will receive such materials, see that they are properly labeled by contributors, and arrange periodically for pick-up.

10. *Maintain order and cleanliness in departmental library and in Conference Room A*

Employee must examine the condition of the departmental library each morning and must shelve books and clean tables as needed. Employee must also be responsible for orderliness and cleanliness of Conference Room A, washing the blackboard each Monday and cleaning table tops as needed. When informed that these rooms will be used for special occasions (seminars, conferences, etc.), employee is responsible for their being in suitable condition for the occasion.

Trouble for County Extension Agents: Improving Progress Reports

The Job of an Extension Agent

"Family Living" is the official designation of the home economics section in the County Extension Service, the governmental unit you work for in Shawnee County. As an extension agent home economist, your job is to provide informal adult education in those areas of home economics where people need help; currently that means topics like aging, stress, nutrition, and ways to save and make money.

Like other county extension agents in every state, you have two bosses: your local section chief and the director in your geographical region. The former is Ethel Larson, the Shawnee County Family Living director. The latter, somewhat more influential, is Cal Shipman, the regional director for the western section of the state. Larson, whom you see a couple of times a week, is a supervisor with strangely little interest in Family Living issues but with a strong instinct for self-survival in the Extension Service bureaucracy. Shipman, whom you see only occasionally, seems to be a reasonable man, but he has responsibility for all sections of the Extension Service and does not devote much of his time to Family Living. (Shipman's office is in Steubenville, some 70 miles south of Shawnee's County Extension Office in the town of Fairport, where you are located.) Larson and Shipman are about as different as two people can be: she is very cool and distant, and he is very talkative and friendly. However, they are alike in one respect: they both always know which way the wind is blowing from Washington. They know what the priorities are at the top of the bureaucracy of the nationwide extension service and how your state's units must satisfy the far-off administrators.

Despite your two bosses' focus on meeting the demands from

Washington, your job description calls for you to meet the *local* public's needs and interests. You attempt to identify these needs by talking to people, reading their letters, answering hundreds of telephone calls every month requesting information on a wide array of topics, and listening to proposals from organizations and informal groups. In response, you design programs, teach courses, give single presentations, and write press releases, newsletters, a newspaper column, and numerous individual letters.

The difficulty of your position—beyond the problems of satisfying two very political supervisors—lies in predicting what kinds of programs the public will actually attend. Frequently, an extension agent assesses a public interest area and plans a program, only to end up with a handful of registrants, sometimes so few that the program is canceled. Even if a program is very well received by those participating, limited attendance turns it into an official failure. Thus identifying objectives in tune with the interests of large numbers of the public is critical to your job success.

Not surprisingly, "Innovation—constant change to meet new needs," is the County Extension Service agent's motto. At the moment you are finishing preparations on a truly innovative training program for all the extension home economists in the western section of the state, Cal Shipman's jurisdiction. This in-service program is a first-time event—a retreat where agents can informally share ideas and problems faced in their jobs in the seven-county area. The retreat idea, which you are sure will assist all agents in meeting public needs better in the long run, was yours, and you managed to sell it to the administrators, first Larson, and eventually Shipman. Cal then appointed Patsy Ferris of the York County office to cochair the event with you.

Although the retreat's purpose is to allow agents to interact freely without administrators around to inhibit the conversation, you realize Cal had to be invited to give some remarks, and after some consideration, you and Patsy decide to invite two Family Living directors as well (including your own supervisor, Ethel Larson, and Patsy's supervisor in York County). Looking over the plans you and Patsy have formulated, you are quite pleased—except for the topic of Cal Shipman's talk: "Your Monthly Progress Report." You cannot imagine a duller or less significant topic.

Monthly progress reports are the most perfunctory writing tasks you perform as an extension agent. The *yearly* progress report is another matter. To receive Larson's and Shipman's evaluation of your performance, you must write an annual progress report which directly influences the number of dollars in your paycheck. But by official policy you must also submit monthly progress reports. The "monthlies" must be sent to both Larson and Shipman, and you know that they also go to some other office. But once they are out, you practically never hear about them again; as a result, after several years on the job, you have come to treat them as just more paperwork, an inconvenience of working for the government. If they have any use at all, you believe it is for yourself, forming a chronological record of what you have accomplished over the month and a reference for preparing the important yearly progress report.

So, why Cal Shipman should choose to talk about monthly progress reports at the retreat baffles you. He will probably bore everyone to death. What a way to start the retreat!

The Retreat

The Home Economists' retreat begins Friday evening, September 16, 1983, at the Bayfield Conference Center at Mille Lacs, a resort about 20 miles from Fairport. All 14 of the home economists in the area are at dinner by 6:30 P.M., along with the three supervisors who are going to deliver their pronouncements early in the evening and then depart. The real give-and-take will be on Saturday. The first speaker tonight is Cal talking about the monthly progress reports. So when, after pie and coffee, you are contacted by the Bayfield manager about a mix-up in the number of registrations (producing problems in both catering and bedrooms), you are not unhappy to tell Patsy to take care of introducing Cal while you attend to the reservations. About a half hour later, you arrive in the meeting room to hear polite applause for Cal's talk. During the brief break to get refills on coffee, you ask Patsy to fill you in on Cal's presentation.

"What, if anything, did he have to say?" you ask.

"His big message was that we should no longer treat our monthly progress reports in an offhand way. They are important, and we should take them seriously."

"What's the big deal? Why should we take them seriously all of a sudden?"

Patsy gestures impatiently. "Oh, you know, all that accountability stuff from Washington. They want more documentation, proof that our programs are valuable, doing what we claim they are."

"So?"

"We've got to supply more evidence in the monthlies. Show how people saved money, or prove they learned something, or changed their attitudes. Evidently we've just been too casual about them."

"And they just noticed?"

"For some reason they've gotten the word to start cracking the whip," she replies. "Cal was pretty explicit about what we should do. Provide details on each item to show programs are working and exactly for whom—especially minorities, low-income people, and men,[1] of course—and that we should explain everything a lot more, especially with an eye to the results."

"Sounds like just one more piece of paperwork dictated by Washington so that we have less time for the real work," you counter.

"He also talked about how we should write them," Patsy continues. "We're supposed to gear our remarks to our key objectives, the major programs, and arrange things so that the big points can be found easily. Seems like most of us have been just listing everything by the calendar."

"I guess he's telling us that somebody is reading these things now."

"And that from now on they will count in our evaluations," Patsy adds. "He made that pretty clear," she whispers before walking up to the front of the group to introduce Ethel.

Cal Shipman's Telephone Call

Back at work on the next Monday (September 19), you get a pat on the back from Ethel Larson for the retreat. The other agent in the Shawnee office raved about the session, so Larson lets you know that's a good sign. Then an hour later you get a phone call from Cal Shipman in Steubenville. He was very pleased with the Friday dinner and meeting and asks you how the rest of the retreat went. After you give him a rundown and bask in his praise for your good ideas and effort in setting up the conference, you are surprised when he changes the subject quite abruptly.

"Say, I was reading over your monthly progress report for August," Cal says. "I was most pleased to see several men and quite a number of low-income people in your groups. Good job also on the use of volunteers."

---

[1] Traditionally, County Extension programs in the Family Living area ("home economics") have served white women. Today policy dictates that agents attempt to equalize their coverage to both sexes and extend services to minority groups. Reporting on programs should include participant makeup whenever men or minorities are significantly represented.

"Thanks," you mumble, while trying to digest this second evidence of the newly developed interest in monthly reports. Now you wish you had been able to hear his talk on Friday night. Patsy gave you the main ideas, but you would like the details as well.

"One problem, however," Cal changes his tone, "You seemed to have to cancel quite a number of programs because of poor registration. That's a lot of wasted planning effort. Hope we can expect to see a turnaround this month on that score."

"Well, of course, that's a problem for all of us," you shoot back. "In our attempts to move into populations never before served by County Extension, we don't always meet with instant success."

"Yes, yes, I know," Cal interrupts. "But all the agents must get on top of program planning to ensure they're meeting real needs and interests. Just wanted you to know that we're concerned about the accountability issue," Cal drones on in his most official tones, and then closes insinuatingly, "It's so important in the evaluation of each agent you know."

After hanging up the phone, you feel a bit chagrined at Cal's final remark. Glancing at the calendar, you note that you have two weeks before you must submit the September monthly report. After a moment, you wonder what the Performance Review Guidelines say about monthly reports. So you turn to your personnel file and pull out the new rating sheet with its 180 questions—questions which both Cal and Ethel Larson must answer about your job performance. Only a supervisor who observes you closely on a daily basis could ever fill out this form honestly, but the regulations demand that the job be done by people who see you only occasionally. Clearly, you must convince them that your programs are valuable; otherwise, you will not get due credit for them. The trouble is that any program that cannot be quantified (preferably in dollars and cents) simply does not "count" much on the official record anymore. Flipping through the rating sheet, you note one question asking the supervisors to rate the effectiveness of the employee's written reports, but the rating guide says nothing specific about progress reports. However, the more you think about it, the more obvious it seems that the monthly progress reports are Cal and Ethel's major monitor for answering many questions about you on the performance review. So preparing your next monthly progress report clearly calls for some change in your procedures. For now, you decide to go back and fill in some details on each activity in early September, and then keep more detailed notes for the remainder of the month. At least you will be ready to write the report come early October.

The September Calendar

Two weeks later, during the first week of October, you look over your beefed-up calendar for the month of September (Appendix A) and prepare to write your monthly progress report in a new and better way.

You are proud of your achievements in several areas but upset over the poor attendance in some of your programs and the failure of one to take place at all. On the one hand, the retreat, your baby, was a huge success—with great evaluations and informal feedback. But the retreat was an unusual program and not for the public—no heads to be counted, no dollars saved. Among your regular programs, your "Myths" course on the 28th and 29th went over well. But that program is not news. What is news, however, is the Small Business course—probably your biggest news. You are very confident about it; enrollment is almost full (32 places with a maximum of 35), so you certainly defined the interests of the community right on that score. People want to work for themselves; they have skills, but they need to know how to start up a business. Using the local entrepreneurs to tell their "success stories" in a course panel and also to help plan the series was a good move on your part. Also, it was smart to ask two of them to give presentations (Jim Edsel, a CPA, and Nancy Carpenter, an attorney), along with some small business specialists from the state university. The course will start in November and run for six weeks, but since planning meetings were held in September, you can include it in this "monthly."[2]

On the other side of the coin, a lot of the traditional winners are just not capturing audiences. The diet program on the 26th was poorly attended; Cal is not going to be impressed with that. Worst of all, however, is the cancellation of the Bolton Heights neighborhood program. *That* was something that would have scored with Washington: grass-roots involvement with low-income and several minority groups. It is beyond you what happened there. It seemed like there was local support; the residents came to you with a request to develop these particular programs on the basis of their own extensive survey of the neighborhood. So you designed the sessions, planning for at least 30

---

[2] By convention in the County Extension Service, your own individual planning efforts for an activity are not covered in a monthly progress report until the activity itself takes place. However, meetings with other persons are included in the month they take place, whether or not the planned activity itself occurs in that month.

families. What happens? Only three people preregistered, despite extensive publicity. Shipman will absolutely love that.

Accountability. The State Fair was pretty mundane. Hmm. With the canning center stuff on September 8, you can calculate some estimated savings. Let's see. If the cost of canning 7 quarts of green beans (purchased by the bushel) is compared with the price of purchasing them commercially canned, each person who attended should have saved approximately $3.00. At least there are a few bright spots here and there! Also, there's that flood of requests for the nutrition inputs from your newspaper column. That's a big pool of persons interested in nutrition, a new source of potential registrations for other nutrition programs. Hmm . . . you wonder how much to tell about the "show" for the junior highers on September 9. Dressing up as an auto mechanic, you made the analogy between the maintenance of your car and your own body. No evaluations are in yet, but the girls certainly enjoyed it. During the next couple of weeks you will do a post-testing of the "Nutrition Spot Check" using volunteers to code the information for the terminal and to run the program. Then there's the Health Impact Committee, which began some discussions on expanding its operations and appointed you to meet with Dr. Myers from the state university about applying for a federal grant to educate the rural poor on health issues. Myers mostly listened to you and said he would look into the possibility, but perhaps you can mention it. Main focus of your group is the diet and care of the pregnant mother and newborn.

Then you start recalling the criteria Cal laid out in the retreat discussion. One thing seems obvious: you can no longer just run through the month, listing the main things you did each day. Instead you will have to write a real report, organizing the information by major activities, and detailing things sufficiently so that you will sound fully accountable. Clearly, you must include everything of substance, but you must put it together so that you get credit for the successes you had, without getting too much discredit for the unfortunate head counts that were beyond your control.

Complete either Assignment 1 or 2:

ASSIGNMENT 1
Using the form provided in Appendix B, write your monthly progress report for September 1983. Recipients are Calvin Shipman, Regional Director, Western Section of Kansas, and Ethel Larson, Assistant Di-

rector, Family Living, Shawnee County Extension Service. An administrator who is unknown to you also receives the report.

ASSIGNMENT 2

Write your monthly progress report for September 1983 to the same persons noted in Assignment 1, but create your own format.

ASSIGNMENT 3

A week after you send in your monthly progress report, you receive the following memo:

COOPERATIVE EXTENSION SERVICE
Western State University and
U.S. Department of Agricultural Cooperating
Steubenville, Kansas 00000

October 12, 1983

To: YOU, Extension Agent, County of Shawnee

I have just read your September monthly report. It is one of the most informative that I have read in a long time. You have been very busy, very productive, and several of your new programs are really moving along. I am especially pleased about your Small Business Course.

Unfortunately, most agents' progress reports haven't shown the big changes yours did. Would you help me out by writing a brief set of guidelines for preparing monthly progress reports? Next week I am going to send a memo to all the agents telling them that their monthly reports need a big turnaround. I would like to include your guidelines in that mailing, so that they can see an agent's viewpoint on the matter. Please send me your write-up as soon as possible. Thanks.

Carl Shpn

Comply with Shipman's request for the guidelines. When they are completed, write him a cover memo to accompany them.

ASSIGNMENT 4
Write a very brief feature article on the retreat for the Oregon Extension Service newsletter, a simple quarterly for agents in all sections of the Extension Service. The visiting Family Living agent, Mary Jo Kreiger, from Korbel, Oregon (see September 21 on Calendar), was impressed with the retreat accounts she heard from several agents who attended, so she asked you to write a brief story for their Oregon newsletter, the *Spotlight*. Kreiger's purpose, as she expressed it during her visit, was to generate interest in a retreat so that she could propose doing a similar program in Oregon. After you have completed the newsletter article, write a cover letter to Mary Jo Kreiger, County Extension Agent, Hiawatha County Extension Service, Korbel, Oregon 00000. Your title and address are County Extension Agent, Shawnee County Extension Service, Fairport, Kansas 00000.

APPENDIX A

Calendar for September 1983—
Annotated by You

(*Note*: The calendar contains some bracketed explanations for you that would not have been written by the home economist on the job. They provide background information so that you can understand the elliptical notes. Where the number of participants does not note men or minorities, you can assume all those attending are white women.)

SEPTEMBER 1983

1-2

State Fair. 1st day took volunteers Betsy Rand and Felicia Martinez. Booth featured "Watch Your Dollars." 2nd day—difficulties with terminal so couldn't run programs. Many more people stopping at booth Sept 1st than 2nd. Gave lecture/demo on low sodium cookery for a crowd of 52. Used my handout. Ethel Larson in audience. Lots of questions from audience. Audience interested and attentive. Several people came up at end to ask questions/comment. 2nd day Helen Bigelow (volunteer) went with me. Terminal was operating so ran some "Watch Your Dollars" programs for people. ["Watch Your Dollars" is an interactive program using figures from members of the public to calculate how they should allocate their resources.] Helen learned to run terminal. Fair had slim attendance on 2nd. Governor came through the building, but didn't stop by our booth.

<u>5</u>

Labor Day.

<u>6</u>

Met with Flat Rock Hospital dietitian and nurse from County Health Department to plan 4 programs on special diets. [Special Diet Programs are training plans for the general public on diabetic, low-sodium, low-fat, low-cholesterol, and weight-loss diets.] Did PR for programs: letters and flyers to agencies, stores, family practice docs, hosp. diet. departs., outpatient clinics, + press releases to newspapers and radio. Volunteers dropped flyers at library, chamber of commerce, pub bldgs.

<u>7</u>

Interviewed Hal Miller. [Hal Miller is a frequent participant in County Extension programs. Because he has learned such good budgeting techniques, you have asked him to be a volunteer, demonstrating to others that the principles taught by County Extension work.] Hal volunteered to give talk for Shopper Course. Keeps accurate records of his food expenses so knows he spends about $1.50 per day; very careful maneuvering!

<u>8</u>

Staffed county canning center. 29 people learned how to can, including one man. A do-it-yourself experience. One group learned pressure canning, the other water bath.

<u>9</u>

Volunteer Sally Brunning helped me run computer program on "Nutrition Spot Check" at Flat Rock Jr Hi. ["Nutrition Spot Check" is a computer program that compares an individual's dietary intake for one day with the recommended daily allowances (RDAs) for 16 nutrients. The spot check shows how well the person typically meets his/her needs.] Spoke to 3 classes to explain individualized printouts. Girls' diets alarming. Some only 1100 calories. Lack nutrients. Put on show to teach nutrition painlessly. Total students 84. Approx 40% minorities.

12

Worked on plans for the retreat.

13

Met with A. T. "Buzz" Washington, instructor Morgan Community College. Discussed ideas and plans for Small Business course—for people to set up in own homes. The course is "Starting Your Small Home Business." Designed flyer that reads: "If you have been thinking about starting a small home business, but weren't sure how or where to begin, this program is for you." The 5 topics: "Getting Started"—costs and procedures; "Marketing and Pricing"; "Taxes and Records"; "Managing Time"; and "Legal Concerns." Concluding the series, a panel of 5 experienced business persons to discuss their starts in small home businesses.

Discussed Health Impact Committee with Marty Myers, of Western State U's Dept. of Public Health. Possibly will submit federal grant proposal on health education in rural areas. Try to get some maternal and newborn training to low-income families. [Health Impact Committee is composed of field agents, a campus administrator from Western State University, and a volunteer participant in Extension Service programs. They meet twice a year to discuss current resource materials in the health area, to suggest in-service training in health for extension agents, and to design health courses for college week, during which the agents give training on campuses.]

14

From my newspaper col., "Morgan Morning Health" (in the *Morgan Herald*), on "Nutrition Spot Check" got a flood of requests for the information forms for the computer program. By end of week we had received about 200 forms. [The "Nutrition Spot Check" (see September 9 above) allows members of the public to send in their individual dietary intake for one day and get a printout showing how well their consumption compares to the RDAs for 16 nutrients.]

15-16

Completed arrangements for retreat. Cochaired retreat at Mille Lacs, beginning Friday evening, Sept. 16. All 14 family home economists attended. Positive evaluations. Goals on initiating new program ideas accomplished. Also cross-county planning. Program plans and agent problems shared. Camaraderie. Good time.

19-20

Enrollment only about 5 for October Shopper Class. Very poor. [The "Shopper Class" is an in-depth series of classes on how to shop for nutritional value, quality, and low cost in supermarkets. Each participant agrees to devote some hours volunteering in extension programs after he/she has completed the training and earned the designation of "master shopper."] Made efforts to increase enrollment for Shopper Class: did a radio spot on KROR and contacted the *Herald* for a news release. Met with Community Early Childhood staff to interest people in Shopper Class. (The Early Childhood folks can only come evenings, so program would need to be condensed or run for several weeks.) By afternoon of Sept 20, enrollment up to 21 people so we will go ahead without Early Childhood people this time. (Contact Early Childhood for another month.)

21

Dry Run for first of special diets programs scheduled for 26th. Met with Mary Jo Kreiger, Family Living agent from Oregon who is visiting Extension offices all over country on a study leave. Explained our operation to her. Kreiger specially interested in our retreat. Asked me to write newsletter piece for Oregon agents.

22

Gave program on budgeting for retirement at Morgan Comm. Col. Used their terminal, ran about 20 programs, explained output. Attendance—29. All women, but about one-third minority.

23

Spoke on panel at Hennepin Clinic (a low-income facility) on "Alternative Living Styles for Seniors." My topic: "Shared living as an option." Three other panelists, including rep from HUD. About 37 people, but mostly women (4–5 men). Approx. half of total were minorities.

26

First Diet Program: "Weight Loss." Only 7 people showed up. Disappointing. Weather was rainy and cold. Middle-aged and older women. No minorities. Didn't appear to be people who work downtown. [This Diet Program was intended to target the downtown worker, not the rural and suburban people who were the Extension Service's traditional clients. The series was offered without preregistrations, so the numbers could not be known prior to the event and the audience can only be described impressionistically by the agent. "Acceptable attendance" for the event would be about 15 persons.]

27

Canceled remaining Diet Programs. Lack of attendance. Buzz Washington and I met with the 4 entrepreneurs from town who will participate in a panel for the Small Business Course: Alice Edsel, Larry McKay, J. L. Carpenter, and Billy Bales. Planning for small biz course for Nov. [See September 13, above.] Also attended "Returning Women's Group" at Middletown College to announce the small business course & answer questions.

28–29

Gave course on "Myths of Middle Age" for 3 counties: Shawnee, Lincoln, and Erie. [The "Myths of Middle Age" course focuses on the realities of aging and sexuality and compares them with the myths and stereotypes in our society. You have given the course several times, but not recently.] 65 women attended who will reteach course to their study groups. ["Study groups," a long-time Extension program, are groups of women in rural areas who meet every month for social and educational purposes. Each group sends a representative to the Extension home economists' programs who takes the monthly "lesson" back to her group to teach it to everyone.]

<u>30</u>

Canceled planned Bolton Heights Neighborhood programs on health, diet, and parenting. Plans based on surveys and formal request by community group (Bolton Neighborhood Center). Flyers distributed to 600 homes; only 3 parents had preregistered for course scheduled to start October 3, Monday.

Throughout the month: answered 231 phone calls, most on canning and food preservation. Wrote "Morgan Morning Health" column 3 times. Wrote "Family Spotlite" with agent Irene Henning.

APPENDIX B

Monthly Progress Report Form

```
    MONTHLY PROGRESS REPORT      _____
                                        (month)


    NAME OF AGENT _____

    COUNTY _____


    Summarize your accomplishments for the month. Report on
    key objectives accomplished in your programming, other
    programs and activities conducted during the month, and
    any other information you wish to share with your
    supervisors. (Attach an extra sheet if necessary.)


    Approximate Number of Program Audience Contacts:

        Total _____

        Male _____   Female _____   Minorities _____
```

Quality Control at Standard Steel, Inc.: Reporting on Molybdenum Recovery

"Standard Steel of America, Inc.," the huge sign over the plant, catches your eye as you drive into the parking lot. After almost two weeks on the job, you still cannot believe your good fortune to have landed a co-op job here in the Specialty Steels Division at Standard. Co-op jobs have been tough to get here lately, partly because Standard has cut down on the number of assignments and partly because the University has tightened its requirements for co-op positions earning academic credit. But here you are, prior to your senior year in metallurgical engineering at Central University, enrolled in the cooperative education program for one semester of full-time work; next term you will be back at Central to finish up your last two academic semesters before graduating. If you do well as a co-op trainee at Standard, you will have a good chance at a career position here, and you will also have improved your chances with other steel companies.

Your assignment is in the Quality Control Department of the Specialty Steels Division, where they make several classes of stainless steel, with many different grades in each class. Because there are so many variables in making stainless, the Quality Control (QC) personnel must work to quantify, minimize, and control the variability as much as possible and to guarantee the specifications for each grade of steel. Your own tasks are mostly statistical, compiling and averaging operation times, yields, and materials.

Although you have been on the job for only a short time, you have already learned a lot about the operation of a steel mill, largely because Mr. Robert Boylan, the quality control engineer you report to, has been very helpful, discussing things with you at length and willingly answering your questions. Rob Boylan, in his late twenties, is very friendly and an excellent teacher. "It sure won't be Boylan's fault if I don't succeed here," you think to yourself.

This morning, as you walk into the QC Department, Rob announces: "Today you must do the Molybdenum Recovery Report. We issue this 'moly'[1] report every two weeks."

You nod. "Guess you keep track of every pound of the precious stuff, huh?"

"Right. The total monthly cost of molybdenum is tabulated carefully. But the moly report that you'll be preparing covers only those grades of stainless with at least 0.75 percent moly. You see, we only check those grades of stainless to which moly is added. It's expensive enough so we can't afford to waste it, but keeping track of it throughout production costs money too."

"How many grades contain over 0.75 percent moly?" you ask.

"Just the four grades with the highest moly content," Rob replies. "We compare the weight of all the moly added to the steel during production with the calculated weight of the moly in the final product to see if we have lost any."

"Oh. So the recovery is how much moly remains in the final product of what you put in during the processing?"

Rob nods at you. "We determine the recovery by sampling the chemical composition at the end of the processing. Here's what we do overall. We keep track of exactly how much molybdenum is added throughout processing. Then we calculate the weight of the moly present in the final product by sampling the steel as it's poured into ingot molds and analyzing its chemical composition."

"So the moly recovery is simply the final weight divided by the initial weight?"

"Yes," says Rob. "More precisely, it is the ratio of the weight of moly charged during processing and the final weight of moly in the product. You calculate the moly final weight from the chemical composition and the total weight of the final product."

"So I assume some moly is lost in the process, otherwise you wouldn't be keeping track of it all the time. How much do you ordinarily lose, and what happens to it?" you wonder.

"Well, we aim for a recovery of 95 percent," explains Rob, "but the acceptable range is between 90 and 110 percent. Some moly is

---

[1] Molybdenum (Mo), sometimes called "moly," is a hard white metal resembling iron that is added to stainless steel to improve corrosion resistance under high-temperature, acid environments. It is very expensive.

actually lost through oxidation[2] and carry-over into the slag—that's the scum that forms on the surface of the molten steel. But there are lots of other things that can lower the recovery as well, and some of them are not losses at all."

"What do you mean? That it was never there in the first place?"

"That's one thing," answers Rob. "Often the steel scrap used to make the stainless has a lower moly content than it's supposed to. On paper it looks like we lost moly in processing, but in fact it was never there at all. The moly report will show that, help identify the poor quality scrap as the culprit."

"Does that mean dishonest scrap dealers, or what?" you say with a frown.

"Not necessarily dishonest. Scrap dealers must estimate the amount of moly from samples taken from truckloads of scrap, so you can't expect that their figures will be highly accurate. Our scrap supplies will often have somewhat more moly, or somewhat less, than the records say. That will, of course, influence the recovery. Occasionally a dealer will deliberately claim a much higher percentage of moly than the scrap contains, but frankly, most of our problems are less fascinating than chasing dishonest scrap dealers."

"Problems like what?"

"Like locating inaccurate record keeping at either the furnace or the vessel stage of production.[3] As I said before, when you go to meas-

---

[2] Oxidation means to combine with oxygen to form an oxide, a substance with different properties from the original metal.

[3] Stainless steel is made in two stages. First, an electric furnace melts down carbon steel scrap and stainless steel scrap containing ferroalloys until the mixture reaches a specified carbon content and temperature. Second, an argon-oxygen vessel decarburizes the steel and refines it to exact chemical specifications. (Each grade of steel within a class has a slightly different chemistry dictated by the intended use of the final product.)

The plant in the Specialty Steels Division at Standard Steel of America, Inc., in Lisbon, Pennsylvania, consists of six electric furnaces and one argon-oxygen decarburizing vessel (or AOD vessel). This steel vessel, lined with brick, is shaped like a cement mixer; its capacity is 70 tons.

In the electric furnace stage, stainless scrap, carbon scrap, and alloys are fed ("charged") into the electric furnace in two loads. (Because the bulk of unmelted scrap volume for each batch greatly exceeds the furnace volume, half the scrap must be melted down before adding the remainder.) The furnace is emptied when the specified carbon content is right and the temperature is high enough.

In the argon-oxygen vessel stage, the liquid steel is transferred by ladle into the AOD vessel where it is refined to very specific chemistries. When the chemistry meets the specifications and the appropriate temperature is attained, the vessel is decanted ("tapped") into a ladle. The steel flows from the ladle into ingot molds resting on railroad cars. After solidifying, the ingots are rolled into slabs.

ure the amount of moly in the finished steel, you may think you've lost a lot, but in fact it was never there in the amount the records claim."

"More moly on paper than in the steel?" you smile.

"Exactly. Or vice versa, of course: more moly in the steel than in our records. Either way, it's not good: we're either wasting the stuff or we're not meeting specifications and will have to add moly."

"How does all the moly get added to the steel?" you ask.

"Moly is added in the form of alloy steel scrap fed (or 'charged') to the furnace. Some of this steel scrap comes from dealers, but some is scrap left over from the plant's own production, the crops and the grinding dust—what's cut and ground from finished slabs.[4] The furnace melter decides what combination of scrap and raw materials is needed for charging the furnace for each batch—deciding what to use depending on which grade of steel he's making, of course, but also on what's available that day. The moly content of each source—the scrap and the raw materials—varies a lot, so it's a tricky business, takes tremendous experience."

"So the furnace melter is supposed to calculate and keep track of everything fed into the furnace, exactly as he does it?"

"That's right," replies Rob. "And there are lots of chances for mistakes, both at the furnace stage and then later at the vessel stage. It's in the vessel that they make all the additions to meet the specs for each particular grade. Most of the moly is added at the end of the vessel stage because it's too easily oxidized away."

"How do they add it?" you ask.

"They toss in steel cans containing ferro moly (FeMo) alloys or moly oxides (MoO_2), literally just throw 'em in," Rob smiles. "The cans can penetrate the slag layer on the top of the steel batch and get through to the liquid steel where they melt. If raw moly were added directly to the liquid steel, it wouldn't get through the slag layer and mix in thoroughly with the steel. Couple years ago, before we started using this technique, we had problems. Lost lots of molybdenum. Recovery rates often ran as low as 40 to 50 percent."

"And now you get 95 percent?" you ask incredulously. "That's some improvement!"

---

[4] Crops are the ends of the rolled slabs of steel which are cut off to square the ends. The dust is made up of the particles ground from the finished slabs. (Grinding off surface defects removes about 5% of the slab weight.)

"It really does work well," Rob agrees. "But there's still a lot of mistakes in the records. The vessel melter takes samples three times during the final steel-making process in the vessel, the first two to see how much moly to add, and the last one, after the final moly charge in the teeming ladle,[5] to see how much they've got. A final steel sample is taken while teeming the ingots (molds) that give the mill certification showing the steel meets the specs for molybdenum.[6] The Chem Lab analyzes these samples, as well as those at the furnace and vessel stages.[7] So if there seems to be an error, the Lab's records can be used to check the production logs."

"So my job is to go over all of the moly that was charged to the electric furnace and the AOD vessel and compare that to the amount contained in the final ingots."

"You got it," says Rob approvingly. "The ratio of moly in the final ingots to the amount added is the recovery rate—essentially how efficiently the process uses molybdenum."

"And if there is any problem in the recovery—that is, anything under 90 percent or over 110 percent—then I check to see if the production logs and Chem Lab records agree. Okay, I have the idea. Now tell me exactly what to do."

"All the data you need are right here in Quality Control," Rob begins. "You take the standardized form called 'Molybdenum Recovery Report.' Here's one," he says handing you a sheet. (See Figure 1.) "Take a look at it. It'll tell you everything you need to collect. What's asked for is the number of the heat,[8] the grade of the steel,[9] the sources for the initial charges to the furnace—like the home scrap

---

[5] The teeming ladle is a bottom-spouted, crane-operated device used to empty the steel from the vessel and pour it into the ingot molds.

[6] Mill certification is based on an average of the samples from the first, middle, and last ingots poured.

[7] The Chemistry Laboratory is responsible for certifying the chemistry of all the steel produced by the mill. The lab, part of the Quality Control Department, is connected by pneumatic tube with all the various stages of the production line; it automatically monitors the process and sends data back to each unit on the line. These data are recorded on the report forms at each production stage, along with the production crew's own data, and these forms are retained in the QC office for one year.

[8] A "heat" is a batch of steel; the heat number is the particular batch being processed.

[9] Grade is the type of stainless steel with specifications for all the contained elements, including the exact quantity of molybdenum.

		DATE							
		HEAT No.							
		GRADE							
SCRAP AND ADDITIONS									
TYPE	SOURCE	WT%Moly							
215-444	HOME	1.8							
313-316	HOME	2.0							
308-316	DUST	1.3							
307	PURCHASED	2.5							
329-316	PURCHASED	1.0							
344 80/40	NiMo	4.0							
306 304/316	PURCHASED	1.0							
313-316	PURCHASED	2.6							
SUBTOTAL	POUNDS OF Mo FROM ALL SCRAP CHARGED								
MoO_2		100%							
FeMo		100%							
TOTAL MOLY ADDED									
PERCENT Mo IN FINAL									
FINAL WT									
AMOUNT OF MOLY IN FINAL									
PERCENT Mo RECOVERY									
COMMENTS									

Figure 1. Molybdenum Recovery Report Form

and dust from the plant here,[10] and all the scrap supplies. See, the percentages of moly are listed for each possible source."[11]

"I see that," you reply. "Now the next two items here are the canned moly added to the vessel, right?"

"Yes. MoO_2 is molybdenum oxide, and FeMo is an iron molybdenum alloy. These are the two forms in which molybdenum is added at the vessel stage."

"Okay, I got it," you say.

"Then you calculate how much moly was added to the heat from all sources. That's the next entry, 'total moly added,' and it's followed by the percentage of moly in the final product."

"Where do you get the final weight?" you wonder.

"That's on the pit report,"[12] Rob says. "It's figured according to the number of ingots poured from each heat. Then you calculate the total pounds of moly in the final product.[13] Finally, then you can come up with the percentage of moly recovered,[14] the last item on the chart."

"And that, of course, is the key item—what they want to know," you say.

"That's it. That's what they want to look at. And if that number is not on target, they want to know why. Which is what the report is all about, of course."

"Rob, you said the aim is for a moly recovery of 95 percent, but

---

[10] Home is the scrap from the home plant: croppings of the slabs and the bottoms and tops of ingots. Dust is the steel particles remaining after the grinding operation on the finished steel.

[11] Each grade of scrap steel has a set percentage of molybdenum guaranteed by the supplier, but the moly is not evenly distributed throughout. Nevertheless, if a supplier sells 100 tons of scrap at 1% Mo, he is obligated to be selling a total of 1 ton of molybdenum.

[12] The pit report is made at the final production stage when the ingots are poured. The weight of the heat (or batch) is determined by the number of ingots.

[13] "Amount of moly in final" is the total pounds of molybdenum calculated to be in the final product according to the chemical composition. To calculate the total pounds of moly, multiply the final percentage of molybdenum times the total final weight: (% Mo in final) × (total final weight) = (pounds Mo in final).

[14] "Percent Mo recovery" is the percentage of the molybdenum added to the heat during the process that is recovered in the final product as determined by chemical composition. To calculate the percentage of moly recovered, divide the pounds of moly in the final product (based on the chemical analysis) by the total pounds added during the process (and multiply by 100).

that the acceptable range is perhaps 90 to 110 percent. Does that mean I only have to account for anything below 90?"

"Well, frankly, they get nervous about anything under about 94 percent, and they won't ignore the high rates either; they'll want to know about any recovery over 110. They don't want to waste it."

"Say, who is 'they,' anyway?" you ask with a grin. "From what I've learned around here up to now, all the production people—the superintendent in the melt shop,[15] the furnace melter, and the vessel melter—all these guys are responding constantly to the analyses throughout the process. What do they care about a report two weeks or more after the fact?"

"The point is the long-term view, the big picture. Naturally, the production people in the melt shop are mostly interested in what's happening by the minute, and in what they must do about it immediately. 'Minutes are money' around here. But they're also interested in whether they should make some big adjustment in the process."

"I guess they want to know the probable causes for any moly recoveries that are 'out of spec' so they can spot any negative trends or problems before they get too big."

"Of course they aren't the only people who get the report," interrupts Rob. "Mr. Larkey and Mr. Barkovich[16] are the ones who would make any decisions if you came up with any significant conclusions."

You raise your eyes questioningly. "Like if I say that the moly content in a load of scrap seems low, they might decide to trace a supplier?"

"They'd decide if it seems worthwhile to check him out. You don't worry about things like that. It's your job to give them the moly recovery figures and to try to pinpoint the cause of any funny ones. They'll make the decisions."

"Okay. Now to get started. Which grades of steel do we keep track of anyway?"

"Just the 316, 317, 434, and 444 grades. But you must check every heat for those grades, of course. Of the thirteen or so heats per day, that means only one or two per day usually, and some days none at all."

---

[15] The melt shop comprises the furnace and vessel stages, the major production stages in the liquid metal processing of stainless steel.

[16] Mr. Larkey is the plant superintendent, the boss of all bosses here, and Mr. Barkovich is the quality control manager, Rob's boss.

"You told me that only the steel bearing over 0.75 percent moly is checked, but what are the specs for each one of these grades?"

"Here," Rob says, handing you a chart (Table 1).

"So I first go and collect all this information for the Moly Recovery Report from the electric furnace and the vessel logs and the Chem Lab records in our office."[17]

"Yes, and once you get it all down on the chart," Rob says with a wave of his hand, "come back and I'll go over it with you so that you can see how to check out any problems."

Early the next morning, you come back to Rob's desk to show him your completed moly recovery chart for the period June 10–June 25. (See Figure 2.) Handing him the chart, you comment: "Seems like I've got a few things to account for here. There's a percentage that is sky high, and there's a couple that are very low."

"Let's take a look," Rob says. "What luck. You really pulled some humdingers the first time around. Well, with those low recovery rates of 77 and 80 percent, you should first go to check the scrap sources on the Chemistry Lab report."[18]

"Yes," you say. "That's on my agenda."

"If the scrap's okay, then check the numbers throughout the production process by comparing the moly additions reported at the fur-

TABLE 1.   Stainless Steel Grades Bearing High Molybdenum Contents

Grade	Molybdenum Range
316	2.00–2.25%
317	3.15–3.35%
434	0.80–1.00%
444	1.75–1.95%

---

[17] The electric furnace log lists the date, time, temperature, and the composition of the initial and second charges to the furnace: the tons of crops, dust, and the ore. At the bottom of the log is the data from the Chemistry Lab on the samples they have taken during the furnace process. The vessel log is similar.

[18] The moly content in any scrap load can be checked on the Chemistry Lab report on incoming scrap and raw materials. Random samples, taken from the railroad cars delivering scrap steels, are analyzed and recorded by the Chem Lab. (Although the Chemistry Lab keeps these records, audits are not performed on any regular basis.)

	DATE		6-10	6-11	6-20	6-23	6-23	6-24	6-24	6-25	6-25
	HEAT No.		50417	19901	21788	42585	42586	42587	42588	42589	42590
	GRADE		317	434	444	316	316	316	316	316	316
SCRAP AND ADDITIONS											
TYPE	SOURCE	WT%Moly				Pounds Added					
215-444	HOME	1.8		27,200	42,200						
313-316	HOME	2.0	43,000			52,000	42,000	25,900	50,000	43,400	31,500
308-316	DUST	1.3				10,000	8,500	10,900	20,000		
307	PURCHASED	2.5									
329-316	PURCHASED	1.0								43,100	
344 80/40	NiMo	4.0									
306 304/316	PURCHASED	1.0	44,800			20,600	19,700	80,200	51,000	23,800	41,300
313-316	PURCHASED	2.6					18,500				
SUBTOTAL	POUNDS OF Mo FROM ALL SCRAP CHARGED		1,308	490	760	1,376	1,629	1,462	1,770	1,537	1,043
MoO$_2$	100%		3,700	680	2,140	1,660	1,200	2,240	2,380	1,860	2,100
FeMo	100%		660	60	240	450	180	420	150	419	210
TOTAL MOLY ADDED			5,668	1,230	3,140	3,486	3,009	4,122	4,300	3,816	3,353
PERCENT Mo IN FINAL			3.24	0.85	1.85	2.14	2.11	2.12	2.12	2.10	2.10
FINAL WT			154,300	137,600	158,000	158,800	162,500	163,400	156,200	145,400	160,200
AMOUNT OF MOLY IN FINAL			4,999	1,170	2,923	3,398	3,429	3,464	3,311	3,053	3,364
PERCENT Mo RECOVERY			88.2%	95.1%	93.1%	97.5%	114%	84.1%	77%	80%	100.3%
COMMENTS			LOW	OK	LOW	OK	HIGH	LOW	LOW	LOW	OK

Note: All numbers are in pounds, except for those marked percentage (%). The records are taken from the vessel and the electric furnace logs, and the pit report. Refer to the text and footnotes for explanation of entries.

Figure 2. Molybdenum Recovery Report

nace and the vessel against what the Chem Lab reported in their samples. All the information you need is right on the reports filed in our office."

"I know," from you.

"Frankly, the scrap doesn't look so sharp on some of these," Rob notes with interest.

"What about that heat no. 42586?" you ask.

"Well, with that recovery rate of 114 percent, I would guess that the purchased scrap containing 313 had a higher percentage of moly than the 2.6 listed here. Just check the Chem Lab reports on the scrap material analysis to be sure."

"Right," as you jot down a note on your pad.

"Also this Heat 21788 looks suspicious for the scrap. The recovery is only a bit low at 93 percent, but it has an enormous furnace scrap charge. You just can't guarantee that the entire 42,200 pounds was 1.8 percent moly. Since this is home crops, most likely the charge was a mix of plain scrap with some Mo-bearing scrap. Check to see if this was a single- or a double-charged load; if double, it's almost certainly a mix with plain scrap so that the two loads didn't average out to 1.8 percent moly. . . ." Rob pauses. "Boy, even this first heat (heat 50417) is low—only 88 percent."

"Yes. And I noted one funny thing about it," you say, pointing at the chart. "The ferro moly charge was pretty big."

"Good observation," observes Rob. "My guess is that the ferro moly was added too soon, so it was oxidized to the slag layer. To make sure, check the time of the ferro moly (FeMo) on the vessel log. If it was earlier than 10 minutes before the tap, then it was too soon."

"Yes, because I was suspicious about the ferro moly, I did check that, and you're right. It was 15 minutes before the tap. Actually the melter put it in at the proper time—about 8 minutes before the tap was due, but then there was a delay of 7 minutes before the ladle was brought up. I got that from the pit report. So altogether it was a full 15 minutes from the time the ferro moly was added until the tap."

"Good work," Rob says. "Now what about these lovelies at the end of the chart?"

"Yes. I noticed that there were three consecutive low-recovery heats, beginning with heat 42587. Look: 84 percent, 77 percent, and 80 percent. But the thing that really struck me," you continue, "is that they all had high scrap charges of the same purchase of scrap—scrap 306 304/316, which is supposed to be 1.0 percent Mo."

"Excellent," smiles Rob. "Chances are they were all made from the same shipment of scrap. If you add up those pounds it equals 155,000 pounds or 77.5 tons of scrap. That's a typical size for one scrap load. It was probably a poor load. Check the scrap shipment, and also check the Chem Lab reports to get the analysis on this load. Especially note to see how many random samples were taken and whether it was over the weekend. I suspect that Standard Steel may have been shorted in this case."

"So maybe dishonest scrap dealers are still a problem," you laugh.

"Can't say for sure, but see what the sampling suggests," Rob says. "As soon as you have everything pulled together, go ahead and write the report. I want to see what you can do," Rob smiles encouragingly. "Just set it out the way you think it would be helpful to everybody. And when you're done, I want you to do something else. These explanations to the co-op trainees take a lot of time. I have decided I'm going to write up a book of procedures for all the regular technical reports they must do. Since you're new at this, you have a better view than I do what somebody right out of school needs to know. Besides, I've just told you in detail what to do! So I want your draft of the procedures for doing a Molybdenum Recovery Report—as soon as possible. If they're good, I'll just use them 'as is.'"

"Give them the instructions so you will have to be available just for unusual matters?" you wonder.

"Exactly. You've got it."

You are still thinking hard about the Moly Recovery Report itself and solving those few loose ends, so writing up the procedure seems rather remote. It is something you will worry about later.

Back at your workstation you look over your notes and set about tying up the few remaining questions. It does not take you long. Heat no. 42586 did have scrap with a higher moly content than 2.6. The Chemistry Lab report of the scrap material was listed at an unusually high figure of 4.1 percent, which means that the recovery was high—about 104 percent—but nothing like 114 percent. Then heat 21788 had a double charge instead of the single one reported. Just as Rob had guessed, that home-crops charge was probably a mix with plain scrap so that the moly content in the two charges was not as high as the recorded 1.8 percent. As for the three consecutive low loads taken from the same scrap shipment, there were only a couple of random samples taken on that shipment, and they were over a weekend. Moreover, they were very low, registering moly percentages of only 0.7 percent and 0.6 percent. So it seems you have the culprit for heats 42587, −8 and −9! A bad shipment of scrap had about 0.4 percent less molybdenum than claimed. Evidently it was not caught because the sampling over the weekend was insufficient. Probably with no supervisor around, they did not bother to take another sample, despite those low percentages.

Now it is time to start figuring out how to write all this up. Rob said he wanted to see what you could do. You will have to show him.

ASSIGNMENT 1

Write the Moly Recovery Report. Attach the chart in Figure 2 to your report. Address the report to M. R. Giullini, Melt Shop Superintendent. The distribution list should cover J. L. Larkey, Plant Superintendent; B. B. Barkovich, Manager of Quality Control (head of your own department); R. P. Boylan, Quality Control Engineer (your immediate supervisor); and A. O. Ewald, Jr., General Melting Foreman. (The furnace melter and the vessel melter both work under Ewald, but they are not on the distribution list. Rob Boylan would look over the report before you sent it out.) Memo letterhead is Specialty Steels Division, Standard Steel of America, Inc., Lisbon, Pennsylvania 00000. Your position is Cooperative Education Trainee.

ASSIGNMENT 2

Write a draft set of instructions for the next and all subsequent co-op trainees on how to prepare a Molybdenum Recovery Report. Provide a memo for Boylan to cover your draft, requesting his advice if necessary.

ASSIGNMENT 3

The Cooperative Education Program at Central University has been under some attack by engineering students and faculty. Too many co-op assignments have been "gofer" jobs with students earning academic credit for spending hours at a photocopying machine or simply running errands. Aiming to eliminate such co-op assignments that do not afford students adequate opportunities to apply their academic knowledge, the College of Engineering has established a Co-op Education Review Committee which has been monitoring the co-op assignments.

As part of this college review, your advisor and committee member, Professor Abner Abramowitz, schedules a conference to question you about your activities. You tell him about several projects, including the Molybdenum Recovery Report, especially noting your preparation of the instructions for future co-op trainees. Throughout, you let him know about Robert Boylan's efforts to teach you about the steel industry.

Abramowitz is obviously pleased about your assignment. "This is the kind of co-op job that our Review Committee should hear about," he exclaims. "A couple of professors on that Committee would like to kill the whole co-op program because some students have had such lousy assignments, even at Standard Steel, by the way. They should know more about good assignments like yours. Look," he continues, "I want you to write a letter to the Co-op Review Committee. Tell them about your experience with the Molybdenum Recovery Report, and especially about writing the procedures. Also tell 'em about this Mr. Boylan. You can say you're writing on my request."

Write the letter to Professor Wayne Hibbard, Chairman, Cooperative Education Review Committee, College of Engineering, Central University, Hillsdale, Pennsylvania 00000.

Representing Accounts for Adler Advertising: A Rationale for a Logo

You have just been hired as an account representative[1] at Adler Advertising, an ad agency located in a suburb of Minneapolis. Though the company is small, with only ten employees, it handles a range of advertising for upper midwest firms, including billboards, newspaper ads, company brochures, and annual reports. For the time being, owner and art director Mary Adler has asked you to assist John Fiorini, one of the firm's two account representatives, so you can learn the ropes. Later you will be handling a third of the firm's accounts by yourself.

You have been sitting in on Fiorini's meetings, listening to him make phone calls, helping him plan strategies for gaining new accounts, and watching him write letters to clients. You are beginning to feel comfortable at your new workplace, and you would like to start handling accounts yourself. It has been helpful watching Fiorini in action, however. For one thing, you have learned a lot about how the company works with clients.

Whenever possible, Adler Advertising involves clients in "idea generation" before presenting a design solution. The owner and account representatives will show clients several "rough layouts"[2] that

---

[1] An account representative conducts business transactions between the ad agency and its customers. Each client is called an "account."

[2] A rough layout is a drawing that shows what the printed design will look like without using or simulating the print processes to be used for the final product. Rough layouts are often done in black and white to show general design concepts and to show the client how the design will look if it is printed in black and white. The artist sometimes suggests colors for the client to consider.

have been prepared by the firm's designers. The account representative discusses alternative solutions, submits an informal design rationale,[3] and then asks clients to choose a design for comprehensive presentation. The "comprehensive" presentation, complete with full-color layouts on illustration board, shows *exactly* how the finished product will look, and it may·be accompanied by an extensive written design rationale. You like the fact that Adler encourages clients to select from alternatives while the solution is in progress. Often that makes them more satisfied with the final product.

Today, as you are organizing notes you took while discussing a plan with Fiorini for establishing more business with local banks, Mary Adler surprises you by dropping by your workstation.

"How's it going?" she asks.

"Pretty good," you answer. "I'm learning a lot from John, but . . ."

"You're eager to do a few things on your own," Mary finishes, smiling.

"That's right," you answer, encouraged. "Do you have something in mind?"

Mary takes a seat and sets a stack of layouts on your desk.

"John is going to be leaving on vacation in three weeks. You'll be taking over his accounts while he's gone. When he gets back, you'll start developing accounts on your own. I know you haven't handled an account by yourself yet, and I think it's time you did."

"Sounds good to me," you say. "Where do I begin?"

"Well, let's start with these layouts," Mary says, pointing to the stack she left with you. "Last week, John picked up a new client, the Northway Management Guild, Incorporated. The firm represents a group of management consultants serving Minnesota and the Great Lakes area. They want a company logo to use on stationery, but they're

---

[3] A design rationale is a verbal description of design concepts. In the rough layout stage, the rationale often is given orally in a client meeting. If a meeting is not possible, the rationale may be written up. When comprehensive layouts are presented in person to the client, the agency usually accompanies the designs with a written rationale.

Rationales are composed by the account rep, who gets input from the designer. An effective rationale gives practical and well-supported reasons for design choices. For instance, in defending color suggestions, an account rep's rationale may cover how color selection affects printing costs; it may also discuss how different colors symbolically represent an idea or philosophy. A good rationale does not simply state that the designer "liked" the way the image looked or "had a feeling" this design was right for the client.

pretty vague about what the logo should show. It's a small job—I told John that I'd get started on it and hand the account to you. In fact, I notified the company last week that you'll be their new account rep."

"So it'll be my baby," you say, smiling.

"That's right," Mary says. "Right now I'm dealing with Jason McClough, who's Northway's marketing VP. All he told us was to design something that would emphasize their location in the north. I gave the job to Susan Lewis[4] and here's what she came up with."

Mary separates the drawings on your desk.

"Sue's got these five black-and-white layouts completed." Mary pauses a bit to think things through. "Let's see, today's Tuesday and McClough wants to see what we've got before the end of this week. Unfortunately, we can't arrange a meeting with him before next Monday. So—," she says, still deliberating, "I'd like you to send these designs to him *today* and attach a letter. In the letter, you should introduce yourself to the client and spell out the rationale for the design concepts. Keep your rationale short, however. Let the Northway consultants know that we're interested in their opinion, but that we have some clear reasons for selecting these designs for them to choose from. You'll have to talk to Sue to find out what she had in mind. Think you can handle it?"

"Sure," you say, thinking this is just the kind of project you'd like to start off with.

As soon as Mary leaves your workstation, you walk back to the art room to talk to Sue. You catch her just finishing up a keylining job for a brochure. Sue's happy to stop and talk to you now; keylining is meticulous work, and the break is welcome.

"Mary Adler just brought me these rough layouts you did for the Northway Management Guild logo," you begin. "I'll be sending them out today, and I need to include the rationale to help the client choose a design. Can I go over these with you?"

"Sure," Sue says. "I liked doing this assignment, but they didn't give us much to go on."

---

[4] Susan Lewis and one other employee work as layout-artist/keyliners under Mary Adler, who acts as art director and designer. Generally, Mary Adler develops visual concepts; the layout-artist/keyliners both execute concepts for presentation to clients and keyline, that is, prepare finished art for production printing. Because this job is small, Mary Adler has let Susan Lewis handle the development of visual concepts, as well as their execution.

"I know," you answer, taking out the first drawing. "What can you tell me about this one?" (See Figure 1.)

Figure 1.   Sue's First Layout

"Well, it shows a logotype[5] and the company name. It reads very nice in black and white. If they want it in color, I'd like to see the logotype done in bright red and the company name in process blue[6] to give it that all-American look."

"I assume you designed an arrow pointing up as part of the *N* in the logotype because the company wants to emphasize their northern location," you comment.

"That's right. Also, arrows show progressiveness. . . . Not much else to say about that one."

"What about this?" you ask, showing Sue the next layout (Figure 2).

Figure 2.   Sue's Second Layout

"Well, I've got an arrow pointing north again. This design is more rounded than the first one, so I'd suggest using colors that blend, rather than contrast sharply. I would print everything that appears black here in dark brown. Brown looks real nice on stationery that's white or cream, and they're primarily interested in a design for stationery. Also,

---

[5] A logo designed in type often is called a logotype. Logos conceived as pictorial designs often are called symbols.

[6] Process blue is a premixed turquoise-blue ink color. It is called "process" blue because it is used with red, black, and yellow to create other colors in the printing process.

some people feel warmer colors imply a friendlier, earthier look. I'd suggest red-orange for the arrow proper, which shows as white here. The red would make it stand out—the color has a lot of energy—and yet it still would blend with brown. Of course, using those colors, this design could be done a couple of ways."

"Oh?"

"We could do the printing using black and red-orange inks. A light tint or screen of black printed over the red-orange will create brown. If we do that, the client could elect black as a color in the design too, maybe for the address on the letterhead, and get three colors for the price of two.[7] Of course, it might be better not to screen colors and just use brown and red-orange inks."

"Why?" you ask.

"It's more difficult to register colors accurately when one's screened over another, especially if the logo's reduced, like on a business card. It might look sloppy and unprofessional."

You jot down a few notes.

"Of course," Sue says, interrupting your note taking, "you might not want to discuss that printing problem with the client at this stage in the game. It would probably be better just to find out if they like the general ideas."

You nod as if you agree, but actually you're not sure about Sue's suggestion. You decide to ask Mary what she thinks later. You take out the next layout (Figure 3). "What did you have in mind here?"

Figure 3.   Sue's Third Layout

"This is a simple one. The pine tree, of course, grows in the north. The one I've designed here looks a bit like an arrow pointing north, emphasizing northness once again. The company would always have

---

[7] Printers charge extra for using more than one ink color when a design is printed. Black is considered a separate "color."

to use the symbol with the type, however. They're not big enough for potential customers to recognize them by the pine tree alone. In fact, that's true for most of these designs—the symbol has *got* to go *with* the type," Sue reflects, and then continues, "I'd suggest forest green for the tree, of course, and black for the company name. Clean and simple."

"Okay," you say. "And this next one?" (See Figure 4.)

Figure 4.   Sue's Fourth Layout

"This works well as a one-color design," Sue begins. "The star is there because I was thinking of the north star. This star, in fact, looks like it's taking off and heading north. I'd suggest doing the whole design in reflex blue,[8] which kind of looks like the night sky. The shading below the star is created by printing the color in a tiny dot pattern which makes the color look lighter when printed on white paper. And, of course, the dot pattern shows a nice contrast in black and white too. The shading makes the star look like it's moving upward. The italic typeface for the company name has that sense of action too."

"I see you've repeated the star motif in this last design," you say showing Sue the layout (Figure 5).

Figure 5.   Sue's Fifth Layout

"Yes, here the star is incorporated in the logotype. I think the logotype would look good in process blue with the company name in black. By the way," she says, thumbing through the layouts, "you

---

[8] A standard premixed color that looks close to navy blue.

might have noticed that I'm suggesting premixed ink colors for three of these designs; all the ones in blue. That's a good thing to do because then the printer uses the ink 'as is' right out of the can. You don't have to worry about printers' color-mixing standards, which sometimes vary."

Sue returns from this aside to examine her last design. "You know, I'm a little worried about this design. I think I might have seen this idea somewhere before."

"What do you mean?"

"I have the feeling I've seen that concept of putting a star shape inside one letter and combining it with two other letters to form a logo used somewhere else. I don't think that really matters now, though. We're just showing them these designs for discussion's sake. Of course, we'd have to check that out later, if they liked it."

"You mean that it's worth it to get Northway's reaction to the design to give you a better idea of what they want?" you remark.

"Of course. If a client doesn't give us much to go on to begin with, you've got to make a stab," Sue says handing the layouts back to you. "Will that do it for you?"

"Sure," you say. "You've been very helpful."

Sue gets back to her keylining, and you return to your desk to mull things over. You know that Mary Adler wants this sent out in today's mail, which will be going out in three hours. You've got plenty of ideas for introducing the layouts, but since you're not sure whether to write about the printing problems Sue raised, you drop in on Mary to talk about it. After you tell her the gist of what Sue said about the designs, Mary gives you a little advice.

"You have to think about how we want our client to respond to these designs," she suggests. "We want McClough to tell us what appeals to him. It'd be perfect if he'd just select one of our five designs, but he may not. He may prefer aspects of some designs combined with others. We're really asking for an open-ended response."

"So maybe I shouldn't discuss the printing problem?" you ask her.

"Well, the printing issue may be too complicated to talk about now. After all, if Northway likes parts of one design and parts of another, we may have to start from scratch anyway. On the other hand, some clients like to know we've done our footwork. A discussion of some printing aspects shows we're looking out for them. And," Mary adds, "since you are new at this, it might be a good idea to say *more*, rather than less—until you get a better idea of what *enough* is."

You smile, a bit weakly.

"Of course, it's your baby," Mary says. And then she adds encouragingly, "You've got to realize a lot of 'selling' to a client is a judgment call. You want to help McClough and his group make a decision, but you don't want to bulldoze them—Northway's in the driver's seat here. The only way you really learn what's best to do in these situations is to study the options and take your best shot. You'll do okay."

"Well, I'll do my best," you respond, and then ask, "When do we want McClough to get back to us?"

"Tell him to call you to set up a meeting with him. If he doesn't call by the first of next week, you call him. And don't forget to introduce yourself in the letter—let him know you're eager to meet him!"

"Okay," you agree and thank Mary for her advice.

When you get back to your office, you review what both Sue and Mary said before sitting down to write that letter.

ASSIGNMENT 1

To prepare yourself to write the design rationale for the alternative NMG logos, make a rough chart organizing the information you received from Sue about each logo under categories of your choice. Indicate which information you will include in the written rationale.

ASSIGNMENT 2

Write the letter that Mary Adler assigned you to write to Jason McClough of Northway Management Guild, Inc. A copy will go to Adler. McClough's address is Jason McClough, Vice-President of Marketing, Northway Management Guild, Inc., 601 Arch, Minneapolis, Minnesota 00000. Your firm's address is Adler Advertising, 7520 Hiawatha, Bloomington, Minnesota 00000.

Design of the Phototherapy Room: Addressing an Issue for the Health Department

When you became a registered nurse, you never imagined that you would be working for an architectural firm. Sometimes you actually think your job as a health facilities planner for Kraft Engineering and Architectural Services (KEAS) has taught you more about the various kinds of nursing practice than you would have learned if you continued to do front-line nursing in a hospital or clinic.

KEAS is a major health facilities designer. Managers for the firm's projects assign you to investigate how facilities are used by nurses in all kinds of health services. Before architects design a space for a specific functional unit staffed by nursing personnel, you interview the people who will be working in the space and find out exactly what they need. Before you came to KEAS, project managers and their architectural staff did this "functional programming" themselves, but they felt they could do a better job if they hired a nurse to help plan nursing areas. Also, they felt a nurse could best answer questions from Michael Fallon of the State Department of Public Health (SDPH) about the adequacy of Kraft's designs.[1] Early today you were assigned to work on just such an inquiry from the SDPH.

When you arrived at work at 8:00 A.M., Greg Jackman, manager for the Northwood Hospital renovation project, handed you a sheet of paper with several State Department of Public Health "issue state-

---

[1] The SDPH determines whether a health facility meets Health Department guidelines for space and equipment requirements. For instance, the SDPH may specify a certain amount of clearance around beds or exam tables or may require storage units for supplies or parking space for stretchers and wheelchairs. Space and equipment guidelines vary depending upon how a room is to be used.

ments" from Michael Fallon, all requiring a response from KEAS. Jackman asked you to respond to "Issue No. 0132" (Figure 1). He also gave you a blueprint of the Inpatient PTU room which Fallon referred to in "Issue No. 0132" and told you that John Salinger, an architect no longer with KEAS, handled the design for this room. Salinger apparently discussed his plans with Nurse Shirley Hieple, Clinical Supervisor No. 1 in the Photochemotherapy Division of the Hospital's Dermatology Department.

Jackman now wants you to reexamine the design and to report back to him with the narrative[2] Fallon asked for. His usual procedure in handling SDPH requests is to get you and others of his staff to respond in writing to the SDPH "issue" statements. Jackman then prepares a report which compiles all responses and sends it to Fallon. You know Greg trusts you to follow up carefully; he will probably incorporate without changes whatever you come up with in his report to Fallon.

The blueprint (No. 9AB310) Greg gave you shows part of KEAS's proposed design for the renovation of the ninth floor of Northwood Hospital. This floor houses inpatient dermatology services. When you located the Phototherapy Room on your blueprint (Figure 2), you immediately understood why Fallon is concerned. The cubicle[3] desig-

---

[2] The "narrative" Fallon asks for is a step-by-step description of the procedures which take place in the Inpatient PTU. The document must show how hospital personnel and patients use the spaces and equipment designated for this room. In particular, it must include information which addresses the problems Fallon has identified.

The term "narrative" is derived from the term "program narrative," which refers to the document which all health facilities must submit to the Health Department when they are planning to build, expand, or renovate. "Narrative" as defined here should not be confused with the rhetorical form "narrative." General guidelines for writing a program narrative for health facilities are published by the U.S. Bureau of Health Facilities, Finances, Compliance, and Conversion in *Minimum Requirements of Construction and Equipment for Hospital and Medical Facilities* (DHEW Publication No. [HRA] 79–14500). A typical program narrative is a large document "describing space requirements, staffing patterns, departmental relationships, and other basic information relating to the fulfillment of the institution's objectives" (p. 10). A program narrative for a large health facility might not include a detailed statement describing the function of every room. Fallon's request for a narrative on the Inpatient PTU room demonstrates that the program narrative for Northwood Hospital's renovation did not include the detail he needs relating function to equipment and space for this area.

[3] Each cubicle is separated by a privacy curtain indicated by the broken lines (-—-) on the blueprint. Dashed lines (– – –) indicate equipment, such as the phototherapy booths and the exam table.

Issue No. 0132

Inpatient PTU* – Rm 9N-30120 – SDPH requests a clear
narrative of tasks to take place in this room. One area
is described for "exams" though this space appears less
than 50 square feet (easternmost cubicle). This space is
substantially less than any "criteria for space" for any
level of exams. Storage location for clean linen and
towels in this room is not clear; space for supply carts
with creams, applications, etc. is not clear; area for
patients to rinse/wash off creams is not clear. If this
area is for inpatients only, then space for transport
vehicle (wheelchair) will be needed. Further study is
needed for this activity.

* The Phototherapy Treatment Unit (PTU), also referred to as the Phototherapy Room,
is used for treating patients with skin disorders by exposing affected areas to ultraviolet
light.

Figure 1.   Issue Statement

nated as an "exam" area is clearly less than 50 square feet in size, and
health department regulations require exam areas to be at least 120
square feet. They also must be equipped with special supply and
writing areas and often a variety of special equipment, such as patient
gases. The exam area or cubicle on the blueprint shows only an exam
table and minimal storage space—a shelf on one wall. The print also
shows three other cubicles, each with a shelf. You do not see any
enclosed storage unit that could be used for storing skin creams. That
seems a bit unusual to you as patients who receive ultraviolet treatment for skin disorders generally apply creams and lotions before they
get the treatment.

You decide not to waste your time guessing what might be going
on here and instead contact Shirley Hieple in the Photochemotherapy
Division of the Dermatology Department. Shirley supervises those
who work in the present PTU. You manage to get an appointment with
Hieple this afternoon.

Armed with a copy of Fallon's issue statement and the new PTU
blueprint, you begin your interview by telling Hieple that the State
Department of Public Health has questioned how your firm has designed the PTU for the hospital and has asked you to explain how the

PTU will function. You then ask Hieple if she indeed had told John Salinger last fall exactly what was needed in the PTU.

"Oh, yes," Hieple insists. "I went over everything with him quite carefully."

"Well," you answer, spreading out the blueprint (Figure 2), "then I have a few questions. Salinger has designed an exam area here with nothing in it but an exam table and a small shelf."

"That's odd," Shirley immediately responds. "There won't be any exam areas in the new PTU."

"No?"

"There are supposed to be four treatment cubicles. Let me take a look at that." After examining the print, Shirley says, "Okay, I see what's going on here. See the treatment cubicles marked on the print? Three have booths with permanent ultraviolet light fixtures in them; the fourth just has an exam table in it. That's the one that Salinger has labeled an 'exam space,' but it's *not* an exam space."

"What is it?"

"It's a treatment area. The patient comes in and lies down on an exam table. Then we bring in a portable lamp which emits ultraviolet rays. The patient turns around so we can direct the lamp on affected areas. We use a regular exam table because it's padded and comfortable for the patient. Plus there is storage space underneath the table where we can keep patient linens. We also keep linens on little shelves attached to the walls in each treatment cubicle. You can see those marked on the blueprint."

"I see. Don't you need additional storage for the creams the patients must apply prior to treatment?"

"Oh, no. That's not how it works. You see, the patients are given creams to apply in their rooms before they enter the Phototherapy Room."

"So they don't apply anything in the cubicles?"

"Well, sometimes we have them put on a little suntan lotion in there, but that's all."

Hieple stops a moment and reexamines the blueprint. "You know," she says, "we asked for those little shelves in each cubicle because that's what we have now. But I just realized we could really use an enclosed storage unit in each cubicle—say about the same width and depth as the little shelf[4] but, oh, seven feet high, I guess.

---

[4] The shelf is 3 feet wide and 12 inches deep.

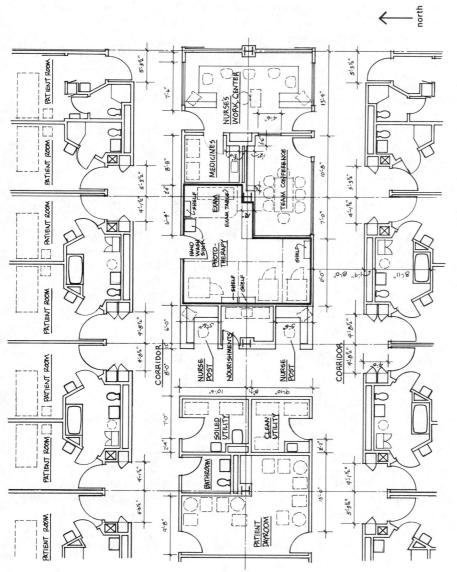

Figure 2. Portion of Blueprint No. 9AB310 Showing Phototherapy Unit

133

It should have adjustable shelves and a robe hook. Then the patients would have a place to hang their clothes or hospital gowns, and we'd have the flexibility to store more linens."

You decide to investigate the situation directly, and ask Hieple if you can see the shelves she's complaining about. Hieple walks you down to the existing Phototherapy Room. Its design is similar to the renovated unit, except that the new unit will have two additional treatment booths. You note that the little shelves in the existing treatment cubicles are top-heavy with linens. It looks like more than a little shelf is needed to store them. And, of course, sitting out in the open, these supplies can get dusty. You tell Hieple that you agree the storage closets she wants would be better than the shelves. While touring the room, you also notice that there is no place for patients to wash up other than a small handwash sink. The blueprint for the renovated unit also shows a single small handwash sink.

"Do patients wash the creams off in this room?" you ask.

"No, we send them back to the bathroom next to the patient day-room just down the hall or to their own rooms. This arrangement will be the same for the renovated unit. You can see the dayroom marked on your blueprint."

"So this entire room is just a place for treatment. No patient exams take place in here at all?"

"That's right."

"And the same will go for the new Phototherapy Room?"

Hieple nods.

"What's the little sink for?"

"That's a handwash sink for staff."

"And where did you say the creams come from—for patient application?"

"Each patient has a supply of creams kept near his or her bedside."

You think that most of your questions have been answered, but in rechecking Fallon's issue statement you see that you have forgotten to ask about the wheelchair accommodations. You ask Hieple about that and she explains how all patients, including those in wheelchairs, are handled.

"Patients on the unit[5] are scheduled for treatment and usually

---

[5] When patients are admitted to the hospital they are assigned rooms in "units" according to the treatment they are getting. Patients receiving dermatology services are placed in that unit on the ninth floor. When this unit is full, they are assigned rooms in other units on other floors.

walk to the Phototherapy Room, so they're not lining up in the corridors or anything. Dermatology patients off the unit who are scheduled for treatment can wait in the patient dayroom in a chair or wheelchair and be called with a two-way intercom."

"Is there room for wheelchairs in the PTU when they get there?"

"No," Hieple answers, "but we don't need to store wheelchairs
there. We can collapse them and set them in the corridor. Only occupied wheelchairs—you know, if lots of patients were lined up—
would cause a problem in the hall."

"Okay," you say. "That sounds reasonable."

"I hope everything is okay now with the plans for the PTU," Hieple says.

"I'm sure everything will be fine. I think the SDPH will be satisfied with our explanation of the procedures as they work with the
design of the unit. Of course, I'll work to see if we can get those storage
units you need."

"Good," Hieple says. "That will make quite a difference."

Satisfied that you have all the information you need, you thank
Hieple for her time and return to KEAS. Before you plan what you
will write up, though, you stop by Jackman's office to ask him about
the shelves in the treatment cubicles which Hieple complained about.
He tells you that there will be no problem changing the shelves to
the storage cabinets Hieple wants.

"Just write a memo to me which includes the narrative Fallon
asked for—you know, do your usual thing relating the procedures to
the design as we now see it—and also tell why the design change will
improve how the room functions."

"Will do," you promise, and get back to your office to begin planning your response to the issue statement.

ASSIGNMENT

Write a memo to Greg Jackman, Project Manager, which responds to
Michael Fallon's inquiry from the SDPH. Remember that Jackman
will incorporate this document in a longer report to Fallon. A copy
goes to Nurse Hieple. Your title at Kraft Engineering and Architectural
Services is Health Facilities Planner.

The Vacuum Freeze Dryer Problem: Communicating with a Vendor

Part 1

Sterling Foundation Research Laboratories is an old, basic research facility in Rockville, Maryland, supported by a private endowment and federal research grants. Led by a very aggressive research director, Dr. Morris Greene, Sterling has recently become well-known, especially for its work in recombinant DNA. Though the laboratories now employ more than 200 scientists and various technical support personnel, Greene keeps his finger on the pulse of each department, pushing hard for significant results and making many of the business decisions himself, probably too many.

As a junior research scientist, you work in Sterling's Department of Biochemistry (one of seven such units). An important piece of equipment in your work is a freeze dryer that you use to concentrate solutions to a solid.[1] Lately, the freeze dryer in your lab has broken down several times—in fact, twice in the last two weeks. First the gauge did not work; then the hoses leaked; and frequently the vacuum was weak or nonexistent. Even when the dryer functions well, you often must wait for several hours because many people need to use it. These delays, slowing down your schedule, irritate you, especially because a small group in Biophysics (in a team headed by Dr. Bart Wilson) has been requesting privileges on the freeze dryer very often of late, privileges which your boss, Dr. Jason Smythe (head of the

---

[1] Freeze drying, or lyophilization, extracts water from prefrozen material under low absolute pressure (high vacuum) and converts the ice to a vapor without passing through the liquid state.

Department of Biochemistry), automatically approves, no matter what the work load in your own group.

Finally, the freeze dryer situation becomes too much for you to take. On Monday morning, the Biophysics technician, Brenda McLaren, is using the instrument at 8:45, in fact, using all ports.[2] She assures you that she will be done shortly after 10:00. When you return at 10:15, you find that Brenda has left, and the vacuum on the freeze dryer has all but disappeared too.[3] You call Harry Pace, the in-house serviceman, to report the weak vacuum right away, but it is well into the afternoon before he gets it going strong again. No one knows how long it will keep going.

After stewing a while, you decide to see Dr. Smythe with the message that the lab needs a new, up-to-date freeze dryer with enough capacity to serve both your own group and Dr. Wilson's people in Biophysics too. You point out how unreliable the vacuum has become, noting that the hoses are worn out and that problems with the pump probably mean that it will have to be replaced very soon. A new model not only would end most of the downtime, but also should handle more samples all at once and process everything faster. Surprisingly, Dr. Smythe agrees with you right away. The dryer is almost 15 years old, and he could not expect it to last much longer. After checking with his administrative assistant, he tells you to go ahead and get the instrument as soon as possible. His instrument budget has a couple of thousand dollars left, which should cover the cost of the dryer.

Consulting several catalogs shows you that freeze dryers cost much more than Dr. Smythe figured. Even Freeze-It, a key supplier known for their competitive pricing, quotes $3,800 in their new catalog, a price which you quickly calculate to be an increase of several hundred dollars over the price in the old catalog, which was current up to a couple of weeks ago. Also, you quickly realize that to accommodate significantly larger loads you will need to substitute a one-half horsepower pump for the customary one-third hp model, thereby adding several hundred dollars more onto the bill. (A one-third hp pump costs $750; a one-half hp unit, $1,050. Either pump's price is added on to the freeze-dryer cost.)

Undeterred, you put in a call to Freeze-It Enterprises in Chicago.

---

[2] A port holds one sample; this dryer has six ports.

[3] A high vacuum is required to convert the ice to a vapor without passing through a liquid state.

After some discussion with Larry Hoch, a sales representative, you persuade him to allow you the price out of the old catalog. That brings the price of the dryer itself to $3,520—hardly a bargain, but better than you had thought 15 minutes before. Once the call is complete, you write down the information (Figure 1).

Armed with the good news about Freeze-It Enterprises' concession on the old prices (making their figure slightly lower than any other manufacturer), you go back to Dr. Smythe with the bad news about the total cost. Smythe remains silent upon hearing a price tag of over $4,500. But he says nothing about the money; rather he questions you closely about how advantageous the new instrument would be. You compare the new dryer's 12 ports with the old unit's 6, and you emphasize that the larger pump means greater capacity, as well as faster processing. Finally you remind him of the big point: the older dryer has an erratic and often maddeningly slow vacuum, and its pump, hoses, and gauges are all nearly worn out.

Smythe doodles on a pad and then abruptly announces that the freeze dryer is a necessary purchase, but $2,000 is all he has for equipment needs that were not foreseen when planning this budget. The answer is to convince Morris Greene (the director of research) that purchasing the freeze dryer *now* would be in the best interests of

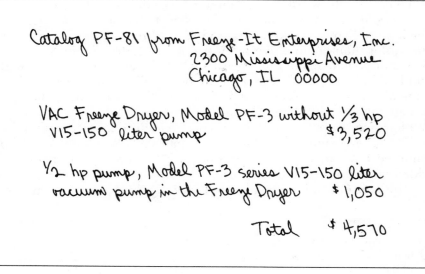

Figure 1.   Notes from Freeze-It Catalog

Sterling Labs. Clearly Wilson in Biophysics needs a dryer, but not enough to warrant purchasing his own; his free ride up until now has been such a good deal for him that it is unlikely he will voluntarily help pay for a new instrument. Smythe concludes, therefore, that it is up to Greene to get Wilson to contribute to Biochemistry's new dryer, perhaps about 20 percent of the total. However, that will still leave a fairly big bill for the research chief to pick up on the general equipment budget. The tightwad Greene will want the purchase justified in terms of improved efficiency for both Wilson's and Smythe's groups. Plus the financial advantages of buying *now* will have to be convincing. Smythe guesses that the repair costs for the old dryer over the past several months must have been sizable, and clearly they will only increase in the future. Persuading Greene will need a clincher, though—perhaps potential benefits to other groups, like Microbiology, which has an old, makeshift dryer that needs dry ice to operate. The people in Microbiology could freeze down microorganisms on this new unit much more quickly and easily, but Dr. Ohanian, the chief, will never buy a dryer as long as the old model works. Upon hearing this news, you only hope that Microbiology will not need the dryer too often.

Despite all this ammunition, Smythe is not so confident that the chief will buy this plan. Nevertheless, he directs you to draft a memo to Greene, attempting to convince him to act now. Smythe reminds you that he does not want to ask Bart Wilson for a contribution, so this memo to Greene will be the first Bart hears of it. On the other hand, he assures you that he will talk to Janet Ohanian in Microbiology, so you can assume her moral support for the purchase, but no funds.

Back at your office, you begin to think about the memo, but before you begin to write, you decide to call up Accounting to find out the repair costs on the old dryer. For servicing the freeze dryer alone, the Shop Department was credited for a total of 13 hours of Harry Pace's time last month, 9½ hours the month before, and 7 the month before that. (Pace's time is figured at the rate of $17.50 per hour.)

ASSIGNMENT 1
Write a memo to Dr. Morris Greene, Director of Research, for Smythe's signature (Dr. Jason Smythe, Department Head, Biochemistry). Copies should go to Dr. Bart Wilson, Biophysics Research Section Leader, and also to Dr. Janet Ohanian, Department Head, Microbiology. Add your name as "Writer" with the title Research Scientist.

Part 2

After receiving your memo, Greene approved the purchase of the freeze dryer with Smythe paying $2,000, Wilson $1,000, and the general equipment fund the balance. The instrument arrived two weeks ago. Because the lab space available from the old dryer is too small for the new instrument (which is 28 inches wide by 22 deep by 30 high), you set it up in the hall, using the only available electrical outlet, a plug adjacent to a safety shower.[4]

Following the instructions in the owner's manual included with the instrument, you remove the front aluminum panel, exposing the gauge and switches. First you fill the vacuum pump with oil up to the "fill line" on the gauge, and then turn the refrigeration switch on. Within 30 minutes the temperature of the trap (where the water condenses) reaches −50°C (the temperature required before switching on the vacuum). Next you turn on the vacuum switch activating the pump. Immediately the instrument starts up a terrible metallic clanking noise. Worse, no vacuum registers on the gauge. After several attempts to get the dryer to work, you call Harry Pace, the lab serviceman, who checks the oil level and then the electrical system, but with no luck. Perplexed, Harry finally just gives the whole housing a good shake. Suddenly the pump gurgles briefly, the noise stops, and the vacuum begins to register. Within 5 minutes the gauge registers 35 microns of mercury—a good vacuum. However, when you stop the unit and try to start it up again, the instrument only makes a racket, refusing to function until given a good shake. After many stops and starts, it becomes evident to both you and Harry Pace that every time the pump is turned on, the operator must shake the housing to get the instrument to work properly.

Pace goes back to the shop, and you call the Freeze-It people to report the difficulty. Larry Hoch, the sales rep, is very surprised when you describe the clanking noise and the lack of a vacuum. After you have answered questions about the oil level and the electrical system to his satisfaction, Hoch suggests that since the company has no regional service, you should remove the vacuum pump and ship it back to Freeze-It for repair or replacement. After expressing your displeasure at the inconvenience and loss of time, you agree to send them

---

[4] A safety shower, which is similar to a conventional bathroom shower, is used for flushing chemical burns.

the pump. You really have no choice. In closing you tell Hoch that you will confirm this call in a letter describing the problem and the shipping plans.

Back in the lab discussing deadlines with Dr. Smythe, however, your arrangements with Hoch do not seem so wise. Together you and Smythe decide to retain the dryer "as is" for a week or two—just to take care of the current heavy work load. As long as you shake it, the instrument works just fine. Smythe suggests that you write to Freeze-It informing them of the change in plans for repair of the pump, as well as his intention to hold up Sterling's payment until the problem is corrected.

ASSIGNMENT 2
Write a letter to Larry Hoch, Sales Representative, Freeze-It Enterprises, Inc., 2300 Mississippi Avenue, Chicago, IL 00000, for Smythe's signature, with copies to Dr. Bart Wilson in Biophysics and Dr. Janet Ohanian in Microbiology. Add your name and position after "Writer" and use the following address as the letterhead: Department of Biochemistry, Sterling Foundation Research Laboratories, Rockville, MD 00000.

Part 3

After the dryer has been situated in the hall for ten days, an upset Jerry Hill, the institute's safety officer, calls Smythe to point out that the freeze dryer is stationed too close to the emergency shower; in fact, it blocks full and easy access to this safety device and must be moved immediately.[5] What Hill is most upset about, however, is that Dr. Greene passed through this hall last evening and observed the offense before Hill caught it.

Smythe comes out into the lab and tells you to get an electrician to install a new outlet further down the hall, well removed from the safety shower. For the moment, you must disconnect the dryer and get it out of the way. Greene is a busybody and a stickler on safety.

---

[5] Because Sterling Laboratories has numerous federal grants from various agencies, violations of safety codes mean heavy fines. The institute's safety personnel are responsible for policing the scientific staff to make sure that they observe all the applicable codes.

As Smythe leaves, he asks you to draft a conciliatory response to Hill, describing Biochem's immediate compliance with the safety requirements and, of course, sending a copy to Greene.

ASSIGNMENT 3
Write a memo to Jerry Hill, Safety Officer, with a copy to Dr. Morris Greene, Director of Research. Write for Smythe's signature and add your own name as "Writer."

Part 4

Late the next day the new outlet is installed about 15 feet down the hall. In checking over the instrument in its new location, you spy an additional oil gauge on the side of the pump, halfway back into the housing, well hidden from the operator and the front of the instrument (where the switches and other oil gauges are located). The side gauge shows that the oil level is low, so you add to the line and turn on the pump. Eureka! There is no mechanical clanking noise, and the unit operates perfectly. You cannot be sure whether the trouble was caused by the level of the floor in the old location, or the inadequate oil, or what, but you are sure that you are disgusted with the Freeze-It owner's manual, which said nothing about the other oil gauge, and with Larry Hoch, the Freeze-It rep, who never mentioned it in your telephone conversation. Under the pressures of work, however, you are simply pleased to use the smoothly running freeze dryer, and you quickly forget about the problems it gave you at first.

Part 5

About six weeks later, Dr. Smythe receives a letter from Larry Hoch at Freeze-It. (See Figure 2.)

Dr. Smythe routes the Hoch letter to you, after red-penciling in the margin: "Didn't you ever write to Freeze-It? Reply to Hoch immediately about what happened with the freeze dryer. Also let him know I've authorized payment today."

By now you are happy with the freeze dryer, as well as a little embarrassed that you did not remember to contact Hoch when the oil gauge problem was solved. At the same time, however, you are still

FREEZE-IT ENTERPRISES, INC.
2300 MISSISSIPPI AVENUE, CHICAGO, IL 00000

August 30, 1984

Dr. Jason Smythe
Department of Biochemistry
Sterling Foundation Research Laboratories
Rockville, MD 00000
    RE: Purchase Order No. Z75309

Dear Dr. Smythe:

According to your letter of July 9, 1984, confirming
the problems of the 1/2 hp pump installed in your Vacuum
Freeze Dryer Model PF-3, shipped on June 29, 1984, you
planned to return the vacuum pump to us for repairs
within a week to ten days. Almost two months have now
passed, yet we have not received the pump. Since we have
received no other communication from you, we assume that
the pump has been lost in transit.

Please advise us immediately whether you sent the
pump to Freeze-It Enterprises, and, if so, the carrier,
freight bill number, and date. We at Freeze-It regret
the inconvenience the pump malfunction caused your
laboratory, and we hope that a shipping error has not
further delayed your research. If the pump cannot be
located and the problem corrected immediately, we will,
of course, supply you with another pump while the
shipment is traced.

Figure 2.   Hoch's Letter

−2−

Thank you for your attention in this matter. Freeze−It Enterprises wants to serve your instrument needs. We hope to have your vacuum freeze dryer operating to your complete satisfaction as soon as possible.

Sincerely,

FREEZE−IT ENTERPRISES, INC.

Larry Hoch

by Larry Hoch,
Sales Department

LH:pp

Figure 2, *continued*

disgruntled when you recollect all the energy you and your co-workers had to put into getting this instrument to run properly, especially because you believe that Freeze-It's ineptitude and poor communication were largely responsible. Moreover, you realize that you are still in the dark about the second oil gauge and why the pump made all that racket, refusing to work until it was kicked. Although the instrument now operates beautifully, you wonder if it will continue to do so. The thing ran without oil for a couple of weeks; who knows what terrible thing that did to it? Perhaps your letter to Larry Hoch should do *more* than report that the dryer works fine now, the pump is not lost in transit, and their money is coming soon.

ASSIGNMENT 4
Write a letter to Larry Hoch at Freeze-It for Smythe's signature. Add your own name as "Writer." Use the addresses furnished in Assignment 2.

The Farnsworth Paper Works Case: Requesting a Permit from the Department of Natural Resources

Part 1

What could be more beautiful than September in the state of Washington, you think, as you gaze out of your office window at Farnsworth Paper Works, Inc. The sun hangs a bit lower in the sky now, even at 10 o'clock in the morning. The location of the paper mill almost makes you forget that you are at work. The mill sits beside the Nargansett River overlooking Tituba Lake and is surrounded by 1,000 acres of natural forest. Quite a sight! You are happy working here as an environmental engineer—first, because you have found a good career in Washington, applying your hard-earned forestry degree, and second, because you believe in Farnsworth. This company has done its best to maintain a clean plant operation that is nonpolluting and safe. And you like Sol Weidman, your supervisor and area manager of Environmental Engineering, who, as you can see by glancing over the front partition of your workstation, happens to be making his way to you now. Sol is scratching his head and mumbling to himself. He starts talking to you even before he reaches your office door.

"We've got a little problem here that I think you can help us clear up."

"What is it?" you ask. You have learned in working with Sol that this chief engineer likes to talk through his thinking on a problem before he assigns projects, so you are prepared to listen for a while.

"The DNR is giving us a runaround."

"The DNR?" you say with surprise. It is not like Sol to complain about the Department of Natural Resources. Farnsworth has always had cordial relations with them. The company runs a clean operation and meets all pollution control requirements without any trouble.

"Oh, our regional DNR office[1] seems to be stalling on a permit to let us dump our fly ash[2] on our landfill. We've got 40 acres just waiting to take it."

"Hmmmm. Why has this problem cropped up just now? We've produced plenty of fly ash over the last ten years. What have we been doing with it?"

"Well, for the last couple of years we've been letting it pile up behind Shed 3A. That was supposed to be a temporary solution until we figured out where to dump it permanently. Well, the stuff's been out of sight there, and so it's been out of mind. We're at a critical point now. In a few months, there will be no room to store more ash behind the shed. Besides, we'd like to clean up that area. We've worked hard not to disturb the landscape around the mill, and we want to keep it that way."

"So what can we do?"

"Well, we could sell about half of what we produce as low-grade fertilizer; we'd have to pelletize[3] it first though, so it can be handled easily. That'd get rid of about 500 tons a year."

"Why not pelletize and sell all of it?"

"The rest of the fly ash is unsuitable to recycle this way. It's mixed with fused sand that's been cleaned off the furnace grates. That stuff can't be pelletized. I think we could get DNR approval to pelletize and sell the good stuff in small quantities as garden fertilizer. It's similar to potash, which is used widely as a fertilizer now." Sol stops to think a moment. "But we haven't bothered to propose this to the DNR yet."

"Because we'd still have to get rid of the rest."

---

[1] Farnsworth is regulated by the DNR office for Region No. 4. This is one of four regional offices reporting to DNR headquarters in the state capital. Each regional office is managed by a degree-holding environmental engineer. The state offices, officers, and laws described here are typical of many states and do not refer to real offices and officers in the state of Washington.

[2] Fly ash is the noncombustible inorganic residue remaining after wood waste has been burned. Fly ash is entrained in a gas stream and includes such substances as ash, cinders, and sand. In paper mills, fly ash is the by-product of wood waste burned for heat.

[3] Pelletizing is a process in which fly ash is mixed with enough clay (for example, bentonite) and water to cause particles to stick together; then the mixture is agitated to form round pellets or extruded through a punched plate to form cylindrical pellets. Fly ash that is not pelletized has the consistency of fine flour and cannot be spread without creating a dust hazard.

"That's right. We won't make much off the fertilizer sale, and we'd still have the disposal problem. I'd like to dump that useless stuff on our 'back forty.' A few years ago that's what we used to do. But the DNR won't permit it now."

"Why?"

"Our back lot is a permeable landfill. Back in '79 the state gave it a Type III classification. That was in response to a DNR investigation prompted by local homeowners. Some people in Ossentuck were using the lot as a general dump, throwing metal, trash, tires, and whatnot into it. And, of course, we were dumping our fly ash there. After some residents complained, the DNR told the city to give citations to residents who dump there and they told us to haul our fly ash to a Type II fill. We've been storing it behind Shed 3A ever since, and, of course, that site's not a Type II landfill."[4]

"Hmmmm. I think I'm beginning to see how all this fits together," you say. "We got cited during a general crackdown. Of course, that could have happened to us whether the residents complained about the dump or not. Up to a few years ago environmental protection agencies weren't too concerned about where anyone dumped organic substances, like wood products. But now they are . . ."

"That's right," Sol interrupts. "The leachate[5] from fly ash is high in alkalies,[6] and we've got Tituba Lake sitting right behind us. The DNR is concerned about drainage into the lake, even though they shouldn't be; we've got land surveys which show there is negligible groundwater flow out of our landfill area."

"Oh, yes?" you note with interest. "What kind of data do we have?"

"Well, two months ago, we hired a consulting firm, Terra Engineering, to analyze the area surrounding our landfill. They drilled test wells at several points between the landfill and the lake and found no detectable level of alkalies in the groundwater, even though we'd

---

[4] A Type III landfill is any unprepared land area used for waste disposal. A Type II landfill is clay lined and otherwise prepared to keep substances from filtering out.

[5] Leachate is the product which is removed from a substance, such as fly ash, when water percolates through it.

[6] Fly ash contains 10–25% alkalies measured by weight as sodium oxide (Na_2O). High levels of alkalies in soil can raise the groundwater pH (a measure of the acidity or alkalinity of a solution). If groundwater with a high pH runs into a lake, it could raise the pH of the lake, encouraging algae growth and cutting the oxygen supply for fish.

been dumping the fly ash there for years before the DNR put a stop to it. The firm also did a hydrogeologic study of the area which showed that the groundwater flows away from the lake. Even if there was anything leaching from the ash dump, it wouldn't go into the lake."

"I assume we sent that data to the DNR."

"Of course, but they didn't act on it. Yesterday I called Vern Fenkel, our regional DNR manager, to check up on it. He says the office is 'taking it under advisement.'"

"What's that supposed to mean?"

"It means they're sitting on it. You see, a lot of the environmental engineers working for the DNR take a very conservative approach to these things. They don't want to make a decision now and be caught with their pants down later. DNR engineers don't want some environmental group to locate an ecological hazard and pin it on them."

"Well, what kind of risk are they taking if they okay our dump?"

"That's what's so frustrating," Sol answers as he suddenly starts to pace back and forth. (You can tell that he is ready to get to the crux of the matter now.) "They are taking absolutely no risk at all!" he says with a great deal of emphasis. Suddenly he walks back to your cubicle and impulsively sits down at your desk.

"This is what's going on," he continues. "As can be expected, the DNR engineers are following state law to the letter. Where state law isn't clear, they are proceeding with extreme caution. No one wants to make a move until someone else does. We've got state law on our side here; the state public law says nothing about dumping fly ash in unprepared landfills. Plus we've got our land surveys. The only reason I can figure that Fenkel is keeping us from dumping ash in our back lot is because some other regional manager won't let some other company do something like that. And that's what we're up against."

"So what are our alternatives?"

"That's what I wanted to go over with you," Sol answers. "I've got an idea, but I'd like to see if you see it the way I do." Spreading his hands on your desk, he begins laying out his plans. "If worst comes to worst, we can simply conform to what they want and have our ash hauled away to a Type II landfill," he begins.

"But that'd be expensive," you counter.

"Of course. I bet it would cost us $25,000 a year to cart the stuff away. The nearest fill with a Type II permit is 35 miles from here."

"What about converting our landfill to a Type II fill?"

"We could, but that would be costly too. We'd have to put a clay cap on it and start over." Sol gets up, shaking his head as he speaks.

"The point is, I don't think we should have to do that; we've got the evidence that says we can dump it safely right here."

"But you've already said the DNR won't approve it."

"I also said that's because some other regional manager must have said 'no' to someone else. But," Sol adds animatedly, "I have a hunch that there's an engineer somewhere in our state regional offices who has let some other company do just what we want to do—sell some of the ash and dump the rest in the back lot."

Sol smiles broadly at you, clearly anticipating that you can see what is on his mind.

"And you want to know what company got permission to do that and from whom," you respond.

"That's right."

"And you want me to find that company."

"Uh-huh. And this is how you could go about it. Call the DNR in Olympia and get a list of all those companies in Washington that burn wood products for power or heat[7]—you know, do a survey of who generates fly ash, who dumps it, who recycles it, whatever. Find out what their permits to dump say."

"Right," you say. "That should be no problem. When do you need the data?"

"I'd like it tomorrow. I want to keep pushing Fenkel so he knows we're not going to let this go. Whatever you find out, put it on a page. I'll use your memo to support my written request for a permit to dump, say, five to seven hundred tons of ash on our landfill each year and sell the rest as fertilizer. They know our situation is getting critical, and a plan to sell almost half the ash instead of dumping it should please them. I'll just tell them exactly what we want, why we should get it, and ask for an immediate response. Your data should give us the edge there."

"Okay," you say. "I'll try to get the information you need by tomorrow."

For the moment you try to forget about how you are going to find

---

[7] Companies that might burn wood waste for power and heat include paper mills, sawmills, and particle-board plants. Wood waste can be burned for power to fire steam boilers. It can also be burned to provide heat for production processes. For example, heated gas from the furnace flu is mixed with cooler air and used to dry such products as bark, lumber, veneer, and wood flakes.

out "by tomorrow" how all the other companies in Washington that produce fly ash get rid of it. You also try to ignore how you are going to handle this little investigation with all the other work you already have scheduled.

"If my hunch is right," Sol continues, interrupting your pondering, "you'll come up with just the information we need."

"I'll try," you reply.

"Oh, I'm counting on you," Sol say as he heads back to his work-station.

You decide not to waste any time and begin your investigation by calling the main office of the DNR in Olympia. Mary Rollofs of the DNR Public Information Office refers you to the Northeastern Council of Washington Governments. Cynthia Balinger of the council's Public Services Department gives you a list of 14 companies that burn wood waste for power or heat. You decide to call those companies that seem likely to produce as much or more fly ash as Farnsworth.

Your first call is to the Richter Corporation, a packaging company in Kent which is in the same DNR region as Farnsworth. Jim Flesh-man, their chief environmental engineer, is immediately helpful.

"We're in the same boat as you," he tells you. "Fenkel wants us to dump our fly ash in a Type II fill. We've been dumping it in any nearby fill that will take it. We also give some away as fertilizer to locals who ask for it. Haven't thought of pelletizing it and packaging it for retail sales though."

"What's Fenkel done about it?" you ask.

"Well," Fleshman responds, "nothing so far. He's pressuring us to haul it to a Type II fill. We've just declined. There've been no complaints from residents near the landfills. We have no guarantee how long he'll be willing to let us keep on as we have been, though."

You thank Fleshman for his information and jot down some notes in your phone log. You find it quite interesting that Fenkel is letting the Richter Corporation do what they want.

You continue to go down your list making calls. By 3:00 P.M. you have called the last company and have typed up notes from your phone calls. (See Appendix A, Phone Call Notes.) It looks like Sol was right. Different DNR engineers in different regions have given companies permission to dispose of fly ash in different ways. With your infor-mation as part of his proposal to the DNR, Farnsworth should have a good case for taking care of the fly ash on their own property. You quickly write up the memo telling Sol of your findings.

ASSIGNMENT 1
Write a memo to Sol Weidman, Manager, Environmental Engineering, telling him the results of your investigation. Your title is Engineer.

Part 2

This morning you drop off your memo at Sol's workstation as soon as you come in. You had to type it yourself at home last night, but this is not the first time you have had to handle a rush job this way. No sooner do you sit down to read your in-box than Sol gives you a call and asks you to come down to his cubicle.

"Just read your info," he says as you walk in. "Well, we don't have much, but we do have something. This might be enough to give us the edge."

"I think it might," you say, wondering what else Sol has on his mind.

"I'm glad we had the chance to discuss this whole problem yesterday," he continues. "I'm not going to be able to write that proposal to Fenkel. George Flaherty in our Products Engineering Office called late yesterday afternoon and has got me working on a rush job. Seems we're going to introduce a new paper products line, and he's concerned about the chemicals required to produce it. We've got to make sure we can dilute them and run our pulp-processing water into the Nargansett River with no problem."

"I see," you say, guessing that Sol is going to ask you to write that proposal for him.

Sol begins searching quickly through his files as he talks to you. "I've got that land survey which Terra Engineering did for us right here someplace, and you've got this data on what other companies are doing. You also understand that ideally we want to pelletize maybe three to five hundred tons a year and dump maybe five to seven hundred tons. We want permits to do both." Sol continues searching through files for the Terra Engineering land survey.

"I suppose you'd like me to write that up as a proposal for Fenkel," you say, again anticipating his request.

"I'll be here to go over it when you're through," Sol says, acknowledging your tacit understanding of the assignment. He spends a minute more thumbing through his files and then suddenly slaps his forehead. "I gave that land survey to Janet Ridley in the Main

Office. She wanted to see it for an article she's writing for the company newsletter on our use of outside consultants. Look," he says, gesturing toward you, "you won't really need this land survey to write the proposal. Simply give an overview of the conclusions as we discussed them yesterday. Fenkel's seen the survey before, and, of course, I'll append another copy to this proposal."

"Fine," you say.

"Keep the writing simple," Sol advises. "Those DNR people shuffle through a lot of paper, and we want them to get the message fast."

Sol tells you about a few other matters he wants you to take care of while he works with Flaherty and leaves you to write the proposal. Well, at least you have the opportunity to follow through on this project and to make all that phone calling pay off. You begin planning your proposal by sketching out a discussion that will support the major requests you make of the DNR. Then you decide how you will work in the information from your memo to Sol. With that figured out, you think you are well on your way to getting the proposal drafted before the morning is over.

ASSIGNMENT 2

Write a proposal to the DNR requesting a permit for future disposal of fly ash according to the plans you discussed with Sol Weidman. The document will be addressed to Vern Fenkel, Manager, Department of Natural Resources Region No. 4, Fredonia, Washington 00000. It will come from Sol Weidman and you will be named after "Prepared by." Your firm's address is Farnsworth Paper Works, Inc., 20 Tituba Lake Road, Ossentuck, Washington 00000.

APPENDIX A

Phone Call Notes

1. Richter Corporation—Jim Fleshman—In the same boat as we are. At this time they go to any nearby landfill and they also give it away as fertilizer. However, the DNR regional (Fenkel's office) wants them to go to a Type II landfill. They have declined. So far so good.

2. Ashland Products—Al Banti. Landfill the ash from a bark—burning boiler. Were told by DNR that a Type III was OK. Received a letter confirming less than 2 months ago. Produce about same amt. of fly ash as us. Ashland is in Region 2; Julia Lipsett, Manager.

3. Abco Cleansers—do not burn a significant amount of wood.

4. Joe's Sawmill—Springfield—two-bit operation.

5. Maisle's Sawmill—Allentown—ditto.

6. Freedom Power Co.—Richard Fowler. They have a current permit to dump wood fly ash; they compact the ash before dumping it on unprepared land (their property). About 300 tons per yr. DNR Region No. 3; Francis Wong, Mgr.

7. Friedlanger's Construction—No Wood.

8. TWP Wood Products—small business, not comparable.

9. Valley Forest Products—our region; fly ash hauled to Type II in Four Rivers. Maybe 1000 tons per yr.

10. Smith—Mentag—Ossentuck—Frank Angelo—Chief Env. Engineer. Run ash to dredged-out pond. This is a municipal landfill (Type II). Mostly coal ash, but some wood ash mixed in. Monitoring of groundwater is going to start at the landfill in the near future. Fenkel requested this; Bass Lake is nearby.

APPENDIX A—*continued*

11. Richland Co.—our region; dump same amount of fly ash as us in a Type III landfill. Coal ash only. Not like ours. Coal burning companies have no trouble disposing ash at any landfill type.

12. Druger and Hayes—plastic tableware; no wood ash; ash from polyethylene.

13. Welsh Container Corp.—nobody in who knew anything.

14. Pittman Products, Inc.—Waste Control Department—Henry Kopp, Supr. They will seek approval to pelletize some fly ash as low grade fertilizer from DNR. DNR has so far indicated there will be no problem with the fertilizer approach; nothing in writing though. If it does not work out, they will dispose of all ash in local municipal landfill (Fowlerville—Type II), as they're doing now. They produce as much fly ash as us. DNR Region 1; Elmore Blanchard, Mgr.

The Industrial Relations Cases: Coping with Change at Howard Brothers, Inc.

(*Note*: After reading the introduction, a student can prepare any one of the following three cases without reading the others.)

Introduction

Your plant, part of Howard Brothers, Inc., a giant of the soap industry, manufactures several household cleaning products in the small town of Braden outside of Atlanta. Your position at the Braden Plant, which has about 1,500 employees, is assistant manager of the Industrial Relations (IR) Department. The department has three sections: Labor Relations, covering all the hourly workers; Salaried Personnel/ Training; and Employee Services, covering mail, telephone, security, benefit programs, and food and medical services.

Because your plant is halfway across the country from Howard corporate headquarters, your department handles public relations tasks that typically would be the responsibility of corporate PR people. Your boss, Jack LaPresle (manager of the Industrial Relations Department), represents the company on many boards and activities like the Airport Review Committee, the Chamber of Commerce, and the board of the United Way, and he deals with the town council and the mayor of Braden on company matters. For some time he has delegated many IR writing tasks to you, jobs such as presenting the Howard

Brothers' position on legislation for local and regional officials (with the benefit of position papers from the corporate legislative section), and writing for the plant manager, Mr. Will P. Gormann, as he represents the corporation. Recently, LaPresle has been so occupied with community activities, including chairing the fund-raising drive for the United Way, that he has been assigning most of his writing to you, even the communication within the department. (You have a feeling that Jack likes to talk more than write.)

So, you do some writing for LaPresle's signature and some for Gormann's. (Rarely do you sign your own name to anything.) Jack LaPresle and Mr. Gormann have very different styles as people, as managers, and as communicators. LaPresle is very talkative, a real politician, a guy who is always "greasing" operations, facilitating things, keeping folks happy so that everything proceeds smoothly. Gormann is quite open for a plant manager, and, though he tends to be a little direct—not always as diplomatic as he could be—he is a prince of a fellow. In fact, both men are great to *write* for. They give you a pretty free rein. Filling you in and telling you what they would like to see happen, they then let you handle things; rarely do they second-guess your solutions or make significant changes in your writing.

Your job at Howard Brothers would be fine, therefore, except that the sales picture has not been good lately. Moreover, the Braden Plant has contributed to the sagging sales with a case of product contamination a few months ago, an incident with many negative ramifications. Just over three months ago, the Spaly Chemical Company sent your plant a shipment of contaminated material for part of an order. Sample testing did not detect the error. Consequently, the material, a component used to manufacture a fabric softener, contaminated a whole production run at the Braden Plant. By the time the error was discovered, the fabric softener was already coming onto the shelves in stores in several parts of the country. The product was recalled immediately, but the unfavorable publicity from the recall depressed sales even further. Although no allergic reactions have been reported from consumers (and no lawsuits filed), some plant workers did suffer minor reactions, and that whole issue is still an unknown. In short, Howard Brothers has a host of problems arising from the contamination episode, and you are frequently part of the troubleshooting efforts. In fact, many of your recent writing assignments have dealt, directly or indirectly, with the spin-off from the contamination problem.

CASE 16A

Yesterday, the manager of the plant, Mr. Gormann, received a letter from Braden's mayor. (See Figure 1.) Mr. Gormann hands you the letter this morning and tells you to answer it for him.

"Main thing," Gormann says emphatically, "is to tell him the truth. Let him know that we're glad he's interested in finding out the truth and stopping the spread of false rumors."

You raise your eyebrows questioningly.

Gormann senses your discomfort and says: "This letter doesn't say a word about the contamination issue, but I'm sure that's what's on Frank Kelly's mind. Nobody was much worried about the plant shutting down a few months back, and sales weren't so hot then either."

"So we should tell Mayor Kelly that our fabric softener was contaminated by a bad component manufactured by an Atlanta vendor?" you ask.

"Yes. Rumors arise from some people saying that the contamination was caused by a conspiracy or some crazy nut or inadequate controls on our part. We have to keep saying that it was a single component from one source with inadequate quality control at their end, and that we no longer are using them as a source. . . . All these facts help to stop rumors."

"Do you think it's wise to go into all that again?" you ask.

"Well, the press releases and the newspaper reporters have covered most of the ground, but not everyone believes newspapers. Look, the point is to calm things down by my making a personal statement to the Mayor. He's worried about the plant closing. The most important thing here is to reassure Kelly that we are not planning to close the plant. We want to stop any rumors about the plant closing without making any promises, of course."

"Okay," you nod. "Certainly we won't say anything about the allergic reactions of some of the workers, then."

"Hardly," Gormann shakes his head. "That's a matter for the attorneys."

"What about all the bad publicity?" you wonder.

"Hmm. Frank is certainly aware of that. It's part of his concern. Tell him that the company is responding with a public relations campaign that will help put things into perspective. But the big point is that we expect sales to head upward very soon."

"You want it to sound really upbeat?"

"Of course, because we *do* expect sales to head up. But," Gormann

Office of the Mayor

TOWN OF BRADEN
33 Missouri Avenue
Braden, Georgia 00000

February 21, 1984

Mr. Will P. Gormann
Plant Manager
Howard Brothers, Inc.
P.O. Box 32
Braden, Georgia 00000

Dear Will:

As you are well aware, rumors are circulating concerning the future of the Howard Brothers plant in Braden. Several of the workers at the plant have expressed such concerns to me recently.

I realize that it is impossible for you to predict the future, but I would appreciate it if you could tell me what the current projections are concerning the activity of the Braden plant. I would certainly appreciate anything you could tell me.

Thank you for your continuing cooperation.

Kind regards,

Frank R. Kelly

Frank R. Kelly
Mayor

FRK:pa

Figure 1.   The Mayor's Letter on the Braden Plant's Future

continues, "I also want him to know I am concerned about the workers' anxieties, and that I am doing what I can. You know, all those meetings I've held to answer their questions, tell them what's going on, reassure them. At least we're trying," he says, staring out the window.

"Fine, I'll let him know that you share his concerns, and that we, at Howard Brothers, are optimistic. Things should turn around soon."

"Yes. That's right," Gormann nods. "Things are going to turn around soon. And we want everyone to know that." He pauses. "After all, it's three months since this bloomin' contamination thing happened. The general slump in the market and the resulting layoffs were bad enough without a contamination incident—but don't go into much detail on that score. We just can't predict what might happen. Main thing is to let him know that we certainly do *not* expect the plant to close," and he underlines the "not" with a jab of his index finger. "We aren't even considering such a move."

As he hands you the Mayor's letter, Gormann concludes, "Let him know that I welcome his help on containing the false rumors."

As you prepare to write the letter to Kelly, you are not quite sure what Gormann wants in this one. His openness is genuine and an appropriate way to represent him, but in this case his openness is somewhat guarded. The problem is that the issue is very delicate, and Gormann simply cannot say whatever he would like. "Open but not too open," might be the real bottom line here.

ASSIGNMENT
Write a letter to the Mayor, Mr. Frank R. Kelly, from Will P. Gormann, Plant Manager, Howard Brothers, Inc., Braden Plant, P.O. Box 32, Braden, Georgia 00000. The mayor's office is in the Town of Braden, 33 Missouri Avenue, Braden, Georgia 00000. (Write your name on the upper-right corner of this paper to identify it for your instructor.)

CASE 16B

About a week ago, you took a call for Jack LaPresle, who is out of the office attending a training seminar for ten days. The telephone call was from Fred Markley, a production engineer who wants to know if some men from Standard Products (your biggest competition in detergents) can come to look over some new equipment in the plant.

The vendor of the equipment, Parker and Company, has been very helpful to the production people at Braden for a long time. Now Parker wants the Standard Products people to take a look at the new Parker centrifuges for isolation of detergent crystals and see what a great job they do at the Howard Brothers' Braden facility.

Although Markley sounds very eager to comply with Parker and Company, you doubt that Gormann would allow this request even in the best of times. Considering the difficulties following the contamination problem, especially the allergic reactions of some of the workers, he is unlikely to want visitors prowling around the plant, but you're not certain, and you would prefer to have LaPresle discuss the issue with Mr. Gormann. So you stall for time, telling Fred Markley to have Parker and Company contact LaPresle directly by mail. Unfortunately for you, the Parker letter for Jack arrives today (Figure 1), and you cannot delay a decision until your boss gets back to the office.

After reading over the letter, you put through a call to Mr. Gormann and explain that Parker and Company wants to bring in some Standard Products folks to take a look at the new Parker centrifuges in the plant. Gormann hears you out and then says evenly, "No, we certainly don't want any visitors around here at a time like this."

And you reply, "That was my assessment, Mr. Gormann, but since Mr. LaPresle is gone, I thought I better check with you."

"Fine; that's just fine," answers Gormann. "The way I see it, when did these fellows at Standard ever let us come and look at *their* equipment? And they always have the same nice answer too. 'Proprietary processes' just won't allow it. Well, you just tell them that our exclusive manufacturing rights won't allow it either." Then he pauses a moment. "Boy, I am sorry about the Parker people. Pat Johnson has been especially good to us. I really regret that we can't give him a hand."

"Fred Markley was very eager to do the Parker people a good turn, that's for sure," you reply.

"Of course. But we just can't do it. Do let Pat down easily on this, however."

"Right," you answer.

ASSIGNMENT 1

Write a letter for the signature of Mr. J. P. LaPresle, Industrial Relations Manager, to Mr. P. O. Johnson, Equipment Division, Parker

Parker & Company
P.O. Box 777
New York, New York 00000

March 1, 1984

Mr. J. P. LaPresle
Industrial Relations Manager
Braden Plant
Howard Brothers, Inc.
P.O. Box 32
Braden, Georgia 00000

Dear Mr. LaPresle:

With reference to my telephone conversation of February 28, 1984, with your Mr. Fred Markley (Engineering), I would like to bring engineers from Standard Products, Talbot, Alabama, to your plant to see your Parker A 31 Centrifuges which isolate detergent crystals.

Standard Products is working with us on an application to use our A 31 Centrifuges at their Talbot, Alabama, plant.

The Standard Products' personnel I would like to bring with me are:
Mr. Milton Berkowitz, Senior Plant Engineer
Mr. Tim Fraleigh, Plant Engineer
Mr. Lance Smith, Maintenance Supervisor.

Figure 1.   Parker's Letter of Request

-2-

We would like to arrange the visit at your earliest convenience. Your valuable help in this matter is much appreciated by Parker and Company.

Sincerely,

Pat Johnson

PARKER AND COMPANY
P.O. Johnson, Equipment Division

cc: F. M. Markley — Howard Brothers Braden Plant
    M. Berkowitz — Standard Products Talbot Plant
    T. Fraleigh — Standard Products Talbot Plant
    L. Smith — Standard Products Talbot Plant
    K. O. Manoogian — Parker and Company New York
    P. A. Teleman — Parker and Company Atlanta
    O. P. Husby — Parker and Company New York

Figure 1, *continued*

and Company, P.O. Box 777, New York, New York 00000. Copies go to Mr. W. P. Gormann, Plant Manager; Mr. F. M. Markley, Engineering Department; and Mr. J. P. Lawton, Chief of Industrial Relations Division, Howard Brothers, Inc.,—Corporate Offices. (Mr. Lawton needs to be apprised of your public relations activities at Braden.) Sign the letter for the absent Jack LaPresle, and initial it with your own initials. (Write your name on the upper-right corner of this paper to identify it for your instructor.)

ASSIGNMENT 2

Write a cover memo for the letter to inform Jack LaPresle, your supervisor, about the circumstances for your writing the letter to Parker and Company. (The cover memo and letter will be ready for him on his return to the office next week.)

CASE 16C

Hard times at the Braden Plant have caused several general reductions in force, and now they are affecting your unit directly. Industrial Relations is losing a receptionist, a clerk, and a secretary. Although the reduced number of employees in the plant does lessen your department's work load, the reduction does not lessen the work enough to compensate for the IR personnel loss. Jack LaPresle describes the problem as "how to get the same amount of work done with three less people."

Focusing attention on the Labor Relations section, Jack asks you to brainstorm with him for ways to do the job without one clerk and part of a secretary (Labor Relations' share of the personnel cut in the IR package).

Right away you suggest eliminating the "open-door" policy, under which the hourly personnel come in at any time of the day to get help with just about anything they want, including filling out forms and making applications and requests. "As I see it," you say, "our open-door policy has turned into a string of constant interruptions. In many respects we're running a drop-in counseling service. A couple of staff members, Jerry Krueger especially, have become kind of big brothers or uncles for a steady stream of workers all day long. If we could think of some way to curtail these discussions, it could free up several hours a day to make up the work load of the clerk we've lost."[1]

"No doubt you're right, particularly about Jerry Krueger," Jack says with a grin. "Good old Jerry. About half his time goes for chatting away with folks, makin' 'em feel good, providing an ear for their problems." Then his tone gets serious. "But that's good, of course. He performs a real service, sort of an in-house, free 'shrink.'"

"I realize he's doing something valuable for the hourly personnel," you protest, "but I thought that this time block was a potential saving for the jobs we *must* do."

"Unfortunately, you're right," Jack says with some chagrin. "I just hate to do it, but it's the obvious move. The big question is, how? We sure can't say, 'Now look, Krueger. Stop talking away with the folks. Just get the job done.' Everybody would think we weren't providing the good service any longer. . . . Besides, it isn't just Jerry, of course."

"There'll have to be some changes in our system, I guess."

Jack laughs. "Obviously. Got any brilliant suggestions?"

After some discussion that does not get you to first base, Jack decides to call a meeting of all the Labor Relations people to try to solve this problem together. "It's better than imposing some decision they'll all follow begrudgingly. Send out a memo to announce the meeting," he says to you, glancing at his calendar. "Let's see, this Thursday at 2:00 P.M. looks open. We'll meet in the LR conference room. Tell them what the problem is in the memo and that we must figure out an answer—*together*."

As you get up to go back to your desk, Jack says, "Hey, wait a minute. Better let 'em know that no significant services can be dropped. I don't want some bright guy to figure out a great solution that cuts the work load by eliminating an essential service!"

ASSIGNMENT 1

Write a memo announcing the meeting. Address it to all Labor Relations staff members: P. Cordozo, J. Krueger, R. Larson, M. Pile, L. Preston, D. Rezmierski, B. Varner, and A. Wallace. The memo is from J. P. LaPresle, Industrial Relations Manager. (Write your name on the upper-right corner of this paper to identify it for your instructor.)

---

[1] The clerk's job responsibilities include providing general information to workers, helping with address changes, health forms, shift preferences, leaves of absence, unemployment forms, pay shortages, and job postings.

At the meeting on Thursday, Jack LaPresle makes some remarks about how regrettable the reductions in LR personnel are. He also says that the problem they face is how to offer roughly the same services with the reduced staff. He gets the ball rolling by asking everyone for suggestions on redistributing the work load, making adjustments in the system, or doing whatever else they believe might help.

More than an hour of discussion identifies many problems, a few suggestions, and a consensus that the "open-door" or "on-demand" policy puts the most strain on the staff's time. Everyone gets interrupted in the midst of tasks because of this free-access system. This slows people down, and everyone accomplishes less of his or her required duties. Moreover, the clerks spend so much time responding to people's problems that they do not get much else done, and their work must be absorbed by other staff members.

"There's no doubt that we all spend a lot of time holding people's hands," Roger Larson comments.

"Probably more time than in assisting them with the specific tasks we're assigned to do," Mike Pile admits.

"Now look," Jack says with some authority. "There's no doubt that we serve a special function around here, and it's one that Mr. Gormann approves of strongly. The trouble is that I'm afraid we can't afford it any longer. We have a set of specific jobs we have to get done, and if we eliminate all this time spent 'holding people's hands' as you put it, Roger, well then, I think that we'll be able to get all the required jobs done—even with less staff."

"We all seem to think that the open-door policy disrupts staff members' work and expends too much of some staffers' time in informal discussions with the workers," you say. "So what do we do about it? How can we change the system?"

"How can we stop people from dropping in whenever they want?" asks Lou Ann Preston. "Bar the door?"

"Yah, I like that," grins Bruce Varner. "Let's bar the back door to the plant. If people didn't have such easy access into our offices, they sure wouldn't be wandering in and out so often."

"No doubt the physical layout of the offices is one of our big problems," says Jack. "Let's look at this sketch of our setup and see what we might do to improve things," and he points at a floor plan of the Labor Relations Offices. (See Figure 1.)

"Certainly we've got to stop people from coming in the back door," comments Arlette Wallace, a secretary. "That's where all the wandering comes from."

"What about building a sliding glass window, a so-called pass window, where they would have to *stand* to talk to us?" asks Roger Larson. "We could post hours for specific services, and that way we wouldn't get interrupted all the time."

"Where would you put these 'pass windows'?" asks Krueger.

Roger is all excited now. "Put them in the conference room, opening to the aisleway to the plant. Simply lock up the plant door that comes directly into the office," he says, pointing to the chart (Figure 1). "Make 'em all come through the Main Plant door. Then they could stand here in the aisleway for help from Labor Relations staff. The pass window would be right here," and he marks the spot for the Labor Relations window between the conference room and the plant aisleway with a big **X**. (See Figure 2.)

"I can see that we would get fewer disruptions with specific posted hours, and I would guess that people won't chat much if they have to stand up at a window," says Jerry Krueger. "I guess we'd have much greater efficiency, but I wonder about the quality of our service."

Lou Ann Preston agrees. "Some people need a lot of help just to survive. With the reading and writing skills many of these workers have, it can end up taking over half an hour just to help a guy fill out a health form."

"Of course," Jack says frowning. "But that is legitimate. We can't cut down on the help they need with specific tasks. But I think that the pass window would encourage people who just want to 'chew the fat' to move on."

"It won't be near the same," Lou Ann says quietly. "Not near the personal contact. I don't care about losing the conference room, but I do care about giving personal service."

"Unfortunately, person-to-person stuff takes time and costs bucks," says Bruce Varner under his breath.

"Look," cuts in Jack, "we are not in any way going to reduce essential services to the workers in this plant. And that includes helping them fill out any forms they need assistance with."

"Say, why don't we think of some ways we could give them roughly the same help without so much direct contact?" says Roger. "One thing—we could make some posters with giant, blown-up forms on them, complete with very simple instructions."

"That'll help some folks, but others won't be able to follow them," remarks Jerry.

"Still," Jack nods approvingly, "it's a good idea."

Although the new system does not meet with universal approval,

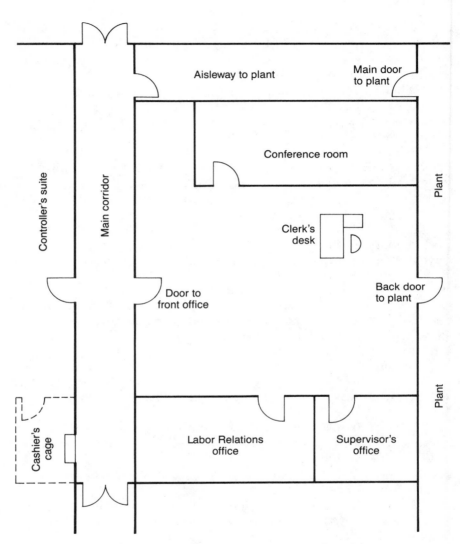

Figure 1.   The Labor Relations Offices at the Braden Plant

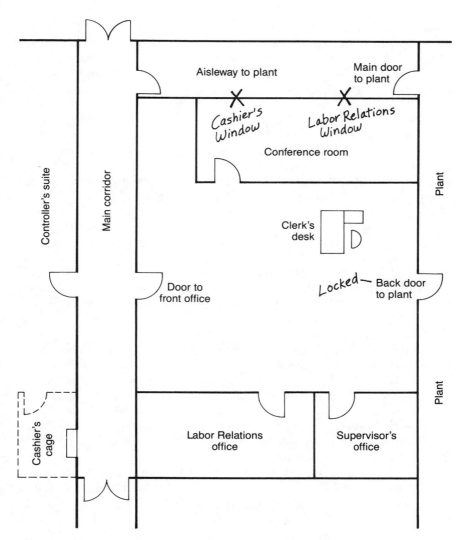

Figure 2.   The Labor Relations Offices at the Braden Plant:
Suggested Changes

nobody can come up with a better idea to solve the problem of a greater work load in Labor Relations. Eventually everyone agrees to give up the conference room and allow posted hours and limited access a try. Certainly the strolling in and out of the office, accompanied by constant disruptions, should end, and the LR staff should be more efficient.

"What about the limited hours?" you ask. "What are we going to limit them to?"

Jack has the major responsibilities listed on a flip chart, and after a brief discussion everyone agrees that the big areas have to be covered all day. However, the Suggestion and Apprentice area and the Unemployment Compensation and general clerk matters will be limited severely. After some slightly heated exchange on who is going to do what, everyone agrees on two hours in the morning and two in the afternoon for each of these areas. The chart of limited hours is then complete. (See Figure 3.)

"Wait a minute," says Bruce. "What about the cashier's cage?[2] Many of the people trotting through here are just interested in chatting a bit on their way to getting a paycheck problem taken care of. If we lock the 'back' door to the plant, everyone will use the Main Plant door to get to the cage."

"And they'll still expect cashier's service at any hour of the day," Paul Cordozo remarks sarcastically.

"Not if the cashier won't open up for them," Jack responds. "The new 'specified hours system' should take care of this problem beautifully. All we must do is get the controller to establish limited hours like we're doing. . . . Say, maybe we could get him to move the cage out of the main corridor and put it in the aisleway to the plant, perhaps next to the Labor Relations window."

"Now you're talking!" Bruce says enthusiastically. "We can put a pass-through window for the cashier on one side, and the Labor Relations window on the other." And he marks a second big cross on the chart, labeling it "Cashier's Window." (See Figure 2, page 169.)

---

[2] Currently the cashier's cage for hourly personnel is located near the Labor Relations Offices, even though it is under the controller's supervision, not Jack LaPresle's. Employees are accustomed to simply knocking on the controller's door to get service when the cage is not open.

> ROGER LARSON, MICHAEL PILE — SUGGESTION AND APPRENTICESHIP PROGRAMS, 7:30–9:30 am AND 1:30–3:30 pm
>
> BRUCE VARNER, DON REZMIERSKI — HOURLY BENEFIT ADMINISTRATION, TRAINING/TUITION REFUNDS, RETIREMENT COUNSELING 7:30am to 4pm
>
> LOU ANN PRESTON, PAUL CORDOZO — WORKERS' COMPENSATION 7:30am to 4pm
>
> JERRY KRUEGER — UNEMPLOYMENT COMPENSATION, HOURLY PERSONNEL ADMINISTRATION MATTERS, 7:30–9:30am AND 1:30–3:30 pm

Figure 3.   Limited Hours Jotted on Flip Chart

"The controller and his people should love this," comments Jack. "They've been going out of their minds in the cashier's office with the constant demand. If we end our open-door system, they should be able to end theirs too."

"Nobody pays any attention to the official hours;[3] people just knock on the cashier's door any hour of the day and expect service.

---

[3] The posted hours for the cashier's service are as follows:

> 7:30 A.M. to 8:30 A.M.
> 10:30 A.M. to 11:00 A.M.
> 1:00 P.M. to 1:30 P.M.
> 2:30 P.M. to 3:00 P.M.

Nobody is very familiar with these hours, however.

Usually they get it," you remark. "It would be tough for us to establish a limited access and stick to it if the cashier's cage maintained service all hours of the day, no matter if they moved into the LR suite or not."

"Good point," says Jack, running his hand through his hair. "We must make sure that Diamond, the controller, goes along with our plan."

Then he winds up the meeting by announcing that the new limited hours system will begin as soon as he can talk to Gormann and the controller, Lee Diamond, and get the shop people going on the construction of the windows, and, of course, notify everyone in the plant of the change in procedures.

After the meeting, Jack LaPresle says enthusiastically to you, "Went pretty well, don't you think? Okay. We've got a lot to do, especially you because I have to go to a meeting tomorrow morning in Pittsburgh. Anything I can't tie up this afternoon, you'll have to pick up."

"Got it," you nod.

"I'll speak to Mr. Gormann at 4:30. Got an appointment already because I anticipated some change. I'm sure he'll approve. He's big on listening to employees, but right now he's most interested in cutting costs. When I'm done with Gormann, I'll try to see Lee Diamond to make sure he'll agree with putting the cashier's cage into the Labor Relations office. Oh, I almost forgot, I must convince him about sticking with the officially posted hours. I don't think there'll be much problem convincing him. The problem will be getting to see him at all. If I do, it won't be for long. So, what I want you to do is write me a memo you can send to him tomorrow morning and draw a clean diagram of the offices with the changes clearly marked. [See Figure 4.] My secretary will let you know if I got through to Diamond, and if so, what he said."

"So that memo should be to explain everything?"

"Yes. Because even if I do see him, I'll never be able to go over all the details," replies Jack. "Then tomorrow check with the union president, Matt Brierly. Apologize for my not being able to see him personally before I left for Pittsburgh. Write him a letter for me too, but also go over the whole thing when you see him. The union must be told why the change was necessary and how it will affect the membership. They'll want to make sure that sufficient advance notice is given."

"The advance notice to the employees should be a week?" you ask.

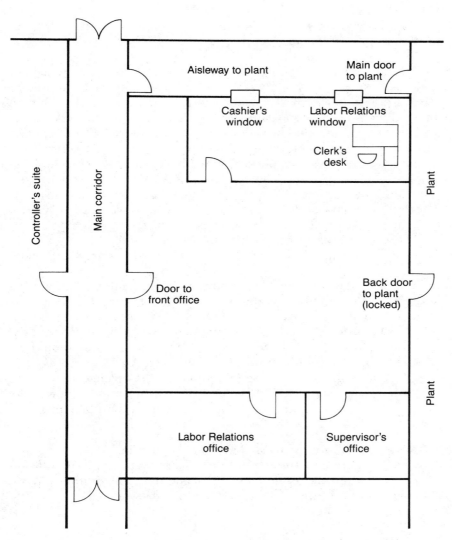

Figure 4. The Labor Relations Offices with Changes Incorporated

"Right. One week before we're ready to roll, we must notify the employees of the change."

"Do you think the union will balk at all?"

Jack stops for a second. "Naw. They know the company has got to save bucks, and this really is a small inconvenience. It's more observing the proper form to consult Brierly than anything else. But we do need them to agree in writing to the changes." And he looks down at his notes. "Moving on here, let's see. Write to Lawton at Corporate Offices. Any procedural change like this must have his approval to implement. He'll want to know that we have the concurrence of the union, the plant manager, the controller. *And* he will most definitely want to know that the new plan was developed out of a 'consensus decision process'—he loves those words! Well, it was a consensus of the whole staff, right down to the clerks and secretaries."

"How do I present the cashier's hours to him?"

"Just as a connected issue. He has no jurisdiction over the controller."

"Next I suppose I must contact the plant carpenter about putting in the pass-through windows, or whatever they're called. I gather this is such a small job we can go right ahead?" you ask.

"Right. Call Art, the maintenance supervisor, in here and he'll help you figure out exactly where to put 'em, how big they should be, all that stuff. That'll be no problem. Good guy, Art!"

"The last thing is notifying everybody of the change, I guess."

"Yes. Write a memo to all hourly workers so that they'll know about the limited hours and all, the change and when it will take place."

Note: All the following assignments are for Jack LaPresle's signature: J. P. LaPresle, Industrial Relations Manager. You should sign his name for him on Assignments 2–4 and add your initials. (Write your name on the upper-right corner of all these papers to identify them for the instructor.)

ASSIGNMENT 2

Assume that Mr. LaPresle's secretary tells you that LaPresle was not able to speak to Mr. Diamond before the controller left for the day. Write a memo to Mr. L. L. Diamond, Controller, to get him to cooperate on the cashier's cage component in the Labor Relations' new plans for limited hours.

ASSIGNMENT 3

Write a letter to Mr. Matt Brierly, President of Union 349, to hand to Brierly when you go to see him on LaPresle's behalf. The union must concur (in writing) to the change in services to hourly workers.

ASSIGNMENT 4

Write a memo to Mr. P. L. Lawton, Division Chief of Industrial Relations, Howard Brothers, Inc., Corporate Offices, to secure his approval for implementation of the new procedures.

ASSIGNMENT 5

Write a memo for distribution to all hourly workers to announce the new procedures and schedule. (Assume that Lee Diamond has agreed with the Labor Relations' plan and that he has asked you to announce the new procedures of the cashier's cage in your memo. The cashier's cage will now follow the old official hours.)

A Missing Deposit Verification: The Lost Mortgage Case

Atlantic National Bank, headquartered in Boston, is one of the largest and most influential financial institutions in the Northeast with branches throughout New England and the Mid-Atlantic region. For several months you have been a management trainee assigned to a new position every two or three months. Currently you are in the Area Management Office for Area V-B in Boston. Your new boss, Bill Hatton (the area credit manager) is friendly to customers but fairly hard on his subordinates, from what the grapevine has told you. Your own observations and experience of Hatton over the last few days bear out his reputation. Hatton is quick to jump on employees, but he is "hail-fellow-well-met" with customers and associates.

This morning Hatton gets a telephone call from a woman who banks at the Pilgrim Heights Branch in Foxbluff, a suburb of Boston. The customer announces herself to Hatton's secretary as Mrs. Clara Peters and asks to speak to the head manager because she wants to register a "serious complaint."

Before taking the call (which his secretary describes as a "customer complaint"), Hatton tells you to switch on your phone to "conference call" so you can listen to his conversation.[1] "I want you to handle this complaint after I speak to the woman," he says. "Write the report, and take care of any follow-up needed."

Switching on your phone while grabbing a yellow pad and felt-tip pen, you immediately hear Hatton's voice booming—both in the telephone and from his desk.

---

[1] This large bank regularly uses a "blind" conference call hookup so that support personnel can hear pertinent conversations.

"Good morning, Mrs. Peters. This is Bill Hatton, the area manager of Atlantic National Bank. What can I do for you today?"

"Mr. Hatton, my late husband, Mr. John Peters, and I have been customers of the Atlantic National Bank for over 35 years. Since he passed away eight years ago, I've been banking at the Pilgrim Heights Branch. I've been an excellent customer of your bank, and I'm very angry at the way I've been treated. I feel that you've let me down."

"I'm very sorry to hear that, Mrs. Peters. Would you please tell me what happened?"

"I certainly will," Mrs. Peters replies. "I've been embarrassed in Florida, in the town where I stay in the winter. Worst of all, I lost my chance to buy a lovely condominium in a new area being developed just west of town. This was a wonderful deal because the condominium had very favorable financing, not just a conventional mortgage. Anyway, I went to the Florida Savings and Loan Association in Belle Beach to apply for this special mortgage. I had to fill out lots of forms, answer questions, and so on. Well, they wanted to know about my account here at Atlantic National in Massachusetts. Asked me how much money I had on deposit—to make sure I had the down payment and all, of course. I told them I had over $95,000 in this account, and then I filled in the address, you know, the account number at the Pilgrim Heights Branch, all those things they needed."

"So what was the difficulty, Mrs. Peters?"

Hatton sounds so cool and controlled that Mrs. Peters would never guess how busy he is this morning, and that three people are waiting to see him.

"Well," continues Mrs. Peters, "the man I was dealing with there in Florida, a Mr. Lopez, he wrote to Atlantic National for what he called a deposit verification. Yes, that's right—*deposit verification*. He was sure I would be approved for the mortgage to buy the condominium in Chelsea."

"Chelsea?" Hatton asks.

"Yes, didn't I tell you? That's where the condominiums are located. Now, can you imagine," she continues, her voice rising, "Mr. Lopez's request to Atlantic National was never answered! After all these years banking with you, Atlantic National never even replied to the people at Florida Savings and Loan. Of course I didn't know that, until I went in to ask Mr. Lopez about my mortgage application. When I told him how surprised I was that you hadn't written, he called the Pilgrim Heights Branch. But, you know, he made me feel as if maybe I didn't have an account at Atlantic National at all. As if I made up my deposit figure or something. Can you imagine how I felt, Mr. Hatton?"

"Yes, Mrs. Peters," Hatton says sympathetically, "I'm sure you felt very uncomfortable, and I regret that very much."

Mrs. Peters continues. "Yes, well on the phone, the Pilgrim people did assure Mr. Lopez that I had an account with over $95,000 in it. But then Mr. Lopez said that he had to have written verification before he could proceed with the mortgage processing and all that. So he gave them the address of the Florida Savings and Loan, and asked them to send the verification right away."

"I trust that everything went okay then, Mrs. Peters?" asks Hatton.

"No, it did not," she answers in a voice beginning to quiver. "It most certainly did not, Mr. Hatton. Florida Savings and Loan in Belle Beach didn't hear from the Atlantic National Bank in time, and so they turned down my mortgage application. Can you believe that? I have almost $100,000 dollars in your bank, Mr. Hatton, your bank. But I lost this wonderful condominium because your officers didn't write that letter verifying my account."

Hatton now commiserates with Mrs. Peters, but despite his sympathetic tone, he does not concede that Atlantic was at fault in any way. He *does* say that he will look into the matter immediately, and asks Mrs. Peters for Lopez's telephone number in Belle Beach. He closes by telling her that she is indeed a valued customer of Atlantic National and that she will hear from the bank soon.

After hanging up, Hatton calls Lopez at Florida Savings and Loan, and with you still listening in, he proceeds to chat about the Florida weather and how he wishes he were down there right now playing golf. Eventually, he does confirm that Mrs. Peters did not, in fact, get the financing on her condo, and yes, it has taken more than a month to get the financing info from Atlantic National.

"But we've got it now," Lopez says. "In fact, we've got two deposit verifications. So everything is just fine. Although Mrs. Peters lost her condo, it was *not* Atlantic National Bank's fault. We weren't able to get private mortgage insurance[2] on more than a few condos in that

---

[2] Private mortgage insurance is to protect the lender in those cases where the borrower pays a smaller than usual down payment, say, less than 20%. Since it is risky to have very many mortgages with such small down payments, private mortgage insurers often restrict the availability of insurance coverage to a limited percentage of units in a specific condominium development—perhaps allowing only 5% of the units to be purchased

development. Unfortunately, Mrs. Peters and several others had to be turned down. We may be able to arrange some conventional financing for her later on, however." He finally winds the matter up by saying, "I have tried to explain this situation to Mrs. Peters, but I'm afraid that she just doesn't understand. She believes that there was some fault on Atlantic National's part, and that if we had received the deposit verification from you in time she would have gotten the mortgage. She'll probably get another chance later.[3] So don't worry about it. And if you're ever down here in Belle Beach, Hatton, come look me up."

After Hatton hangs up, he sits quietly for a few moments, staring straight in front of him. He looks perturbed. Then he dials the phone again and soon you hear: "Hello, Ken." (Kenneth Lee is the branch manager at Pilgrim Heights.) "Few minutes ago I was on the line with one of your customers, a Mrs. Peters. What's going on with her?" he asks rather sharply.

There is a pause on the line. Apparently Lee is as surprised by Hatton's challenge as you are. Though Hatton never let on during his phone call with Lopez, he evidently did not believe the Florida Savings and Loan man's sweet words that Atlantic National was in no way to blame for what happened to Mrs. Peters.

Finding his voice, Lee acknowledges his involvement in Mrs. Peters' case and expresses regrets about what happened to her. He confirms that, indeed, she is a long-time customer. "I tried my best for her," he claims. But then he becomes very defensive, insisting that he never saw the original request for the deposit verification from Florida Savings and Loan Association.

"Now look here," snaps Hatton. "It sounds to me like Atlantic National blew it. It sounds like Mrs. Peters didn't get her mortgage because her application was incomplete. I want the straight story on what happened here. How come we didn't respond to these deposit verification requests?"

"We did," says Lee. "When Mr. Lopez called from Florida, won-

---

on this special plan (what Mrs. Peters referred to as "this wonderful deal"). With such a small number available, a developer would typically have more potential purchases for these special deals than he could accommodate; thus completing an application later than others *could* be a factor in not getting the mortgage.

[3] Although there were not enough of the mortgages with small down payments to accommodate Mrs. Peters, the Florida Savings and Loan Association will probably be able to offer her a conventional mortgage on the condominium. That higher-down-payment financing would be her second chance to purchase the condominium.

dering why we hadn't responded to the written request for verification, I told him that Mrs. Peters was a good customer with a substantial account with us and that although I had never heard from him before, I would mail the verification off immediately. Unfortunately, my letter evidently got lost because Lopez gave me the wrong zip code, but I only found that out when he called me back several weeks later to ask why he hadn't received the verification. Of course, I insisted that I had sent it, and I read off the date, address, etcetera, from my file, when he noticed that the third number on the zip was wrong. So again I promised to send him a verification immediately, but this time to the correct address," Lee gulps for breath.

"Evidently," Hatton breaks in, "he received both the verifications at about the same time. It took about three weeks for the one with the wrong zip code to arrive. But, in any case, they both got there too late. By that time the Florida S&L had denied this lady with $100,000 in our bank the mortgage she wanted."

"I'm really sorry about that, and I wish I could help Mrs. Peters, Mr. Hatton, but it's not my fault that Lopez gave me the wrong zip code. And I am certain that we never did receive the written request at all."

"Well, who knows who misplaced that written request? As for the zip code, you either heard wrong or Lopez gave you the wrong number; there's no way of knowing for sure," replies Hatton briskly. "But there's nothing to be done about it now. Probably Mrs. Peters will be able to get a conventional mortgage through Florida Savings and Loan in Belle Beach." And with that he abruptly hangs up.

Motioning you over to his desk, Hatton tells you to write up a customer complaint report, as well as a letter to Mrs. Peters, but he does not tell you what to say. In fact, within two seconds he has answered another phone call, and you realize that you will have to decide how to handle this.

Who was at fault, you wonder. Whatever happened to the written request for the deposit verification? Whose fault was the zip code mix-up? It might have been Lopez's, but it might have been Kenneth Lee's. Yet, perhaps none of this mattered; at least Lopez said it did not matter. On the other hand, even Hatton seems to think that maybe Mrs. Peters did not get her condo because her application was incomplete. That certainly seems like a distinct possibility; in your own limited experience you have known several instances when somebody's application lost out because of some missing item. Lopez seemed to be waffling a bit there. He said she would not have gotten it because there was insufficient private mortgage insurance, but why did they make a negative decision in such a hurry, right after they made that second long-distance call to Pilgrim Heights? Perhaps they just "oversold" the special mortgages, expecting more deals to fall through than actually did.[4] Maybe that is why Lopez said that Atlantic National's failure to respond did not matter. The Florida S&L probably did not have enough of the special mortgages to accommodate Mrs. Peters, even if her application had been complete.

After constructing this possible scenario, you realize that there are other possibilities as well. You wish you could call Lopez yourself and ask him a few questions. Unfortunately, your position as a trainee will not allow it. You also wish you could ask Hatton some questions, though to judge by the way he talks, it seems that he believes there is a strong possibility that Kenneth Lee made a mistake. Still, Hatton does not impress you as the type of person to find Atlantic National in the wrong on anything—unless it could be proven so. On the other hand, Mrs. Peters is not going to easily accept the notion that Atlantic National served her well in this case.

However, you cannot sit shifting back and forth on this issue all day. You must write up the report and the letter now. After a moment's consideration, you decide to begin with the letter; then you will be able to describe it in the report.

ASSIGNMENT 1
Write a letter to Mrs. Clara B. Peters III, 2051 Tower Road, Foxbluff, MA 00000, from W. Z. Hatton, Credit Manager, Area V-B, Atlantic National Bank, Boston, MA 00000. A copy should go to Kenneth Lee, Branch Manager, Pilgrim Heights, Foxbluff.

Complete either Assignment 2 or 3:

ASSIGNMENT 2
Write up the customer complaint form (Appendix A) for your boss's signature, W. Z. Hatton, Credit Manager, Area V-B. List Hatton in the "Received by" designation. The "Employee Involved" (who will re-

---

[4] Just as airlines may "overbook" a flight because they expect that a certain number of ticketed passengers will not show up, a bank may "oversell" its available mortgages because they expect a certain number of the applications to be withdrawn or denied.

ceive a copy of the report) is Kenneth Lee, Branch Manager, Pilgrim Heights, Foxbluff. The customer whose name, address, and telephone are listed is, of course, Mrs. Clara B. Peters III, 2051 Tower Road, Foxbluff, MA 00000 (account no. 702–554–23; telephone 444–9908). All customer complaint reports from the area are filed in the operations manager's office for access in case of lawsuits and for periodic audits checking for patterns of complaints.

ASSIGNMENT 3

Write a customer complaint report, constructing a document to best meet the requirements of reporting this complaint to the operations manager's office. This report would substitute for the complaint form in Appendix A. All the reporting information in Assignment 2 will be the same, except that you should address your report to B. L. Garth, Operations Manager, Area V-B.

APPENDIX A

Customer Complaint Form

```
                    REPORT OF CUSTOMER COMPLAINT
      Walk-In _____        Justified _____
      Telephone _____        Unjustified _____


      Date _____ Time ____  Name _____
      Branch _____   Address _____
      Employee Involved _____   Telephone _____

      GENERAL NATURE OF COMPLAINT:




      COMMENTS:






      BANK RESPONSE:






      RECEIVED BY _____  Region _____
      Referred to _____  Date _____
           Use blank sheets if additional space is needed.
```

Specifying Materials for the Fire Marshal: A Problem at Grant Designers, Inc.

Part 1

For you, this is a red-letter day. Early this morning, you made a site visit to the North Corners Mall, where workers had just finished laying the carpeting for the large central mall space. You designed the interiors for the mall, and you were eager to see how the grid-patterned carpet you chose for the mall's center looked when installed over 2,000 square feet. It looked pretty good, if you did think so yourself, especially the gently sloping carpeted ramps leading to the fountain in the middle. Seeing the completed job made having to sit at your drafting board hours on end worth it. And, to top things off, you have the next few days free to attend the Interiors International Conference in Honolulu. Lucky you.

All in all, your design work for Grant Designers, Inc., of Atlanta has been pretty smooth going. The firm has a wide range of clients from banks, schools, and shopping centers to individual homeowners. Grant Designers provides services which include partitioning a building shell, specifying interior surface finishes, and selecting furniture, floor coverings, lighting, and artwork. Lately, the company has been doing a lot of work for Solar Building Corporation (SBC), a new architectural firm just outside Atlanta. You really admire George Filipac, the young principal who heads SBC. He took a pretty big chance starting a firm that builds only solar-heated structures. Filipac has encouraged Grant Designers to be innovative and creative in specifying interior finishes for SBC projects. You have found it most challenging to design interiors for buildings which bring in a lot of outside light, a concept central to passive solar design.[1]

---

[1] Passive solar design incorporates features which maximize the lighting and heating effects of sunlight and minimize the use of energy from another source (for example, mechanical, electric, or gas-generated power).

This afternoon, after you have finished a few rough sketches, you intend to show Curt Winkler your latest ideas for the lower-level public spaces of a new office building which SBC is designing in Macon, Georgia. Curt, who is both your supervisor and the owner of Grant Designers, should be particularly pleased about what you did with the building's main corridor, its so-called "Main Street."[2]

It takes you an hour and a half to complete your sketches. When you are done, you smile to yourself, pleased with the results. You pick up your tracings and vendor brochures on the furnishings you have chosen and trundle down to Curt's office.

Your discussion of the furniture for the building's lobby with Curt goes very well. He likes your choice of benches from Join-Rite and your suggestion that planters be constructed in the floor of the lobby. However, when he sees your design for the building's corridor, the "Main Street," he does not look very pleased.

"I see you're using the same bench system here as you've specified for the lobby of the building," Curt says, a note of slight discouragement in his voice.

"Yes, I did," you answer. "I planned to use the same benches, with planters in between them to connect them. That way the lobby and 'Main Street' would look like one continuous space, oriented to the outside."

"You're quite right that the design would do that," Curt answers. "But I'm afraid we can't use the benches in that area."

"Why not?"

"Oh, they'd look great," Curt says, sensing your disappointment, "but it's a good bet that Rob Lasker won't let us do it."

"Rob Lasker, the fire marshal for the city," you say quietly, recalling the last time you tried to work with him on a job Grant Designers was doing in Macon, the same town where the new office building is going up. Rob Lasker is in a class by himself. When you last worked with him, he would not let you specify a particular brand of tackboards for office spaces. He is one of those old-guard fire marshals who enjoys wielding power. Of course, all builders and interior designers know they must satisfy fire codes for new construction. You would think it would be just as simple as looking up the code and

---

[2] The "Main Street" is a corridor located adjacent to an all-glass exterior wall on the south side of the building. The interior wall defining the corridor is constructed of masonry to collect solar heat gained through the glass exposure to the outside. This corridor, in effect, appears from the inside of the building to be part of the outside space.

doing what it requires, but nothing is ever that simple. The local fire marshal has quite a bit of leeway in interpreting just what those codes mean. And Lasker is a great one for between-the-lines interpretations. Since his word is the law, Grant Designers must go along, no matter what you or Curt or others may feel is a "correct" interpretation of the code. Of course, you could appeal Lasker's decision, but that would be time consuming and costly.

"We might as well find out now if we can go with the benches," Curt says. "I'm going to call George Filipac and see what he says."

Curt calls George and explains your design concept for the office building's main corridor to him. The conversation is short. When Curt hangs up, you ask eagerly, "So what's the bad news?"

"Well, George reminded me how tough Lasker is . . ."

You nod, remembering the tackboards.

"As I might have predicted, George says we can't have any furniture designated for the 'Main Street,'" Curt continues.

"You mean we can't have anything in that corridor that isn't part of the building's construction," you say, recalling from previous bouts with Lasker what the fire marshal regards as "furniture" and figuring that is the rule George is going by.

"You got it. But wait a minute; there may be a way to get around this." Curt asks to look at the sales brochure for the benches, and you locate it among the materials you brought with you (Figure 1). He then asks, "Can these benches be bolted to the floor?"

"Don't know," you say. "I'd have to call the sales rep for Join-Rite."

"Well, if they *can* be bolted, Lasker might let it pass, providing that he can approve the materials specifications[3] for the bench system components. Unfortunately, the brochure doesn't give materials specifications."

"You're right," you say, looking again at the Join-Rite publication (Figure 1). "Not a word about what this stuff's made of. Looks like the surface is either painted or finished with a wood veneer, but it doesn't say, so who knows what's underneath it."

"Or what material that planter liner is made of," Curt adds, "and what holds the parts together, what kind of glues they use for the veneers, or what they finish them with."

---

[3] Materials specifications give detailed information about the components used in a product; in this instance, the product dimensions, methods used for reinforcing and joining materials, and the kinds of woods, plastics, glues, or other materials.

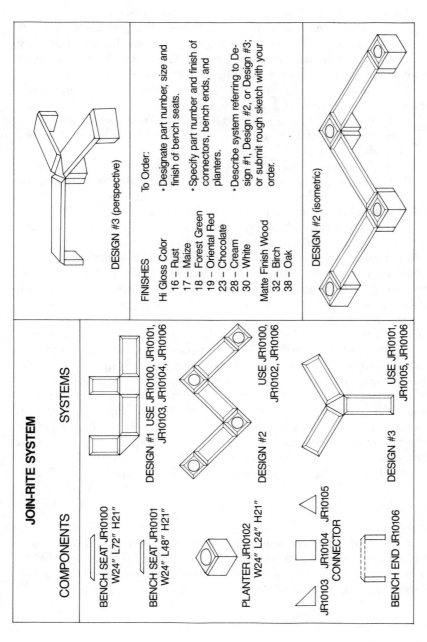

Figure 1. Join-Rite Brochure

187

"Can't tell," you agree. "None of that stuff's here."

"Besides those materials specs, we'll need fire and smoke ratings on the product, too," Curt says. "Hang on a minute, let me check my file on Lasker." You wait a minute while Curt sifts through memos and notes in his file of correspondence with Lasker. "When you specified those tackboards, he wanted to know how much smoke they produced when the material burns, and—let's see—whether and how much fuel the stuff adds to a fire, and how far the flames would spread. You'll have to get that info, too. Join-Rite should have a UL[4] rating for each of those characteristics."

"Got it," you say.

"That data should be available from the sales rep. You should get on it in a hurry. The rep may have to contact Join-Rite's main office, and that could take some time," Curt warns you.

"I'll do what I can today," you say. "Guess I'll have to—I'm leaving for that design convention in Honolulu tomorrow."

"What a shame," Curt says, with a slight smirk. Curt decided not to go to the convention this year and that left the way open for you. "Well, see if you can get hold of that Join-Rite rep before you put on your Hawaiian lei—that is, if you can keep the ukuleles and the ten-foot surf off your mind!"

You leave Curt's office thinking that it will not be hard to forget the ukuleles, but that surf! Back at your own work cubicle, you try to get Alice Toepfer, the sales rep for Join-Rite, on the line. Alice works for Richter-Spencer and Company, Inc., a firm that handles sales for several carpet, textile, and furniture companies. She is a pleasure to do business with. She has a great sense of humor, and she is quick to get what you want when you want it. Unfortunately, Alice cannot be reached. You now have no choice but to write her a letter asking for the materials specifications. You drag out the Join-Rite brochure once again and type a letter to Alice requesting the information you need.

ASSIGNMENT 1

Write a letter to Alice Toepfer, Sales Representative, Richter-Spencer and Company, Inc., 3000 Montclair Street, Atlanta, Georgia 00000. Your title is Interior Designer. Your firm's letterhead is Grant Designers, Inc., 736 Magnolia Boulevard, Atlanta, Georgia 00000.

---

[4] Underwriters Laboratory.

Part 2

It has been at least a month since you wrote Alice Toepfer asking for materials specifications for Join-Rite benches. One week after she got your letter, right after you got home from Hawaii, she called to say that she would have to write Join-Rite's United States headquarters in New York for the materials specifications. Because Join-Rite is based in Helsinki and because Alice was not sure *what* the New York office might have, she said it could take a while.

Today Curt has found another possible application for the Join-Rite benches—seating in a private art gallery in Atlanta. The gallery owner, Katherine Woodson, wants furniture in her gallery that will not overpower the artwork and will allow for flexible arrangements. For instance, she would like to be able to put seating either along walls or in small groupings, depending on how she sets up her exhibits. You and Curt both think the colors, sizes, and arrangement possibilities of the Join-Rite components meet these criteria. Fortunately, you do not need fire marshal approval for this application! Curt asks you to send Ms. Woodson the Join-Rite brochure along with a letter describing the advantages of the bench system for her purposes. Both of you plan to meet with Ms. Woodson to discuss colors and finishes after she has had a chance to review the brochure. To get things moving quickly, you take out the Join-Rite brochure and draft the letter to Ms. Woodson right away. Your letter will go out on a Grant Designers "transmittal form" which is used whenever someone in your office sends materials to a client.

ASSIGNMENT 2

Write a letter introducing the Join-Rite bench system to Ms. Katherine Woodson, Woodson Gallery, 201 Cotton, Atlanta, Georgia 00000. (Copy and use the transmittal form, Appendix A. The document goes to Ms. Woodson and is from you. Under "Items" you must specify the quantity and kind of material you are sending. Under "Remarks" you will begin the letter.)

Part 3

When the mail arrives this afternoon, you are happy to see an envelope with Alice Toepfer's return address. When you open it, you find a cheerful note from Alice (Figure 2) attached to a sheet of furniture specifications from Join-Rite (Figure 3).

TRANSMITTAL
RICHTER - SPENCER AND COMPANY, INC.
Sales Representatives: Carpets, Fabrics, Furniture
3000 Montclair Street, Atlanta, GA 00000

MESSAGE	REPLY

To: YOU
Grant Designers, Inc.
736 Magnolia Blvd.
Atlanta, GA 00000

Date:

Date: May 14, 1984

Dear YOU,

Hallelujah and pass the wine! As you can see by the enclosed, Join-Rite has finally provided me with a specification for the bench system. Also, found out these benches can be bolted to the floor. Sorry, they don't have fire ratings. Let me know if this will do.

Best regards,

Alice Toepfer

Alice Toepfer

Signed: _____

Figure 2.   Alice's Note

JOIN-RITE INTERNATIONAL, LTD.

Showroom: 180 W. 74th St., New York, N.Y. 00000
Office: 500 E. 50th, New York, N.Y. 00000
Telex: Helsinki 300-2398 Telephone: 212-896-3546

Model Nos. 10100 — 10106

All core materials either 3/4" or 1–1/8" densest baraboard*

All solids — poplar, kiln–dried, minimum moisture content

End panels are splined & grooved & bolted†

All veneers premium grade — book matching standard‡

Thickness of veneer varies — minimum 1/36" approx., maximum 1/28"

Veneers applied with urea based glues. Surface finish stain and scuff resistant

Planter liners are smoke–grey colored fiberglass

Hi–gloss color denotes polyester finish

Matte finish denotes lacquer finish

* Particle board.
† A wood slat (spline) on one panel fits into a groove on another panel. Panels are bolted for stability.
‡ All wood grain patterns match up when sheets of veneer are placed together.

Figure 3.   Specifications from Join-Rite

You immediately take the specifications to Curt. He says exactly what you were thinking when you first looked at the specs.

"Lasker won't go for this. They've listed the materials specifications, but there are no flame-spread, fuel-contribution, or smoke ratings."

"I know," you say. "What should we do?"

"Well, we can't go with that product. If we want benches in that corridor, we'll have to find some with UL ratings."

"I think I'll call Alice Toepfer and ask if she has UL fire ratings for bench systems produced by other manufacturers."

"Okay," Curt says. "It's a shame that Join-Rite won't work out for that office building. We're lucky we can put those benches in the Woodson gallery."

You agree, telling Curt that you'll be sure to tell Alice Toepfer about your disappointment with Join-Rite.

When you later get Alice on the phone, she tells you she can get UL fire ratings for bench systems produced by three other manufacturers, and then she says, "You know, I think the Join-Rite system is actually superior to many on the market for applications in large public spaces. I think that company should get their products tested and UL rated. I could probably get them to move on that if I had a letter or two from designers who rejected their products because they weren't rated."

You tell Alice you'd be happy to write such a letter.

"I'll forward your comments directly to Join-Rite," Alice says, "and add a few words of my own."

You approve her plan, and Alice tells you that she will send you the fire ratings on products from other bench manufacturers as soon as possible.

ASSIGNMENT 3

Write the letter to Alice Toepfer that she requested regarding your experiences with Join-Rite. A copy will go to Curt Winkler. Use the addresses furnished in Assignment 1.

APPENDIX A

Transmittal Form

GRANT DESIGNERS

736 Magnolia Blvd., Atlanta, Georgia 00000

DATE: **TRANSMITTAL**
TO:

FROM:

RE:

ITEM(S):   NO.   DESCRIPTION

_____   _____

_____   _____

PURPOSE:

___ AS YOU REQUESTED   ___ REVIEW AND RETURN

___ FOR YOUR INFORMATION   ___ REPLY TO SENDER

___ FOR YOUR APPROVAL   ___ OTHER (SEE REMARKS)

REMARKS: (Use back if necessary)

Evaluating Polyglop: EconoAuto Expands Its Car Accessories Market

Background

"How do you make it good *and* inexpensive?" That seems to be the question you face every day in your work as a staff engineer in the Process Development (PD) Department of the Manufacturing and Engineering Development Office of EconoAuto Corporation. (See Organizational Chart, Appendix A.)[1] The PD Department is a "staff function" that provides research and development services for the major divisions of EconoAuto. Most of your work for PD involves improving manufacturing procedures to result in better products or more efficient production. You find this work challenging and worthwhile, particularly since EconoAuto is dedicated to making simple and reliable products for the economy-class auto market.

EconoAutos are popular, inexpensive cars that "keep on runnin'" and are easy to fix when they don't. In fact, the Sprinter line of midsize cars has such a good reputation for being easy to maintain that it has developed a substantial market for accessory products that help Sprinter owners do their own mechanical and body repairs.

Lately, the Product and Services (P&S) Marketing Plans Department of the Sprinter Division has become very interested in marketing a plastic body filler called Polyglop. The product is manufactured by Phoenix Chemical Company, Ltd., Sarnia, Ontario, and is sold through auto supply houses and auto dealers. Apparently Canadian dealers of

---

[1] Study the Organizational Chart now to enhance your understanding of relationships among divisions, departments, sections, and the personnel within them.

EconoAuto cars have shown some profit in selling this body repair product to do-it-yourselfers. Consequently, management in the P&S Marketing Plans Department of the Sprinter Division believe the product should be purchased from Phoenix and marketed in the United States under the Sprinter name. Polyglop would then be sold through Sprinter's Parts and Accessories (P&A) Supply Department to U.S. auto dealers.

Polyglop promises to gain an even larger share of the auto accessories market for Sprinter through appealing to Americans who like to do their own "garage" work. So far no decent substitute for lead body filler (60% lead, 40% tin) has been found for soldering body parts or filling dents. Lead is toxic and it practically takes an artist to apply it using a blowtorch. Polyglop can be applied at room temperature with a putty knife; it is nontoxic and a lot cheaper than lead, too. Of course, a plastic filler cannot be expected to have the structural strength or durability of lead, but it could be just the thing for surface repairs. And it could save car owners costly trips to a body shop after minor bang-ups.

Ordinarily, products are tested thoroughly before EconoAuto makes a large-scale purchase. Tests are done to verify the quality of the product and to gather data for marketing purposes. After a product is purchased, the same tests may be used later to ensure quality control. In the case of Polyglop, this procedure has been temporarily side-stepped.

Six months ago, John Kaczmarek, manager of the P&S Marketing Plans Department, learned from a vendor about an option to buy Polyglop from Phoenix Chemical at an unusually low wholesale price. An initial purchase of 20,000 three-pound cans of Polyglop at $4.76 a can could be made by Sprinter's P&A Supply Department, headed by Alex Stevens, if Stevens signed the purchase order within 30 days. Kaczmarek recommended that Stevens sign the purchase order and that he also request an additional shipment of 20,000 cans to be delivered to the P&A Supply Department six months after the first shipment.

Kaczmarek knew he jumped the gun in recommending that Stevens make the Polyglop purchase, but risk taking had paid off for him in the past. Sprinter Division upper management has given handsome salary increases to executives like Kaczmarek who move fast and work out the details later—as long as the details *do* work out. Most of Kaczmarek's past decisions have stood the test of time. He believed that the Polyglop purchase would also prove fortunate. He had read sales summaries in the *Automotive Retailer* which showed that $24 million worth of the product was sold through auto supply houses and dealers in 1984, and EconoAuto's own sales reports for 1984 showed that Canada's 860 EconoAuto dealers sold $300,000 worth.

Two months after making his recommendation to purchase 40,000 cans of Polyglop, Kaczmarek began "working out the details" of testing the product and developing a marketing strategy. He learned from Henry Clancy of the Planning and Research Section of P&A Supply that Process Development had done a lot of work in testing plastic solders. Clancy suggested that Polyglop be tested by your department. He also gave Kaczmarek a list of 11 other polyester body fillers which could be potential competitors for Polyglop.

After his communication with Clancy, Kaczmarek wrote a letter to Irving Faulbaum, manager of PD, asking that your department develop tests which will show Polyglop's superiority over comparable products now on the market (Appendix B). Along with the letter, Kaczmarek included samples of the 11 competing products which Clancy had named. In a later phone conversation, Kaczmarek told Faulbaum that he would like to use PD's test data in an advertising campaign directed at EconoAuto's dealers to get them to buy Polyglop from the P&A Supply Department of the Sprinter Division. The campaign would be particularly important in securing a share of the body filler market for the company. (Sprinter auto dealers now have the option of stocking EconoAuto service products or those of competitors.)

Faulbaum gave Kaczmarek's request for tests of Polyglop to your boss, Jan Leahy, supervisor of the Nonmetallic Section of PD. Leahy assigned the task of evaluating Polyglop to you because you had tested a plastic solder, P.S. 183, for production use a couple of years ago.

One week after you received your assignment, Leahy told you that Alex Stevens of P&A Supply assigned Susan Johnson of the Quality Control Section in Body Engineering (Metal Stamping Division) to provide testing services for future shipments of Polyglop. Johnson's tests will be used to ensure the functional material quality of shipments purchased from Phoenix Chemical. Johnson contacted your department to develop suitable tests. (Quality Control staff do not design their own tests, but use tests developed by your department or outside sources.) Upon receiving Johnson's request for service, Jan Leahy assigned you the additional task of designing your tests for evaluating Polyglop so that they could be considered for future use in quality control testing.

Your Technical Investigation

In your previous work with plastic solder, you learned that plastic body fillers had been proposed for use by American auto manufacturers since the end of World War II. Using plastics was first prompted by the scarcity of lead, but other qualities such as nontoxicity, lower cost, lower weight, and lower processing temperatures continued to make plastic popular in auto manufacture.

In 1980 you completed the final report on your testing of the plastic solder, P.S. 183, which was an epoxy solder developed for use in metal bonding. Your tests evaluated P.S. 183's ability to withstand the rigors of production paint-processing ovens and rough handling. You examined the plastic solder's weathering properties, impact resistance, flexibility, and toughness. In short, you examined whether it could serve as a substitute for lead as a production-line solder.

You decided that you could use some of the same tests to evaluate Polyglop; however, you did not expect this polyester to meet the durability standards required for production-line use. As you planned the tests for Polyglop, you kept in mind that polyesters are particularly suited for home use in minor repairs because of their lower cost, heatless cure (product hardens at room temperature), and greater slip (product does not stick to putty knife in application). At the same time, however, they could never be suitable for factory use or for structural repairs.

You sketched out plans for five tests of Polyglop which would give equal importance to product durability and ease of use. All tests were to be completed using standard EconoAuto body stock (0.036 inch thick) to which the filler would be applied.

Among the five tests you planned to use were two of the durability tests which you had used to test P.S. 183: a "cold reverse-impact resistance" test and a "tensile shear strength" test. You figured that the filler product had to be durable enough not to crack or pop out when the car body was hit, particularly in cold weather when the product is likely to be more brittle. To test this property, you would take a panel of body stock, put a dent in it, fill the dent with the polyester, refrigerate the panel, and then drop a steel ball on the reverse side of the dent to see what happens to the plastic filler. Dropping the steel ball on the reverse side of the filled dent just as the panel came out of the refrigerator would show whether the filler in its most brittle state would crack or pop out when the car body is jarred or hit.

After you checked your past report on P.S. 183 to see if your memory served you right on the general procedure for the cold reverse-impact resistance test, you wrote some specs for it in your logbook, including general instructions for mixing and preparing the filler (Figure 1, page 199).

When testing tensile shear strength for P.S. 183, you used body stock panels joined by a standard reinforced E joint which was filled with the plastic solder. To form the E joint, two panels were fitted together and reinforced by another panel spot-welded to the back. To perform the same test on Polyglop, you decided that you would again use 6 inch by 6 inch panels, this time cutting them in half and joining their 3-inch ends in a standard E joint. You would then fill the joint with polyester and metal-finish it.

After you worked out the details of panel preparation for the tensile shear strength test, you prepared a sketch for your logbook (Figure 2, page 200).

To conduct the tensile shear strength test on the joined panels, you decided to use a standard tensile shear testing machine.[2] Based on your past experience with fillers used to make structural repairs, you figured that the filled surface should resist up to 250 psi before it shears. You realized that your standard is a bit arbitrary; in fact, tensile shear strength is not of critical importance for a surface filler. Nevertheless, for comparison purposes, it would be a good idea to see how tough the body fillers are. You noted your standard as well as specs for the test in your logbook (Figure 3, page 201).

Because Polyglop would be used to repair exterior painted surfaces, you decided to test how smoothly it would sand or metal-finish for painting and how well it would stand up to various weather conditions after it was enameled.

To do these tests, you planned to use 3 inch by 6 inch panels joined by an E joint, just as for the tensile shear test. To check for a smooth finished surface, you simply would observe what happened when the panel was sanded a full 15 minutes after the filler had gelled.[3] You could be sure the surface was well prepared if the filler

---

[2] The tensile shear testing machine holds the joined test panels vertically: the bottom of the lower panel is secured and remains stationary. The top of the upper panel is clamped to a movable jaw which pulls the panel upwards. The amount of force which the filled surface resists before it shears or separates is measured in pounds per square inch (psi) of adhered surface.

[3] A filler is considered "gelled" when it is stiff enough to be sanded.

COLD REVERSE IMPACT RESISTANCE

1. 0.036" body stock, 6" × 6" square, spherical depression – 3/16" deep and 1¾" in diameter.

2. Panel degreased and sandblasted before filler applied.

3. Fill depression with polyester; set until can be worked.*

4. Panel metal finished (sanded) w/ 12" disc grinder, 50-E garnet disc.

5. Refrig. at –10 F for two hr.

6. 2" steel ball dropped on center of dimple on reverse of panel at 1' and 2' heights.

7. Observe for cracks.

Standard: No cracks.

Mixing

— Samples mixed at room temp. (76 F) w/ 3" glazing knife on flat surface. Mixing time = 1 minute.

* A filler has set enough to be worked when it does not stick to the sander during metal finishing.

Figure 1.   Cold Reverse-Impact Resistance and Mixing Specifications

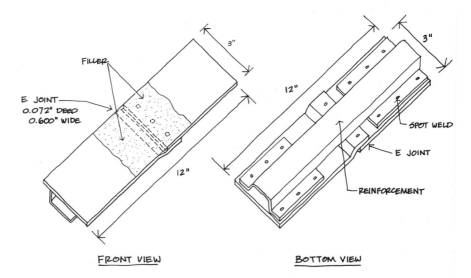

Figure 2. Panels Joined and Reinforced with Standard E Joint

"feathered" well, that is, if it remained intact after being sanded to minute thicknesses. You recorded specs for this feathering test in your logbook (Figure 4, page 202).

To test for weathering you decided to run panels with the filler through the weathering test which is conducted routinely on paint samples by the Body Materials Unit in Susan Johnson's Quality Control Section. For each filler type you would prepare two test panels. Each test panel would consist of two 3 inch by 6 inch pieces of body stock joined by an E joint filled with plastic solder. You would clean and metal-finish the panels as for the other tests, and then send them to Gus Kantner in Body Materials to have them painted with a prime coat and a finish coat using the standard EconoAuto baked enamel procedure. As for his standard testing of body paints, Kantner would subject your test panels to 250 hours in a weathering machine that your department developed for weathering tests.[4] To determine

---

[4] The weathering machine is used to test how objects respond to environmental changes. Materials placed in the weathering machine are exposed to ultraviolet light, temperatures ranging from below 32°F to 110°F, and variable humidity from 0% to 100% in alternating cycles. EconoAuto has previously established 250 hr. as the standard exposure time for acceptable exterior body materials.

TENSILE SHEAR STRENGTH

1. 0.036" body stock, two 3" x 6" pieces joined by a standard E joint, 0.072" deep and 0.600" wide.

2. Three test runs per product.

3. Degrease and sandblast joined panels, fill joint w/ product.

4. Set, metal finish as for cld. rev. impact test.

5. Test adhered surface w/ tensile shear machine.

6. Note psi at separation.

Standard: resist 250 psi

Figure 3.   Tensile Shear Strength Specifications

whether any weather damage is directly related to the application of the filler, rather than to some weakness in the paint, control panels without the filler would be run through the same test. You noted specs for this test along with the others in your logbook (Figure 5, page 203).

You then jotted a note reminding yourself to write a memo to Gus Kantner requesting the weathering tests: You will prepare the panels with the filler; he will prepare control panels, arrange for all painting, and conduct the tests; you will be ready with your materials for him next week; he should do the tests a week later.

The last test you planned was the gel time test. For this test you would simply time how long it takes the filler to set once it is mixed

FEATHERING

l. Joined panels prepared as in #l and #3 for Tensile Shear.

2. Metal finish l5 min. after prod. gels. Observe for chipping, gumming, loss of adhesion. One test per product.

Standard: No chip., gum., loss adhes.

Figure 4. Feathering Specifications

and applied.[5] Your common sense tells you that 3 to 5 minutes is about the optimum gel time for home-use body filler. After this time the filler should appear hard enough to be worked. Any longer setup time would discourage the user. No one wants to wait all day to begin working the material. Less time would make the product too hard to handle; it would set up before it could be applied properly. With these considerations in mind, you noted your standard and specs for the gel time test in your logbook (Figure 6, page 204).

After designing the tests, you went ahead and ordered panels of body stock from the Metal Stamping Division. You then set up all equipment to conduct the tests on Polyglop and the other 11 products named in Kaczmarek's letter to Faulbaum. You also sent a memo to Kantner in Body Materials requesting the weathering tests.

---

[5] The time it takes a material to harden is an important factor in judging polyester solders. These organic materials are thermosetting. They begin to gel when two components, a hardener and a base, are mixed triggering a chemical reaction. Once the gelling process starts, it is irreversible; you cannot soften the product again. One of the reasons lead is such a workable solder is that, unlike polyesters, it is thermoplastic. When you apply heat to it, lead immediately softens; when you remove heat, it hardens. The hardening process is totally reversible.

WEATHERING TEST

1. Prepare E joint panels w/ filler as in #1, #3 and #4 for Tensile Shear. Two E joint panels per filler.

2. Panels painted w/ prime coat, color coat (standard EconoAuto baked enamel procedure).

3. Per test run: one control panel (6"x6") degreased, sandblasted, painted w/ prime coat and color coat; two test E joint panels ea. w/ same filler, prepared as in #1 and #2 above.

4. Check each hour @ 50-250 hr. Examine for damage to color coat/prime coat.

Standard: No damage @ 250 hr.

Figure 5.   Weathering Specifications

ASSIGNMENT 1
Write a memo to Gus Kantner in Body Materials requesting the weathering tests on the polyester fillers. Leahy and Johnson are on the distribution list for the memo. Refer to Appendix A for positions and heading information.

You decided the best order in which to conduct your tests was gel time first, then cold-reverse impact, tensile shear, weathering, and feathering. As you did the testing, you found that some products failed

GEL TIME

1. Mix filler using procedure specified.

2. Filler immed. applied to panels w/ stand. E joint (as for tens. shear test). One test per prod.

3. Note time it takes filler to congeal @ room temp. (76° F).

Standard: 3-5 minutes.

Figure 6.   Gel Time Specifications

the first three tests by such a wide margin that it was not worthwhile to do the remaining tests. You had to make some judgment calls here, but your decision to quit testing halfway through the series for some products was also inspired by past experience in working for your supervisor. Leahy has always expected you to be thorough; she also has urged you to avoid needless tests that increase the costs of a project. After completing the gel time, cold reverse-impact, and tensile shear tests, you decided to discontinue testing for 4 of the 12 products. You then called Kantner in Body Materials to let him know that you would be sending only the remaining 8 products to him for the weathering test. You hoped that these decisions on testing would satisfy Leahy.

Last week, after you had completed all your tests and had received the weathering test results from Kantner, you made a table to compare results (Appendix C). You found that the tests certainly distinguished the quality of the products. Leahy and Johnson would be happy about that. Unfortunately, the results may not be as pleasing to Kaczmarek. After this initial assessment of these results, you asked Jan Leahy to contact Bob Stover, manager of Central Testing in Technical Services, and to find out if his department could conduct a field test of the eight fillers. You explained that for this test the company should get employee volunteers to use the fillers on their own cars. For each product, employees should note how well the product mixes, applies, and finishes; they also should note anything else that might affect the product's salability, for instance, strange odors or skin irritation. As you wanted these results quickly, you suggested that only one employee test each product.

When you outlined your design for the field test for Leahy, she approved your plan. She also asked you to write a memo for her signature requesting the tests from Central Testing.

ASSIGNMENT 2

Write a memo to Bob Stover from Jan Leahy requesting field tests of the polyester body fillers. See Appendix A for positions and heading information. (Write your name in the upper-right corner of your paper to identify it for your instructor.)

Your Report

It is now three weeks since you requested the field tests. Bob Stover reported yesterday that the tests are still in progress. Today you get a surprise request from Jan Leahy for a report on your investigation *now*. The report will be from Faulbaum (for his signature) and will be addressed to Kaczmarek. Apparently Kaczmarek is pushing Faulbaum for answers so he can cover his tracks on that Polyglop purchase fast. Of course, Faulbaum will want to show Kaczmarek that he can count on PD to come up with the information he needs when he needs it. Leahy will review your draft and then send it on to Faulbaum for his approval.

Before you have time to think about your report-writing strategy, you get another request from Leahy to write to Johnson in Quality Control and describe the test procedures which that section might use to test future shipments of Polyglop. Leahy tells you to describe your tests, your standards, and Polyglop's performance. Later, you, Leahy, and the people from Quality Control will meet to decide which tests will be useful for their purposes and to develop product performance standards.[6]

You are not too happy about getting these two requests to write before the field results are in, but you think that you have data that will be useful to Kaczmarek, and the tests are easy enough to describe for Johnson. Though you have to write two reports, with careful planning, you might make some sections work for both. On that happy note, you get started.

ASSIGNMENT 3

Write a report addressed to Kaczmarek from Faulbaum (for Faulbaum's signature). Leahy will be listed under "Approved by." You will be listed under "Prepared by." Make sure you review Kaczmarek's original request for services before you start. Study the case and Appendix A and decide who else should get the report.

ASSIGNMENT 4

Write a report outlining suggested procedures for Quality Control testing of Polyglop. The report will go to Johnson. Faulbaum and Stevens will be on the distribution list. Study the case and Appendix A and decide who else should get the report.

---

[6] At EconoAuto, Quality Control decides which tests to use and sets quality control standards after consulting with your department or outside sources. QC then meets with company specification writers who provide written specifications for Polyglop to be sent to the manufacturer. When specifications are set, QC regularly tests shipments to see that they meet the written specs for product quality.

APPENDIX A

Partial Organizational Chart for EconoAuto Corporation

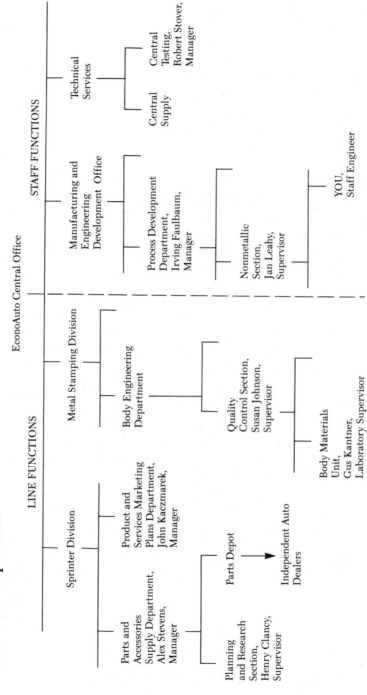

EconoAuto Central Office

LINE FUNCTIONS

STAFF FUNCTIONS

Sprinter Division

Metal Stamping Division

Manufacturing and Engineering Development Office

Technical Services

Parts and Accessories Supply Department, Alex Stevens, Manager

Product and Services Marketing Plans Department, John Kaczmarek, Manager

Body Engineering Department

Process Development Department, Irving Faulbaum, Manager

Central Supply

Central Testing, Robert Stover, Manager

Planning and Research Section, Henry Clancy, Supervisor

Parts Depot → Independent Auto Dealers

Quality Control Section, Susan Johnson, Supervisor

Nonmetallic Section, Jan Leahy, Supervisor

YOU, Staff Engineer

Body Materials Unit, Gus Kantner, Laboratory Supervisor

207

APPENDIX B

Kaczmarek's Letter Requesting Service

ECONOAUTO COMPANY

Intra-Company Communication

November 9, 1984

Mr. I. Faulbaum
Process Development Department
Manufacturing and Engineering Development

cc: Ms. J. Leahy
     Process Development

     Mr. A. Stevens
     Parts and Accessories Supply Department
     Sprinter Division

SUBJECT: Plastic Body Filler

We are interested in merchandising an acceptable plastic
filler for body repair work. We believe one product, in
particular, shows promise for this use: "Polyglop,"
manufactured by Phoenix Chemical, Sarnia.

We are submitting with this letter samples of Polyglop
and of eleven other types of filler listed in an
attachment. All filler types are now available to the
trade.

We would like you to appraise these samples strictly as
a service repair item.

APPENDIX B—*continued*

-2-

Will you please advise us regarding durability, paint
retention, surface pits or air bubbles, or any other
properties you consider important. Specifically, note
measurable superiority of Polyglop over competing
products.

An early reply will be appreciated.

s/John Kaczmarek, Manager
Product and Services Marketing Plans
Sprinter Division

ATTACHMENT

JK/jy
Project XL — 78-B

(continued)

APPENDIX B—*continued*

ATTACHMENT

Polyester Body Fillers Now on the Market

Polyglop	Phoenix Chemical Company Sarnia, Ontario CANADA
OK Filler	James Schaefer Co. Albany, New York
Flexiputty	Apollo Chemical Co. Ltd. Toronto, Ontario CANADA
Fiber	Plastics Division Flexfast Company St. Petersburg, Florida
Patchup	Mandell Corp. Boston, Massachusetts
Plastice	The U.S. Sealtight Company Orlando, Fla.
B.F. 100	Beardsley Petroleum Houston, Texas
Bondrite	The Phillips—Carver Company Chicago, Illinois
Superfill	Fiber—Plastics Company Livonia, Michigan
Superfill Paste	Fiber—Plastics Company Livonia, Michigan
Filler Formula	All—Purpose Plastics Company Detroit, Michigan
Superslik Paste	Polyco Chemicals Newark, New Jersey

APPENDIX C

Test Summary for Polyester Service Kits

		Mix Ratio			Reverse Impact	
Material	Cat.	Base	Hard-ener	Gel Time @ 78° F	1' Drop	2' Drop
Polyglop	Liq.	96 gr	2 dr	4 min	OK	1" Crack
OK Filler	Liq.	50 gr	22 dr	5 min	OK	Cracked
Flexiputty	Liq.	54 gr	14 dr	3 min	OK	Cracked
Fiber	Powd.	50 gr	7 gr	7 min	OK	Cracked
Plastice	Powd.	75 gr	10.5 dr	6 min	Cracked	Cracked
Patchup	Liq.	55 gr	30 dr	120 min		
B.F. 100	Liq.	55 gr	30 dr	9 min	Popped out	Popped out
Bondrite	Liq.	50 dr	12 dr	30 min	OK	Cracked
Superfill	Powd.	50 gr	1.25 gr	11 min	Cracked	Cracked
Superfill Paste	Liq.	50 gr	8 dr	4 min	OK	Cracked
Filler Formula	Liq.	64 gr	28 dr	5 min	OK	Popped out— cracked
Superslik Paste	Paste	150 gr	3 gr	9 min	Popped out	Popped out

dr = drop
gr = gram

(continued)

APPENDIX C—*continued*

Material	Tensile Shear				Weathering (250 hr)			Feather
	1st	2nd	3rd	Ave	Control	1st	2nd	
Polyglop	238	242	250	243	cracked in prime	OK	OK	OK
OK Filler	440	435	360	412	OK	2 cracks in color 164 hr	1 crack in color 229 hr	OK
Flexiputty	390	400	325	372	OK	cracked in prime	cracked in prime	OK
Fiber	375	455	439	423	OK	cracks in color 164 hr	cracks in color 164 hr	OK
Plastice	162	109	141	137				
Patchup								
B.F. 100								
Bondrite	262	310	288	287	cracked in color	fine cracks in color 68 hr	fine cracks in color 68 hr	gummy
Superfill	595	770	550	638	cracked in color	cracks in color 50 hr	cracks in color 50 hr	OK
Superfill Paste	435	680	760	625	OK	OK	OK	slight flake
Filler Formula	297	308	360	322	cracked in prime	cracked in prime	OK	OK
Superslik Paste								

Cashing in a Bright Idea: The Government Employee Suggestion Case

Elizabeth L. Malone with
Barbara Couture and Jone Rymer Goldstein

You left your college and its engineering program at the end of your second year and accepted an entry-level position with the U.S. government as a Quality Assurance Representative (QAR). For the first year, a QAR is assigned to various inspecting duties in different manufacturing plants. However, you are assured of receiving promotions to more responsible work after both the first and second years on the job; you will then be inspecting more complex items and possibly supervising other inspectors. You like working for the government and are looking forward to your promotions, even though responsibilities are limited to making sure that the literal terms of contracts are carried out.

In your first job as a QAR, you worked out of another inspector's office, visiting "mom-and-pop" companies that sell simple, nuts-and-bolts items. The work was pleasant, though not demanding. To make your job more interesting during this time, you attended a training class, did some background reading on quality control, and submitted several written "suggestions."

The Suggestion Program is the government's official mechanism for rewarding employees who recommend "ideas which contribute to . . . overall effectiveness and efficiency," as the official booklet says. Suggestion awards look good on your record, give you some recognition for your initiative, and may earn you some money if what you suggest saves the government measurable dollars. Most government employees never submit suggestions, or they give up after a rejection, but you are both interested and persistent. Trying to improve the system challenges you and focuses your energies.

The first suggestion you submitted, that government inspectors use a form you devised to streamline reporting, was rejected with some polite language about the form's "very limited value." Realizing that there must be a more specific reason, you called Gene McCrory, the Recognition and Awards Coordinator, who processes all Quality Assurance (QA) suggestions.

After you talked with him a bit, he seemed to realize that you were sincerely interested and would submit more suggestions if he gave you some advice. He hesitated a bit, then explained that the tone of your suggestion had offended both John Heberlein, the evaluator in Quality Assurance, and Frank Smith, the Executive Secretary for Incentive Awards in Personnel, who makes sure all suggestions have been processed according to established procedures.

"Heberlein," said McCrory, "just plain didn't like the fact that some person who'd only been on the job for a month thought a new form would be better than the one that's been used for ten years or more. If what you're suggesting is an improvement, fine; but don't run down what's already in place."

You'd taken McCrory's advice and tried to avoid stepping on anyone's ego in your second and third suggestions, ways of improving QA procedures on a short assembly line. Result: both were accepted. You even received $50 for the third one, which was "of moderate value," but savings could not be calculated in hard dollars. Fifty dollars is not exactly a substantial sum, but the more money you save the government, the more you get awarded, since a percentage of the savings goes to the suggester.

Your job of monitoring mom-and-pop operations ended when you were transferred to an inspection job working in the International Truck (IT) plant. IT is assembling trucks for the government under a four-year contract (contract number DEA306–83–C–7077); the trucks will be used by all military departments in the United States and abroad. For a contract of this scope, Uncle Sam often stations reliable inspectors right in the manufacturer's plant, as you are now stationed. You feel this inspecting job is definitely a step up; you feel that your professionalism, indicated in part by your suggestions, has helped you get the job.

One of your responsibilities at IT is to make sure that the company safeguards and documents the government-furnished property (GFP). When the government provides items to be used with the manufacturer's product, the contract requires that the GFP be kept in a separate location and that separate records be kept for it, giving you and IT some tedious paperwork to fill out. Since IT has never had any GFP before this contract, IT employees are not sure what to do. As a result, you are in a position to help the company. Moreover, you have a sense of responsibility; you are protecting the government's interests, even if the GFP on this contract is not very valuable. It consists of two items for each truck:

1. Black, three-ring notebooks, called logbooks, used to keep track of mileage and maintenance when the trucks are in use.
2. Canvas maintenance cases, which hold and protect the logbooks.

The first items, the logbooks, cost $4.40 apiece, except for some excess stock received from government supply depots. The excess stock is theoretically free, but it has caused you no end of trouble. For some reason, the free logbooks never seem to come when they are supposed to, and on one occasion the delays actually held up the production line. On delivery, about 600 free logbooks turned out to be green; the contract specifies black logbooks. Because the green ones did not meet contract requirements, they had to be scrapped and new black ones bought. Soon after beginning the IT job, you realized that placing and tracking the logbooks cost the government plenty in time and trouble.

Both the purchased and free logbooks go into the second GFP items, the maintenance cases, which cost $5.80 each. At the end of the IT assembly line, an IT employee puts a logbook into a maintenance case and inserts this package into the glove compartment of each truck. Part of your job is to inspect the end of the assembly process to make sure the GFP is being handled and installed correctly in the maintenance case in the glove compartment.

On your first visit to this inspection point, you watch George Vicars, the IT employee who installs the logbooks and cases, set up his station. He rips open several cartons of logbooks, then several of maintenance cases. You notice that the cartons containing logbooks are smaller than the cartons containing maintenance cases. Making a mental note to find out why the logbook cartons are small, you go back to watching Vicars. He pulls out a logbook, which is encased in a heavy-duty plastic bag open at the top. He strips off the plastic, throwing it on the floor, pulls out a maintenance case and inserts the logbook into the maintenance case. Within a few minutes Vicars has a pile of logbooks in maintenance cases, ready to go into trucks—and a pile of plastic bags.

"Hey, George," you inquire, "what happens to all these plastic bags?"

"These here? They're for the garbage."

"You mean they're just packaging?" you ask.

"Yup. Every darn logbook is in a heavy-duty plastic bag."

"So you take the logbooks out of the plastic bags, put them in maintenance cases, and throw away the bags," you sum up for him.

"You got it."

"Sounds like a lot of extra work," you say.

"Sure is. Waste of time, if you ask me. And here's another waste of time—taking logbooks out of these miniature-sized cartons. Only four logbooks per carton—you'd think they were china dolls or something. Those free ones we get, they aren't packed in plastic bags—and there's 24 to a carton, too. Heck of a lot easier to handle and install."

"Well, I'll see what I can find out about this," you say. "Maybe we can make your job easier. Or maybe there's a reason for the way this stuff is packaged."

You go back to your office and start wondering whom to call. After some thought, you decide on Sam Straith, the government engineer assigned to the contract. Presumably Sam knows why certain requirements were written into the contract.

"Sam," you begin, "logbooks we buy—they come only four to a carton, and they're in plastic bags that seem to be made to fit and protect them. Why? And why does the contract call for the maintenance cases when these things already come in heavy-duty plastic bags?"

"Why the protective packaging on the logbooks?" Sam repeats. "Well, mostly that's for the logbooks we've ordered for the parts supply depots. They're going to sit on the shelves for awhile, and they'll deteriorate quickly if they aren't packed well. As for the canvas maintenance cases, they're required by military users on all vehicles with open cabs."

"But these trucks don't have open cabs," you remind him.

"So they don't," he agrees. "Then I don't know why they're there."

And neither do you. After the phone call, you begin to consider what to do. Should you bring the matter up to your quality circle or submit a suggestion yourself? The kinds of matters the circle considers have not included contractual changes. You decide that recommending an amendment to the contract is really outside the scope of the circle. You'll submit this suggestion on your own.

You feel confident that you can make some real money from this suggestion, since the government's laying out hard dollars for GFP.

You begin to work out the details. Using the plastic bags to protect logbooks in the trucks would eliminate the need for maintenance cases. The government will not have to buy the maintenance cases, the logbooks will still be protected, and all George Vicars will have to do is take the plastic-bag-encased logbook out of its shipping carton and put it in the truck.

You do some quick calculations. Just counting vehicles left on the contract for which cases are not already in stock, you figure as follows:

$$22{,}060 \text{ maintenance cases} \times \$5.80 = \$127{,}948$$

You also decide to recommend packing the logbooks 24 instead of 4 to the carton. You call the supplier, Marin Office Supply, and get an estimated savings of $1,544.20 for packing all the logbooks 24 instead of 4 to a carton. Total savings are now $129,492.20.

Patting yourself on the back for your brilliance, you suddenly remember that free logbooks do not come in plastic bags. "Naturally!" you think to yourself, "if anything would ruin the plan, it would be the free logbooks!" Just as you are about to recalculate the savings to take into consideration the fact that free logbooks will need maintenance cases to protect them, you remember all those plastic bags on the floor by George Vicars' station. You are sure there are more than enough there to cover all the free logbooks for this contract. You decide to ask George to start saving the plastic bags.

Before reaching for a suggestion form (Appendix A) you think a moment about the egos who will be on the other side of it. Jerry Rutkowski, the government contracting officer, will make the final decision, but he will ask for advice from many people: Sharon Beasley, the head of your section; Sam Straith and possibly other technical people; and users from all the military departments, who by now have some trucks with the logbook–maintenance case combination. Then, of course, there's Frank Smith, who will audit the suggestion to make sure all the procedures have been followed. That is a lot of people to think about, but you feel sure you can write a suggestion that will not offend any of them.

ASSIGNMENT

Fill out the suggestion form in Appendix A with your suggestion for improved efficiency on the International Truck, Inc., contract. Your title is Quality Assurance Representative. Your phone extension is 7-2312.

APPENDIX A

Suggestion Form

1. Name:
2. Title:
3. Topic of Suggestion:
4. Your Signature:
5. Signature of Executive Secretary:
6. Home Address Where Acknowledgment Will Be Sent:
7. Describe Suggestion. (Explain current situation and your suggestion for change. Discuss any benefits which would result from adoption.)   (Use additional pages if necessary.)

Wastewater Treatment Planning: Analysis for the Federal Government

You are a field engineer for Borden, Craig, and Hicks, an engineering consulting firm with headquarters in Madison, Wisconsin. After nine months on the job learning as much as you can about the business of wastewater treatment facilities, you are assigned the fieldwork for a wastewater treatment project for the city of Wikonac, a small resort and industrial town of just under 8,000 people located on the shores of Lake Michigan in the state of Wisconsin. Wikonac must upgrade and expand its municipal sewer system and wastewater treatment plant because of the stringent requirements mandated by the federal Clean Water Act. Accordingly, city officials have hired Borden, Craig, and Hicks to design the new facilities and prepare a "Facilities Plan," an elaborate document that will enable the town to apply for federal support for the expansion and improvement project. The money is available from the Environmental Protection Agency's Construction Grants Program.

One of the first steps in completing this feasibility and design study is conducting an Infiltration/Inflow Analysis. An I/I Analysis evaluates the current wastewater collection system to see if either infiltration or inflow[1] into the sewers is excessive. If the ground water and storm runoff prove too much for the treatment facility, then the EPA guidelines require that the city get a highly detailed analysis specifying the exact sources of the problem. This report, called a "Sewer System Evaluation Survey," is then included in the full "Fa-

---

[1] Infiltration into the sewers is ground water entering through faults in the system, such as bad joints. Inflow into the sewers, on the other hand, is water from storm runoff or melting snow, or from bodies of water such as lakes and rivers.

cilities Plan," along with the "Infiltration/Inflow Analysis." The I/I
report itself shows whether it is more cost-effective to handle infil-
tration/inflow of water by eliminating it at its source (that is, by pre-
venting it from entering the system) or by treating it. The report also
recommends the most cost-effective ways to improve the system, and
it sets the design capacity for the new facilities, based on population
projections.

The project manager for the Wikonac plan, Bob Carlson, is a man
you have not worked for previously. You are a bit apprehensive because you have heard that he is a stickler for detail and tough to please.
Carlson will direct the I/I Analysis, and by incorporating the work of
several people at the main office and you out in the field, he will write
up the I/I Analysis for the Environmental Protection Agency and the
Natural Resources Department of the State of Wisconsin. (Eventually
the report will form an appendix in the final "Facilities Plan" for the
City of Wikonac.) Although Carlson will visit Wikonac periodically
throughout the project's duration, you are the field engineer (with the
title Project Engineer) who will locate any problems with the current
system (such as flooding), check for any infiltration/inflow into the
system, and carry out the Sewer System Evaluation Survey if your
initial analysis shows such an elaborate assessment to be necessary.

Before you leave Madison, you must meet with Carlson to learn
about the situation in Wikonac and to find out exactly what he expects
of you there. It is no surprise to you when Carlson tells you to meet
him in his office at 7:45 on the Friday morning before the week you
are due in Wikonac. After a brisk greeting, your new boss sharpens
three pencils in an electric sharpener, places a yellow pad squarely
in front of him, and sits up very straight in his chair. Then he more
than lives up to his reputation by going over everything you could
possibly need to know and a few other things besides. First, he lectures you on the geography of the area and all the pertinent geological
conditions. He makes a big point about the sandy soil in Wikonac,
noting, however, that the soil in the southeastern section of town is
clay. Then he discourses on the water levels of Lake Michigan for the
last ten years, providing you with the official tables. Drawing your
attention to the rising levels of the lake, Carlson points out that in
August of this past year the water levels were a full 49 inches above
the low water datum.[2]

---

[2] The low water datum is the plane on each lake which serves as a reference point for
depths in lake survey charts and federal navigational improvements.

Next Carlson pulls out the town's population figures for the past 50 years, together with the projections for growth his office staff has already made. Looking them over, you see that Wikonac appears to be a rather sleepy place—not exactly an exciting assignment. Carlson abruptly brings you back to matters at hand by telling you that the population of Wikonac remained at about 8,500 until 1955 when the numbers decreased slightly, only to be followed by a further drop in 1965. Today the population is down to 7,730. The projected population for the year 2005 (the design year for the facility) is set at 8,500.

You comment that this projection will put Wikonac right back to where they were at midcentury, but Carlson forges ahead, grinding out numbers on three small nearby townships that may use Wikonac's system, thereby adding on about another 3,500 people for the year 2005. Finally, Carlson winds up by announcing that the total population to be served by the new wastewater facilities in Wikonac is 12,000.

Scanning the data, you take advantage of his pause to ask some questions.

"What's the industrial use?" you begin.

"A few modest users like a supermarket, a couple of small firms, plus the usual assortment of schools, motels," Carlson offers. "Wisconsin Tool has fairly heavy use. The biggest user of water by far, though, is the Beta Chemical Company. But they don't return their waste water to the city sewers because of chemical pollution. On the other hand, there is a small hospital, called St. Anne's, on the outskirts of town. It doesn't use town water, but it does discharge into the Wikonac sewers."

"And what about the sewer system?" you ask, a question which provokes Carlson to turn his attention to the wastewater collection system itself.

"Wikonac's facilities were built around the turn of the century," he begins expansively. You sense that a history lecture is coming.

"Originally, they built combined sewers for discharge into Lake Michigan and the Gull River. You know, of course," he says raising his eyebrows, "that sanitary sewage treatment wasn't commonly practiced in those days. Combined sewers carried both sanitary sewage and storm-water runoff into some handy body of water."

You nod patiently, realizing that your new boss believes you must start at square one; you hope that after he gets to know you better he will not feel that he has to lead you by the hand.

"Well," Carlson continues, "Wikonac's facilities were added to in bits and pieces over the years. In 1938 they constructed a primary wastewater treatment plant, and also an interceptor sewer along the lake and the river to the plant. Diversion overflow structures[3] were put in along the interceptor for rain and melting snow. The interceptor sewer just couldn't handle all the storm runoff because it was designed principally for dry-weather flow."

"How do things look today?" you wonder. "Any problems?"

"There seem to be only a few problems, and they're caused by the combined sewers. I don't think you're going to find anything serious," Carlson says, as he strokes the top of his slightly balding head. Then he abruptly stops and leans forward in his chair. "Of course you must not assume anything. I want a first-rate job."

"Of course," you reply. "By the way, what are the city officials like?"

"They're okay, but they all sound like walking advertisements for Wikonac. The city manager is a fellow named Ben Williamson. He seems satisfied with most anything we do or say—just so long as it makes Wikonac look good. The mayor is a nonstop talker who thinks Wikonac is a tourist Mecca. Then there's the 'super' in the Wastewater Treatment Plant, Henry Monroe. He's been with the system for almost as long as it's been in operation and boasts that it's the finest facility all up and down the Michigan shore."

"Is it?" you ask.

Carlson laughs dryly. "Listen. The major reason Monroe thinks it's so great is that he gets very few complaints about basement flooding. A couple of superintendents from nearby communities are harassed by irate citizens with wet basements, and talk about little else. Frankly," Carlson continues seriously, "the Wikonac system isn't bad, but Monroe thinks of it as his private property."

"So the idea is not to offend him—or the other town officials—while still getting all the information we need," you observe.

"Right," says Carlson. "Get all the facts, without poking any more holes in Wikonac's pride than you have to."

You believe that you are up to that task, and you also believe that

---

[3] A diversion structure is a manhole or special structure below ground where an extra pipe is installed above the normal flow-carrying pipes. The extra pipe is to divert flow to the river when high-flow levels would otherwise flood basements or flood the ground surface. Often the overflow pipe is not higher, but is separated from the normal flow pipes by a weir (a dam). During periods of excessive flow, the combined storm runoff and wastewater rises over the weir and flows out the overflow pipe.

you are going to like working for Carlson. He is a stickler, but he is very straightforward, and he surely has provided you with good background on Wikonac. As you finish up your other tasks and prepare for your trip, you begin to look forward to seeing this town for yourself.

Driving into Wikonac on Sunday evening and settling in at your motel, you think to yourself that this is not a bad place for a field assignment—an attractive resort town which the locals have a right to be proud of. The next morning you head out to the Wastewater Treatment Plant to pay a call on Superintendent Henry Monroe. You find old Monroe just as Carlson described him: full of praises for Wikonac's facilities—"Basements here are dry as a bone," and, "Finest system on the Michigan shore." The sewers, according to Monroe, do a "great job" of carrying the storm runoff, and there is "no infiltration, absolutely no infiltration at all." Under your repeated questioning, however, Monroe finally admits that when Lake Michigan is high, Lake Nebagamon is also high and allows some inflow. Also the Gull River occasionally backs up into the pumping station. "But," the old man insists, "it's almost nothin' to speak of."

Nodding to him but wondering to yourself, you ask him if you can see the records on the system. You find that today the Wikonac wastewater system consists of three major sewer subsystems with a total of 10,170 feet of sanitary sewers, 12,090 feet of storm sewers, 167,020 feet of combined sewers, and 625 manholes. Checking out the maps, you identify key manhole locations and diversion structures. Then you begin to analyze the flow records. When you finish, you conclude that Monroe's rosy opinions might be quite close to the mark: the system looks fine, at least on paper.

The next day you arm yourself with the maps of the system and head into the town to look for signs of infiltration or inflow and any other problems such as dry-weather overflow[4] and inoperative overflow devices. You examine 23 potential overflow points on the interceptor sewer where combined storm-water runoff and wastewater overflow when it rains. Next you check out the seven pumping stations

---

[4] Dry-weather overflow comes from a sanitary sewer through an overflow pipe to a watercourse or storm sewer during a time when no storm-water inflow is present. The cause of dry-weather overflow may be blockage in the sanitary sewer, inadequate size of the sanitary sewer for the normal dry-weather flow, or excessive infiltration. (See Footnote 1.)

(lifts) on the system. Finally you make the rounds of the key manholes you had selected while reviewing the records at the plant.

Overall, things look good. The diversion structures seem to be in fine shape, most of them having an overflow pipe with a masonry dam inside to control the level of the overflow. However, you do observe that during dry weather, some water overflows into the river at two of the diversion structures (at manholes 23 and 27). You suspect sloppy housekeeping, so you write yourself a note to ask both Monroe and the Department of Public Works (DPW) people about that later.

You also find some evidence for Monroe's admission of river water backing up into the pumping station. At diversion manhole 9 (located on the corner of Elm Avenue and M Street), you notice what appears to be sanitary sewage. This must be the backup Monroe mentioned. Evidently when the lake is high, the Gull River rises and backs up into the pumping station; then when the river water flows back into the north side of the river channel, it carries along diluted sewage. Checking this out at the pumping station, you easily find the culprit: the top boards on the wooden weir[5] have deteriorated so badly that they allow the river to back up into the pumping station. Easy remedy for that inflow, you smile to yourself.

Later in the day you find another problem. This time it is at the $5\frac{1}{2}$-foot box sewer[6] in L Street between 14th and 15th Avenues. There is a steel-plate overflow device where water is entering the sewers at high lake levels. You start wondering where it is coming from, and then recollect what Monroe had said about the small inland lake, what was that strange name? Lake Nebagamon or something. By now you see quite clearly that high levels of Lake Michigan are causing some problems in the Wikonac sewers. However, you are quite sure that minor repairs will take care of things, and you jot down some notes (Figure 1).

Back at the treatment plant, you check with Monroe about the dry-weather overflow to the river at the diversion structures at manholes 23 and 27. After some hemming and hawing, Monroe admits that perhaps the upstream sewers need cleaning, and he advises you to speak to Vic Ling, the superintendent at the DPW. In a telephone conversation, Ling finally reveals that there has not been any recent cleaning

---

[5] A weir is a dam or vertical wall which prevents overflow until the water level rises to its top.

[6] A box sewer has a square or rectangular cross section.

-REPLACE BOARDS ON WOODEN WEIR AT THE MAIN ST. PUMP STATION

-RAISE THE STEEL PLATE ON THE L ST. BOX SEWER

Figure 1. Repair Notes

of the sewers upstream, but only after you first listen to a lot of talk about the "bad winter this year" and "all the road sanding we had to do this January."

No big problems that you can see—just poor maintenance. This Vic Ling sounds sloppy to you and also pretty defensive about his operation. Sand buildup in the sewers is causing those overflows at manholes 23 and 27. Despite that fact, altogether things look almost as bright as Carlson predicted. The city needs to improve its housekeeping of the sewers, and the DPW needs to make a couple of repairs to prevent the inflows from Lake Michigan when it is at high levels. Certainly the inflows you have found resulting from the combined sewer system are clearly known and reasonable, so a sewer survey does not seem likely.

Convinced that the I/I Analysis for Wikonac is going to be easy, you pay a visit to the Water Department to collect the records on the amounts of water pumped to the Wikonac system. You pull together the daily records and calculate the monthly averages in millions of gallons of water per day (mgd) for the last four years. Then you append the yearly averages to your lists, plus the maximum and minimum days (Table 1).

Next you pull out the figures for water pumped to the Beta Chemical Corporation. Recalling Carlson's remarks about Beta not returning its water to the city sewers, you realize that you must consider all the water the chemical company uses; then you will be able to calculate the amount of pumped water that must be accounted for at the wastewater plant. Unfortunately, city records for Beta are incomplete, the company having reported them for only the last three years.[7] Well, at

[7] Later you learn the reason: Beta had not replaced a faulty meter until three years ago.

TABLE 1. Pumped Water to the City of
Wikonac (mgd)

	1981	1982	1983	1984
January	1.22	1.22	1.16	1.33
February	1.40	1.19	1.53	1.29
March	1.20	1.24	1.23	1.34
April	1.33	1.26	1.19	1.20
May	1.30	1.40	1.45	1.26
June	1.64	2.12	1.68	1.52
July	1.79	2.23	1.58	1.61
August	1.93	1.78	1.40	1.70
September	1.31	1.60	1.35	1.44
October	1.11	1.24	1.26	1.25
November	1.22	1.22	1.26	1.18
December	1.10	1.16	1.32	1.18
Average (year)	1.38	1.47	1.37	1.36
Max. day	2.96	2.88	2.44	2.29
Min. day	0.84	0.74	0.91	0.98

least you can figure out how much pumped water has been returned to the sewers in each of these years; perhaps that will be enough to check out the system. You rough out another table (Table 2).

After compiling these figures on the pumped water, you return to the Wastewater Treatment Plant and pull the monthly averages on wastewater flow recorded for the same years (Table 3).

Looking over the data, you are quite surprised, especially at 1981 and 1982. During those years, Wikonac not only did not have excessive inflow or infiltration, but instead large amounts of water were literally disappearing from the system. Your comparison of the figures on water pumped to the city and the recorded wastewater flow shows that in 1982 there was a lot more water being pumped into the system than was flowing through the wastewater treatment plant. The yearly average of actual pumpage was 1.47 mgd, but subtracting the 0.25 mgd used by Beta Chemical, you figure that on the average 1.22 mgd should have been pumped and returned to the sewers. You find the recorded wastewater, however, averaged only 0.91 mgd for the year. That is a substantial loss, and a very peculiar one. You ask yourself: Where did the stuff go?

Turning to 1983, things look more normal. The figures for pumped

TABLE 2. **Pumped Water Not Returned to the Sewer (mgd)**

	1981	1982	1983	1984
January	(data not available)	0.30	0.32	0.41
February		0.22	0.26	0.44
March		0.19	0.25	0.40
April		0.26	0.30	0.20
May		0.28	0.23	0.18
June		0.22	0.30	0.06
July		0.33	0.45	0.82
August		0.14	0.38	0.29
September		0.25	0.41	0.27
October		0.25	0.33	0.23
November		0.28	0.37	0.22
December		0.24	0.37	0.34
Average		0.25	0.33	0.32

TABLE 3. **Wastewater Flow Recorded (mgd)**

	1981	1982	1983	1984
January	0.54	0.86	0.90	1.08
February	0.55	0.80	0.78	0.89
March	0.59	1.07	0.99	1.45
April	0.54	0.86	1.03	1.23
May	0.54	0.89	0.94	2.31
June	0.54	0.88	0.95	3.46
July	0.56	0.96	1.07	2.72
August	0.65	0.99	1.35	1.97
September	0.89	0.99	1.33	1.66
October	0.86	0.86	1.13	1.50
November	0.90	0.85	1.00	0.95
December	0.97	0.93	1.01	0.92
Average (year)	0.68	0.91	1.04	1.68
Max. day	1.10	1.41	2.20	5.42
Min. day	0.40	0.57	0.54	0.61

water and sewage are about even at an average of 1.04 mgd. But after that year, you note that everything turned around totally. By 1984 the recorded wastewater flow was higher than the pumped water by a whopping margin: an average of 1.68 mgd wastewater and only 1.04 mgd pumped water (that is, 1.36 mgd minus the 0.32 mgd of Beta water not returned to the sewers).

The big question you face: Why were there such large losses of water from the system in 1981 and 1982? And to add to the confusion, why was there a big turnabout in 1984 with large amounts of wastewater? The latter sure looks suspiciously like excessive infiltration of water into the sewers.

Perplexed, you begin to mull over the possibilities. Shuffling through the records, trying to make some sense of the discrepancies between the pumped water and the wastewater flow recorded by the treatment plant, you start looking at the water levels of Lake Michigan which Carlson gave you. (See Table 4.) As the figures show, the level of Lake Michigan has been rising, and is certainly higher in 1984 than in either 1981 or 1982. The answer for the big difference in pumped water and wastewater flow in 1984 seems obvious enough: the high lake levels are causing inflow of both lake and river water into Wikonac's system, thereby increasing the recorded wastewater. But at least you know where the water is coming from, and the repairs will take care of most of it.

TABLE 4.   Lake Michigan Water Levels*

	1981	1982	1983	1984
January	578.69	578.81	579.1	579.89
February	578.55	578.69	578.9	579.92
March	578.49	578.97	578.9	580.02
April	578.63	579.24	579.1	580.38
May	578.99	579.55	579.6	580.65
June	579.26	579.80	579.8	580.98
July	579.35	579.91	580.0	580.99
August	(data missing)	579.86	580.2	580.96
September	579.21	579.70	580.3	580.68
October	579.08	579.47	580.2	580.44
November	578.99	579.22	580.02	580.12
December	578.92	579.1	579.87	579.97

* These data represent actual lake levels, but the years have been changed to conform to the case chronology.

But that does not help you much with the crazy figures from 1981 and 1982, the years in which so much water just seemed to evaporate. You review the possibilities for dry-weather overflow, the textbook answer, but nothing in your direct observations of the facilities points to that as the cause of such a large discrepancy. After some brainstorming, you decide to check out the water meters in the Water Department. That effort proves fruitless; the meters are well calibrated, with the actual and recorded pumpage in agreement.

Next you drive back to the treatment plant to see about the wastewater flow meter. Stopping by the superintendent's office, you chat with Monroe about the wonders of beautiful Wikonac, casually mentioning that you are on your way out to test the meter recording the wastewater flow. Out in the plant you use a surveyor's level to measure the actual head on the rectangular weir which measures the wastewater flow.[8] Your first measurement shows the actual flow to be 1.4 mgd. So then you check the wastewater flow *recorded* by the meter. The record shows it to be only 1.1 mgd! A difference of 0.3 mgd. You believe you have found the culprit, a poorly calibrated meter. Your second test confirms your suspicions. Actual flow is 1.3 mgd, whereas the plant's recorded flow is 1.0 mgd.

Doing some quick calculations, you figure that the reported rate has been about 300,000 gallons per day less than the actual wastewater flow. That is an *average error of about 29%* and is probably the reason the *recorded* levels for 1981 and 1982 are so low.

Now you have a touchy situation on your hands: how to find out how Monroe got this all fouled up without damaging his pride and causing him to clam up about his great system. You knock on his door with some trepidation. Monroe looks up and asks, "Suppose you found the meter just fine, eh?"

Deciding to be indirect, you toss him a question: "How long since the meter's been calibrated, Mr. Monroe?"

"Let me see. Been a while."

"Can you recall the last time you did it?" you urge.

"Not precisely," Monroe shakes his head. "Few years, I guess."

"Could it be as long ago as 1979 or '80—say, four or five years ago?" you venture.

"Maybe," Monroe says, looking out the window.

"I'd like to see the way you calibrated the meter. If," you add politely, "you wouldn't mind."

---

[8] The "head" is the height of the water above an established point on the weir.

Looking surprised at your request, Monroe remains silent for a moment. Then he clears his throat and answers. "Well, actually, I didn't calibrate that meter myself. Wasn't just sure how to do it, so I called on Dick Hughes. He's the city engineer, so I figured he'd know how."

You gulp, thinking that this simple matter is becoming rather complicated. But there is no turning back now. You excuse yourself to Monroe and immediately pay a call on Mr. Hughes in town. After a friendly exchange, you tell Hughes you need to know how the meter was calibrated. Not surprisingly, Hughes first has some difficulty recalling this event. When he does, his friendly manner turns cool. However, after a few minutes of gentle persuasion by you, he shrugs and agrees to go to the treatment plant with you.

Back at the plant, Monroe looks up as you pass his office, seemingly quite surprised to see Hughes in your company. Immediately, Monroe pops up and follows you out into the plant.

Hughes, replying to your question about calibrating the meter, points somewhat vaguely and describes setting the meter at the weir. In a flash you realize what has caused the problem with the recorded figures. Rather than positioning the meter to measure the water upstream where the flow hits its peak, Hughes had set it directly at the weir itself. So the wastewater flow has been undermeasured for the last several years—who knows just how many years, you think to yourself—all because of a simple error in setting up the meter.

Gently you point out the problem to both Hughes and Monroe, making as light of it as possible, while still attempting to make sure that they both realize that the meter must be recalibrated to measure the flow properly.[9] Though he seems embarrassed, Hughes shakes your hand briskly, nodding in agreement to everything you have said. After he makes a hasty retreat, Monroe strikes quite a different posture, expressing how pleased he is with your discovery: "Glad you figured this out. We'll get this meter set right. Want to make sure everything here in Wikonac is shipshape, you know."

Relieved that you have not alienated Monroe, and convinced that he will get the meter recalibrated soon, you turn once again to the

---

[9] Although you can see that the place where the meter was positioned to measure the water is inaccurate, you do not actually go into the instrument itself at this time. A technician could calibrate the meter in a couple of hours, but this task is not something you would typically do.

records. Now you know why you have a seeming surplus of water pumped into the system during the periods when the lake was low. In fact, you realize that *all* the figures on the recorded wastewater flows are inaccurate; they are way below actual flows for all the years you are looking at.

But you still do not know precisely how the amount of water pumped relates to the wastewater flow, a fact you assume Carlson will be eager to know. So you get down to the task of figuring out the exact differences between the two figures. You take selected weeks in February because there is no runoff or lake inflow to speak of then. After some reflection about the 29% daytime error rate you set previously, you decide to raise it to an average of 31% to account for lower flows at night.[10] Selecting the week of February 15–19, 1982, as a first case, you calculate the average recorded wastewater flow to be 714,000 gal/day, add 31% (or 221,340 gal/day) for the recording error, and come up with a total wastewater flow of 935,340 gal/day. However, there is that small hospital Carlson mentioned, St. Anne's, just outside Wikonac. It does not use town water, but it does discharge into the sewer system, so you must subtract the wastewater flow of 33,000 gal/day to come up with a figure of actual wastewater flow from city users. Your calculations show it to be 902,340 gal/day.

To compare this actual wastewater flow with the water pumped into the system, you take 1,254,400 gal/day, the average water pumped between February 15 and 19, 1982, and subtract the 256,138 gal/day used by the Beta Chemical Company but not discharged into the sewers. Thus you arrive at 998,262 gal/day as the actual water pumped. Thus the average excess water pumped (that is, pumped water not received at the wastewater plant) is only 95,922 gal/day (or 0.096 mgd). This represents a water loss of only 7.65% (based on recorded water pumped).

You are beginning to think that you have a handle on the problem. However, because you need more evidence, you select another week to sample, this time February 13–17, 1984. Here the average recorded wastewater flow is 796,000 gal/day, and the total wastewater flow with the 31% estimated error of 246,760 gives a total of 1,042,760 gal/day. The hospital uses approximately 33,000, so the actual wastewater flow is 1,009,760 gal/day. The average recorded water pumped during Feb.

---

[10] The error is a higher percentage at the lower wastewater flows typical during the night.

13–17 in 1984 was 1,314,200 gal/day; subtracting the Beta Chemical Company's use of 282,714, you arrive at 1,031,486 as the actual water pumped. Therefore, you conclude that the average excess water pumped for this week is only 21,726 (or 0.022 mgd). Wow! you say to yourself. That is only a loss of 1.65% (based on recorded water pumped)—a really minuscule amount. With a big smile on your face, you underline 1.65%.

Immediately you put through a call to Carlson in Madison. You go over the story with him. After a moment of silence in which you can almost hear him thinking, he compliments you for finding the cause of the discrepancy between the pumped water and the waste-water flows so quickly. Then he comments that since a well-managed system has water losses of anything up to 10% (based on recorded flows delivered to the system), Wikonac's looks pretty fine with figures ranging between 1.65% and 7.65%. The losses are minimal; the levels of water pumped and wastewater flow are almost the same.

"Seems there's nothing to worry about there," Carlson concludes.

"So since the losses are okay and the infiltration/inflow are known, we can dispense with the Sewer System Evaluation Survey?" you ask.

"Yes, of course," Carlson replies. "The infiltration appears to be as negligible as I predicted. The inflows are clearly known—caused by high levels of the lake. They can easily be prevented by the repairs. Wikonac doesn't need a full survey. We can go right ahead."[11]

"So things are in good shape," you heave a sigh of relief.

"Well, we'll see how they look on paper," Carlson replies. "Before you get busy on the analysis of the industrial-use levels, I want you to write up your analysis of the system so I can take a look at that right away. Tell me exactly what you observed and the problems you found, together with your assessments."

"Okay," you say.

"Make sure you cover those discrepant figures caused by the meter, and explain the numbers along with the lake levels and so on, so I can include them in the I/I Analysis."

"Of course," you answer.

---

[11] Despite the high wastewater flows in 1984, a full Sewer System Evaluation Survey is not required. The inflows resulting from the combined sewers (in which catch basins for storm runoff and lake inflows are connected to the sanitary sewers) are clearly known as coming from Lake Michigan when it is at high levels. No further attempt to locate inflows is, therefore, necessary. Moreover, the repairs to the Wikonac sewers that you have designated will prevent the excessive inflows caused by these high lake levels.

"Then you must write Ben Williamson, the city manager," Carlson continues, "to tell him and everyone else about the housekeeping jobs and the repairs the DPW must make to stop those inflows caused by the high lake levels."

"Right," you say hesitantly. "That's a notification for the city? To let them know what's wrong?"

"You've got it," Carlson replies. "They'll know what to do. You just need to make the problems clear for the record and to let Vic Ling, the DPW superintendent, know. He needs to get his men going on these repairs and the sewer maintenance, instead of something else he happens to think is more important."

"Okay," you reply, while jotting yourself a note to enumerate the problems and the solutions.

"Also tell them what you've been doing and where things stand now. Uh, let them know the system is sound and that the survey isn't necessary."

"Okay."

"Come to think of it, I guess you'd better tell them about the meter problem, too. They might've heard rumors about the 'funny figures' or the faulty meter—things like that get around fast in a small town, so fill them in—without embarrassing Hughes, or Monroe, or Ling, or anybody else for that matter."

"Of course not," you answer, as you scribble down his instructions. "The letter will be out for your signature this afternoon. I'll try to get the report ready to mail to you tomorrow."

ASSIGNMENT 1

Write a letter to the City Manager, Mr. Ben Williamson, Town of Wikonac, Wisconsin 00000. Copies go to Richard M. Hughes, City Engineer; Henry Monroe, Superintendent of the Wastewater Treatment Plant; and Victor O. Ling, Superintendent of the Department of Public Works. The letter should be signed for Borden, Craig, and Hicks, Consulting Engineers, Research Circle, Madison, Wisconsin 00000, by Robert P. Carlson, Project Manager, and you, Project Engineer.

ASSIGNMENT 2

Write a report to R. P. Carlson, Project Manager, Borden, Craig, and Hicks, Research Circle, Madison, Wisconsin 00000.

Facilities Planning for Southfork Public Schools: No Room in the Computer Room

John Slocum, chair of the Southfork Public Schools Building Committee, checks his watch and scans the faces of the others seated at the conference table in front of him. It is a hot June night, and the cramped quarters of the boardroom in the school district's old administration building make everyone at this Building Committee meeting look as uncomfortable as they probably are. You can tell that the group has worked long and hard together. All present have that let's-get-down-to-business look that is characteristic of people with too much to do in too little time with too little money.

"I guess we can begin," John Slocum opens, glancing around the table. "I'd like to start," and he smiles toward you, "by welcoming our new facilities planner from Croake and Stern, Incorporated."

Slocum then proceeds to introduce you to the rest of those present. Of course you have met Jack Marcotte, the superintendent of schools, and also Margaret Marshall, who sits on the Board of Education with Slocum. You've known Susan Rebuck of the Jensen and Freeland architectural firm for a long time. New to you are Douglas Powaser of the school district's business office and Bud Greysack of Tri-County Construction Management.[1] Everyone is cordial enough, though they all look a bit drawn, and a few appear discouraged. Slocum quickly gets things moving after the introductions.

---

[1] Rebuck, Greysack, and you are consultants to the Southfork Public Schools. Marcotte, Marshall, Powaser, and, of course, Slocum are members of the Building Committee. This committee was established by the SPS Board of Education specifically to handle new building projects for the school district.

"To make sure that everyone here is up to speed," he says, "I think it would be helpful to review briefly the events which led to our hiring a facilities planner for the Administrative and Curriculum Services Building project."

Straightening a stack of paper in front of him, Slocum continues, "As you all know, five years ago Southfork Public Schools' Board of Education approved plans to build a new Administrative and Curriculum Services Building. Three years ago, voters approved by three to two a bond issue to fund the new construction. Since then, building costs have gone up far more than we anticipated. We are quite certain now that the bond dollars won't be enough to build the structure we planned on."

Everyone at the table appears to be listening politely to facts you know they've all heard too many times.

"Of course," John Slocum continues, smiling wanly, "our architect and our construction manager have both suggested a number of changes in materials for our new building to save money, but it looks like these savings won't be enough. There's no way out. We simply have to design a smaller building. Sue Rebuck and Bud here, along with members of their firms, concluded last April that we had to reduce the size of the building by 20 percent. To give ourselves some room to negotiate, we told all administrative and curriculum services departments assigned to the new building that they would have to accept a 25 percent reduction in the total space we originally allotted to them. We announced this cut across the board knowing that we can cut some services more, others less, and that we can't cut some at all. With a little juggling, though, we should come up with that 20 percent reduction." Here Slocum pauses and gestures toward you. "And, of course, here's where our new consultant comes in."

You smile while recognizing what a difficult job you've been hired to do—replan a facility 20 percent smaller than the users originally thought it ought to be, and worse yet, thought it would be.

"Two weeks ago," Slocum adds, "we requested *all departments* that will be housed in the new building to tell us in what areas to cut space allocated to them to come up with a total reduction of 25 percent. That included everybody from the superintendent's office to our Educational Media Department. To make things easy for each department, we suggested that each could simply choose to accept a 25 percent reduction in the size of each room allocated for a specific departmental purpose. Needless to say, we've had a lot of agonized responses to this suggestion. However," Slocum quickly adds, smiling at the superintendent, "Dr. Marcotte and his staff have responded positively by suggesting exactly where they could get along with less space."

Marcotte smiles with approval.

Pointing to an accordion file he has placed on the conference table, Slocum says, "It seems that almost no one else can get along with less space, however. So we're going to have to make some unpopular decisions. Of course, each department did their own space planning over a year ago. Using departmental input, our central administration staff put together a Functional and Space Program[2] for the proposed building. Even though each department worked hard under the Building Committee's directive to be conservative, we think now that professional help will lead us to a better plan for every department. Our new consultant from Croake and Stern will review all responses to our recent request to cut space and then review and revise the Functional and Space Program from a year ago. If all goes well, we should have a new program for our architects to work with in about a month."

Slocum asks all present if they have any questions for you about how the functional programming will proceed.

"I just say best of luck to you," Margaret Marshall opens, cynically. "Getting our administrative and curriculum service people to think realistically is not going to be easy."

"That's why we've got a professional," Doug Powaser remarks in your support, and then adds, "I'm sure our new consultant will be conscious of our budget and at the same time recognize our need for an up-to-date facility. We'll find the fat in those space allocations, but we'll also know where space just can't be cut, like in our Data Systems Center,[3] for instance. We can't afford to jeopardize our computer services."

Slocum interrupts Powaser saying, "Our Data Systems Center is important, Doug, as you've reminded us many times before, but the DSC is just one of many important functions to be housed in that new

---

[2] A Functional and Space Program tells how much space is needed for each different function carried out in the building. For instance, it will tell how much space is needed for storing records, providing secretarial services, housing educational films, and so on.

[3] The Data Systems Center (DSC) takes care of computer services for the whole school district, including student records, payroll, equipment maintenance programs, testing services, and so on.

building. If there's a legitimate cut to be made there, we'll have to make it."

"Let's hope we won't be cutting our throats in the process," Powaser adds, a bit under his breath.

Slocum attempts to move the meeting on by asking if there are questions from anyone else. There are none, so he continues with the next item on the committee's agenda. Later, when the meeting breaks up, Slocum sits down to review with you the departmental responses to the Building Committee's directive to cut space.

"The departmental response I'm most concerned about," he begins, "is from our DSC people. I know Doug Powaser thinks we should give them just what they ask for, but take a look at this."

Slocum shoves a memo under your nose addressed to the Building Committee from Fred Kline and Ramon Mendez, the chief administrators of the Data Systems Center (Figure 1). Meanwhile, he opens his briefcase and takes out an overstuffed three-ring binder labeled "Functional and Space Program for Administrative and Curriculum Services Building." He flips the pages until he comes to the section describing the needs of the Data Systems Center.

"Let me fill you in on what's going on here," Slocum continues. "When we completed our Functional and Space Program a year ago, the Data Systems Center had a total of 4,380 square feet allotted for their function. We, of course, have suggested that they can reduce their total to 3,285 by simply cutting the space in each room in the DSC by 25 percent. That includes the computer room, which would be reduced from 3,060 square feet to 2,295." Slocum points to the memo which he handed to you earlier (Figure 1). "As you can see, Kline and Mendez claim they can hardly fit new equipment that we have ordered in their present computer room in the old school board building. That room's just under 2,000 square feet. Plus they say here that they need some additional hardware to go in there beyond the two mainframe CPUs."

You scan the memo, noting reference to space for "terminal controllers" and "disk storage" in addition to space for central processing units (CPUs).

Slocum interrupts your reading saying, "Of course, it's hard to tell exactly what they want space for here. The whole thing is so poorly written."

You agree that it is a terrible memo, but decide to ignore Slocum's remark.

SOUTHFORK PUBLIC SCHOOLS
Tempe, Arizona

MEMORANDUM

To: Building Committee

From: Fred Kline
                       Head, Systems Support
                       SPS—Data Systems Center

                       Ramon S. Mendez
                       Head, Computer Operations
                       SPS—Data Systems Center

DATE: April 30, 1984

SUBJECT: Space Reduction—SPS Data Systems
                       Center

The present reduction of 1095 square feet in total space for the Southfork Public Schools Data Systems Center is reasonable if it is consistent with the reduction in space for the rest of the school district's administrative and curriculum services.

However, the major concern is the reduced space for the Computer Room (reduced to 2295 sq. ft.) which has come to our attention in our attempts to accommodate the second 2469 computer and the disk modules in the existing computer room which has 1928 sq. ft. This hardware, scheduled for delivery in October, 1984, will require getting rid of the worktable behind the printers and the control section area. If we do this, there would be space for upgrading one CPU to a 2469AP processor. (We expect to have two 2469AP processors altogether when we

Figure 1.   Letter from the Data Systems Center Staff

-2-

move into the new buiding.) Our current storage of paper in the existing computer room and the control section will need to be relocated sometime next year to make space for the additional disk modules.

The computer room space in the new Administrative and Curriculum Services Building should be increased to accommodate upgrading the two CPUs, adding terminal controllers, and disk storage. The recommendation is to increase the computer room space from 2295 square feet to 3000 sq. ft.

FK:mh

Figure 1, *continued*

"How much space do those CPUs take?" you ask.

"Well, I don't know," Slocum answers. "Kline and Mendez don't really say in this memo. I thought I could find out how big all this equipment is by looking at the Functional and Space Program from a year ago. Look here," Slocum says to you, pointing to a section of the Functional and Space Program (Table 1). "Here's what the program says about the computer room and the control room."

"As you can see, the list doesn't describe what computer hardware is going in there. We've got one 2469 processor in our computer room now and are supposed to get a second one in October, as they say in their memo. Now when we move to the new building, we will have two 2469AP processors—the upgraded machines they mention. Kline and Mendez say they could only fit one of the new processors in their existing space if they had to, but even if we reduce the computer room to 2,295 square feet, we're giving them over 350 square feet more than they have now in their old computer room. What do you think?"

"I don't know," you answer, feeling a bit helpless. "It's pretty

TABLE 1.   A Portion of the Functional and Space Program for the DSC

| | | | Units | |
| | | | Number of Rooms | Square Feet per Room |
Code Number	Space Name	Remarks		
1436	Computer room	Computer hardware. Air conditioning units. Office for Supervisor-Computer Operations I. Adequate work space for peak staffing of 4 computer operations staff. Raised flooring. Fire protected. Water supply. Humidity control.	1	3,060
1437	Operations control room	2 workstations for control clerks. Each work-station with desk, chair, filing area. 1 report dissemination area.	1	120

hard to judge computer space. The trend seems to be that as technology advances, smaller space is needed for the CPU. From what I know about the 2469 processor, however, the upgraded version—that is, the 2469AP your staff talks about here—is actually larger. Don't know by how much though."

"Well, neither do I," says Slocum, "and they sure don't enlighten us in their memo."

"And another thing," Slocum goes on, "I don't understand what they mean by adding those terminal controllers—see this in the last paragraph?" he says, pointing again to the memo. "What's that equipment for? Had they anticipated it before or is this new stuff? It also isn't clear how much disk storage they need in the computer room. The Functional and Space Program [Table 1] doesn't say anything about disk storage and paper storage in that room. Do they need space for that in the computer room or what?"

"Probably," you suggest. "It would be inconvenient to locate that stuff someplace else. But how much space they need for all of this really isn't clear. I think their request for 3,000 square feet seems somewhat arbitrary," you add, looking again at the Functional and Space Program. "Their original program called for 3,060 square feet for the computer room. You'd think they'd ask for that."

"I don't know why they didn't," Slocum answers. "Perhaps they were trying to compromise by accepting a little less space. You know, another thing that bothers me is that they don't suggest whether they could make up for some of that lost space in the computer and control areas by cutting other areas."

"Well, they hint that they're just tolerating the 25 percent cut in the rest of their department," you say, reading from the memo again.

"True," Slocum says. "Though I doubt that these guys even looked at what could be cut elsewhere. Take a look at what the Functional and Space Program says about space allocations for the other rooms in the DSC" (Table 2).

You scan the program and then say, "I wonder why they've planned 100 square feet for the director's office and 200 square feet for the assistant director's office."

"Beats me," Slocum says.

You are both silent for a moment. It is clear that it's impossible to deal with the DSC's request for more space in the computer room. You require more information about their space needs. You suggest a plan of action to Slocum.

"I think I should write these DSC administrators," you say, "and

TABLE 2. Other Rooms in the Functional and Space Program for the DSC

			Units	
Code Number	Space Name	Remarks	Number of Rooms	Square Feet per Room
1430	Director's office	Enclosed. Seating for 4. Worktable.	1	100
1431	Assistant director's office	Enclosed. Seating for 4. Worktable.	1	200
1432	Administrative assistant's office		1	60
1433	Reception	Seating for 6.	1	60
1434	Programmer/ analysts' offices	Workstations for programmers and analysts. Seating for 3. File and cabinets, bookshelf, CRT capability.	12	60
1435	Supervisor's office		1	60

ask them to answer some specific questions. I can't be of help to you without precise information."

"I couldn't agree with you more. You should write Kline and Mendez, but make it clear that you have the Building Committee's backing," Slocum says as he begins packing up his briefcase. "I'd suggest beginning your letter by introducing yourself as the new consultant appointed by the Board. And say that you are investigating the DSC computer room space at my request. Send copies to all the Board members, too."

"Sounds good," you answer. "I'll draft a letter to Kline and Mendez first thing in the morning."

"Fine," Slocum says handing you the memo from Kline and Mendez. He also gives you the pages from the Functional and Space Program on the DSC, saying, "Don't be afraid to make demands on the computer people. These guys have to straighten up their act."

Because it is getting late, Slocum says that he will review the responses to the space cut directive from the other Administrative and Curriculum Service departments and send copies with his comments to you. He remarks that the response from the DSC was the most confusing and potentially the most sensitive. He reminds you of Doug Powaser's remarks earlier this evening, saying, "Doug is a real supporter of our Data Systems Center. He thinks our DSC staff is innovative and efficient, and he doesn't want to see their services curtailed."

You remark that Margaret Marshall may differ with Powaser.

"Well, she thinks none of our administrative and curriculum staff takes planning seriously," Slocum responds. "There are days I agree with her. I know one thing for sure, Kline and Mendez didn't show a very impressive planning effort in this memo."

With that last remark, Slocum shakes your hand and bids you good night. On your way home you think about how you will put together that letter in the morning.

ASSIGNMENT 1

Write a letter to Fred Kline, Head, Systems Support, and Ramon S. Mendez, Head, Computer Operations, Data Systems Center, Southfork Public Schools, Tempe, Arizona 00000. A copy of your letter will go to all members of the Southfork Public Schools Building Committee, and their names will appear on your letter. Your job title is Facilities Planner. Your firm's address is Croake and Stern, Inc., 158 Sunset Drive, Tempe, Arizona 00000.

ASSIGNMENT 2

All facilities planners at Croake and Stern submit monthly progress reports to George Stern, Chief Consultant. Stern requests employees to write the report with separate sections describing progress on each project assigned. Assume that your progress report is due in two days. Write a section describing your work on the Southfork Public Schools project.

The Staff Development Case:
A Proposal for
New Guidelines for Nurses

Your three-person unit, the Staff Development Office for Medical/ Surgical Nursing, serves the continuing education needs of nurses on the medical and surgical staff of the University General Hospital of the City of New York. With only four months of service in the position of educational nurse specialist, you are the newest employee in your department, but the other two nurse-educators are eager to share responsibilities with you, and so you have been assigned to several hospital committees. Recently, you started a two-year stint on the Educational Planning Committee, a group with one representative from the staff development office of each department (for example, Pediatrics, Obstetrics/Gynecology, Psychiatry). The committee's function is to develop basic in-service training and programs for upgrading nursing knowledge and skills.

The nine-member committee is chaired by the director of Central Services for Nursing Development (CSND),[1] Helen White. Although you do not know White well yet, she is one of your two bosses. (The other is the head of Medical/Surgical Nursing, Bonnie Schlect.[2]) Serving on the Educational Planning Committee is giving you the chance to get to know White firsthand, not just through the grapevine. For most of the first meeting you attended, you were quite impressed by

---

[1] The CSND supervises the training and continuing education for all the nursing specialties.

[2] The organization of the hospital gives you two completely independent supervisors, one in training (the chief of the CSND, Helen White) and one in staff nursing (the chief of Medical/Surgical Nursing, Bonnie Schlect).

her. Helen White seems to be a very articulate person, and she was certainly well prepared for the meeting. Attractive and poised, she smiles a lot, and you cannot quite see why people do not care for her. By the end of the meeting you began to get a glimmer, however. She talks well, but she talks interminably, and she does not listen to others much. In fact, she is pretty aggressive—so much so that people do not like to confront her even on procedural issues such as the endless meetings she holds without scheduling any breaks.

In your mail this morning, you find a short memo from Helen White (Figure 1), together with the draft of the guidelines for a new policy that your committee will consider at its next meeting. (See Appendix A, "Proposed Guidelines for Mandatory Development Programs.") Glancing over the draft for the policy on mandatory development programs, you feel that the statement looks innocuous enough, but after another minute, a couple of points strike you as ambiguous. Exactly what is a "mandatory program" anyway? From this list in section I of the draft, it sounds as if just about anything Helen White might want to make mandatory could be slipped into the required list. Looking further down the page, you wonder about the issue under II, B that reads, "Unit programs may be planned. . . ." Does this statement allow each department to substitute programs of its own for the mandatory ones set up by the CSND, or are supplementary programs all that the policy allows? It does not sound clear to you what the rights of departments would be under these guidelines. Hmmm. With a fuzzy policy like this, an authoritarian chief in CSND could ride roughshod over the individual nursing units.

You decide you need some advice, so you plan to get your two co-workers in Medical/Surgical Staff Development, Larry Coe and Janice Quigley, to look over the Proposed Guidelines with you. Their long experience at University General should help you to assess the whole situation better and to know how to approach the topic at the committee meeting next week.

Later this morning you get a chance to show both Larry Coe and Janice Quigley the draft of the Proposed Guidelines from Helen White. You soon learn that your suspicions about the policy were well founded; at least Larry and Janice both think so. In fact, they both believe that the policy needs revision for several reasons. Larry comments that the crucial issue is whether the policy will allow departments to substitute other programs for the mandated ones and whether it will permit any outright exemptions. The current unwritten policy—which Larry notes has been observed for several years and which

UNIVERSITY GENERAL HOSPITAL ━━━━━━━━━
━━━━━━━━━━━━━━━━━━━ CITY OF NEW YORK

Central Services for Nursing Development
MEMORANDUM

To: Educational Specialists, Nursing Staff
         Development Offices

From: Helen White, Director
         Central Services for Nursing Development

Date: October 15, 1984

RE: Educational Planning Committee Meeting
    Our next meeting will be Friday, October 19, 1984,
1:30 to 3:30 pm in Room P-446.

                        Agenda

Topic	Time	Leader
Information Sharing	20 minutes	Everyone
NY Nursing Assoc. Information	15 minutes	Helen White
New Thermometer	30 minutes	Helen White
Critique of Mandatory Development Programs	20 Minutes	Helen White
Open Topic	30 minutes	Everyone

    enc: "Proposed Guidelines for Mandatory
Development Programs"*

* See Appendix A.

Figure 1.   Helen White's Memo

seems to be implied by the criteria listed in II, B—allows each nursing department the right to propose program substitutions of its own whenever the mandated training does not meet its needs very well. Each nursing department can also request exemption from any required program that is not relevant to its specialists.[3]

Janice agrees with Larry that the substitution issue is the most important problem with the proposal, but she is also very critical of the way the guidelines were put together. Helen White did not follow guidelines for writing policy in "Format Requirements: Administrative Policy and Procedures" (Appendix B) and, in Janice's opinion, the results are pretty serious. Policies are supposed to include definitions wherever there might be disagreement or misunderstanding, but no "definitions section" appears in White's draft. "Who knows for sure what a 'mandatory program' is?" Janice asks.

After scrutinizing the Proposed Guidelines, Janice concludes that the whole write-up seems just plain sloppy, so sloppy that she cannot believe Helen White did it herself. "You can say a lot of bad things about Helen, but she's not stupid and she's not sloppy," concludes Janice. "I think 'Red' Larson did the job. This whole third section on procedures is so vague, it's almost a joke. It's supposed to set out exactly what each personnel category does, very explicitly. Also, I'm concerned that there's no mention of the Division of Personnel and Human Services[4] here."

"Sounds like a typical Helen White power play to me," laughs Larry.

---

[3] For example, the Outpatient Ambulatory Care Service might request exemption from a mandated program on eliminating electrical hazards caused by operating many pieces of equipment.

[4] The Division of Personnel and Human Services ("Personnel") is not connected with Helen White's Central Services for Nursing Development. Personnel is charged with conducting training and education for all hospital employees. Because their offerings in certain subject areas overlap with those of the CSND, the *informal*, unwritten policy for several years has been for each specialty to determine whether the Personnel course or the CSND course best met its practitioners' needs. Currently a fair number of mandated programs in management are provided for nurses by Personnel instead of CSND. Moreover, Personnel courses in the management area are frequently elected by departments rather than the CSND offerings. (The current informal policy allows individual departments to seek CSND approval for substitutions of Personnel for CSND courses if the alternative program's goals are comparable to the mandated ones. This option to select Personnel's offerings is one that Larry Coe and Janice Quigley are afraid would be lost under the "Proposed Guidelines for Mandatory Development Programs.")

Janice retorts, "But it's not funny, Larry. White can't bear to lose an ounce of control, and since Personnel isn't under her jurisdiction, she'd rather that nobody even knew that they exist—that they are a source of legitimate alternative programs."

"The truth of the matter," Larry chimes in, "is that Helen is jealous that some of the management-type programs offered by Personnel are better than the stuff coming out of CSND."

"True," says Janice. "And part of that is simply professional jealousy. She doesn't like the idea that educational specialists in Personnel are all management folks, not nurses. After all," she quips, mimicking White, "what can those business types know about nursing?"

At this point in the discussion, you ask Janice and Larry if there is anything you can do about all these issues. Janice believes you can critique the Proposed Guidelines quite readily at the committee meeting because, "White will let Red Larson take the flack." Larry is not so sure about that, advising you to be careful about stepping on Helen White's toes; she does not like criticism much. Yet Larry wants you to get across the idea that individual departments should have the right to substitute programs for the CSND mandated ones, and the policy must state that clearly. Janice also believes that point is essential, and since this confirms your original idea, you agree to present that position at the committee meeting.

Three days later, all nine representatives are at the Educational Planning Committee meeting at 1:30 P.M. After a brisk half hour of what the agenda calls "information sharing" but which turns out to be Helen White expounding on a long list of small issues, the topic turns first to the New York Nursing Association's new guidelines and then to the new equipment of the hour: the electronic thermometer just purchased for all nursing services at a cost of more than $900,000. White's office has gotten a videotape to train everyone in its use, and discussing the thermometer training ends up taking almost two hours. By 3:50 P.M., when everyone is quite worn down, Helen White finally brings up the "Proposed Guidelines on Mandatory Training Programs." After a short introduction in which she refers to "my thinking when I wrote this up," White asks if committee members have any questions or comments on the draft of the new policy.

So, you think to yourself, Helen White evidently wrote the policy draft herself. This is a nice turn of events. Janice Quigley's notion that Red Larson prepared this sloppy proposal was not true at all, and it will not help you to avoid sounding critical of White. Quickly you begin to rethink your points, while waiting to hear what the other committee members say. The room, however, is silent, save for the heavy breathing of the coffee machine. After a minute you realize that all the others are shaking their heads in answer to White's request for comments: no, they have nothing to say about the draft, which they are staring at very quietly. After meeting for most of the afternoon, people are just too tired to care, you think ruefully. Finally someone from Pediatrics breaks the silence by mumbling that the draft, "Looks fine."

Helen White now smiles more broadly than usual. The policy discussion is finished, and everyone is satisfied—obviously. If you are going to say anything at all, you must move quickly, and you do. You comment that your department thought some definitions were required by the official format for administration policies. Your unit felt that "mandatory programs" should be defined—"just so there wouldn't be any confusion on exactly what was mandatory." Helen White's smile fades, and she curtly informs you that the new format for writing policy statements does not require any definitions. When you appear surprised at her reference to the "new format," she coldly suggests that you get a copy from the Finance Department, from a Miss Teison there.

Although you are momentarily stopped by wondering why the Finance Department is the specialist on administrative policy format, you plunge ahead, telling White that your department believes that part II, B of the policy draft does not make it clear that units can *substitute* their own training for the mandatory programs. The draft makes it sound like the individual units can only offer *additional*, or supplementary, training, not substitutions. After hearing you out, White with icy politeness tells you that she will look into this matter to see if any clarification is required. As she turns to move on, you say that you have one more point. "The Personnel/Human Services Division should be included in the units listed as eligible to offer the substitute programs."

Bristling at the mention of Personnel, White stares at the proposal a moment, and then poses a question she clearly does not expect to have answered: "Why should the CSND write a policy for them?"

You murmur something about "just wanting Personnel noted as an alternative," but White closes the issue by reiterating her intention to review the question of individual department substitutions for mandatory programs. At that point, Johnny Blair of Obstetrics/Gynecology comments that instructors for substitute programs should be evaluated by the CSND, just as the curriculum itself is. Helen White nods approvingly, jotting down *that* comment in her notes. Then she declares the meeting over.

On your way back to the office, you stop in to see the Finance person, Miss Teison, whom White mentioned as the guru for administrative policy formats. You show her the draft guidelines and tell her your story. After you finish, Miss Teison drily comments that the format change was just for *clinical* and not for administrative policies. Then she pulls out an old set of "Format Requirements: Administrative Policy and Procedures" (Appendix B), and points out that, yes, in answer to your question, definitions are most certainly required, and also, yes, Mrs. White seems to have followed the wrong guidelines in writing up this policy on mandatory development programs. Evidently White used the clinical policy/procedure format rather than the administrative one. As it stands now, White's draft (at least according to Miss Teison's judgment) is incomplete and in the wrong order, and the items are in overlapping categories.

Back at your department, Larry Coe and Janice Quigley are much amused by your story of the meeting and your visit with Miss Teison in Finance, but they are not so amused by its ramifications. Larry suggests that you should get well prepared for the next committee meeting. In his opinion, White may try to ramrod the policy through the way she wants it. Each department's right to propose alternative programs to mandatory training programs and to apply for exemptions is a key issue. It is paramount to your department's ability to run a quality program, to avoid becoming the lackey of the CSND. "Look," Larry warns, "Helen White may have her bad points, but a policy must work with whoever is in the job. Her successor could be far worse, and then where would we be with an ambiguous policy?"

To avoid all the nightmare scenarios the three of you have imagined, Larry suggests that you should revise the guidelines for the mandatory development programs yourself. That way you will be absolutely clear about all the problems in White's draft, and if necessary, you will have an alternative draft ready, not just criticisms of hers. Janice Quigley agrees but advises you that White is not the sort of person who will respond well to suggestions once she has publicly taken her own position. If you are going to get anywhere with Helen, in Janice's opinion, you will have to communicate with her privately before the next committee meeting. Either you should go talk to her (taking your revised guidelines along, of course), or you should send the revised draft to her, with a nice memo explaining your position.

You agree with their advice, saying that you will revise the policy, and then either take it to her or send it to her. But you do not have enough information to write up the section on staff responsibilities, and you are not certain about some of the other issues.

Larry suggests checking the "Administrative Manual" for help on the staffing section. Flipping through the manual, he advises you to photocopy the second and third pages of the policy statement, "Staff Development Activities." (See Appendix C.) Then you can just make some simple adjustments to the sections covering the responsibilities of the CSND and the educational nurse specialists, so that you can use these pages more or less as they stand in your policy draft.

Larry also starts giving advice about the central issues. He says that the policy should make it clear that not only does the CSND give programs itself, but it also evaluates proposals for program substitutions and coordinates these alternatives. In addition, the departmental educational specialists plan alternatives to the mandatory programs.

Janice interrupts to suggest that you carefully check over all the pages of the "Administrative Manual" before using them in your policy write-up. She notes that the manual's overall plan is fine and most of the entries are okay, but the Personnel/Human Services category is very incomplete; your version should include something about providing programs, not just keeping records.

In discussion with Larry and Janice, you decide that the option to substitute programs designed by individual departments or by Personnel is of first importance in writing your draft. Each department must have the right to set up its own training and use Personnel's; no matter what Helen thinks of the Personnel courses, many nurses regard them highly and want to be able to take them rather than CSND-sponsored programs. Next on the list is the notion that a department can request exemptions to specific programs that are not relevant to its staff. The power here would still reside with the CSND, but at least the possibility for exemption would be established. Of far lesser importance, you all believe, is the sloppy definition of the mandatory programs. Mandatory programs, according to Janice, are listed in the *CSND Nursing Manual* and also in the "Nursing Practice Guide" for each department. The policy should just state that clearly and note exactly who requires the mandated training.

"It's the regulatory agencies," says Larry. "The Allied Commission on the Accreditation of Hospitals, the New York Department of Public Health, and then all the specific hospital departments with their own rules and regulations."

Back at your own desk, you go over your notes and the Format Requirements, checking each item still requiring more information. The Format Requirements are anything but clear, so you decide to compare each section with White's draft. The very first item in the Format Requirements, the "Policy Statement," and the second one, "Definitions," are lumped together in White's version under "Policy/ Procedure." The Format Requirements' third item, "Policy Standards," is more-or-less covered in White's section II, "Policy Statement." However, the Format Requirements' section IV, "Procedure," is not adequately covered at all in White's "Procedure." She does not make the nurses themselves sound responsible for meeting the mandatory requirements; instead she makes it appear as if the head nurses are responsible for everything. Finally, the Format Requirements ask for a "References" section, but White's draft omits this item altogether. To put together a list of items for the reference section, you review your files and come up with the *CSND Nursing Manual,* the "Nursing Practice Guide" for each department, the *Personnel Department Manual,* and the standards of the New York Department of Public Health and the Allied Commission on the Accreditation of Hospitals—all relevant to the mandatory program issue.

Preparing to write up a revised version of the policy, you hit on one more idea: you will include the suggestion of Johnny Blair of OB/ GYN that the CSND should evaluate the credentials of the instructors of all substitute programs, as well as the programs themselves. That is one thing that might make Helen White a little less unhappy about your suggested revisions. And you are quite sure you will need all the help you can get to persuade her to accept your version of the policy.

Before you begin to write, you walk over to Larry Coe's desk for a final review of your plans. "Okay, Larry. Let me review this whole thing with you," and you tick off the following. "In rewriting this policy, I am going to make it square with the Format Requirements, and that means dropping some things, adding some things, and moving others around. I am going to make sure that substitution and exemption issues are covered explicitly, I'm going to get the mandatory programs properly defined, I'm going to cover the Personnel programs as an option, and finally, I'm going to spell out actions of all the staff members by lifting some pieces out of the Administrative Manual. Does that cover everything?"

"Sounds fine to me," smiles Larry. "Have you decided whether you'll try to talk to White before your meeting?"

"No," you admit. "Haven't had time to think that one through yet. What do you advise?"

"I'd write to her. She can think about it alone and maybe come to some reasonable way out without losing face. Also, by writing you can make sure that you'll get to her before the meeting. She may not even have time to add you to her busy schedule."

"Sounds good to me," you say. "That means I'll have to write a very clever memo to convince her to accept the revisions in my version."

Larry chuckles. "You're going to have to be more than clever; you're going to have to be a magician!"

ASSIGNMENT 1

Rewrite the "Proposed Guidelines for Mandatory Development Programs" (in Appendix A).

Complete either Assignment 2 or 3:

ASSIGNMENT 2

After either rewriting the guidelines or discussing their revision in class, write a cover memo to send your draft to Mrs. Helen White, Director, Central Services for Nursing Development. She should receive your draft prior to the next meeting of the Educational Planning Committee. Blind copies (that is, copies not marked on the original to White) go to Larry Coe and Janice Quigley. Your title is Educational Nurse Specialist, Medical/Surgical Nursing—Staff Development Office.

ASSIGNMENT 3

After thinking over the suggestions of your co-workers and looking over the Proposed Guidelines more carefully, you decide that to rewrite the new procedures yourself seems somewhat presumptuous. Therefore, you decide to write a short report to White explaining in full the reasons that the guidelines should be rewritten. That way, she can do the job herself, if she wishes, or assign it to someone else. White should receive your report prior to the next meeting of the Educational Planning Committee. (Blind copies go to Larry Coe and Janice Quigley.)

ASSIGNMENT 4

One week has elapsed since you sent your draft and memo to Helen White. Although the Educational Planning Committee meets tomorrow afternoon, you still have not heard a word from White. The agenda she has distributed to the members does not mention the issue of the proposed guidelines.

In your discussion of the situation with Larry Coe, he suggests that you should prepare to speak at the full meeting in case White brings up the subject of the proposed guidelines. Janice Quigley suggests that you should try to make an appointment to see White before the meeting. Ultimately, the decision is yours, however.

Prepare a communication plan covering your overall strategy to deal with the problem and outlining your ideas for implementing it. Conclude your communication plan with a statement defending it.

ASSIGNMENT 5

Assume that you did not discuss the proposal with White, either before or during the committee meeting. Since the original meeting three months ago at which she asked for members' comments, the proposal has never appeared on the agenda, never even been mentioned at a meeting. Your department members, Coe and Quigley, are getting concerned about the proposal because there is a rumor that White might move up into the central administration. They would like to see the mandatory development program guidelines written up and approved before a new chief comes in. Write a memo to White or prepare a set of notes to discuss the issue with her in an interview.

APPENDIX A

Proposed Guidelines for Mandatory Development Programs

University General Hospital of the City of New York

Continuing Educational Services for Nursing

Mandatory Development Programs

I. Policy/Procedure Purpose and Mechanisms
   University General Hospital's Nursing staff shall
   meet mandatory training education program
   requirements. Mandatory Development Programs are
   required for nurses by Regulatory agencies.
   Programs may also be mandated for:
   A) Entry into practice (to include role changes).
   B) Reinforcement of emergency and safety skills and
      knowledge on an annual basis.
   C) Changes in nursing practice.
   Listing of mandatory programs and specific nursing
   personnel who must attend will be located in the
   Central Services for Nursing Development Nursing
   Manual under "Mandatory Programs."

II. Policy Statement
   A) Mandatory program objectives and methods for
      meeting these objectives will be stated within
      each program in the CSND Nursing Manual.
   B) Mandatory training/educational programs are
      under the directive of Central Services for
      Nursing Development. Unit programs may be
      planned if all of the following criteria are
      met:
      1) Individual program objectives are compatible
         with mandatory program objectives.
      2) Program objectives are reviewed by CSND at
         least 3 weeks prior to the session.

(continued)

APPENDIX A—*continued*

—2—

   3) The centralized mandatory program computer
    number must be assigned to the program.
  C) Head Nurses are responsible for insurance of
   compliance with this policy.
  D) Successful completion of the individual's
   computerized educational record.
  E) In specific circumstances, individuals who are
   physically unable to achieve the required
   competencies may be granted a waiver of a
   particular program. Waiver approvals must be
   signed by the Head Nurse and the Directors of
   Nursing.
  F) Any employee who does not meet the requirements
   of mandatory training programs is subject to
   disciplinary action up to and including
   dismissal.

III. Procedure
  A) CSND and/or units meeting policy requirements:
   1) Provides training opportunities.
   2) Maintains computerized records on each
    individual.
  B) Head Nurse
   Enforces compliance with the standards set forth
   in this policy.
  C) Nursing Staff
   Responsible for meeting mandatory program
   objectives.

APPENDIX B

Format Requirements

Format Requirements
Administrative Policy and Procedures

Some occasions will require answering all of the sections. For example:

If there is no policy established or referenced by a proposed procedure, indicate "none" under *Policy Statement* and *Policy Standards*.

If there is no procedure involved with the proposed policy, indicate "none" under *Procedure*.

I. *POLICY STATEMENT/PROCEDURE*

A concise statement of the Unit's position on the involved objective, with a short explanation of the applications of the policy and/or procedure.

II. *DEFINITIONS*

Specification of what is meant by words or phrases in the policy which otherwise would be open to various interpretations.

III. *POLICY STANDARDS*

Expansion upon the policy statement and specification of the principal measures for accomplishing a Hospital objective.

IV. *PROCEDURE*

Specification in detail of the actions, in sequence, for accomplishing the Unit's position on the involved objective. Where applicable, the position responsible and the timing for accomplishment of each action shall be indicated. The following format shall be used:

Position Responsible[5]   *Action*[6]

---

[5] The "Position Responsible" is the job title for each position involved in implementing the policy/procedure.

[6] The "Action" covers the responsibilities of the job holder, those actions necessary to effect the policy/procedure.

V. *REFERENCES*

Organizational principles, Hospital policies and procedures, laws, professional standards, regulatory agency standards, which are the basis for and/or caused the policy and procedures to be developed.

Identification of the policy and/or procedure author, including position and/or department.

APPENDIX C

"Staff Development Activities" Section of the "Administrative Manual"

IV. *PROCEDURE*

Responsible Person	*Action*
Nursing staff member	1. Meets on-going mandatory program requirements on a regular basis.
	2. Attends programs which meet professional continued learning/growth needs.
	3. Attends programs identified by supervisor as important for improved/enhanced job performance.
	4. Attends programs identified by supervisor as necessary for implemention of new programs or procedures.
	5. Completes staff development attendance records.
Supervisor	1. Assists nursing staff to attend *mandatory* programs by granting Business Time.
	2. Assists nursing staff in identifying professional continued learning/growth needs on Performance Plan.

3. Identifies areas where staff development programs would improve/enhance job performance.
4. Identifies programs where attendance is necessary for implementation of new programs/procedures.
5. Enforces compliance with the standards set forth in this policy.

Educational Coordinator/Educational Nurse Specialist

1. Provides information to staff regarding upcoming staff development/continuing education programs.
2. Plans/coordinates staff development programs to meet unit/department needs.
3. Provides appropriate program attendance records for staff to complete.

Central Services for Nursing Development

1. Provides mandatory staff development programs.
2. Provides educational programs to meet educational/professional development needs.

Personnel and Human Services Division

1. Provides annual computerized Educational Records of all nursing staff members' attendance at staff development programs for their personnel files.

Evaluating a Cost Proposal for EMI Suppression: A Government Contract Case

Elizabeth L. Malone with
Barbara Couture and Jone Rymer Goldstein

In your last semester before graduation at your university's College of Technology and Engineering, you follow your uncle's suggestion to apply for a job where he works, in the Systems and Engineering Branch of a federal Contract Administration Services Office. His office is part of the Defense Logistics Agency, which handles all aspects of administering contracts for the U.S. military departments.

In your job interview you can tell that the chief of the branch is interested in you, and you are interested in what he has to say. He explains parts of the contract administration process which will involve you: When companies submit cost proposals for contract bids or as a result of changes in a contract, this office evaluates the proposals. A cost analyst visits the contractor's plant and looks at the record books, systems, and bids from subcontractors. Then the government analyst recommends to the contracting officer which costs to accept, which to disallow, and which to try to negotiate downward. In this process, the contracting officer (CO) and the cost analyst often need the expertise of an engineer to evaluate technical aspects of a cost proposal. The usual job of the engineer in the Systems and Engineering Branch is to answer two questions:

1. Is the material that the contractor wants to use "reasonable and allocable"?[1]
2. Are the labor hours allotted "reasonable and allocable"?

---

[1] "Contract Cost Principles and Procedures," a section of the *Defense Acquisition Regulation*, defines the terms:

"15–201.3(a) A cost is reasonable if, in its nature or amount, it does not exceed

The engineer does not concern himself with costs per se; he submits his report to the cost analyst, who translates the material and labor hours into dollars and evaluates prices and rates.

The job sounds good, and when it is offered, you accept and start just a week after graduation. The first few months on the job go well, and you begin to be enthusiastic about the work. You like going out to company plants, usually with a cost analyst (your favorite is Joe Coughlin, a happy-go-lucky sort of guy); you like the feeling that many dollar decisions are influenced by your opinions; you like talking frankly about the issues with your uncle.

One day you get a formal request for assistance from Joe Coughlin in a case involving electromagnetic interference (EMI) suppression on 1¼-ton trucks made by U.S. Motors. After glancing at the proposal, you call Joe.

"What's the deal on this proposal, Joe?"

"Well, do you know about this contract, uh—let's see, number PRA603–84–C–0098?" Joe asks, checking his notes.

"I know U.S. Motors deliberately bid low to get the contract because the company needed the business so badly," you reply.

"That's right," Joe says. "Those 44,000 trucks on the contract will be a big boost to the company for three or four years. But now every time the government decides to change the requirements and U.S. Motors gives us a cost proposal to make the change, the CO, Georgia Millian, wants us to take a close look to be sure U.S. Motors isn't trying to make a little extra profit on the contract changes. After all, they can't be making much on the main bid, so they may try to make a high profit on a change."

"So Georgia thinks we'll find something wrong with it?" you ask.

"Well, let's just say that she wants us to be able to justify our evaluations, especially if we approve the proposed costs."

"Okay. Give me a few days to study the proposal. I could go on a plant visit with you next Tuesday or Wednesday," you offer.

"Good," says Joe, "because I already made the appointment for Tuesday. I'll get a government car."

---

that which would be incurred by an ordinarily prudent person in the conduct of competitive business. . . .

"15–201.4   A cost is allocable if it is assignable or chargeable to one or more cost objectives . . . in accordance with the relative benefits received or other equitable relationship."

The next day you clear everything off your desk so that you can immerse yourself in the proposal. You also look at a copy of the contract modification, in which the government directs U.S. Motors to make the changes. Buried in contractual "witnesseth that's" and "whereas's," the gist of the modification is that the government wants 11,893 trucks to meet the EMI characteristics specified in Notice 4, MIL–STD–461A, RE05 and CE07. In other words, the government wants the engines of these vehicles quiet enough so that radio equipment can be installed and used with no interference from engine vibrations or noise. Fine. The company has already done that; the initial vehicles have been accepted by the government as meeting the specifications. U.S. Motors has waited until the work was completed and the money spent before turning in a cost proposal. Now the question is whether the amount U.S. Motors spent, $3,119,296.04, represents costs that are "reasonable and allocable."

The first step in the process is to review the proposal yourself, comparing the company's times with generally accepted standards in the industry[2] and formulating questions you need to ask. The U.S. Motors proposal contains five categories that you have been asked to analyze: parts (a bill of materials), production time (time added to substitute parts for standard parts), tooling, engineering labor (to make design changes and to test the EMI levels), and publications (to change the owner's manual because of the changed parts).

You decide that a precedent case would help you analyze this one, so you dig out a similar EMI-suppression case from several years ago and compare the older bill of materials with the current one from U.S. Motors. Most of the changes result in shielded wires or parts. Considering the changes in truck engines in the last decade, you decide that, as far as your desk review is concerned, the current bill of materials looks all right.

The next category is added production time. The contractor proposes 36.98 minutes extra production time per vehicle, including

---

[2] The government requires that the contractor show some documentation to back up proposed times—either standards developed by the company or published, industry-wide standards. The government has not itself developed standards for production times, but it does have a reference manual for engineering tasks. The manual, *Technical Analysis of a Cost Proposal* (TACP), gives a range of hours for specific tasks; the engineer determines how complex the task is in order to judge whether the contractor's proposed time is reasonable.

26.15 for modifications to the engine and 10.83 for truck modification. You feel that three or four of the truck-modification operations have high time allotments and make a note to check on them. The rest of the times fall within industry-wide standards, but you must verify that all times fall within company standards, too, since the latter may be different.

Tooling costs also seem to be routine. If the parts listed are necessary, the tooling certainly is: a die mold, coil-bracket tooling, a multiple-cavity mold with a rotor assembly, and a few minor items. No problems there, you think.

Turning to the next part, however, you see where the major problem might be—engineering labor. The company is claiming 1,465 hours of engineering department labor and 4,225 hours in testing and laboratory work. Both of these look high to you, especially when you compare them to the earlier case, which itemizes about half that number of hours. Of course, the engineering labor category represents the company's best chance of stretching the figures; materials and production times are pretty closely controlled, but who is to say for sure how long the testing actually took? Furthermore, U.S. Motors has provided no backup in the proposal itself; all that the proposal contains is a list of 16 tasks and the times. (See Table 1.)

Well, you may have found your can of worms. You hope that U.S. Motors will be happy to show you all the backup data you need for their claimed hours: the engineering logs, the tests results, the reports, and so on.

The last category, publications, itemizes three pages revised in the truck-owner's manual at five hours per page. Your standards for tech manual publication show a range of five to nine hours, so this time looks pretty good. You will just have to see about the engineering labor on Tuesday.

When you and Joe arrive at U.S. Motors, Paul Fisher, the contracts manager assigned to this government contract, is there to greet you. He says he is a very busy man, but he has cleared his calendar for today to show you around to get any information you need. He is smiling during these introductory remarks, but both you and Joe get the point: do not take any longer than one day.

You and Joe part company; Joe goes off to the Purchasing Department to look at vendor quotations; you go to Design Engineering, then to Production Planning. You spend the morning looking at drawings for various part changes, department standards for production times, and tooling requirements and requisitions. For some reason

TABLE 1.   Proposed Engineering Hours, U.S. Motors

Engineering Department Labor

Body & Electrical design and engineering (five subtasks)	1,115 hours
Body & Electrical release	49 hours
Chassis Engineering	193 hours
Chassis release	34 hours
Graphics	74 hours

Testing and Laboratory Labor

Testing	2,089.5 hours
Data evaluation and analysis	800 hours
Laboratory time	500 hours
Vendor interface	300 hours
Certification tests	120 hours
Lost time	100 hours
Report writing	80 hours
Calibration	72.5 hours
Maintenance	60 hours
Devising of test procedures	53 hours
Status review meetings	50 hours
Total	5,690 hours

one set of drawings is not available, and you still think three production times are high. But basically you have seen the information which supports the materials and times specified on U.S. Motors' proposal.

You go to lunch with Joe, who is also having a reasonably successful time. In general, both of you feel that people are cooperating with you as well as they can and that most of the data to verify the proposal's figures are in place.

Next comes engineering labor. Fisher takes you up two floors to meet Mark Liddy, an engineer who has collected the work orders on this contract. You study the work orders, and they agree in every respect with the cost proposal. Since it is not your business to look into U.S. Motors' time-collection system (which is Joe's responsibility), you decide to assume that the hours were actually booked to this contract, that is, that the hours are "allocable." Now you only need to find out what U.S. Motors did with that time, that is, whether the hours are "reasonable." You explain to Liddy that you need to see evidence of what the engineers accomplished.

"I don't understand," he says, seemingly puzzled. "The engineers logged these times, and they were approved by the department heads. That's proof enough."

"Well, no—let me give you an example," you reply, trying to stifle your irritation. "The proposal lists 500 hours for lab time. I need to know what tasks your people performed during those 500 hours, maybe by talking to them but certainly by seeing the written documents that resulted from what they did. If a lab experiment was run, say, I'd expect that I could see the lab report."

You are being cordial, but you want to take a strong position. You figure Liddy will have to give in, at least partially; he and you both know that the written backup should exist and that obviously the government wants to know what actual work it might pay for. So you persist. And finally Liddy consents to introduce you to some department heads, and you and he go to the Body & Electrical Department in Design Engineering.

From Chris Magnusson in Body & Electrical you get a look at drawing and configuration changes. He confirms the task breakdown: 500 hours to prepare engineering drawings, 50 hours of seven configuration changes, 120 hours to design drawing changes, 250 hours for vendor coordination, and 195 hours to engineer six changes. However, he politely refuses to separate tasks into parts, provide approximations of time spent on each task, or let you talk to the engineers whose logs you had hoped to see.

"You know how it is," he says, gesturing vaguely. "Some things you think are going to take a long time turn out well the first time, and vice versa. Average times really don't mean anything. On the one hand, you've seen the hours that were logged, 1,115. On the other, I've shown you the products of the hours we worked. Those engineers are working on different projects now; they wouldn't remember a project they finished six months ago, and digging in those logs is like trying to make sense out of hen scratchings."

Magnusson will not budge from his position on the first item on the engineering hours list, but he does explain the items listed as release function (49 for Body & Electrical, 34 for Chassis): this is time used to translate all part changes and design changes to computer language and to communicate the changes and status to the entire company. You feel that the Body & Electrical release time is certainly justified, but you wonder aloud about the Chassis time, since that department did not originate any changes. In response, Magnusson takes you to the Chassis Engineering Department and leaves you with Andy Jacobson.

All Jacobson can offer in support of the release time and the other 193 hours on the proposal for chassis engineering is that his department made sure no changes were necessary. He enumerates generalized tasks, such as making sure the engine assembly would go under the hood and "some" board layout. He, too, remains cordial but firm; he is not going to dig out any hard data to show you. He says it is not part of his job to give information to company outsiders.

By this time you really begin to wonder. These people seem to have all agreed that they are not going to cooperate. But each one has a different reason. You wonder what the real one is. You are getting tired of being polite, but you know what you are supposed to do in a situation like this: clarify the areas that need more supporting information and report deficiencies to Joe and through him to the CO, who is supposed to convince the company to produce the necessary information.

The rest of the engineering hours were booked at the Test Track: 2,089.5 hours to measure electromagnetic radiation from trucks, 2,135.5 hours in support work. Total hours on the submitted proposal are 4,225, which represents a substantial amount of money. You tell Fisher you would like to visit the Test Track; first he hesitates, but then agrees. He makes an appointment with Art Forney, Assistant Head of Testing, for the next day.

You meet Joe to drive back to the office. "I wish these days in the field were the lazy, pleasant times everyone else seems to think they are," you grumble. "And tomorrow might very well be worse."

"I can't complain," says Joe. "There was no way we could oblige Fisher and finish up today, but I'll probably finish up tomorrow by talking to him about overhead and profit. By the way, the time collection system looks bona fide to me."

"Terrific," you say gloomily. "So if I can't accept the hours, I'll be way out on a limb. They've spent the money and booked the hours. It'll just be a suspicion on my part that they shouldn't have had to use all that time."

At the Test Track the next day, you get about the same reaction you had gotten from Liddy, Magnusson, and Jacobson. Same glib oral explanations, a little valuable information—and almost no hard data to back up the proposed hours. Art Forney is especially good at this game, being cordial but evasive for hours on end. At the close of the day you look over your notes. You have written down U.S. Motor's description of the tasks performed, your description of the data you have seen, and what you need to follow up on. As you go through what you wrote, you underline those items with insufficient backup. (See Figure 1.) As you leave you tell Forney that you or the CO will probably be in touch with him. He appears neither surprised nor worried, so you figure he must have the company's support for his non-cooperation.

Back at the office the next day, you decide to discuss this case with your uncle. "I figure I've got to ask for help in getting more information," you tell him, "but I don't want to ask for any more than I have to. The testing and data evaluation, for instance: I guess I can do the divisions into time per sheet myself and see if the average is within standards. Let's see, that's 1.6 hours per sheet for testing, about 0.7 hours per sheet for evaluation. That's a little less than was allowed in that older case and certainly within the current standards. And some of the rest of this stuff I think I can accept without documentation, stuff like the calibration time and the lost time. The lab time, though, *that* I can't accept at all. Even if U.S. Motors does come up with something to support that amount of time, it shouldn't be engineering time; you can bet their engineers weren't out there gassing up trucks! Vendor interface, again, looks suspicious to me; the parts are standard, and they wouldn't show me any files of correspondence to show special efforts were required. I suppose they wrote reports, but why wouldn't they show them to me? Why wouldn't they show me maintenance documentation or test procedures? I don't understand what's going on!"

"Well, companies can have several reasons for not cooperating with us," says your uncle. "First, U.S. Motors has never before had to give out any more information than what goes on a bid—just the bottom line price and a few external details. Second, since truck manufacturers are so competitive, U.S. Motors is naturally leery of letting anyone dig into how they work; some other truck maker might find out about it, too. Third, the company doesn't want to be bothered. Now, all of these are understandable reasons for not letting us see all the info we need. But you've got to consider other possibilities, too . . ."

You finish for him, ". . . that either their engineers just plain took too long doing the job, or their record keeping is sloppy, or they're deliberately padding the record, which means we shouldn't be paying all they're asking for."

Testing:	Saw 2 books of data sheets from semiautomatic measuring equipment—supposed to be 1250 sheets. Each sheet showed field intensities in range specified by MIL–STD for radiated & conducted emissions. From each sheet 2 manual antenna changes were made: no time per sheet given.
Data evaluation analysis:	Include data sheets above; Time per sheet?
Lab time:	Described as maintenance of vehicles, e.g., gassing, checking oil. No support—trip records, mileage, etc. Note: why is this called engineering time?
Vendor interface:	Searches for vendors (why not regular vendors, who certainly make such parts?) for 12 items. 2 of 12 produced by U.S. Motors. 2/3 of time spent with one vendor. Says getting parts was "sizable task."
Certification tests:	Final measurements on radiated and conducted emissions; saw reports & curves: looks good.
Lost time:	Test program halted because of weather, maintenance, etc., equipment failure. No maintenance or other records.
Report writing:	Produced 3 reports w/ composite curves; none shown.
Calibration:	of radiation measuring equipment and/or frequencies with 2ndary standard. Done daily ("quickly") & periodically (1/2 hr.).

Figure 1.   Notes from Visit to U.S. Motors

Maintenance:	Maintained test equipment, including 3 antennas & 4 coaxial cables. No maintenance records shown.
Test procedures:	No written procedures shown.
Meetings:	Prep time and meetings, groups of 3–10. No meeting minutes or documentation for action related to project.

Figure 1, *continued*

"Right," nods your uncle. "Now, keep calm and just write down what info you need and from what departments. Since you got your assignment from Joe, write to him and send a copy to the CO. And better ask for an extension on the report deadline; you won't get it out by next week."

After going over your notes again, you decide to ask for further data from Design Engineering (breakdown of time into particular tasks from Body & Electrical and from Chassis) and the Test Track (support for tasks under lab time, vendor interface, report writing, maintenance, test procedures, and meetings). You also decide to ask Joe for a two-week extension on the deadline for your report.

ASSIGNMENT 1

Write a memo to Joe Coughlin, Cost Analyst. Send a copy to Georgia Millian, Contracting Officer. Your title is Engineering Analyst in the Systems and Engineering Branch, Contract Administration Services.

Two days later Georgia Millian sends you a copy of her letter to Fisher at U.S. Motors, mailed right after she read yours to Joe; in the letter she asks (almost verbatim) for what you requested and also for some information Joe needs. Not long after, you get a call from her.

"We're in a fix," she tells you frankly, "and I need as much help from you as I can get. The money that's set aside for this change order has to be written into the contract in two weeks, or it goes back into the general appropriations fund and we'll have to ask for it all over again. It could take a year or more to get it back, and U.S. Motors has already completed the work a good four months ago. The company expects a payment, and we should pay. Now, none of this is our fault, but . . . we need to negotiate this change order next week."

"Meaning there's no chance of getting any extra data," you say.

"I'm sorry," she replies. "Really, I don't think there's much chance anyway, no matter how much time we have. I talked to Paul Fisher today; he told me U.S. Motors isn't willing to have us dig any deeper than we have. The company's worried about information leaks to its competitors. I realize that your main troubles center on engineering hours. I know you can't write a full-blown report by three days from now—but would you write up what you can about the engineering hours? This would be a preparatory report; you'll still have to write a full report in a couple of weeks, especially if we don't negotiate a price next week. But you'd be able to use this report as the basis for the final one. Meanwhile, Joe can use it to write the preliminary cost analysis I've asked him to write for next week."

"So you want me to detail my judgments just on engineering hours, *not* on parts, production time, tooling, or publications?" you ask.

"That's right," replies Millian. "At this point I don't want you to waste your energies on stuff we can accept. Just give me what you have on the engineering hours."

"You know," you state frankly, "without the backup information, I'm on pretty shaky ground in a couple of areas. Some of my report will be just educated guesses."

"Well," she responds, "if U.S. Motors hasn't given you data and you can't make an independent estimate, just state that the hours for that particular task aren't allowable because they haven't been supported; we'll try to deal with that in the negotiating session. We may be able to use that as a lever to get more information. By the way, you should plan to attend the negotiation next week. I'd like you to lead off with a statement summarizing your findings."

You reluctantly agree to both requests and hang up. Then you turn to your desk and go through your notes a third time. You look to see what you can estimate from the standards and from what you know about the complexity of the work. You finally come up with a sketch plan of the numbers of hours you can accept versus U.S. Motors' pro-

TABLE 2.   Supported Hours versus U.S. Motors' Proposed Hours

Task Description and Rationale for Nonacceptance	Supported Hours	Proposed Hours
Body & Electrical (0.434 of proposed hours supported)		
Engineering drawings (TACP* guide)	184	500
Seven configuration changes (4 hours each)	28	50
Design drawing changes (4 @ 20 hours)	80	120
Vendor coordination	120	250
Engineering of six changes (noncomplex; 8–40 is standard, recommend 12 hours each)	72	195
Body & Electrical release	49	49
Chassis & Chassis release (since same type work as body & electrical, use same ratio of 0.434)	98.5	227
Graphics	74	74
Testing	2,089.5	2,089.5
Data evaluation & analysis	800	800
Laboratory time (no support, should not be engineering tasks)	0	500
Vendor interface (noncomplex task, parts readily available, no documentation)	0	300
Certification tests	120	120
Lost time (2.6% of supported hours—well within standards)	100	100
Report writing (3 @ 15 hours; none shown)	45	80
Calibration	72.5	72.5
Maintenance (necessary task, consider amount of test time which generated 1,250 data sheets)	60	60
Test procedures (no documentation, standard semiautomatic process)	0	53
Meetings (no objective evidence of productivity)	0	50
Totals	3,992.5	5,690

* Technical analysis of a cost proposal

posed hours. (See Table 2, page 271.) You cannot use your table as it is. It is little more than notes, and you have jotted down your judgments just for yourself. However, you hope you can use it as a starting place for the report Millian wants.

You look at your work. You are not happy. Too many "soft" spots, too many unknowns. You think to yourself that the standards are so flexible they could almost justify anything. Look at the one for engineering changes! But in the absence of cooperation and information from U.S. Motors, this is the best you can do.

As you look at the figures, though, you begin to think of them another way. "Almost 1,700 hours I'm questioning," you realize. "That's almost a year's salary for some engineer—and the overhead will more than double that figure. Negotiating's going to be tough—but I'm going to hang in there."

ASSIGNMENT 2

Write a report to Joe Coughlin, Cost Analyst, and send a copy to Georgia Millian, Contracting Officer. Your branch uses a strict format for reports to cost analysts: Part 1 is a Statement of Work, background and identification of the proposal, and any specific technical questions that were answered. Part 2 is called the Extent of Coordination and Examination, that is, what the engineer did in order to answer the technical questions. Part 3 contains Findings, and Part 4 consists of Conclusions and Recommendations which can be used by both the analyst and the CO.

ASSIGNMENT 3

Prepare an oral presentation for the negotiation session. Your audience will include Georgia Millian, Contracting Officer; Joe Coughlin, Cost Analyst; Paul Fisher, Contracts Manager at U.S. Motors; and probably at least one, possibly all, of the engineers you talked to at U.S. Motors. You need to clarify what costs you cannot currently accept as "reasonable," why the government cannot accept them, and what U.S. Motors should provide as backup. Your presentation will serve as a starting point for the negotiation and as an attempt to enlist cooperation from U.S. Motors' representatives.

Controlling Pollution: The Great Eastern Oil Refinery Case

Part 1

"We're the conscience of the refinery" is the slogan of your boss, the manager of Technical Services at the Cleveland refinery of the Great Eastern Oil Corporation. Although considered a bit self-righteous even by you and the other employees in Tech Services, Larry Koegel vigorously pursues his mission: making Great Eastern run as well as possible, not only for the corporation's benefit, but for the good of the community as well.

"Everyone else around here just wants to run the plant without causing any problems," Koegel frequently proclaims to you and your co-workers. "Our job as troubleshooters means we actively *look* to find things going wrong. We don't wait for them to happen."

"Everyone else" around the Cleveland refinery means the whole plant management team, a group of "good old boys" (excepting Koegel, of course, and a couple of other young fellows) who meet weekly to make all decisions about running the plant together. In these meetings, Earl Sampson, the plant manager and a 30-year veteran at Great Eastern, sits and listens—saying little, waiting to hear out his team so he can rule by consensus. Among his cohorts are the operations manager, Gordon Borowski, a shy old-timer who says even less than his boss; the product control manager, Billy-Jo White, who in Koegel's pet phrase "goes with the flow"; and the maintenance department manager, Fred LaRue. Each of these men in his own quiet way vigorously protects his own turf and pushes for his own priorities. Last, but most certainly not least, there is the lab manager,[1] Hank Zoller, whose volubility contrasts sharply with the senior members of the

---

[1] The Analytical Laboratory is a unit in the Product Control Department that is concerned with matters affecting product quality.

team.[2] Zoller enjoys bellowing his views, particularly his complaints about the lab's lack of automated equipment, the heavy work load demanded of his 30 staffers, and his contempt for the chief of Technical Services (Koegel), who, Zoller likes to say, "acts like he's out trying to save the world."

Pollution control, one of Koegel's major responsibilities as head of Technical Services, is only partly the cause of his reputation with Zoller. As lab chief, Zoller must come up with the support services Koegel requires for many of his unit's projects; not surprisingly, the two men's mutual hostility has grown through several years of problems where Koegel simply wanted more out of Zoller's staff than the lab chief was willing to provide. Your part as an associate refining engineer casts you as an assistant to Koegel in his pollution control efforts; as a result, you are not exactly popular with Zoller either. Your job is to keep the pollution control devices running well enough so that the plant's stack emissions will not offend the nearby residents in Mendota Heights. Many local citizens seem to know that if they find the smell offensive from Great Eastern's chimneys, all they have to do is telephone the county Air Pollution Control Commission. Thus you are constantly vigilant to any pollution problems, even slight matters which might go unheeded if your plant were located in the middle of a cornfield.

Great Eastern Oil has more than the good will of Cleveland's citizens at heart in controlling its emissions, of course. Every time some inhabitant of the Mendota Heights area calls the Control Commission to complain about Great Eastern's stacks, the regulatory agency issues a written confirmation of the complaint and delivers it to Koegel. If the pollution is not brought under control right away, the commission levies fines of $250 per day; if the condition continues for any length of time, they eventually issue a citation against the company. If necessary, they can jail the plant manager for extended noncompliance.

Worse than fines, however, is the possibility of the corporation coming under formal review by the Control Commission if the commissioners judge that they have received too many complaints about your firm, even fairly minor ones. Because regulatory review can mean much trouble and expense, Great Eastern obviously tries hard to avoid it. In a review, the county Control Commission can check over all your company records and fine you. They can also require you to place monitors on your equipment if their inspectors suspect your records

---

[2] All of the managers, including the Technical Services head, Larry Koegel, are on the same level (except for Zoller of the Analytical Lab).

are faulty, or they can direct you to change company procedures, following their dictates. If you do not comply, they can even seek a court-decreed closure of your plant. In short, the negative repercussions from citizens' complaints can be great.

Protecting Great Eastern against the damages which can be caused by citizen complaints is thus a high priority for Tech Services—top priority, in fact, for you. First, you must prevent large fluctuations in stack emissions, thus keeping the number of complaints down to a minimum, and second, you must correct any problems that do occur, and do so as quickly as possible.

Lately things have not been going so well in your domain. Despite your best efforts, the plant has received numerous official complaints about the stack emissions. You know the cause of the bad odors lies in the sulfur recovery unit (SRU) and the tail-gas treater/absorber unit. These units clean up the sulfur in the amine acid gas coming out of the refinery process before it flows out of the stack as an effluent.[3] (See Appendix A.) Inevitable fluctuations in the operation of the hydrodesulfurization unit[4] (which feeds the amine acid gas into the cleanup system) cause variations in the concentration and rate of flow of the gas into the SRU and absorber units. If these swings in the amine-gas feed are not immediately balanced by the flow of air into the line, the treater/absorber unit overloads, belching out noxious fumes and orange smoke from the incinerator stack.[5] Unfortunately,

---

[3] The sulfur recovery unit (SRU) removes approximately 96% of the sulfur in the amine acid gas coming from the plant. Then the tail-gas treater/absorber unit recycles the remaining 4% of the sulfur, sending it back to the front of the cleanup process.

[4] The hydrodesulfurizer is a licensed process for sulfur removal from "gas oil" ($R-S-R + 2H_2 \rightarrow RH + RH + H_2S$).

[5] The incinerator stack, 199.5 ft tall, has a twofold purpose: (1) it heats and disperses the off gas (the final environmental discharge), and (2) it acts as a relief valve for the entire process. Any toxic and nauseous H_2S remaining in the off gas is oxidized to less toxic and nauseous SO_2. High SO_2 concentrations result in visually detectable plumes. The overall SRU process works as follows: The acid gas (H_2S) is burned with air, giving elemental sulfur and water vapor. To achieve maximum conversion of the acid gas, the ratio of H_2S (hydrogen sulfide) to SO_2 (sulfur dioxide) should be 2 to 1. The ratio of acid gas to air must be set so that only $\frac{1}{3}$ of the H_2S oxidizes to SO_2. The SO_2 then reacts with the remaining H_2S to give elemental sulfur. Therefore, slight changes in either the H_2S concentration or the flow rate of the amine acid gas require resetting the air flow. The equations describing these reactions are as follows:

$$\text{Step 1} \quad H_2S + \tfrac{3}{2}O_2 \rightarrow SO_2 + H_2O$$
$$\text{Step 2} \quad \underline{2H_2S + SO_2 \rightarrow 3S + 2H_2O}$$
$$\text{Overall} \quad 3H_2S + \tfrac{3}{2}O_2 \rightarrow 3S + 3H_2O$$

the current sampling system, dictated by Technical Services and run by Zoller's lab crew, just cannot control these swings adequately—no matter what you do.

Today, Monday, your supervisor, Larry Koegel, receives official notification of another citizen complaint submitted to the Control Commission. This time it is a problem that developed over the weekend, and one that you are all too well aware of. In fact, you and your sidekick in Tech Services, Jim Pagley, were both called in on Saturday evening. Despite your best efforts in the plant, however, the orange smoke is still pouring out now, and the odor is bad downwind from the plant.

However, the problem is worse than just another official complaint. While talking with the commission official this morning, Koegel and the corporation were put on notice. The commissioners are becoming concerned at the frequency of complaints about the emission problems from Great Eastern's stacks and are considering more drastic measures. The official, Harrison Brown, hinted that they might mandate a review of the refinery, and pointedly suggested that the company put an SO_2 monitor on the incinerator stack—a suggestion that Koegel notes could quickly become an official order. Since the monitor would cost Great Eastern in excess of $40,000, plus absolutely unthinkable maintenance costs every year, Koegel is more than eager to figure out some better way to prevent the frequent fluctuations. He assigns you the task of coming up with a plan to present to management, ". . . something brilliant to bring the problem under control," he says, "and get the Control Commission off our backs."

By later in the afternoon on Monday, you and Jim Pagley solve the immediate pollution problem by tinkering with the system, and you celebrate the disappearance of the vile smoke and odor with a pizza after work. Your relief is short-lived, however, because the next morning you must begin reviewing possibilities to correct this problem once and for all, so that Great Eastern will not periodically be forced to revert to Band-Aid treatments.

If only the automatic analyzers would work as they are supposed to, checking the system continuously, you think to yourself. But getting them to do that is like a pipe dream; practically no plant has them functioning reliably. You surely are not going to start working on them as a practical solution. Instead, you decide to focus your efforts on the current monitoring system in which the laboratory personnel measure the tail gas three times per day and the absorber off gas only once. (Refer to Appendix A.) Obviously fluctuations in the refining process at any time other than those four checkpoints in a 24-hour period will cause problems. The imbalance will take as long as a half hour, or even more, to show up downstream in the system before the operations people can correct it by adjusting the air flow. Simply put, you are not getting information often enough so that refinery process deviations can be corrected before they become big pollution problems. The answer seems clear to you: increase the number of measurements so that you can respond to operations changes sooner.

Pulling the daily operating log sheets, you look over the data from measuring the amounts of hydrogen sulfide (H_2S) and sulfur dioxide (SO_2) in the tail gas three times per day and the H_2S in the off gas once each day. The fluctuations are absolutely wild! Whereas the volume percentage of H_2S and SO_2 together in the tail gas should not be more than about 1.75%, it ranges as high as 6.5%.[6] And then there is the H_2S in the off gas. Whereas it should be at about 200 parts per million (ppm), it ranges above an outrageous 6,000 ppm! Shaking your head, you think to yourself that if these numbers do not convince everyone of the necessity to monitor the system more often, nothing on the wide earth will. Straightaway you copy the data showing the wide ranges in the off-gas samples for November and the tail-gas samples for the first three weeks of December as good representations of what is going on. (See Tables 1 and 2.)

Then you sit down with a can of soda and the figures, trying to judge how many samples per day will really help the situation, what monitoring might help convince the regulatory board, and what you can realistically hope to get out of management. After sketching out some plans, including some clever ways you could present all this data to Mr. Sampson and crew, you drop by Koegel's desk to outline your ideas. You begin by announcing that in your opinion the most important item is to increase the lab measurements of the H_2S in the off gas. You believe that the checks should be raised from one per day to approximately six. One measurement every four hours would allow sufficient feedback to the process operator about any problems in either the SRU or the treater/absorber so that he could make adjustments in the air flow into the system before things get out of hand. Koegel nods and you continue with your plans. The most important

---

[6] When the unit is not running well, the concentration of either the H_2S or the SO_2 is very large. Therefore, if the volume percentage of the sum of H_2S and SO_2 is great (anything above 1.75%), it indicates an off-specification process.

TABLE 1. H_2S in Off Gas as a Function of Throughput
(Data copied from daily operation log sheets)

Date	Units Acid Gas Flow to Sulfur Recovery Unit*	H_2S in Off Gas (ppm)
11–1	8.0	40
11–2	8.6	352
11–3	6.4	23
11–4	8.3	1,681
11–5	5.1	430
11–6	8.4	12
11–7	8.3	11
11–8	7.3	53
11–9	6.3	6,400
11–10	6.4	1,410
11–11	7.3	6,400
11–12	7.8	2,386
11–13	7.3	100
11–14	6.8	95
11–15	5.0	120
11–16	5.6	38
11–17	8.8	3,600
11–18	6.7	295
11–19	8.4	55
11–20	9.1	100
11–21	9.0	95
11–22	8.8	250
11–23	8.9	84
11–24	8.2	230
11–25	8.3	95
11–26	8.2	30
11–27	8.2	35
11–28	7.6	210
11–29	7.8	80
11–30	7.9	40

* Flow is measured on a 0–10 linear scale.

TABLE 2. Total H₂S and SO₂ in Tail Gas as a Function of Throughput

(Data copied from daily operation log sheets)

Date	Units Acid-Gas Flow to Sulfur Recovery Unit*	% H₂S (volume)	% SO₂ (volume)
December 1†	7.6	4.13	0.09
	6.4	0.58	0.20
	9.1	0.15	0.71
December 2	10.1	0.30	0.25
	10.0	0.30	0.25
	7.0	0.14	0.13
December 3	10.5	0.28	0.18
	9.3	0.15	0.46
	9.5	1.41	0.11
December 4	7.4	1.16	0.16
	8.0	0.29	0.15
	4.8	0.14	0.32
December 5	4.7	0.37	0.11
	10.1	0.90	1.00
	10.2	0.13	0.78
December 6	6.9	0.15	0.63
	10.1	0.30	0.14
	7.9	0.35	0.33
December 7	7.7	0.29	0.25
	9.0	0.33	0.11
	5.7	0.31	0.12
December 8	6.5	0.30	0.21
	9.9	1.39	0.74
	7.1	0.27	0.16
December 9	7.7	0.28	0.23
	7.3	0.69	0.06
	9.6	1.82	0.12
December 10	8.9	0.26	0.19
	10.2	3.66	0.30
	9.0	1.66	0.32
December 11	9.4	2.01	0.09
	6.2	6.25	0.25
	5.9	0.29	0.13
December 12	8.6	0.27	0.23
	7.7	0.36	0.30
	9.5	0.15	0.98
December 13	8.6	3.44	0.10
	6.4	0.28	2.12
	6.8	0.23	0.15

(continued)

TABLE 2, *continued*

Date	Units Acid-Gas Flow to Sulfur Recovery Unit*	% H_2S (volume)	% SO_2 (volume)
December 13 (*cont.*)	6.2	0.29 N.S.‡	0.25
	7.3	0.12	1.89
December 14	7.8	0.18	0.60
	7.3	5.20	0.29
	7.4	2.29	0.07
December 15	8.0	1.81	0.28
	9.0	0.44	0.14
	10.4	0.27	0.25
December 16	9.2	0.23	0.62
	6.4	0.40	0.18
	9.0	0.41	0.12
December 17	8.4	1.76	0.08
	8.9	3.49	0.32
	8.8	0.28	0.08
December 18	8.3	0.16	1.32
	7.4	0.18	0.53
	6.2	1.46	0.11
December 19	6.9	1.74	0.08
	7.8	0.78	0.12
	8.0	1.94	0.09
December 20	5.8	0.75	0.46
	6.3	0.30	0.15
	8.3	0.45	0.18
December 21	8.2	0.28	0.23

* Flow is measured on a 0–10 linear scale.
† Three measurements are made each day.
‡ No sample.

reason for increasing the number of off-gas checks, in your opinion, is that this move might persuade the Control Commission members that they do not need to require Great Eastern to install the SO_2 monitor. This is because you would be checking the off gas for H_2S so frequently that you would be able to correct for any pollution before it became a problem.

This time Koegel smiles in agreement, but then he pauses, and leaning back in his chair says sarcastically, "Sounds good. Just wonderful, in fact. But there's just one little problem. I'm sure that good old Zoller will also think it's wonderful. Why I can just hear him shouting about how it will take his poor, overloaded lab two whole hours per day to measure the off gas six times.[7] How do you expect they will ever get all their other work done? And before you can say anything to justify your proposal, he'll start in complaining again about the off-gas sampling procedure itself. He'll say it's lousy; yah, that's the word he'll use: lousy! They only do it once a day now and it's an impossible procedure and we have the nerve to suggest they do it six times per day. Next he'll demand new equipment to do the job. After all, we can't expect the lab to do all this extra work with their old equipment. Finally, he'll finish us off by announcing that the sampling will do little or nothing to control the problem anyway, so there's no use doing it. Period."

By this time you're laughing out loud at Koegel's attempts to bellow like Zoller, but the impersonation also leaves you somewhat anxious; your boss's words hit pretty close to the mark. No doubt Zoller will fight like a tiger to protect his budget and his staff's work load, and there is no use denying that his influence with the management team is formidable. If nothing else, you know he can simply wear them down. He just hollers away until people agree with him just to get some peace and quiet.

Koegel is not done yet, however. After catching his breath, Koegel says thoughtfully, "Zoller will probably bring up his favorite refrain, namely 'Why haven't we got the automatic analyzers to work right? After all, if they functioned properly we wouldn't need to do this manual sampling at all.'"

"Well, he's certainly right on that score," you admit ruefully.

"You know," Koegel says screwing up his face, "to get back to the issue, Zoller wouldn't accept the six off-gas checks gracefully even if he got new equipment to do the job. In fact, he'll probably rant and rave about how his poor workman has to go out and take a sample from almost 20 feet up in the air, on the platform. Then after they get it analyzed in the lab, and the telewriter sends the results to operations, what happens? Often, *zilch*. Absolutely nothing. The operators are *supposed* to make immediate adjustments in the air flow, but half the time they do absolutely nothing."

"Well," you interpose, "and what are *we* supposed to do about

---

[7] It requires one workman 15 to 20 minutes to make each measurement of the H_2S in the off gas for a total of about two hours labor time per day.

that? True, the operations people often neglect making adjustments, unless they get specific instructions from the foreman, but you'll have to admit that the lab techs are often sloppy and don't send them any information to work with. Frankly, I think that the lab people are the biggest source of the trouble. The sampling system works great if it's done properly, and it'd certainly solve most of the pollution problems if everyone cooperated fully. It seems to me we just have to get Zoller to do the six daily checks of the off gas and get him to do them right and report the info to the plant. After that we can worry about the operators doing their job."

"Okay," Koegel agrees. "But we have to find some way to pressure Zoller to do the extra off-gas analyses. Let's see, hmm. We'll push hard on the leverage the extra checks would give us with the Control Commission.[8] That's probably our only ace. Let's see. We can suggest that the six measurements per day should also provide us with a solid data base. Just in case the SO_2 pollution ever comes under formal review. But we need something else to sew up our case."

"Hey, I've got it," you grin. "I'll bet if we ask Zoller to take extra samples of the sulfur recovery unit tail gas, he would be happy to settle for just the off gas. We can ask him to increase the number of SRU tail-gas checks from three per day to, uh, say, why not—six, same as the off gas. Yah, that's it! It wouldn't be a bad idea at all, and we could certainly justify it easily enough—though I suppose it's not very realistic to ask him to do it, especially if we add on these extra five samples of the off gas per day."

"Boy, you can say that again," Koegel chuckles. "He'd go crazy! After all," Koegel continues in a serious vein, "if we measure the off gas often enough, that will not only tell us whether we have a pollution problem from the stack, but indirectly we'll track the air flow and also the concentration of H_2S and SO_2 at the front of the process. So we can certainly get along without the tail-gas checks."

"In the best of all worlds," you reply, "we should have both the off gas and the tail gas checked regularly. I think we should increase both the tail-gas and the off-gas analyses, and we should stagger them,

---

[8] From the commission's point of view, the off gas is more significant because it is the environmental discharge, whereas the tail gas is an internal stream indicating less than optimum economic operation. From the plant's perspective, high H_2S in the off gas indirectly indicates improper air flow to the front of the sulfur plant, as well as improper discharge into the environment.

so that we would have checks every couple of hours—like 2 A.M. the off gas, 4 A.M. the tail gas, 6 A.M. the off gas again, and so on. That's really the best plan, and the one the refinery should have. It would keep the operators honest on the off shift so that they'd make adjustments immediately instead of waiting until several hours later. But I admit that even if it's a good idea, it will absolutely blow Zoller's mind. What do you think? Will he accept the extra samplings of the off gas? That is, if we request the tail gas too but then back down in the meeting and accept just the off gas?"

Now it's Koegel's turn to laugh. "You're a dreamer. Everyone else may buy that, thinking it sounds like a good compromise. But Zoller isn't going to roll over dead just because we suddenly appear somewhat more reasonable face-to-face with him in the meeting than we sound in the written report."

"Well, the truth of the matter is that as long as the automatic analyzers don't work satisfactorily . . ."

"And who knows if they ever will work," Koegel interrupts.

"As long as they don't," you continue doggedly, "the manual sampling of the tail gas and the off gas are good substitutes."

"The only problem with these substitutes is that they take forever," complains Koegel. "About a full half hour from the time you complete the sample of the tail gas before you can make a correction."

"But the off gas isn't so bad," you counter. "Although the sampling takes at least 15 minutes for either the tail gas or the off gas, the off gas takes only about 10 minutes from completing the sample to making a correction."

Koegel comes back smartly. "The off gas is certainly easier and faster than the tail gas, but it's definitely no substitute for an automatic system that would do the whole operation in less than four minutes."

"Yah. We know that the ideal answer is the automatic analyzers that sample all day and correct immediately, but how about being realistic, huh? Half a loaf is better than none."

"True," Koegel nods. "But Zoller is sure to start singing his old song about the automatic analyzers, even if we stay mum. For years— as long as I've been here, and probably much longer—he's been griping that if we could only get. . . . Say, I just thought of something. Those analyzers have been in place for almost eight years. Let's see, where was I? Zoller's been saying that if we could only get them to work properly we could drop all this lab sampling and testing. He's hardly going to change his tune when we propose increasing the lab analyses, you know."

"Maybe we could offer him some trade-off," you say brightly. "Like some relatively useless chromatography analysis we could drop so he wouldn't see this as an increase in his work load."

"Nah. Wouldn't work," frowns Koegel. "I have a better idea. Why don't we admit that the best thing all around is to get the automatic analyzers to work? In fact, we could propose that getting them to work properly should be made a high-priority item in the plant. But in the interim, the lab should do these analyses of the tail gas and the off gas so that we can control things right."

You nod, smiling when you think of how Zoller is going to bellow now.

"In fact, this is pretty clever," concludes Koegel. "I can't wait to see your memo that's going to convince everyone at the meeting to support our proposal. Old Zoller is going to have to do those extra off-gas analyses, and he may even have to do the tail gas. Let me see your draft as soon as it's ready."

ASSIGNMENT 1

Write a memo to Billy-Jo White, Product Control Manager. (The memo is addressed to White because it deals with an issue of quality control.) Copies go to Earl Sampson, Plant Manager; Gordon Borowski, Operations Manager; Fred LaRue, Maintenance Manager; and Henry Zoller, Manager of the Analytical Laboratory. The memo is from Larry Koegel, Manager of Technical Services, and you, Associate Refining Engineer in Technical Services.

Part 2

At the next weekly meeting of the managers, your proposal is on the agenda (your memo having been distributed a couple of days earlier), and an all-out battle ensues, much as Koegel predicted. He tells you about it with relish![9] After an hour of sometimes harsh exchange, the group consensus is that the automatic analyzers will have to become an immediate high-priority item, and despite Zoller's roar about the high costs of his staff (now up to almost $45 per person-hour), the

---

[9] Koegel attends these meetings, of course, but you do not.

inadequate equipment, and the heavy work load, the lab is directed to do six, not one, off-gas checks daily. Although the managers readily drop the item on the extra tail-gas samples, Zoller is quite angry, and puts Koegel on notice that he'd better get those automatic analyzers to work right and do it *fast*. Koegel warmly assents, but explains calmly to everyone that finding a solution to that problem is a big order. From what he has heard (via you) about Great Eastern plants in Pennsylvania and Louisiana and about a competitor's operation in Illinois, automatic analyzers require an artist to operate them.

Concluding his story of the meeting, Koegel smiles, saying. "You certainly have your work cut out for you now! But before you begin, I want you to write a memo to Borowski for me. He writes up the minutes from these meetings, and he often doesn't get all the details just right. I want to send him a summary of what we agreed on; then we won't have to argue about it later. From past experience, I guess he will use what we send him, pretty much word for word. Just say something like, ah, this is what we agreed to do on the analyzer problem."

ASSIGNMENT 2
Write a memo to Gordon Borowski, Operations Manager, for Larry Koegel's signature. Larry is Manager of Technical Services. (Write your name on the upper-right corner of this paper to identify it for your instructor.)

Part 3

Not many days later you suddenly learn that you are not going to be able to devote all your efforts to getting the analyzers to work. Zoller is not going to creep back to his lab and dutifully send his people out to do the six off-gas analyses. That would be too much to expect. He begins to complain almost immediately, and soon insists on a meeting with you and Koegel.

In a scrappy mood, he lays things on the line. "There's so much wrong with this lousy system of yours," he begins (he sure likes the word "lousy" you think to yourself), "that I don't even know where to begin."

Koegel is irritated already. "You didn't seem to have too much trouble getting started on telling us about it," he says sarcastically.

Zoller ignores Koegel and plows ahead. "The valves are corroded; the sampling system itself is so terrible that no repeatable words will describe it."

From Koegel: "Hank, could you be more specific?"

"Absolutely. There's water in the line. Whenever it's below freezing, the line is all plugged up."

"Oh," Koegel says with his lip curling, "that's why your men just toss out the sample so much of the time."

Zoller chooses to ignore this rejoinder too and just glares at Koegel as he continues: "Freezing isn't the only problem. Many of the samples are loaded with stagnant residue, stuff from old samples. That line is just too big. It's about a quarter inch. Should be about half that, I'd guess; then it might draw right."

At this concrete suggestion, Koegel changes his tone and becomes more agreeable. "Okay, Hank," he says. "You've got a legitimate gripe. We'll try to fix up these things right away. Regret that it's been so much trouble for your people." Turning to you, he says, "Let's see if we can't get that system fixed up right away."

Nodding first at Koegel and then at Zoller, you whip right out to the platform next to the stack and climb up the ladder to the sampling station about 20 feet in the air to see what shape the system is in. With the wind blasting and the 15-degree cold, you think you will freeze to death if you cannot get the sample fast, but when you attempt to carry out the sampling procedure, you immediately discover that the sample line is in terrible shape. The insulation is falling off all over the place. The valve handles are broken, making it tough to open them. Then you discover that the line is plugged up tight; you would need a steam hose to melt the ice so you could draw a sample. Whew, you say to yourself. It would not take much intelligence to figure out that there is water in this line. And suddenly you feel just a little sympathy for Zoller's men who have to do this job—even if not for Zoller himself, who, of course, wouldn't be caught dead out here.

Back at your desk, you quickly make some notes of what will be needed to fix the sampling station. Then bringing the sheets with you, you drop in to see Koegel, flopping down in a chair to rest after your exertions.

"Things are a rotten mess out there, Larry. Much worse than we ever imagined. Everything Zoller says is true—no, wait a minute, he doesn't know the half of it. I can tell you I wouldn't want to have to try to draw those samples every day."

"Really?" Koegel says incredulously. "Tell me all about it."

"There's water in the line, and the whole thing is falling apart," you answer.

"Well, what do we need to do? As long as it's cheap and quick, we'll just go ahead."

"Oh, it shouldn't cost much to do," you reply. "I figure all we really need is to put in small tubing, one-eighth inch will do. The volume then will be 20 cubic centimeters, compared to 120 cubic centimeters currently. That will eliminate all the residue problems. Then we need to fix up the insulation; it's falling apart so badly that the line is frozen tight."

"You can put a stream tracer[10] around the line, first, and then wind the insulation around the outside," suggests Koegel.

"I think we should also put in a probe in the middle of the line so that they can get a better sample,"[11] you add.

"Are they drawing off the pipe wall now?" Koegel frowns.

"Yah. And is it dirty!"

"That's a good idea . . . the probe, I mean. Also put a bevel on the probe, downstream side. That'll prevent the probe from plugging," Koegel nods.

"Right," you say, making some sketches on your pad. (See Figure 1.)

"Plans sound fine to me," Koegel concludes. "Oh, I think I'd also tell the maintenance people to leave in the disconnected one-quarter-inch tubing. They can just lash the new and old tubing together with some stainless steel wire, and then wind the tracer around the two of them together. The insulation will go around the whole thing, and it will be much stronger."

"Good point," you smile, as you sketch the plan. "The old tubing will help support the new."[12] (See Figure 2.)

"Now write this up right away. Maintenance can get the job done in no time and at least we should have Zoller dampened down enough so that you can get on with the big problem, the automatic analyzers. We've got to get those beasts to work."

---

[10] The steam tracer will keep the line hot so that it will not freeze. If both the insulation and the heat source are working, the water will "gravity drain" out of the line.

[11] A center probe will draw bulk flow, thus producing a better sample than can be drawn on the wall of the pipe. The probe is retractable for cleaning.

[12] The new sampling station at ground level will replace the one 20 feet in the air. (See Appendix B.)

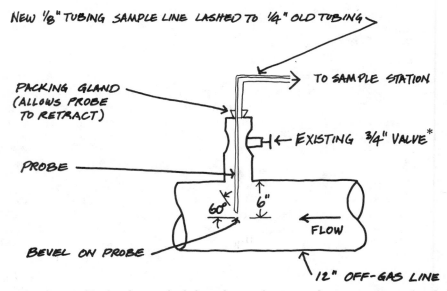

NEW ⅛" TUBING SAMPLE LINE LASHED TO ¼" OLD TUBING

PACKING GLAND (ALLOWS PROBE TO RETRACT)

TO SAMPLE STATION

EXISTING ¾" VALVE*

PROBE

60° 6"

FLOW

BEVEL ON PROBE

12" OFF-GAS LINE

* The existing ¾-inch valve can be left in place without any adjustments. A new ⅛-inch valve to operate the new sampling station will be installed at the bottom of the line (at ground level).

Figure 1. Your Drawing for Repair of the Absorber Off Gas Sampling System: Diagram of Tubing and Probe

You cannot quite imagine ever getting the automatic analyzers to work; as Koegel says, they seem to be more of an art than a science. One plant in Texas you visited has them working beautifully, but they do not seem to quite know why; certainly nowhere else you have ever been has a clue how to keep them going on a reliable basis. But somehow or other you will get them going, you say to yourself—though you wonder when that day might come.

ASSIGNMENT 3

Write a report to the Manager of Maintenance, Fred LaRue, describing the work that needs to be done. Include a sketch for him to follow. Copies go to Billy-Jo White and everyone on the distribution list for Assignment 1; these people will make a decision on going ahead with the work at the next weekly management meeting. The report is from Koegel and you, just as in Assignment 1.

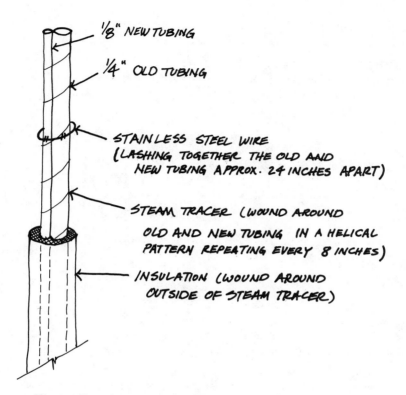

1/8" NEW TUBING

1/4" OLD TUBING

STAINLESS STEEL WIRE
(LASHING TOGETHER THE OLD AND
NEW TUBING APPROX. 24 INCHES APART)

STEAM TRACER (WOUND AROUND
OLD AND NEW TUBING IN A HELICAL
PATTERN REPEATING EVERY 8 INCHES)

INSULATION (WOUND AROUND
OUTSIDE OF STEAM TRACER)

Figure 2.   Your Drawing for Repair of the Absorber
Off Gas Sampling System: Cutaway Diagram of New Tubing
Lashed to Old

APPENDIX A

Removal and Recovery of Sulfur from the Amine Acid Gas

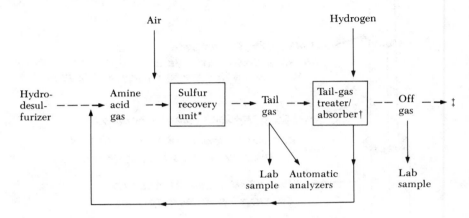

*Removes 96% sulfur.

†Recovers remaining 4% sulfur and recycles to front of process as H_2S.

‡Discharged through incinerator stack to atmosphere.

The refinery sulfur recovery unit consists of two units: an 80-ton-per-day sulfur recovery unit (SRU), designed to recover commercial-grade sulfur from refinery acid-gas streams, and a tail-gas treater/absorber unit, designed to reduce SO_2 in effluent gases to below 250 ppm.

Normal feed to the SRU consists of amine acid gas from the hydrodesulfurizer. H_2S in this stream is converted through thermal and catalytic reaction to commercial-grade sulfur, after which it is condensed and stored in a sulfur collection pit for transport by truck and rail for commercial sales. Under optimum conditions the SRU can recover 96% of the sulfur in the feed.

The tail gas from the SRU feeds the treater/absorber unit, which catalytically reacts any remaining H_2S sulfur-bearing compounds with hydrogen to produce H_2S and inerts. The H_2S is absorbed, stripped, and recycled to the front of the process as acid-gas feed. The remaining effluent gases (off gas), with H_2S content below 250 ppm, are incinerated to meet governmental requirements.

APPENDIX B

Plan for New Sampling Station

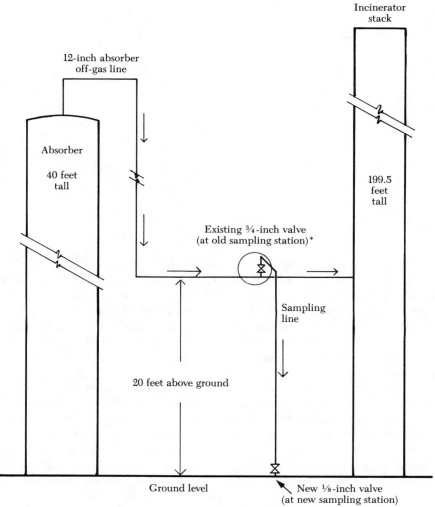

Incinerator
stack

12-inch absorber
off-gas line

Absorber

40 feet
tall

199.5
feet
tall

Existing ¾-inch valve
(at old sampling station)*

Sampling
line

20 feet above ground

Ground level

New ⅛-inch valve
(at new sampling station)

* Figure 1 is a blown-up diagram of the old sampling station area circled here.

The Absence-Reporting Case: Tech Optics, Inc.

Note: Students can prepare Part 1 separately. They can prepare Part 2 without writing the assignments for Part 1, but not without reading Part 1 and analyzing it carefully.

Part 1
August 20, 1984

You are a personnel compensation analyst working for Tech Optics, Inc., a manufacturer of optical supplies in Schenectady, New York. The company's president is Alex Warde, who started the business in a three-room office five years ago. Tech Optics has since grown to just under 500 employees. It has four divisions, each one managed by a vice-president, and a personnel department, called Human Resources, which is directed by Sarah Pounder, who reports to Alex Warde.

You work for Ms. Pounder. Your job entails writing job descriptions, figuring correct salary rates according to local and national salary data, and keeping track of insurance and employee benefits. Problems and questions about wage and salary matters usually land on your desk. In other words, you process recommendations for raises and answer questions of any sort about compensation. Occasionally, the vice-presidents in charge of the various divisions are interested in comparing data on their personnel with information on other employees in the company. You handle these inquiries too.

This hot day in August 1984, you get a phone call from Fred Wells, vice-president of manufacturing. He is a little upset about a report by Lynn Swanson, a former administrative assistant who left the company a year and a half ago. Apparently Wells had asked Swanson to keep track of employee absences in the four departments in his division. He recently discovered that his new assistant, Karen O'Hara, has not been doing these computations. Swanson evidently forgot to tell O'Hara about this task before she left the company. Just now, in looking through Swanson's old reports, Wells discovered a chart giving the weekly percentages of absences for the last seven months of 1982 and the first two months of 1983 in his division's four departments. He is shocked at what the data seem to show. In some weeks, absences were as high as 26 percent in some departments. Understandably, Wells wants to know whether his division's employees are taking more time off or failing to report for work more often than employees in other divisions. He promises to send you Swanson's records right away. He also asks you to give him any recent data Human Resources has collected on absence rates for the Manufacturing Division.

You are a bit puzzled by Wells's call, though you do not tell him so. You do not understand why he would have assigned Swanson to compute absences in the first place. Records of employee absences for the entire company are processed by the Human Resources Department. The administrative assistants in the company divisions simply collect employees' weekly time sheets and make sure absences are reported correctly on the sheets. Human Resources actually computes all the absence statistics. Your payroll clerk, Sam Bergman, should be able to tell you what is going on in Wells's division, since he keeps track of all employee absences at Tech Optics. You plan to discuss Swanson's report with Bergman as soon as it arrives.

August 21, 1984

Today you get Swanson's record for the absenteeism rate among hourly workers in Manufacturing Division's Departments 41, 42, 43, and 46. The report lists the percentage of absences in each department on a weekly basis from June 1982 to February 1983 (Appendix A). You call Sam Bergman and ask him to give you a copy of the report filed by Human Resources on absences for that period. When you get Bergman's report, you realize that you cannot even compare it to Swanson's figures. The "report" consists of a hasty memo and a small table of absence statistics (Figure 1). The statistics cover absence rates for the last five months of 1983, not 1982.

You call Bergman and ask him to bring you the fiscal year 1983 report immediately. He arrives at your desk right away carrying a piece

T E C H   O P T I C S   I N C .

HUMAN RESOURCES DEPARTMENT

TO: YOU
       Supervisor

FROM: Sam Bergman
        Payroll Clerk

DATE: August 23, 1984

Sorry, we didn't keep very consistent records in 1982 since there was such a large turnover of employees. Here are my monthly totals for the last five months of '83. By the way, I did find a report with Tech Optics' overall absenteeism rate for the fiscal year 1983 (August, 1982–July, 1983).* Do you want it? I can't find any of the raw data though.

Sam

Date	% Absent Hourly	% Absent Salaried	% Absent All Employees
August, 1983	1.6	.4	1.0
September, 1983	1.4	.4	.85
October, 1983	2.25	.5	1.4
November, 1983	1.8	.6	1.3
December, 1983	1.85	1.7	1.8

* The term "fiscal year" refers to the period August through July. The number of the year always corresponds with the number of the calendar year for the months January through July. Hence the period August 1982 through July 1983 would be called "Fiscal Year 1983" or abbreviated as "FY 1983" or "FY 83."

Figure 1.   Bergman's Report on Percentage Absent

of paper (Figure 2). You are shocked when you read the figures. "You mean this is all we have on fiscal year '83?" you ask.

"Unfortunately, that's it," Bergman replies. Then he adds quickly, "But I'm now keeping much better records than we kept in the past. I've only been here since last August, you know—just a year ago today." He launches into a monologue on how he is keeping the data much better now when you interrupt.

"I'm sure your efforts will make it a lot easier for us to answer questions about absences in the future," you say, trying to show some understanding of Bergman's situation. "But we need to know now what's going on in Wells's division. Can you show me the percentage of hourly employees absent from Departments 41, 42, 43, and 46 from August to December 1983?"

Bergman looks away for a minute. "Well, I can't immediately," he says. "I haven't been computing absences by department. I've got all of his time sheets, but I'd have to go back over them all. You see, to compute absences, first I separate the hourly and salaried time sheets into two groups, then I alphabetize each group and total them."

"Hmmm," you say. Now you see why Wells had Swanson keeping records of her own. Once the time sheets leave his department, there's no way of retrieving information on his employees. It's beginning to look to you like the whole absence-reporting system could use revamping. Unfortunately, you've got too many other projects going today to have a lengthy meeting with Bergman now.

"Listen," you tell him, "we need to meet to discuss in detail how we're keeping track of absences. I have a feeling we may have a problem on our hands here. I'm tied up with other projects this week and next week, and then there's the Labor Day weekend . . . how about Tuesday, September 4, at 9 A.M.?"

	Salary	Hourly	Average
Average Absenteeism Rate at Tech Optics for Fiscal Year 1983			
(1st 6 mos. of '83)	.07%	3.0%	1.7%
(last 6 mos. of '82)	.06%	2.2%	1.4%

Figure 2.   Bergman's 1983 Absence Figures

Bergman nods and heads out the door.

Once he is gone, you groan. What are you going to say to Wells? You do not know how you are going to compare his data with Bergman's stuff. You cannot do anything about the fact that Wells's figures are for 1982 and Bergman's for 1983. However, since absenteeism patterns tend to be seasonal, comparing data for the same months might be reasonably legitimate, even though they are in different years. Of course, patterns differ significantly between hourly and salaried employees. You get to work rearranging Wells's data to compare his division's absenteeism rate with the overall company data for hourly employees.

After organizing the absenteeism data and roughing out some possible graphics, you realize that there is no way you can make the Manufacturing Division look good. The figures are way out of line compared with the overall monthly averages for all hourly employees at Tech Optics. You are not sure what the reason is, but you suspect that Swanson might have been computing absences with a method different from the one Bergman is now using.

Meanwhile, you discover that Wells has called and left a message with your secretary. He wants the story on the absence data he sent you—now. You grimly set about writing him a memo. You decide to let him know that you will thoroughly review Tech Optics' entire absence-reporting system. You hope that will satisfy him. Unfortunately, you will have to send a copy of this memo to Sara Pounder. She runs a pretty smooth operation, and although she is quick to correct inadequacies in the department, she also does not like making changes. She is sure to feel that Human Resources has slipped up on this one. You do not want her to feel threatened by your review of the absence-reporting procedures; at the same time, you do not want Wells excited about absences in his division. You hope that your memo will let them both know that you are handling the situation well.

ASSIGNMENT 1

Organize the data in Appendix A so that it answers Wells's original question in graphic form: How does Manufacturing compare with Tech Optics overall?

ASSIGNMENT 2

Write a memo to Mr. Fred Wells, Vice-President of Manufacturing, with a copy to Ms. Sarah Pounder, Human Resources Director. Your position is Supervisor, Compensation, Human Resources Department.

Part 2
August 24, 1984

After you finish the memo, you start thinking some more about the implications of your department's method for keeping data on employee absences. You wonder if the way Human Resources computes absences is comparable to other firms. You are aware that Business Researchers, Inc. (BR, Inc.), of Albany keeps personnel data on a variety of industries in the upstate New York area. They produce reports which compare information on employment patterns. You decide to write BR's research coordinator to ask for any reports they may have on absenteeism patterns and to get kinds of absenteeism defined so that you can get your own house in order. You also decide to find out what reports the Bureau of National Affairs (BNA), a private organization in Washington, D.C., has on absenteeism in small manufacturing firms.

ASSIGNMENT 3
Write letters to BR, Inc., and the BNA requesting the information you need. The addresses are as follows:

E. E. Smith
Research Coordinator
Business Researchers, Inc.
300 Research Drive
Albany, New York 00000

Bureau of National Affairs
1231 25th St., N.W.
Washington, D.C. 20037

Your firm's address is Tech Optics, Inc., 850 Industrial Drive, Schenectady, New York 00000.

August 31, 1984

Wells received your memo a week ago and immediately gave you a call. Needless to say he was not happy about the absenteeism rate in his division compared to other hourly employees at Tech Optics. He wants to get to the bottom of this, and he has had Karen O'Hara spend some time rummaging through Swanson's old files. She found a chart that Swanson used for computing absences, and Wells sent it to you through company mail. He thinks it will help you in your review of absence-reporting procedures. Meanwhile, Sarah Pounder dropped you a brief note saying she thought you handled Wells's problem just fine. She also said she approved of your effort to review the absence-reporting procedures. Pounder does not appear to be edgy about your investigation. Of course, now you realize that you really *do* have to complete that review, and you are even pleased at the opportunity. You want to improve the reporting system so that Wells and the other VPs will be better able to keep tabs on absences in their departments.

The chart which Wells found in Swanson's files is really not all that much (Figure 3). The information you requested from BR, Inc., and the BNA comes in this afternoon's mail (Appendixes B and C). You sure are pleased they responded so quickly. You start looking through the information and listing some questions to ask Bergman. Next Tuesday is when you are supposed to meet, and you hope he has his act together.

September 4, 1984

At 9 A.M., Bergman arrives in your office. You think he is pretty worried about this meeting. The record keeping done by Tech Optics' clerks certainly has left something to be desired. You decide to assure him that he cannot be held responsible for what was done in the past, but you make it clear that records must be kept clearly now and that the system must be passed on easily should Bergman leave the com-

---

Computing Employee Absences
% Absenteeism

$$\frac{\text{No. of incidences}}{\text{No. of employees} \times 5 \text{ days}} \times 100 = \underline{\hspace{1cm}}\%$$

No. of incidences include <u>all</u> absences except Vacation, Holiday, and Birthday

---

Figure 3.   Lynn Swanson's Method of Reporting Absences

pany. You barely get a chance to say "good morning" before Bergman starts talking eagerly about what he has been doing.

"Since I was hired last August," Bergman notes, "I have scanned through the files several times to find the raw data on past absenteeism. Mike Short, the man before me, obviously had absenteeism records low on his priority list. I haven't been able to locate any raw data on absenteeism from previous years, but I have found some blank charts on which Short seems to have marked reported absences."

Shuffling his papers, Bergman hands one sheet to you (Figure 4) and announces, "The formula Short was using for computing absences represents the proportion of work days lost in a month, compared to the actual work days available in the month, times the number of employees working."

"Hmmmmm," you remark, looking at Short's chart. After one moment you pull out the chart Wells sent you which shows how Lynn Swanson computed absences. "It appears that Short computed data differently from the way Swanson in Manufacturing did. She seems to have compared the number of incidences of absence to the available days of work. Look at this." You pass Swanson's chart (Figure 3) to Bergman. "Wells sent it over yesterday."

Bergman stares at Swanson's chart in amazement. "It looks like the way Swanson was counting, a person who was tardy on any one day and a person who was absent a full day were counted the same— both as one instance of absence. That's like comparing apples and oranges."

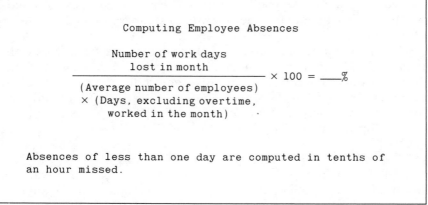

Figure 4. Short's Method of Computing Absences

"I know," you answer.

Bergman turns to you. "I wonder where Swanson got this formula. And why was she computing absences anyway?"

"Probably because our department couldn't give Wells data on his personnel exclusively," you suggest.

Bergman ignores your comment. "Well, I'm now computing absences just as Short did. You can see that he counted absences in terms of tenths of an hour missed. So, a tardiness of ten minutes, for instance, was marked as an absence of two-tenths of an hour and a whole day was counted as eight hours missed."

As Bergman is talking, you review the information you got from BR, Inc., and the BNA. "Look," you say while handing Bergman the BR, Inc., info, "how does the way you're computing absences compare with this?"

Bergman looks at the BR, Inc., "Definitions" (Appendix B) and slowly shakes his head. "Well," he says, "this is close to what we're doing but not exactly it. You see, I've been counting each day missed in long-term absences and calculating absences of less than one day in tenths of an hour missed. It looks like BR, Inc., only counts the first four days of a long-term absence and counts all absences of less than one day as half a day."

"Where did Short come up with this system you're now using?" you ask.

"I'm not sure," Bergman says quietly, "but I found an old memo written to Short from Jay Selznik, VP of our Research and Development Division, indicating that R&D was going to report absences this way. It seems Selznik wanted Short to keep him informed of how his division was doing. Maybe Short liked the system and just adopted it wholesale. That made it easier for him to compare R&D with the rest of the company."

"Well, I doubt that Short did the calculations for anyone other than R&D. It just takes too much time. Anyway," Bergman continues, "the first I heard of it was when I discovered that memo from Selznik yesterday." Suddenly Bergman lights up. "I'll bet Short told Lynn Swanson how she could do the figures for Wells's division, but she got the formula wrong. I'll bet that's how these different methods got started!"

"Could be," you mutter to yourself.

But Bergman tries to smooth things over. "Look, that's all past history. We haven't been doing any internal comparisons for anybody since I got here, and to my knowledge, even R&D hasn't been doing

them on their own lately. What really matters is that I've got the administrative assistants in all divisions reporting absences to Human Resources in tenths of hours on the time sheets now. And they are all doing it in the same way. I've separated data for all hourly and all salaried employees for each month in fiscal '84, but I would have to go back over all the time sheets to calculate absences either by division or by individual department."

Bergman can see that this whole situation is beginning to upset you, and he starts pacing nervously. Though you *are* irritated, you can empathize with Bergman. It would be a tedious job to calculate absences by department, and you are not sure that all departments want or need such records. On the other hand, upper management may find breakdowns by department as well as by division useful for comparing absence patterns within the corporation. Of course, separation by hourly versus salaried is good enough for comparing Tech Optics to other companies. But even to do that properly, it looks like Tech Optics is going to have to adopt a new computing formula—one that conforms with BR, Inc.'s "Definitions." You believe that the computations really should remain in the hands of your department, because Human Resources is ultimately responsible for personnel record keeping. Although Wells's assistant was doing absence statistics on the side, it looks like all the others were simply turning in time sheets to the Human Resources payroll clerk. That should probably stay the same.

You break from your thoughts to find Bergman still pacing. "Look, Sam," you begin, startling him for a moment, "I'm going to have to get Sarah Pounder in on this. It's good we've got all your departments reporting absences to you in the same way, but I should think Sarah would want us to conform with reporting procedures in other companies." (Despite the fact that she does not like change very much, you add to yourself.) "That means the administrative assistants will have to mark both the long-term leaves and the absences of less than a day differently on the time sheets. Meanwhile I'd like that data you have on fiscal year '84. You did start reporting absences using the Short method since you got here in August of '83, right?"

"Sure did," Bergman smiles. "I've got absence data from August '83 to July '84 organized. I suppose you'd like me to show trends from month to month."

"Yes," you say. "Unless the data are erratic from week to week. Wells's sure showed big weekly jumps."

"Well," Bergman responds, "I think the reason for that was that

Swanson reported every incidence of absence without distinguishing tardies from whole days missed. My data show no big jumps from week to week."

"Good," you say. "Now how will you break down the monthly data?"

"I suppose you'd like to see hourly, salaried, and combined percentages of absence, right?"

"Right," you answer, "but don't bother to arrange data by division." You are thinking to yourself that you do not want to make the VPs nervous about how each one of their units stacks up—at least not now when you are thinking of putting in a new reporting method.

"I could also compare the monthly data to the yearly averages I've got for fiscal years '83 and '84," Bergman continues.

"Good idea," you tell him.

"You're aware that I don't have any of the monthly data for fiscal year '83," Bergman adds, tentatively.

"Yes, you've told me that," you remind him, and then add, "I think we can work well with the information you do have."

Bergman smiles, tells you that he will start arranging the data right away, and hurries out. Meanwhile you begin making plans. You believe that the company should immediately start keeping track of absences according to guidelines of the Business Researchers, Inc., of Albany. You also think Bergman should do calculations by department so that data can be compared internally. This might require getting him some clerical assistance, but you think it is worth it to keep the company's house in order. To get the ball rolling, you must first convince Sarah Pounder that this is a necessary change. You start planning a memo which will promote your plan to change absence calculations to conform to BR, Inc., "Definitions." If Sarah says yes, then Human Resources will have to convince the VPs that the new procedure is better, and their assistants will have to be told how to report the absences to Bergman. Of course, while pushing the advantages of your plan in the memo to Sarah, you will also have to mention that Bergman may require some assistance.

ASSIGNMENT 4
Write a memo to Sarah Pounder, Human Resources Director, which proposes your new plan for absence reporting.

September 6, 1984

This morning as soon as you walk in, your secretary lets you know that Ms. Pounder wants to see you right away. You take a few sips of coffee and start down to her office. When you get there, Sarah looks pleased.

"I got your memo yesterday, and I think your plan for the new procedure is fine," she starts out. "But when I announce that we will be computing absences by department to the division chiefs, they may get a bit nervous, thinking that we're concerned about the departmental absence rates in each division." Looking directly at you, Sarah pauses. "Do we have anything to be concerned about or not?"

"Well," you start out slowly, "I don't think we do. I've got Sam Bergman pulling together all data on fiscal year '84 for salaried and hourly employees. As soon as he gives it to me, I can compare it with the stuff we've got on similar manufacturing firms from BR, Inc. I can also compare our data with the BNA statistics, but theirs aren't broken down by salaried and hourly employees; also the monthly data we have from them is for fiscal year '83, not '84."

"But the seasonal trends should be approximately the same for both years."

"That's what I figure," you say, remembering that you thought the same thing earlier when Bergman first told you Tech Optics had no monthly data for fiscal year 1983.

Sarah takes a step forward. "Look," she says, "I want you to draft a memo to all VPs and their administrative assistants explaining that we're now going to compute absences like BR, Inc."

You smile in approval.

"Now about getting an assistant for Bergman . . . ," Sarah pauses and you tense up a bit. You knew that Sarah would get tough about getting help for Bergman. "I don't think we should hire any new personnel," she continues, "especially since it's likely that six months from now Tech Optics will purchase a new payroll software package that can generate absence reports."

You are taken aback by this news and suddenly decide to take a seat. Noticing your surprise, Pounder says, "It wasn't my idea; I think our current system handles payroll just fine. And computing absence statistics hasn't been a high priority around here. Bergman seems to handle it manually well enough. Alex Warde [the president] was sold on the new package. He gave me the lowdown on it last week. He's ordering a lot of other software from the same company for other applications outside of our department."

You're aware that Mr. Warde often makes purchases without consulting his VPs, let alone Sarah. So naturally, Sarah's a bit peeved. Nevertheless, Tech Optics has to update its data processing to keep up with its growth.

"Sounds like a good move," you say. "Tech Optics has grown by leaps and bounds over the past five years; personnel needs to have a data management system that will keep pace with our growth." You pause a minute, and then ask, "What kind of absence report will the new package generate?"

"Well," Pounder answers, "it doesn't do anything fancy; for instance, it won't compute percentage absent, but it will take data from the time sheets and produce totals for each department."

"So data from the time sheets will be entered into the computer," you surmise.

"Yes," Sarah replies.

"And so all Bergman will have to do is to check the sheets before data are entered into the computer and processed, and then apply the absence formula to the totals appearing on the report the computer spits out."

"That's about it," Sarah says. "Providing the program works the way it's supposed to," she adds skeptically.

"Of course," you concede. Then you add, "Whether it works or not, this new software won't help us now."

"You're right," Sarah says. "Besides, it isn't a sure thing that Warde will approve the software purchase anyway. What we must do now," she continues, "is to get each division to fill out time sheets according to the BR guidelines, and then we must get each division to compute their own absence statistics—both for individual departments and for the division as a whole—using the BR formula. We can still have Bergman compute company statistics from the time sheets, but we can use the division computations to make internal comparisons. If the computer software becomes a reality, we can have Bergman do the statistics for each division and department as well."

"Sounds good to me," you say. "Having individual department absence rates should appeal to the division chiefs, even if they aren't pleased about seeing their own units compared to the other divisions. Of course, computing the department and division rates will be extra work for the VPs' assistants."

"Yes," Sarah agrees. "But the time sheets won't be any more work for them. You just have to let the assistants know they are to mark the sheets differently for long-term leaves and for absences less than a day. But the computation of the departmental and division absence percentages is a new task; there's no getting around that."

"There sure isn't," you say uneasily. "And they'll have to compute separate rates for hourly, salaried, and all employees. And of course they have to do it right—right, that is, according to the BR formula."

Sarah stares out her window for a moment. "Why don't you include in your memo to the VPs some information comparing Tech Optics to some other companies? We'd look pretty good, wouldn't we?"

"I think so," you reply. "Depends on what Bergman can come up with."

"Well, we want to let the VPs know they're doing a good job and there's nothing to worry about—if we can, of course. We don't want to alienate them with a new procedure that seems like a threat. Remember," she adds, "you'll need their cooperation in giving you the absence data the way you want it."

"Right," you say.

"Get back to me if you have any problems," Sarah says. "You should really get that report out before the end of the week."

"Sure," you smile confidently.

With the strategy for announcing the new reporting system settled, you quickly leave Sarah's office and hurry down to Bergman's desk to see if he's got that absence data ready. Fortunately, he's there and he's got the chart completed. You look over it eagerly, hoping it will show that Tech Optics' absence rates are pretty low.

Looking at the chart, you immediately see that something's wrong. Beginning in January 1984, the absence rates for the hourly employees increase dramatically (Appendix D).

"Sam, did you notice this big jump in absences starting in January 1984?" you ask, pointing at the graph.

"Yes, but that's easily explained," Bergman answers. "You see, after January '84, individual departments started submitting time sheets for all people on medical or extended leave. Before that time, medical leave and long absences of all kinds were reported irregularly. So time sheets submitted to us by each department since January naturally show more absences."

You shake your head, realizing that when long-term absences are included in division reports, Tech Optics' absence rates look bad compared to other small manufacturing firms reported in the BR, Inc., statistics. More than ever, you are convinced that Tech Optics must conform to reporting procedures used by other companies. There is no other way to get comparative data.

"Thanks, Sam, for finally giving me the whole story," you comment drily. "You're sure you haven't left anything out now?"

"No, that's it." Bergman looks quite pleased with himself.

You send him out and get back to your office. You take a deep breath and start thinking about how you are going to put together the report for Sarah Pounder. Looks like you could use Bergman's comparison data for the period August 1983 through December 1983 anyway. Comparing these figures with the stuff from BR, Inc., and BNA makes Tech Optics look pretty good. The only trouble is that medical leave absences were not reported by Tech Optics during that period; consequently, if you are going to use those figures, you will have to think of some way of noting that fact.

On the other hand, Bergman's analysis of the absences beginning with January 1984 only confirms the need for Tech Optics to follow BR, Inc.'s reporting procedures. Including all those long-term absence days makes the picture look awful, so awful that maybe it would convince the VPs that you need a new system.

It will not be easy deciding how to present Tech Optics' absenteeism rates to the VPs. You wish Sarah had not asked you to include them, but the fact of the matter is that she did. Well, there is no use putting the job off. You must plan your draft of a report for Sarah to send to the division VPs. They will have to get a clear picture of what is to be done differently and why. You just hope that in the process of telling them about the new procedure you will not make them nervous about the comparative statistics Human Resources will generate. Comparing absence figures internally and with other companies should help management make the company more productive, but the VPs might not like the prospect when it comes to others looking at their own operations. Although the assignment is tough, you believe you can get the VPs to see that the change will be for the better.

Complete either Assignment 5 or 6:

ASSIGNMENT 5
Write a report to all vice-presidents heading divisions at Tech Optics. The report will be from Sarah Pounder, Human Resources Director. You will be listed as report author under "Prepared by." The VPs administrative assistants will be on the distribution list. Refer to the

following list of Tech Optics vice-presidents and administrative assistants:

Jay Selznik
Research and Development Division
Assistant, George Dagher

Fred Wells
Manufacturing Division
Assistant, Karen O'Hara

Sylvia Hart
Sales and Promotion Division
Assistant, Jane Fosdick

Ralph Budnick
Customer Service Division
Assistant, Harry Thompson

ASSIGNMENT 6
Write the report described above to the vice-presidents only. Include in the report an announcement of a training session for the administrative assistants to cover the change in procedure. See Assignment 5 for the names of the vice-presidents.

ASSIGNMENT 7
Assume that the vice-presidents responded positively to the report you wrote for Sarah Pounder in Assignment 5 or 6. Sarah assigns you to prepare a ten-minute oral presentation with graphic aids on the new absence-reporting method to train the VPs' assistants.

APPENDIX A

Manufacturing Division Absences for Hourly Workers, in Percent

Date	Department 41	Department 42	Department 43	Department 46
6/7/1982	10.2	10.0	25.7	6.0
6/14	3.6	15.5	20.0	7.0
6/21	10.0	16.1	20.0	10.7
6/28	10.2	7.1	1.0	6.3
7/5	2.5	7.2	6.2	8.1
7/12	7.8	6.0	10.0	8.1
7/19	14.1	10.0	1.0	10.0
7/26	6.0	13.2	13.5	5.9
8/2	15.0	10.1	22.1	10.0
8/9	11.0	13.6	20.0	9.2
8/16	6.8	10.1	16.2	7.3
8/23	10.0	16.5	3.8	3.3
8/30	4.5	8.5	16.0	4.5
9/6	9.0	10.0	7.5	5.5
9/13	16.5	10.0	4.0	3.9
9/20	9.2	10.9	13.8	4.6
9/27	10.5	7.5	1.1	6.9
10/4	4.6	3.2	20.0	5.8
10/11	9.2	8.7	3.5	10.0
10/18	14.0	11.0	33.9	5.0
10/25	16.0	11.0	10.0	5.0
11/1	6.5	7.5	29.9	8.3
11/8	6.8	9.9	24.2	7.3
11/15	5.3	7.6	6.1	3.3
11/22	3.8	3.5	10.5	1.5
11/29	4.6	6.9	15.0	3.0
12/6	4.6	4.8	9.9	5.0
12/13	4.6	3.7	13.4	7.2
12/20*	11.1	9.5	10.0	2.5
1/3/83	4.6	4.5	1.1	7.0
1/10	16.0	5.2	19.9	5.5
1/17	4.5	5.1	7.3	5.5
1/24	7.7	8.0	20.0	1.8
1/31	3.0	6.9	22.5	2.1
2/7	4.6	9.5	20.0	4.0
2/14	7.2	13.1	16.0	3.1
2/21	11.1	9.8	13.1	4.0
2/28	23.0	9.8	26.0	5.2

* Plant closed week of 12/27.

APPENDIX B

Letter from BR, Inc.

BUSINESS
RESEARCHERS, INC.
OF ALBANY

300 Research Drive
Albany, New York 00000

August 30, 1984

YOU
Human Resources Department
Tech Optics, Inc.
850 Industrial Drive
Schenectady, New York 00000

Dear YOU:

Enclosed is the information you requested regarding absenteeism rates in small corporations. As a member of BR, Inc., Tech Optics may participate in our statistical studies and receive monthly research reports on a variety of personnel data.

You'll find on the enclosed sheets a list of definitions which explain variables for our absence statistics and a breakdown of salaried and hourly absenteeism rates for FY 1983 (August, 1982 – July, 1983) and the last five months of 1983 for manufacturing firms. We have not yet completed our survey of absences from January, 1984 – July, 1984. We will send you figures for FY 1984 (August, 1983 – July, 1984) when our reports are complete.

Please call me if you need any more information.

Sincerely,

Eunice E. Smith

E. E. Smith
Research Coordinator

enc.

(continued)

APPENDIX B—*continued*

BUSINESS RESEARCHERS, INC. OF ALBANY

<u>DEFINITIONS</u>

Absenteeism, in this study, is defined as unscheduled job absence whether or not it is excused or paid. Compensatory time off and paid personal leaves are not included if the employee has made arrangements ahead of time. Time lost because of bereavement, sick leave, and discipline are included, as it is usually not arranged in advance.

In the case of long–term absences, only the first four days are included. Absences of less than one day are included as one–half of one day. The absenteeism rates reflect percentages derived from the following formula:

$$\frac{\text{Number of work days lost in month}}{(\text{Average number of employees}) \times (\text{Days, excluding overtime, worked in the month})} \times 100$$

The "number of work days," does not include days which consist entirely or primarily of overtime work (i.e., Saturdays, Holidays).

APPENDIX B—*continued*

Absenteeism Rates for Manufacturing Firms

Firm	Hourly Averages		Salaried Averages		All Employees Averages	
	FY 1983	Last Five Months of 1983	FY 1983	Last Five Months of 1983	FY 1983	Last Five Months of 1983
Firms of Less Than 500 Employees						
A	6.75	6.50	—	—	—	—
B	9.52	15.00	—	—	—	—
C	5.76	5.93	3.70	2.68	5.14	4.96
D	1.71	1.22	0.96	0.58	1.39	0.87
E	—	—	—	—	2.25	1.90
F	1.09	1.51	2.83	1.99	1.34	1.58
G	6.67	5.48	—	0.95	4.44	3.97
H	4.00	4.73	—	—	—	—
I	—	—	0.99	1.30	—	—
J	9.71	5.71	0.49	2.86	3.40	4.76
K	3.04	3.63	2.21	0.91	3.20	3.56
L	2.82	2.16	1.66	2.24	2.15	2.21
M	2.50	2.55	4.13	4.67	3.51	3.87
Mean	4.87	4.95	2.12	2.02	2.98	3.08
Firms of More Than 500 Employees						
N	—	—	2.19	1.60	—	—
O	2.64	3.51	1.59	1.93	2.36	3.09
P	5.00	4.81	2.23	2.06	4.56	4.36
Q	—	—	0.02	0.03	—	—
Mean	3.82	4.16	1.51	1.41	3.46	3.73
Total mean	4.71	4.83	1.92	1.83	3.07	3.19

APPENDIX C

Job Absence Statistics from the Bureau of National Affairs

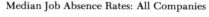

Median Job Absence Rates: All Companies

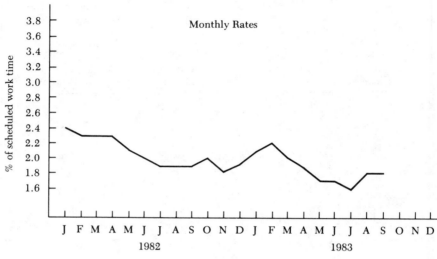

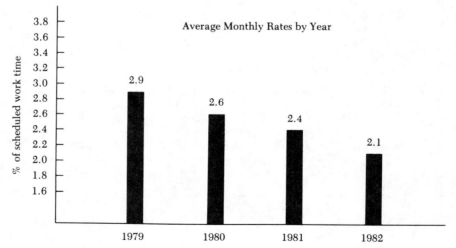

Source: From *BNA's Quarterly Report on Job Absence and Turnover*, 3rd Quarter, 1983, p. 2. Copyright © 1983, The Bureau of National Affairs, Inc., Washington, D.C. 20037. Reprinted by permission.

APPENDIX C—*continued*

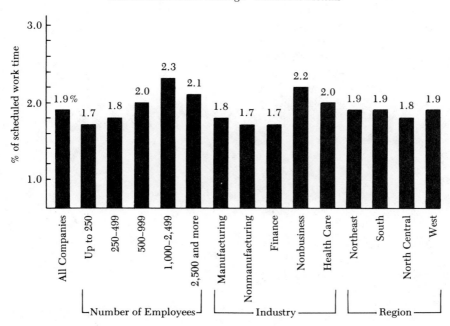

1983 Absence Rates: Average — First Nine Months

Job absence rates during the third quarter of 1983 fell one tenth of a percentage point from the previous three months' average to 1.7 percent of scheduled work time. This third-quarter average is two tenths of a percentage point below the rate recorded for July, August, and September of 1982 and represents the lowest three-month average recorded in BNA's quarterly survey program. As illustrated by the line graph, the monthly rate of unscheduled employee absence declined from a median of 1.7 percent of work time in June to 1.6 percent in July before rising for the first time in six months to 1.8 percent in August and September.

The all-company average absence rate of 1.9 percent for the first nine months of 1983 reflects no change from the first half of the year but is two tenths of a percentage point lower than the figure recorded for the first nine months of 1982. Year-to-date average monthly absence rates range from a low of 1.7 percent in the smallest companies to 2.3 percent in firms with 1,000 to 2,499 employees. (See bar graph.) As in the first six months of 1983, year-to-date average monthly absence rates are highest among nonbusiness establishments (2.2 percent) and employers in the health care subcategory (2.0 percent). Nonmanufacturing businesses and employers in the finance subgroup average a 1.7-percent absence rate for the first nine months of the year, while manufacturing companies are losing an average of 1.8 percent of scheduled work time.

Job absence rates for January through September vary little by geographic region — 1.9 percent of scheduled work time for companies in the Northeast, South, and West and 1.8 percent for firms in the North Central states.

Absence data were provided by 453 companies, of which 72 percent reported rates for all employee groups. Third-quarter median rates average 1.6 percent for companies reporting for their entire workforces and 1.9 percent for firms reporting data for specific groups only — usually plant or hourly employees.

APPENDIX D

Tech Optics Monthly Absenteeism for Fiscal Year 1984

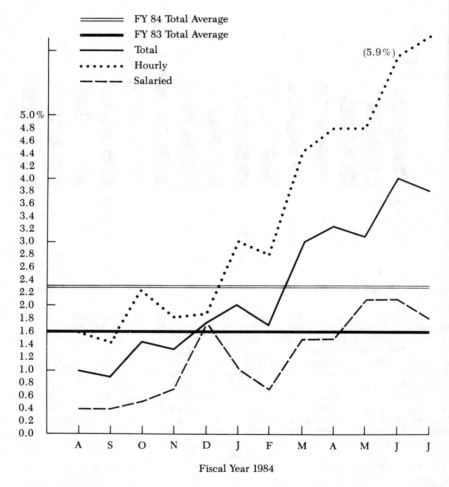

Fiscal Year 1984

Absenteeism: Unscheduled job absence whether or not it is excused. This includes tardiness, unpaid illness, unpaid personal absence, bereavement, absence for disciplinary reasons, medical leaves, and no reports.

The Model Plant at Clarkstone:
The Technical Writer's Case

Erickson/Engelberg, Inc., manufactures precision steel parts for the aircraft industry. With corporate headquarters outside San Diego (in a little town called Tremont, California), the company of 1,800 employees runs four plants: one located in Tremont, about a mile from the corporate offices; one in Texas; one in Massachusetts; and one in Nebraska, in a very small town called Clarkstone. You have been working in the corporate offices at Tremont for exactly three weeks, and you are still trying to find your way around, get to know people, and learn something about the company and its various operations.

Your job title is "Technical Writer," and you are attached to the Product Development Department. Primarily you were hired to document technical procedures, but you were also brought in to assist engineers throughout the corporation with writing jobs. You spend about half your time writing technical documents and the other half helping engineers write client reports about problems in designing new products or preparing variations on standard specifications. So far, then, all your work has been in Product Development.

Today you get quite a different assignment. Your boss in Product Development, Marsha Redding, tells you that the chief of corporate plant engineering, Horace Vandervelt, a man who has been with Erickson/Engelberg many years, has just been told he must have a serious operation next week that will keep him away from the job for about two months. Because Vandervelt has had his hand in so many pies, his tasks are being parceled out, and writing a newsletter article about one of his projects has come to you.

Immediately you tell Redding that you will give the assignment your best effort. Before you report to Vandervelt, you would like a chance to look over previous issues and familiarize yourself with the publication.

Redding laughs and informs you that there is no newsletter in the company; this is a special publication in honor of the firm's 25th anniversary. Perhaps they might do a regular newsletter if this works out well, but there are no definite plans—at least none that she has heard about.

"So there's nothing for you to look at to see how we do it, but rest assured," she adds, "nobody around here knows much about journalism. In fact," she continues, "no one person is editing the newsletter. Mr. Witonski, the CEO,[1] is keeping much of the control himself and has asked several people to write articles. The whole idea is to celebrate the 25th anniversary, make the company look good, and make the employees feel good about the company, and all that other good stuff. I'm supposed to help out from here, but Melinda Brown, our secretary, will do the main job of pulling it all together."

Thinking the assignment will not be too difficult, you get up to leave Redding's cubicle.

"Be at Vandervelt's office by 3 P.M.," she concludes, as you leave.

You report to Vandervelt, a big man in a rumpled shirt with rolled-up sleeves, at 3 P.M. sharp. While attending to the buzzing of his phone and some fellow studying blueprints at his elbow, he motions you to sit down. Although he clearly expected you, he is just as clearly terribly busy, though he eventually turns to you with a warm smile.

"New around here, aren't you? Well, I'm glad to have your help on writing up this newsletter article. Sorry I don't have much time to fill you in on everything about the project at Clarkstone—that's what the article is about. I just have too much to do before I go into the hospital on Monday. But I'll run over the main points."

You take out your yellow pad, and Vandervelt begins.

"We just finished a project at our Clarkstone Plant—the one in Nebraska, in the middle of nowhere. Boy is it cold in the winter on those plains. Oh, sorry, this is Bob McCormick," he says gesturing toward the young man looking at the blueprints. "Let's see. Where were we? Uh, I worked on it over the past few years with Bud Avery, the plant manager at Clarkstone; problem was dirty mist polluting the plant. We finally solved it a few months ago, and we have the control

---

[1] CEO stands for chief executive officer.

equipment going great. That plant is now as clean as a whistle," he says with a proud smile.

You nod, thinking of the local plant, wondering what he means by "clean as a whistle."

Vandervelt removes a mint from a roll of candy in his pocket, and goes ahead. "Witonski wanted us to get some PR for the company on how well we solved this mist problem in the Clarkstone Plant . . . " He stops. "I suppose you realize that when you grind steel and finish it to tolerances in the millionths of an inch, you have to run a lot of coolant over the abrasive wheels. When you run the coolant—either kerosene or water—the high-speed machines throw out all this dirty mist, and the hoods around each machine can't catch all of it. It simply sticks to everything. Builds up on all the equipment and on the building itself. It's a mess."

Nodding, you assure Vandervelt that you understand the nature of the pollution problem in a steel-grinding operation, since you have been over at the Tremont plant several times this past week.

"Oh, Tremont. It's terrible. Old and filthy. It meets OSHA[2] standards, but barely; I can't see how, frankly. But Clarkstone is another world. It's a new plant, only about eight years old now, and it's got all the newest equipment. If the workers at Tremont saw Clarkstone, they'd all have a fit."

"So I gather they don't realize that it could be a lot cleaner here?" you ask.

"Well, that's not quite accurate," muses Vandervelt. "Tremont is an old operation. No matter what we did there, it could never be as clean as Clarkstone. Anyway, I was telling you that Witonski asked me to write up this project and submit it to a plant management journal."

You must look somewhat startled because Vandervelt laughs and says, "Say, you're not going to have to write the journal article! Anyway, I don't mean to mislead you. This is no high-powered engineering journal. Only a pub called *Maintenance for Manufacturers.* Witonski reads the thing, and I think he wanted to brag about Erickson/Engelberg a bit. Anyway, I thought it was a pretty good idea, so one day I sat down and wrote something up. Guess I didn't think about it too much ahead of time—just sort of told the story of what

---

[2] OSHA stands for Occupational Safety and Health Administration.

we did at Clarkstone. Anyway, here's my first effort," he says, handing you a sheaf of papers. (See Appendix A.) "Put it away to read later."

You put the papers in your folder, and Vandervelt continues.

"Soon as I finished, I started to think that I'd like to see what Bud Avery would put into the article. So without showing him my version, I badgered him into writing a couple of pages." Vandervelt laughs out loud. "'Big Bud' hates to write. I knew all along that I would have to do the job myself. Well, here's Bud's write-up." (See Appendix B.)

"After that I got an idea. I decided to call one of the editors at *Maintenance for Manufacturers* and get some advice before I went any further. I told her about our pollution project and asked her if they'd be interested. She was very encouraging. Liked the story, gave me some suggestions for laying it out, which I tried to follow as I started to rewrite the thing." And he hands you a third sheaf of papers. (See Appendix C.)

By now you are wondering what all these drafts for *Maintenance for Manufacturers* have to do with the newsletter article you're supposed to write. Vandervelt is sure getting to the point slowly.

"That's not the whole article," he says with a wave of his hand at your folder. "Just the first few pages, and now it will have to wait until I get back here in a couple of months. But the anniversary newsletter can't wait. So that's where you come in."

You nod slightly and ask, "What is it that Mr. Witonski wants in the newsletter piece? I should think it would be quite different from the journal article you were writing."

"You've got the right idea," Vandervelt heartily agrees. "You'll have to revamp everything because this is for the employees: everyone in all the plants, hourly and salaried, and everyone here at corporate headquarters."

"So it's to make everyone here feel that Clarkstone is the greatest and cleanest plant in the world, and that this shows the employees what a great company Erickson/Engelberg is to work for?"

"Something like that," Vandervelt grins. "But Witonski also wants a lot more than that. He wants to be able to have something to show people *outside* the company that we not only meet OSHA standards, but that we go out of our way to surpass them, that we do the right thing by our employees, that we run a tight, first-class operation, that we are a good-boy company, that . . ."

"I don't understand," you interrupt. "What do you mean by showing people 'outside the company'?"

"Oh, Witonski will want to reprint it so our sales people can use

it. Show customers what a great company we are; more than just pushing the products. Also he might use it to get some PR through the
newspapers. Good publicity in the community—not only here but also
in Clarkstone."

"So I gather what I'm writing is not just for this newsletter."

"Well, I suppose that depends on how good your article is," Vandervelt laughs. "The newsletter is the reason we're doing it, but if
the piece is well done, it'll probably get a lot of distribution. Listen,
the Clarkstone Plant was Witonski's pet project right from the start.
The pollution control project was really his idea. It might never have
been done at all if he hadn't had this grand plan about making Clarkstone a model plant. Now that the project worked out so well, he
obviously wants the whole world to know about it. It's your job to
help that to happen."

"Okay. I've got the idea. What's the Clarkstone plant manager's
role going to be in this?"

"Hmm . . . I guess you can send your finished article to Bud Avery
to make sure you've got all the facts right. Might be a good idea to do
that. But Bud figured that he wrote the whole thing up in that article
I gave you. Wouldn't be any use to ask him to write a piece for the
newsletter. I'd say you're on your own."

"I gather everything I need to know about the project is in these
drafts?" you ask.

"I hope so," Mr. V. frowns, running his hand through his shock
of white hair. "But let me just give you the overall picture. The big
question for us was, should we have a central pollution control system
with all the grinding machines connected by ducts to one system, or
should we have individual machines. We found out that the best was
an individual system. We've got an enclosure, like a shell, around each
machine and a *separate* collector for each one too, so it's totally individual. The enclosure is a box, a beautiful stainless steel and aluminum affair, custom-made for us, not just a simple hood. Has doors,
air inlets, and a hose attachment to the collector. The system is electrostatic." The phone rings, and as he answers it, Vandervelt hands
you a manufacturer's brochure on the system saying, "Read this paragraph." (See Figure 1.)

You quickly scan the paragraph. When Vandervelt puts down the
phone, he looks questioningly at you: "You got it? See how it works?
Simple principle of opposites attract. So the oil ends up on the plates,
and the air is recirculated into the plant. Works beautifully."

"That's sufficient to remove everything?" you ask.

> When the air is drawn into the Klean–Air system, it
> first passes through an electrical field. The airborne
> particles, some as small as 0.03 micron, here receive a
> strong electrical charge. The air then passes into a
> second section containing a metal plate of the opposite
> electrical charge. This plate attracts and captures the
> ionized particles, and the air is returned to the room
> with up to 99% of the impurities removed.

Figure 1. Paragraph from Klean-Air Brochure

"A prefilter takes out the coarse particles first, but that's all. And the whole thing is fairly quiet. Just uses a small motor and a blower to circulate the air."

"Uh, what about those dirty plates?"

Vandervelt smiles broadly. "Excellent question. As the kerosene or water washes over the metal collecting plates, cooling them off, the drops of mist mix in with the coolant. Any solids are just carried along in this flow. The gunk then just drains into a sump,[3] and eventually the coolant is recirculated. The whole thing is self-cleaning."

"Self-cleaning?" you ask incredulously.

"Right," says Vandervelt with enthusiasm. "We never need— well, almost never need—to wash the plates manually."

"Am I to say 'never' needs cleaning or what?" you ask.

"Well, 'almost never' is fine. Just let it go at that. Remember what you're writing this for. Frankly, things like the reductions we made in our whopping fuel bills in those horrible Nebraska winters, that's the sort of thing that matters. Under the old system we were pumping out an enormous volume of air, all loaded up with oil mist. And replacing it with clean air which we had to heat. We're saving almost $50,000 per year on our fuel bills. If you have any other questions, after you've read over all this stuff. . . . Oh, here is some information outlining the system from Klean-Air that might help. [See Appendix D.] As I was saying, if you have questions, call Bud Avery. Best of luck."

---

[3] The sump is a pit at the lowest point in the drainage system into which the solids collect.

You get up, thanking Vandervelt and wishing him luck on his operation and a speedy recovery.

"Don't forget to send a copy to Witonski when it's done," he says with a smile.

Back at your desk, you start looking over Avery's and Vandervelt's material. What had originally sounded like a little newsletter assignment seems to be an opportunity for showing what you can do. Before you are done with this, Mr. Witonski should know who you are.

First you read over everything that Vandervelt gave you (Appendixes A through D). Although some points are not clear at first, you manage to interpret all the ambiguous sections, because explanations appear in later drafts. Once you have made a careful study of the three drafts of the journal paper and the proposal from the vendor, you have a fairly good picture of the Clarkstone project. Then you begin to wonder what the ordinary folks in the company know about it, and also what their opinions are. You decide to talk to a few people to get a better idea of how your readers will be approaching your article.

First you seek out one of the salesmen you've met, an older guy named Doug Whitman, who likes to chat, and you ask him about Clarkstone. "Have you ever been there?"

"Of course. Off and on, over the years. Since it was first built."

"Do you remember what it was like before they put in the pollution control equipment?" you ask.

"Sure do. Frankly, I thought it was a mild embarrassment. Management would have us drag big clients through Clarkstone to show off our state-of-the-art plant, but it didn't look so great, I can tell you."

"So you figured it needed cleaning up?"

"You bet. But now it looks pretty good."

Your next contact occurs accidentally in the canteen. While you are heating some soup, you begin chatting with the chief accountant, who asks what you are doing. You tell him about the newsletter story on Clarkstone, and he immediately offers you what he calls "the real reason" they did this pollution control project. According to him (and he tells you pointedly that he's speaking "off the record"), it was an anti-unionization issue. There was talk of unionizing at the Clarkstone Plant, and management got very scared. They wanted to do something big, a gesture to show the rank and file that the company cared about them. "It's a very sensitive issue, friend, and nobody will give you the straight dope on it. What Witonski wants in this newsletter article is to show the employees how benevolent and fine Erickson/Engelberg is. The truth of the matter is that the pollution problem was there from the time the plant opened up, but nobody did anything about it for something like five years, not until the unionization issue reared its ugly head."

You thank your new acquaintance for his opinion, and later that day you drop in to talk with Marsha Redding in Product Development. You tell her that you've heard that the Clarkstone Plant cleanup was an anti-unionization effort. She frowns immediately and says that she has never heard that, and you had better steer clear of that issue in your write-up. You agree, but you ask her why they went after the Clarkstone Plant when it was clearly meeting OSHA standards for particulate removal. After all, they have several other plants, all of which are older and evidently much dirtier. "Polluted" was certainly the right word for them, if not for Clarkstone.

"Right," says Marsha, "but don't use the word 'pollution' at all here. Any plant meeting OSHA standards isn't polluted. Certainly never mention the word as far as Clarkstone is concerned. The CEO, Mr. Witonski, built Clarkstone with a vision in mind, a vision of having the best plant possible, and best clearly meant cleanest, as well as a lot of other things."

"But what about the employees at all the other plants?" you wonder. "How would they feel about the gunk in their old plants when they know the company has a great new plant that they're spending money on to make even better?"

"Well, nobody said too much about that," Marsha replies slowly. "Management always called Clarkstone a pilot project, suggesting that any benefits achieved there would later trickle down to the other plants. Why are you so concerned about that?" she frowns.

"I guess I figured that the guys at the other plants would be some of the most interested readers of the article I must write. They might just be wondering when they could expect a spanking clean plant for themselves."

"You're right, I suppose," Marsha muses. "They might start thinking about that. Hmm. Maybe you should just play up the angle that the company didn't want to build a new plant that was 'state of the art' and not have it be really clean. You know, meeting government standards doesn't mean much if it still *looks* dirty." She pauses. "It's a dicey matter. Perhaps you can stress the 'flagship of the fleet' notion." Finally she concludes brightly, "I'm sure you'll figure out something!"

"I hope so," you reply.

"By the way," Marsha says as you get up to leave, "don't forget that most of the workers have less than a high school education. Keep it simple. No fifty-dollar words."

"I figured that," you reply. "Say, how long should this article be?"

"About 1,000 words, I should say," replies Marsha.

Note: Assignments 1 through 5 below are a sequence of writing tasks in preparing the newsletter article. However, it is not necessary to write any of the preparatory assignments to complete the major assignment of writing the newsletter article itself.

ASSIGNMENT 1

Collect newsletters from three organizations, preferably medium-sized business or industrial firms. (You can get newsletters through friends, or you can call the public relations office of most organizations and ask for a copy of their newsletter. Although newsletters are intended for internal distribution, most companies are happy to give them to clients and other members of the public.) Look over the newsletters to get an idea of their style and approach to their audiences. Write a brief statement summarizing your ideas about how to write a newsletter article.

ASSIGNMENT 2

Write a draft of a 1,000-word newsletter article presenting management's view of the solution to the pollution problem at Clarkstone. The newsletter article will go to the whole corporation, including salaried and hourly personnel at all four plants and the corporate offices.

ASSIGNMENT 3

Write a memo to B.D. Avery, Plant Manager, Clarkstone Plant, Clarkstone, Nebraska 00000, to cover your article's manuscript. (Recall that Vandervelt advised you to send it to Avery to verify the contents.) You are Technical Writer, Product Development Department, Corporate Offices, Tremont, California 00000.

ASSIGNMENT 4

After one of your class colleagues has reviewed your manuscript (role playing Bud Avery), incorporate any changes you feel will improve it and send it on to Marsha Redding. Write a cover memo to Marsha Redding, Supervisor of Documentation, Product Development Department, to get her comments and suggestions for your final draft.

ASSIGNMENT 5

Prepare a final draft of your manuscript, and write a cover memo to President Walter W. Witonski.

Note: Assignments 6 through 9 are tasks to be completed after publication of the newsletter.

ASSIGNMENT 6

Write either a 200-word press release for the newspaper in the town of Clarkstone, the *Clarion,* or a 200-word release for the San Diego *Daily Herald.* (Tremont, where corporate headquarters is located, is near San Diego.)

ASSIGNMENT 7

The copies of the company newsletter article have been printed up in separate handouts to be used by your salespersons in fostering the idea of Erickson/Engelberg as a first-class manufacturing company. Paul Peters, a young engineer in Vandervelt's group, has been asked by the head of sales to give a five-minute briefing on the Clarkstone project at the next regional sales managers' meeting. (Peters is not very familiar with the history of the Clarkstone project; he is just pinch-hitting for Vandervelt.) Peters' job is to fill in the salespersons on the background for the newsletter article so that they can discuss Clarkstone intelligently with customers.

You are assigned to help Peters, a rather quiet engineer who immediately tells you that he does not like to give presentations. "Since the audience is a bunch of salesmen, I don't even know what they might want to hear," he shrugs. "Perhaps you can give me a plan for it?"

Write an outline for an extemporaneous speech, noting the major points and supporting information that you believe Peters could give in about five minutes.

All of the ten salesmen attending the meeting where Peters will speak will have received the newsletter about three weeks before the briefing. (Whether they will have read it, who can say?) No salesman on the Erickson/Engelberg staff is an engineer, but all have received training in the manufacturing procedures used in your operation.

ASSIGNMENT 8

Mr. Witonski has a business contact, Jay McLeod, who manufactures a precision steel product requiring grinding and superfinishing similar to your plant's operations. This last weekend, Witonski chatted with McLeod at a party and mentioned the individual machine pollution control system at Erickson/Engelberg. McLeod evidently expressed much interest in Witonski's decision to adopt an individualized system because McLeod's own engineers are leaning toward a new centralized system for their plant. Witonski closed the conversation with a promise to get some information on the subject to McLeod.

Today Witonski asks you to prepare a letter, "actually almost a little report, I guess," he calls it, to tell McLeod why Erickson/Engelberg decided to go with an individualized system. "I owe McLeod a favor," Witonski says, "so I want you to tell him in some detail why we decided that the individual system is so superior. I don't know if his situation is much like ours, but I want to share our experience with him. Then he can decide if it pertains to his plant. I wouldn't mind if he learns about our model plant at Clarkstone, anyway!" Witonski smiles.

Write a report for Witonski's signature to Mr. Jason McLeod, Precision Products Corporation, Box 83, San Diego, California 00000. Your letterhead is Erickson/Engelberg, Inc., Tremont, California 00000. (Write your name on the upper-right corner of this paper to identify it for your instructor.)

ASSIGNMENT 9

Mr. Witonski has been invited to present a talk at the annual awards banquet for the Science Fair winners in San Diego. (The winners are junior and senior high school students from the San Diego area.) The choice of topic is up to Witonski (something about the relevance of science to industry), and he has decided to talk about the Clarkstone project. (Evidently he liked your article in the newsletter!) Today his secretary calls and asks you to write a manuscript for a ten-minute talk. (It is common practice for top management to speak from manuscripts prepared by staff.) She tells you to assume that Witonski will spend the first few minutes talking about the Science Fair and then will make an appropriate transition to talking about how industry constantly uses science in the quest for improved manufacturing—which is what he wants from you. You agree and now must write the manuscript to tell about Clarkstone in seven minutes.

APPENDIX A

Vandervelt's First Draft

Mist Removal—Clarkstone Plant

As the plant capacity increased, the oil mist generated by the grinding machines created a problem which required a solution.

In order to determine the best way to remove the oil mist, Bud Avery and I visited the Plant Engineering Show in Chicago. From the information obtained from the various manufacturers of mist removal equipment, those with the apparently best equipment were selected to come into the plant and view the problem, and to make specific recommendations: the Zale Corporation, Ward Co., Fulton, and Klean—Air.

The only stipulation made to these firms was that they were required to provide a performance guarantee, and field tests would be required to substantiate the claimed performance. No other equipment limitations were placed on the suppliers.

The four manufacturers responded with proposals for various types of equipment ranging from a large central mist collecting system with an automatic self cleaning feature which required the construction of an outside shelter for the collector, to small individual self contained units. We considered the various methods proposed to eliminate the oil mist, and the relative merits of a central vs. individual unit collection system.[4]

(continued)

---

[4] Individual units not only have a shell enclosing each machine to capture the mist, but a completely separate collector for each machine. A centralized system would connect many grinding machines to one large collector through an elaborate, stationary duct system.

APPENDIX A—*continued*

INDIVIDUAL UNITS VS.	CENTRAL SYSTEMS
Servicing of any type can be done from floor level. Service would be much quicker and easier.	All servicing would have to be done high in the air.[5] This would require more time.
Service can be performed by one man and would require no equipment.	Service would usually require the time of two men and use of some type of equipment such as a fork lift. Not always available.
Damage to components should be considerably less because of less handling under much more workable conditions. Also, components are much smaller and lighter weight.	Components would have to be handled more times and being larger and heavier would be subjected to a proportionately higher risk of damage.
No ductwork to clean except for small short connecting hoses.	Extensive fixed ductwork that will require periodic cleaning due to settling out of particulate matter.
Individual control of each machine. Any possible breakdown affects only that one machine. Units would be mounted in such a manner as to permit the removal and replacement of a complete air cleaner within a very few minutes. A spare unit would be on hand at all times to minimize downtime. Only one machine would be putting effluent into the air for a very short period of time should this happen.	Many machines would be controlled by one air cleaner. Breakdown would cause all to put contamination into the atmosphere. It is impractical and almost impossible to do anything except the most simple of repairs with the unit in operation. In the case of a major breakdown it is impractical to replace the unit so downtime could be lengthy.

[5] A centralized system collector, suspended from the ceiling, would hang high off the plant floor, approximately 18–20 feet up.

APPENDIX A—*continued*

Each air cleaner would drain the collected oil back into the respective production machine it came from.

Collected oil would have to be drained back into one production machine or discarded.[6]

Since each air cleaner only will service one machine any possible fire hazard would be limited in size and easily contained with the hazard area easily accessible.

Any possible fire hazard would be of much more magnitude and not readily accessible.

Individual units would be much more aesthetically pleasing because there would be no ductwork suspended within the work area. Each unit would appear as an extended part of each production machine.

Numerous ducts both horizontal and vertical would detract from the aesthetics of the interior of the building and present a possibility of interference with existing conveyors and lighting systems.

Entire system would be completely flexible. Production machines could be added, removed, or changed to a different position to fit the ever changing work requirements without affecting other machines or ductwork.

Any additions, removals, or relocating of production machines would require a major change in ductwork.

(continued)

[6] The central system would require extensive ductwork to recycle the coolant back to each production machine; thus the only feasible options are recycling it back to a single production machine or discarding it.

APPENDIX A—*continued*

Since each unit would only service one machine, the air flow on any one machine can be adjusted to fit that particular machine. The ideal situation would be to have the smallest air flow through each separate machine that would still capture the most contamination. Units turned on only for operating machines.	Since there would be a series of production machines connected to one larger unit it is impossible to change the air flow on any one machine without a corresponding change of air flow in all other machines connected to that unit. Also the entire system would be on regardless of the number of machines in operation.
Since the individual units can be serviced from floor level the total maintenance cost should be much less.	Would require periodic manual cleaning. Since cleaners are mounted high in the air, cost would probably be somewhat higher.
The cost of installing an extensive central system would be eliminated.	An elaborate central ducting system would have to be installed.

Based on the above comparison, it was decided to pursue the individual collector approach and to work with Klean–Air of Oakland, California, while they developed their unit under our existing conditions. Although each manufacturer claimed their equipment would clean up the oil mist, none would provide a written performance guarantee, except Klean–Air was agreeable to bring their equipment in at no cost to us and to develop a performance standard under our conditions.

Many initial problems were encountered with the Klean–Air electrostatic collecting unit.

APPENDIX A—*continued*

```
    1) Insulators shorted out.
    2) Etching of the collector plates occurred.
    3) Varnishing⁷ occurred on internal surfaces.
All of the above problems were solved with modifications
to the unit which included:
    Coating the collecting plates to prevent corrosion.
    Relocation of the internal controls
    Using stand off insulators
    Adding a mechanical prefilter
    The above development took place over a considerable
period of time (approximately 6 months). During this
period, individual machine hoods were designed and
ordered.

    On 3/8/83 we had an independent laboratory perform
in and out efficiency tests and the following results
were obtained on the Klean-Air unit - 96.94%
particulates removed.
    We continued to monitor mist collector performance
through June 1983.
    From the tests which were conducted, and the
experience gained during the trial period, the following
concepts were conceived.
    Attributes for Smoke and Mist Control from Machine
Tools.
    1) Source capture, i.e., totally close in the
       machine, not just a hood or curtains; cross
       drafts, etc., will affect a certain amount of
       mist escapement.
    2) Exhaust port location.⁸ Locate the exhaust port
       away from major splashing and agitating of the
       coolant liquids, don't allow anything but the
       fine particle mist to enter the exhaust tube.
```

(continued)

---

⁷ Varnish is the buildup of particles and coolant on the ductwork and the collector.

⁸ Smoke and mist leave the grinding area through the exhaust duct and enter the duct leading to the collector. The port must be located sufficiently far back from the grinding operation so that coolant does not splash directly into the duct.

APPENDIX A—*continued*

3) At least 6 inch diameter exhaust tube or larger, if feasible. This reduces the velocity of the air movement so that only the light mist that does not fall out naturally is entered into the filter system.
4) Use low CFM[9] air flow, 100–300 CFM is adequate to evacuate the mist from 1 machine, if adequately enclosed.
   —The low CFM allows for natural drop out of heavy liquids and particulate.
   —It allows the mist to travel through air cleaners, with maximum contact and coalescing.
5) All ductwork or tubes to be pitched and jointed so that all liquids can drain back and not collect in low spots or leak at seams.
   —Old coolant retained in ductwork will become rancid and create bad odors.

By 6/24/83 the decision was made to use the electro-static precipitator unit made by Klean–Air. The units gave excellent performance and tended to be self cleaning because the collected coolant washed the plates.
Tests proved that manual cleaning of the cells could be prolonged to a period in excess of six months. After the initial correction, the units ran through the test period maintenance free.
   A purchase order was written to Klean–Air on 1/18/84 for $187,435 for 86 electrostatic precipitator type units and spare parts for use on the grinders and superfinishers in the Clarkstone plant.
   This order contained proven performance guarantees.
   The entire project is scheduled for completion by November 1984.

---

[9] CFM is cubic feet per minute, a measurement of the volume of air a blower can draw.

APPENDIX B

Avery's Draft

The first winter after the plant was started, it was evident the impingement type air mist collectors which were bought with the machines were not doing the job.

When the plant was buttoned up for the winter weather, the smoke and mist contaminated the plant atmosphere to such a degree that oil started to drip from the superstructure.

The plant was originally designed with a well-balanced exhaust and tempered fresh air makeup, but as the costs for energy increased, it became uneconomical to exhaust all the heated air. <u>A project</u> was initiated with the objective to clean up the air and retain it in the building for winter heating.

We set parameters to follow to obtain the most efficient equipment available.

1) Best percentage of particulate removal
2) Central system versus a unit per machine
3) Check the need for area ceiling units for collecting any escaped mist from the other sources
4) Return the clean air into the building
5) Keep noise level below OSHA standards
6) Maintenance requirements
7) Filter replacement
8) Interference with work area
9) Cosmetic appearance
10) Manufacturers warranty as to percentage of particulate removal
11) The need for hoods and machine closures for source capture

With all these things in mind, we embarked on a major in-house testing program. We asked several companies to supply their product for evaluation. Most were miserable failures, some were fair, but none met our expectations.

(continued)

APPENDIX B—*continued*

Out of these tests, two types of equipment showed promise and two companies were willing to work with us in revising the equipment and retesting it. After working with the two firms for a few months, however, we asked the Zale Corporation of Chicago, Illinois to withdraw, and we set up a full-scale project with the Klean-Air Company of Oakland, California. Their unit is of the electrostatic precipitator principle and works very well on our machines.

As the coolant and smoke collect on the plates of the cell, it creates a liquid which drains off; thus they have a continuous self-washing effect. In over a year's operation, we have incurred zero maintenance and again the clean air is exhausted in the work area.

Central systems versus a unit per machine: Our studies indicated the individual units had more flexibility allowing ease of changes of plant layout and in case of a breakdown, you only lose the unit. With a central system you have the whole system down.

There is also easy installation with a flexible duct to each machine. With a central system there is a large fixed duct, no flexibility, balancing problems and oil leaks.

A few things which our study pointed out in the selection of equipment and their operating efficiency are:

1) Install good designed machine closures, capture the mist at the source.

2) Use a low CFM blower-only move enough air to evacuate the grinder closure.
   -This allows time for the heavy particulate to fall out naturally and does not overload the mist collector. With a good closure, 400 CFM is adequate even on the biggest machines.

3) Each particular mist problem has to be evaluated and the equipment tailored to suit. This can only be done by actual trial and tests. Our units are 5th generation from the original test units.

APPENDIX B—*continued*

We have 86 units from Klean—Air, some with 200 CFM blowers and some with 400 CFM, depending on the application to heat treatment, grinding, or superfinishing.

Some spin—off advantages we have found are: The grinders hold size better. The air movement keeps the thermal expansion stabilized.[10]

The relative humidity of the cleaned air is equal to outside before the humidity generated in the machines raised it in the plant.

With the new closures on the machines, there is no splashing of coolant out of the machine. We have a clean floor and work area. We return a large number of gallons of grinding coolant back to the system daily. The air in the plant is almost 99% free of smoke and mists.

[10] Steel tends to expand under the high temperatures reached during the grinding process. Coolant (water or kerosene) tends to cool the steel, of course, but the air movement of the blower assists this process.

APPENDIX C

Vandervelt's Second Draft

Problems

The 140,000 sq ft plant in Clarkstone, Nebraska
manufactures precision steel parts for the aircraft
industry. The first winter after the plant started
operation, it was evident that the impingement type mist
collectors which were purchased with the grinding and
superfinishing machines were inadequate for the job. The
high speed grinding and polishing abrasive wheels hurled
large quantities of very finely divided coolant into the
air. Because of inadequate machine hooding, much of this
oil mist escaped into the room. Large quantities of oil
mist still entered the mist collectors, and soon they
became so laden with oil that they became a contamination source. The continuing oil mist and smoke problem
resulting from the manufacturing process was creating a
condition which was not conducive to a first class
operation. The superstructure was accumulating oil,
which not only created a fire hazard; but drippings
prevented cleanliness. Additionally, in order not to
build up oil mist concentrations in the plant atmosphere
during the winter months, large volumes of air had to be
exhausted. This air had to be replaced with heated make-
up air.

Solution

A project was initiated with the objectives of
cleaning up the plant air, and to eliminate the need to
discharge large quantities of air to the outside. In
order to determine the best solution to our problem many
manufacturers were contacted and selected to come into
our plant to view the problem, and to make specific
recommendations. The only stipulation made to these
firms was that if their equipment were selected they
would be required to provide a performance guarantee
which would have to be substantiated with field tests.
All of the manufacturers responded with proposals
for various types of equipment ranging from a large
central mist collecting system with an automatic self-
cleaning feature which required the construction of an

APPENDIX C—*continued*

outside shelter for the collector to small individual
self contained units. Each manufacturer claimed their
equipment would clean up the oil mist, but none would
provide a written performance guarantee at this point.
Several agreed to bring trial units in and work with us
to develop their performance standard under our conditions.

It was at this point that several decisions were
made. First, no matter what type of mist collecting
equipment was chosen, source capture would be used. It
did not make sense to allow the oil mist to travel up in
the plant contaminating everything along the way and
finally collecting the mist in a ceiling-hung mist
collector. Therefore, machine enclosures were designed
and ordered. Secondly, the decision was made to use
individual machine mist collecting units instead of a
central system type. The reasons were many but some of
the major ones were[11]:

With the above considerations we began our evaluation of mist collecting equipment provided by the Klean-
Air Company of Oakland, California. The Klean-Air unit
was a newly developed electronic air cleaner, and seemed
best suited for our needs. The Klean-Air equipment was
tried and evaluated for a period of about a year and one
half on our machines.

Many initial problems were encountered. The Klean-
Air unit experienced shorting across the insulators,
etching of the plates, and varnish build-up. As each
problem occurred it was analyzed and solved by the

(*continued*)

[11] At this point Vandervelt had left a blank space.

APPENDIX C—*continued*

manufacturer. The final equipment evolving as a result
of the trial was several generations beyond the original
design. From the experience gained during the trial
period, the following concepts were conceived:
1) Totally close in the machine. A hood or curtains
   is not sufficient to prevent cross drafts from
   causing mist escapement.
2) Locate the hood enclosure exhaust port away from
   major splashing of the coolant. Allow only fine
   mist to enter the exhaust tube.
3) Use low CFM air. 100-300 CFM (in a 6-inch
   diameter tube) is adequate to evacuate the mist
   from one machine. This allows for natural drop
   out of heavy liquids and particulate.
4) All ductwork should be pitched back to the
   machine for natural drainage.

After the initial design changes on the Klean-Air
unit, it ran through the test period maintenance free.
The unit tended to be self cleaning because the
collected coolant tended to wash the plates. Tests
proved that manual cleaning of the cells could be
prolonged to a period in excess of six months.

The entire project was completed in December 1984.

Results
     Field tests have been conducted both by the manu-
facturer and an independent laboratory. Results show
that over 95% of all particles down to sub-micron size
are being removed. There is a visible difference in the
atmospheres in both the grinding and heat treat
departments. Oil mist is no longer being deposited on
the superstructure.

     Calculations indicate that as a result of reducing
the amount of exhausted air, the savings resulting from
eliminating the need for corresponding make-up air will
be $49,000/yr.

APPENDIX D

Proposal from the Vendor

Klean-Air Company
Travis Street, Oakland, California 00000

November 10, 1982

TO: Mr. B. D. Avery
        Clarkstone Plant
        Erickson/Engelberg, Incorporated
        Clarkstone, Nebraska 00000

SUBJECT: Klean-Air Electronic Air Cleaning Systems

Dear Mr. Avery:

    Thank you for affording us the opportunity to work with you and your company in solving the problem of the heavy accumulation of oil mist in your plant during production hours.
    Klean-Air is the leader in the control of interior air pollution. You can be assured that we represent the finest air cleaning equipment available, backed by the latest in engineering and technical advances.
    We are one of a worldwide network of full service Klean-Air distributors and we are looking forward to doing business with your company in helping to control your in-plant air pollution problems.
    If you have further questions please contact me at 000-415-9927.

                    Sincerely,

                    John Harden

                    John Harden
                    for the Klean-Air Company

(continued)

APPENDIX D—*continued*

SCOPE:

    This proposal has been generated to meet your specific needs, utilizing the information we have discussed during our visits to your Clarkstone Plant.
    This system is designed to effectively source-capture the oil mist that is continuously produced during the operation of the production grinding and polishing machines in your plant. This area contains a possible 106 production machines of which there are now 81 in place and operating daily. All of the machines are high speed operations and generate the oil mist that accumulates throughout the work area on the floors, ceilings, lights, walls, equipment, and other fixtures.
    The Klean-Air Cleaning System will provide a cleaner, brighter, safer, and more healthful place in which to work.

THE PROPOSED SYSTEM:

    Following the evaluation of the above data and the results obtained from test equipment in your plant, we recommend the Klean-Air System comprising the following industrial grade air cleaners.

Seventy seven (77)	Klean-Air Model A 30 Electronic Air Cleaners. One unit to be installed at each enclosed production machine.
Four (4)	Klean-Air Model B 44 Electronic Air Cleaners. One unit to be installed at each of the centerless grinders.
Five (5)	Klean-Air Model D 60 Electronic Air Cleaners. These units to be suspended overhead in a free-hanging pattern in the production area.

APPENDIX D—*continued*

PRINCIPLES OF THE SYSTEM:

Electrostatic precipitation is an operation which utilizes electrostatic forces to separate suspended particles from the air. Based on the principle that all matter can be given an electrostatic charge, our system passes the smoke or oil laden air through an intensive electrostatic field thereby imparting a strong charge to the particles suspended in the air stream. The charged particles are then attracted to oppositely charged metal collecting plates, allowing the cleaned air to pass from the unit. The cleaned air is recirculated directly into the work area.

MODEL A 30

Each Model A 30 is mounted on the floor pedestal adjacent to the production machine. The air cleaner is attached directly to the grinder by a short air duct. The air to be processed is drawn through the openings of the enclosed machines entraining the oil mist in the air stream ensuring capture through the air duct into the air cleaner. The contaminants are collected by the electronic filters and the cleaned air is then discharged through the blower into the immediate area. The collected oil mist forms droplets that drain into the sump and back into the production line for reuse.

MODEL B 44

Each Model B 44 will also be mounted on a pedestal over the centerless grinders and each will be equipped with a capture hood. The hood will be suspended from a movable arm so as to be retracted when the grinder needs to be serviced with the jib crane.

(continued)

APPENDIX D—*continued*

MODEL D 60

The Model D 60 units will be suspended from overhead in a free-hanging pattern to circulate the upper air throughout the area. These units will capture the contaminants that are generated from other sources as well as the small amount that may penetrate the system. The high velocity air being discharged from the blowers of these units will move the air in front of the units toward the suction inlet or capture zone of the next unit. This will provide a "moving ceiling" of air throughout the production area and provide collection for airborne contaminants.

BENEFITS OF THE SYSTEM

1) Clean air in the plant.
2) Increased employee health and safety.
3) Cleaner floors, lights, walls, ceilings, and fixtures.
4) Increased employee productivity.
5) Energy conservation from reduced exhaust and heat system usage.
6) Reduced building maintenance.

For a successful system that provides the desired results of overall effectiveness, ease of maintenance, and aesthetic appearance, this Klean-Air System is the best system for your plant.

The Computer Center Proposal: Evaluating Software/Hardware for DiGiorgio Frozen Foods

Part 1

Fred Marvel clears his throat and leans over to unpack his display boards and set them up on his chrome-plated chart stand. He takes his time, looking confident that he has done a good job of selling DiGiorgio Frozen Foods his consulting services and a lot of Dataterm hardware and software to boot. Now he just has to summarize his proposal and seal the deal. You feel there is not much you can do about it, but then, you are not sure you *should* do anything about it.

You get up and decide to walk around the conference room a bit. The modern teak furnishings and subdued gray and beige decor reflect the recent prosperity of DiGiorgio Frozen Foods. Only eight years in business and already adding new branch offices. With more business and more paperwork, computer data processing really is the only way to go.

Owner Tony DiGiorgio throws a glance your way; he must think that you are planning to leave the room before Marvel sums up his presentation. You put your hand up and smile, signaling that you do not intend to go anywhere, even though you wish there were somewhere you could go. Only two and a half months on the job as Tony's administrative assistant, and already he treats you like his heir. You wish you knew more about purchasing computer systems so that you could help him make the right decision. You know Tony has to computerize his operation immediately, but that urgency could keep him and his staff from seeing the holes in Marvel's computer center plan.

You look cautiously at the others called to this meeting: Al Greenberg, Vice-President of Operations, and Julie Cresback, Senior Accountant. The sales and distribution managers had to cancel because

343

of a backlog of work. Their presence would not have helped in any case. You doubt that any of them has had any time to do some real planning for the company's future; all the top people at DiGiorgio Frozen Foods have been marching double-time since the business started.

When you left Star Foods in Philadelphia for this job in Kansas City, you thought things would be less harried. Things should be a little slower in the Midwest, more considered. You guessed wrong. As a matter of fact, you wish you were back at Star right now. They were switching to a computerized operation too. Sue Collins, the assistant to the operations VP, was in charge of the changeover. It surely would help if Sue were here.

You stop pacing and sit down. It looks like Marvel is ready to come in for the kill. He flashes you and DiGiorgio a toothy grin.

"So you see, Tony," he begins (Geez, you think, he treats Tony like a buddy), "Dataterm and I can provide you with all the computer equipment, software,[1] and consulting service you need to bring DiGiorgio's Frozen Foods into the computer age and meet your expansion needs for the next five years."

You wonder a lot about that. It seems as though Marvel has not been around long enough to take a hard look at Tony's expansion plans.

"So let me sum up what you'll need, Tony, to meet your objective of simplifying product inventory and handling expanded sales and personnel record keeping when you start those four new regional offices." Marvel clears his throat and then begins his analysis. "For data management, you'll need our accounting, payroll, inventory control, and remote distribution[2] software packages. First of all, we will set up the accounting and payroll software systems. These will be the easiest to implement. One to three months later, you can hook up the

---

[1] "Software" refers to a collection of programs and routines that make a computer perform a function or facilitate the programming of a computer. In this case, the software is a series of programs to manage data so that company personnel can use the computer to do such tasks as payroll computation, inventory control, and record keeping of various sorts.

[2] The inventory control and remote distribution software packages are closely integrated. The first handles record keeping for inventory within the warehouse; the second handles record keeping for inventory shipped, including customers, carriers, and dates shipped and received.

DATATERM SOFTWARE FOR DiGIORGIO FROZEN FOODS

PACKAGE	PRICE
PAYROLL	$1,400
ACCOUNTING	$1,200
INVENTORY	$2,400
REMOTE DISTRIBUTION	$800

Figure 1. Marvel's Display of Dataterm Software

inventory and remote distribution software packages. You'll purchase the basic packages from us and redesign them to suit your specific needs. This chart gives you the prices for the four packages you can purchase from us. You know, Tony, our prices are very competitive."

Marvel then uncovers a shiny display board on the chart stand (Figure 1).

You quickly jot the package prices down just before Marvel switches display boards.

"Now, on this chart," he continues, "I've displayed your current work force [Figure 2]. With the Dataterm payroll software you can store all personnel data including health-care deductions, taxes, vacation pay, absences, and bonuses for all your employees. You'll only need to make a few adjustments to the basic package to record 'commission' wages for your sales force."

You wonder what Marvel means by a "few adjustments," but quickly suppress your skepticism as you see DiGiorgio smiling confidently at you. He seems really sold on this Dataterm pitch.

Marvel keeps on going. "From what I've seen of your accounting system, Tony, Form AC–108, one of Dataterm's 150 accounting packages, will handle your account with very few changes."

Surprisingly, Julie Cresback speaks up. "Who will be making the changes, Mr. Marvel, my accountants?"

You are glad to see that someone is on the ball here.

"Why, no. The computer center will make work lighter for your

POSITIONS ON PAYROLL FOR DIGIORGIO FROZEN FOODS

POSITION	SALARY
VP OF SALES	39.9 K
SALES MANAGER	25.9 K
DIST. MANAGER	22.7 K
10 FIELD SALESMEN	18.2 K
DISPATCHING SUPER	20.4 K
6 DRIVERS	16.8 K
5 WAREHOUSE WORKERS	14.3 K
INVENTORY CLERK	12.3 K
VP OPERATIONS	37.1 K
ADMINISTRATIVE ASST.	31.5 K
OFFICE MANAGER	26.5 K
TIMEKEEPER	14.4 K
2 SECRETARIES	14.8 K
MAIL CLERK	9.1 K
ACCOUNTANT	25.2 K
2 ASST. ACCOUNTANTS	19.6 K
3 SALES RECORDS CLERKS	11.2 K

Figure 2.   Marvel's Display of the Payroll Positions

accountants. The adjustments to software[3] will be handled by your company's new computer center personnel." Julie looks like the wind has been taken out of her sails. She is definitely worried about de-

---

[3] Software is designed to handle a specific function, for example, to sort a list of names and addresses alphabetically by last name. If you want to do a different function, such as sort the list alphabetically *and* by zip code, you may have to adjust the software or acquire additional software, depending on the task, the flexibility of the software, and the programming skills of your computer personnel.

creases in her department. With less work to do, who is to say whose job will go?

"Which brings me to my next chart, Tony," Marvel continues, bringing out another crisp piece of cardboard (Figure 3). "To get and keep this operation going you'll need about eight new staff members." He points to the chart. "Now at current market wages, you can get a manager of computer operations for 30 K."

You hate it when salesmen use that computer lingo—30 K indeed. Oh well, you will forgive him if he delivers the goods.

"Now the computer operations manager will make sure all systems are coordinated and generally keep your operations people from having to get their feet wet with data processing."

Tony beams at Al Greenberg, VP of operations. Greenberg does not look pleased. You wonder if he is thinking about who will manage the computer staff, since they seem to control just about everything. It is clear that Tony has not thought of the personnel problems this new computer installation could cause.

"Under the manager of computer operations you will need two analysts," Marvel continues, "a technical analyst to complete operating systems development and a programmer analyst to maintain the programs and to plan future programs you may need. These people will redesign the Dataterm basic inventory control and remote distribution software packages to suit your needs. You'll also need three programmers, one operating programmer and two general program-

---

COMPUTER CENTER PERSONNEL

POSITION	SALARY
MANAGER OF COMPUTER OPERATIONS	30.0 K
ANALYSTS	23.0 K
PROGRAMMERS	19.0 K
COMPUTER OPERATORS	14.5 K

Figure 3.   Marvel's Breakdown of Computer Center Personnel

mers, to handle adjustments to all the software. Finally, you'll need four computer operators."

My gosh, you are thinking, Tony is going to have to hire a battalion. Are all these people needed?

Tony is on your wavelength. "This seems like a lot of new personnel for a company our size. Do we really need all these people?" he asks Marvel. "Why two analysts and three programmers? And why four operators?"

"If things worked ideally, it would take one and a half analysts, two programmers, and three operators to do the job, Tony. But you can't hire half a person, and you have to count on problems. The reason I'm suggesting two analysts and three programmers is to back up the operation—in case of sickness, vacations, and all those other things that come up. It wouldn't do any good to cut your operation to the bone, you know. You'd just end up with the system down a lot. If you start out with four operators, you will get two-shift coverage: two people on days and two on the afternoon shift. The second person on afternoons is extra, but that's your insurance for absences. You can always put this person on the day shift, if you need to, without severe impact on production and work flow. I believe it pays off to have a little leeway."

DiGiorgio says nothing for a moment. You wonder about the system "being down a lot." Marvel mentioned that as if it were an expectation, rather than an exception to the rule. And those salaries!

Tony is way ahead of you. "Are these salaries adjusted for current market sales in this area?" he asks.

"Yes they are, Tony," Marvel answers. "If you go with them, you should have a good selection of applicants to choose from. I think you'll find that these salaries will also fit in well with your organization. If you want, I can assist you in setting up criteria for these positions, or I can even help you with the interviews."

Tony raises his eyebrows.

Marvel plunges ahead. "One thing you might consider is sending one or two of your current employees to school to fill a couple of these positions."

Tony seems satisfied with this answer, but you notice Al Greenberg shaking his head. You suppose that he is wondering who will become the computer jockeys. Will he lose some of his sales people?

Undaunted, Marvel keeps going. "Now let me lay out for you the equipment you'll need and the time frame we can work within to get

DATATERM HARDWARE

EQUIPMENT	COST
CPU MODEL 50	$22,000
2 DISK DRIVES	44,000
DISK CONTROLLER SUPPORTING 2 DISK DRIVES	35,000
6 DISKS (.75 K EACH)	4,500
TAPE DRIVE CONTROLLER	32,000
TAPE DRIVES (2 AT 10.6 K EACH)	21,200
TAPES (200)	2,600
CARD-KEY ACCESS	800
MISCELLANEOUS	11,200

Figure 4. Marvel's Choice of Dataterm Hardware

the system up and running. This chart displays the Dataterm hardware I've selected for your operation" (Figure 4).

Marvel takes out a pointer and starts running through the figures on the chart. He throws in a lot of fancy computer lingo about bits and bytes and memory capacity that goes over most everyone's head. One thing you know for sure, though: he is describing a huge mainframe system,[4] something you hardly expected, given the current size of Tony's operation—a $4 million a year business. Even if Tony expands with four more regional offices in five years, you think the whole shot could be handled on a minicomputer. That is what they did at Star. You decide right then and there to call Sue Collins and review this stuff with her.

---

[4] A mainframe system is a computer system with maximum memory and programming capabilities. Most small businesses can handle data processing on a mini- or microcomputer with less memory and a more limited range of programmable functions.

You break from your reverie to note that Marvel is now distributing some computer printouts. He keeps talking as you read them (Figures 5 and 6).

"These printouts show the project schedule for getting the hardware installed—the time it'll take to get your computer center fully operational—and who will be doing what. I've listed events and tasks sequentially, but of course many of them will be handled at the same time. We'll be able to hire and train staff, for instance, during the 30 days it takes to deliver the computer. We can finish the whole project in about 50 to 55 working days. That includes hiring and training the personnel and completing the hardware installation. The jobs are all listed here, and I've shown which tasks will be handled by the new computer personnel."

Marvel lights a cigarette and waits for the group to glance over the printouts. He takes a few quick puffs and then launches into his closing remarks.

"DiGiorgio Frozen Foods can't do better than to go with Dataterm's software, hardware, and consulting services to start up a computing center. We'll help you to expand services without getting bogged down in paperwork. Our 20 years in the business and national reputation will stand behind you when you make that important move to computerized data processing. I believe I've told you all we have to offer. Any questions?"

Well, that was short and sweet. You note that Marvel's call for questions is met with total silence. Finally, DiGiorgio breaks in.

"What's this 'card-key' item you've got listed on your hardware chart, Fred?" (See Figure 4, page 349.)

"That's your security system, Tony. A card-key pass system allows only users with cards to have access to the system. It will protect you from computer data theft, something I'm sure you've heard a lot about."

After a moment, Al Greenberg breaks in. "What happens if the system goes down. How long is that going to hold us up?"

"You needn't worry," Marvel answers. "Dataterm has an office right in Kansas City. Pavco, Inc., our closest competitor, has a service office three hours away. You couldn't do better for service than to go with us. And we have a comprehensive maintenance contract available on our hardware. I can bring you that information if you like."

Marvel looks around for more questions, but no one offers any. The problem is, no one really knows enough about computers to know what to ask. In addition, the only written material Marvel passed out

```
             Project Schedule for Computer Center


                                              Days to
                     Task                  Complete Task

         1.   Employ manager                     6
         2.   Define site                        2
         3.   Select computer                    4
         4.   Prepare site                       10
         5.   Order computer                     4
         6.   Await delivery of computer         30
         7.   Install computer                   1
         8.   Employ analysts                    6
         9.   Write detailed procedures          5
        10.   Design forms                       4
        11.   Order forms                        2
        12.   Await forms delivery               6
        13.   Employ programmers                 4
        14.   Train programmers                  6
        15.   Write/modify programs              16
        16.   Develop test data                  4
        17.   Complete documentation             4
        18.   Employ operators                   3
        19.   Train operators                    4
        20.   Convert files                      4
        21.   Test and debug programs            6
        22.   Run parallel operations            8
        23.   Run online operations--live
```

Figure 5.   Marvel's Time Breakdown for Computer Installation

```
                 Tasks for Computer Center Staff


                                                   Days to
          Area                 Task             Complete Task


      Analysts           Write Detailed
                         Procedures                   5

                         Design Forms                 4

                         Order Forms                  2

                         Await Forms Delivery         6


      Programmers        Train Programmers            6

                         Write/Modify Programs        16

                         Develop Test Data            4

                         Complete Documentation       4


      Operators          Train Operators              4


      Full Staff         Convert Files                4

                         Test and Debug Programs      6

                         Run Parallel Operations      8
```

Figure 6. Marvel's Analysis of Computer Staff Jobs

was the data on the time schedule. He should have put more information on handouts.

Tony gets up. "Well, Mr. Marvel, you've given us a lot to think about here. I'd like to discuss your proposal with my senior staff and get back to you in a couple of weeks." Tony offers his hand. Marvel shakes it vigorously and begins packing up his stuff. The two of them chat until Marvel has his gear together. After Tony finally ushers him out, he comes back to the conference table where you have all been waiting.

"Looks pretty good, doesn't it?" he says. "Fred really knows his business. Of course, we really have to review this stuff before we make a move."

Al Greenberg taps his pencil and Julie Cresback stares out the window. You decide you have to say something. "I'm not sure, Tony," you begin. "There are a few things that bother me about the proposal."

"Oh? Let's have it."

"Well, from my experience at Star, it seems that you don't need a big mainframe computer to handle your operation. Of course, that depends on how big you expect this business to get. Did you discuss our expansion plans with Marvel? Does he know our sales projections for the next five years?"

"Well, we really didn't get into that."

"It seems funny," you continue, "that he could estimate what we need with the little info you've given him."

Tony puts his hands in his pockets and starts pacing the length of the conference room. "It's true, I didn't give Fred details about our future plans, but I did give him a pretty comprehensive rundown of our current sales, inventory, expenditures, and so forth."

You note that Al Greenberg looks mildly surprised. It appears Tony didn't let Al know what he told Fred Marvel. You decide to push a little further. "I'd like to contact someone from Star Foods who handled a computer changeover there. I think she might help us in examining Marvel's proposal."

"Sure," Tony says looking around the room. You sense that he feels some tension behind Greenberg's and Cresback's silence. "Write your friend at Star. Give her a summary of Marvel's lowdown—prices, the whole bit—and find out what she thinks." Tony smiles at the three of you. "Look, you should all feel good about this. Sure this computer conversion will change our company, but we can't afford to fall behind. Al, Julie, you know we can't keep up with the paperwork now."

Greenberg and Cresback mumble their agreement.

"If there's any problem you two see with this computer center plan, I want to hear it, okay?"

"Sure, Tony," Al responds. Julie smiles weakly.

Tony grabs his briefcase. If he wants advice, he is not planning to hear it now. He glances around the room, decides that everything is settled, and leaves for his office. Julie looks at you, shakes her head and walks out. Al steps over to talk to you.

"You know, Tony hasn't thought much about how all these computer people will change the organization of the company. Who will they report to anyway? And what about my sales and distribution managers? They used to be responsible for all the sales records. Will this computer staff take over their jobs?"

Al clearly does not expect you to answer, and you know that he is not likely to press Tony about it. He leaves the conference room worried and pensive.

You know that Al and Julie are loyal to Tony through and through. When he is sold on something, they know that it is best to let him think it through for himself first. When he is ready for their input, they will sit down with him and talk it out. If they disagree, they will give it to him straight. But right now they know too little to help him. It is clear that you all could use more information.

You return to your office to try and make some sense out of the notes you took during Marvel's presentation. Pretty soon you have the details of his proposal outlined.

You decide that it would be a good idea to summarize the proposal separately as an attachment to your letter to Sue Collins so that you can give the summary both to her and to Tony, who may want to distribute it to Al Greenberg and Julie Cresback for their review. Of course, to save time in putting this information together, you will use Marvel's printouts (Figures 5 and 6) "as is" in your summary report.

After you have written up a summary of Marvel's deal, you jot down questions that occurred to you as you listened to the presentation. You then organize this latter material for your letter to Sue Collins. As you write your draft, you decide to say at the end that you will call Sue in a week to discuss this problem with her. After you drop your letter off with a secretary, you make a note on your calendar to call Collins next week.

Assignments 1, 2, and 3 must be done in order.

ASSIGNMENT 1
Write a summary of Marvel's proposal including his software and hardware selections, personnel allocations, and setup time table. Use Figures 5 and 6 as appendixes. Consider that both Sue Collins and members of your office will review your document.

ASSIGNMENT 2
Write a cover letter to Sue Collins to go with your summary of Marvel's proposal (Assignment 1). The address is Susan Collins, Administrative Assistant, Star Foods, Inc., 400 Grosbeck, Philadelphia, Pennsylvania 00000. A copy of the letter goes to Tony DiGiorgio, President. Your

position is Administrative Assistant. Your firm's address is DiGiorgio Frozen Foods, 800 Arbana, Kansas City, Missouri 00000.

ASSIGNMENT 3
Write a cover note to Tony DiGiorgio, President, to go with the copy of the letter and summary of Marvel's proposal which you sent to Sue Collins (Assignments 1 and 2).

Part 2

It has been a week since you sent the letter to Collins. You decide to give her a call today and find out what she thinks about Marvel's proposal, but before you call her, you drop in on Tony to see if he may have done some more thinking about the matter since you sent him your summary of Marvel's deal. When you get to Tony's office, you find him on the phone with Joe Scarpuza, one of the district salesmen. It seems that there has been a shipment mix-up. Tony and Joe are hashing it out, checking shipment records against the central inventory control. It looks as though they will be at it for a while. Tony notices that you are waiting, however, and asks you to stay.

"A shipment error—the second one this week," Tony tells you as he hangs up the phone and takes out a cigar. Tony has half-smoked cigars all over the office. "We've got to get our inventory control system computerized and fast," Tony says. "This paper record keeping is for the birds. We've just got too much data backlogged. We're missing shipments. . . ." Tony looks up at you and suddenly stops his complaints. "Look, I hope you can get the information you need from your friend in Philly. I'm meeting with Marvel next Monday, and I want to be ready for him. By the way, I've also called a representative from Pavco. I know their service office is three hours away, but I want to hear what they have to offer. From what I've read about maintenance of computer systems, it doesn't matter how far away the service center is. It's the average time between computer breakdowns and the average time for repairs that really counts."

You register some surprise that Tony has called in another consultant, but then Tony is a sharp businessman; it would not be like him to leave bases uncovered. Tony tells you more.

"I've taken a hard look at the summary of Marvel's proposal you put together," he says. "Asked Al Greenberg to do research on computer equipment comparable to Dataterm's. He and I have done sales volume projections for the next five years, assuming we expand by four regional offices. We've also been thinking about where we could house the new equipment and the computer staff." Tony is really going now. "We'll stop renting out that storage space over our warehouse," he continues. "We have a 50-by-100-foot second-floor space to work with there. Plus there's a freight elevator to bring up equipment." Tony rambles on about the space for the computer. "Look," he says, interrupting himself, "you know better than I how your friend Collins can help us. Just write up whatever you find out from her. Do an analysis of Marvel's proposal, based on her input; maybe suggest some guidelines for evaluating what Pavco tells us. Get a copy to Greenberg and Cresback, too. I want their input on this thing." Tony pauses to take a few puffs on his cigar. "I'm taking off in an hour to survey our sales territory around Columbia. Be back Friday afternoon. So just drop your report off on my desk so I can review it before I talk to Marvel on Monday."

You tell Tony you will get something to him by Friday, that is, if you get adequate info from Collins. You notice that Tony has started another cigar.

Back at your office you phone Collins. It is 4:30 in Philadelphia, but when you get Sue, she sounds like she just ate her morning Wheaties. Of course, that is how you remember her, always on top of things, eager, and a hard worker. You are happy to hear that she has reviewed your letter, and you waste no time getting down to specifics.

"Sue, I'm not sure that we really need all this equipment Marvel's trying to sell us."

"That's hard to say," Sue answers. "Your company really must do some solid forecasting and then ask two or three consultants to specify what you'll need. You might want to get consultants who aren't working for computer hardware manufacturers or call in a reputable accounting firm that does computer studies. You want to choose equipment because it fits your needs, not because your consultant will get a cut of the sale. Though I have to admit, the majority of the sales consultants working for Dataterm are pretty much on the level about what they tell you."

"How do we plan for what we need?" you ask Sue.

"Well, first off, you've got to define the firm's short- and long-range plans and write down all of its business functions."

"I think DiGiorgio's done some of that," you interrupt.

"Good. But he and everyone affected by the computer changeover must list every type of data you want to have stored in the computer— company personnel records, customers and addresses, inventory items and the number of each, sales vouchers—everything. That's the only way you'll know how much storage capacity you'll need."

"Why get *everybody* involved?" you say.

"A computer installation is always a scary affair. A lot of people don't like shifting information control over to a machine. You're going to have employees who are worried about losing their jobs."

You tell Sue about Al Greenberg's fear that the company will be turning his salesmen into computer staff.

"Well, that's very real," Sue tells you. "Your company has to decide what employees will control the computer and where they fall on the company organization chart. That should all be out in the open or you could end up with key staff working against the computer department. That's why I say that everyone should be in on the decision making right from the beginning. The accountants should describe what kind of financial statements they need, how they want them printed, how often, and how fast. Your clerks should tell you how long it takes them to process inventory and sales information and what kinds of computations they do. Your managers should determine all the records they want the computer to keep and how much data they want to see in print. Oh, and your personnel department should say how they want employee time to be recorded or checks to be printed." While Sue is talking, you take notes and hope you can keep up with her. "Speaking of hard-copy reports," she interjects, "does the print-out copy you sent me show the kind of print Dataterm might use to print your reports?"

"Uh, I don't know," you admit.

"Well, that's a big point. There are several kinds of printers and to my knowledge, Dataterm's printers don't give you the sharpest image available. Of course, you may not be concerned about that."

"Well, how do we get something better?" you ask.

"When your central staff meets, you're going to want to list all report forms required by each department and decide how you want them to look. Then ask your consultants what's on the market that can get you what you want. Plus," Sue adds, "you should decide whether some information you now have on paper really needs to be printed. Maybe CRT screen access is good enough."

"Really?"

"That's right. If you can call up data on a video screen when you need it, why get printouts for everything? By the way, I'm curious about the equipment Marvel proposed. In your memo you don't say anything about terminals, remote or outside printers of any kind, nor communications controllers.[5] Did Marvel quote prices for these items?"

"Well, I suppose that equipment falls into what he called miscellaneous items," you say uneasily.

"That stuff should be specified exactly in his equipment bid. Of course, your company should determine who needs terminals, how many might be in use at once, and how often you'll need reports printed. All of this influences equipment selection."

"But Marvel must have taken those things into account before he gave us the equipment breakdown."

"Not necessarily. Many vendors offer a standard deal that suits most businesses of a particular size and type. If you want the system to be exactly what you need, you've got to set the specifications and then get him to meet them."

You pause to review some notes you've made on Marvel's proposal. "What about the project schedule for the center?"

"It's hard to say anything about it," Sue replies. "For one thing, you should make sure your consultant supplies a 'precedence' diagram for those events. The precedence diagram will show exactly which events are dependent on others and which can occur simultaneously and so on. His list of tasks doesn't make precedence clear."

"Hmmm . . . and what about those software package prices he listed?" you ask.

"Can't really evaluate them. Are those purchase prices or leasing fees? Do they include maintenance? Does he guarantee he'll fix defects? Will he take full turnkey responsibility?"

"What's that?"

"That means that he'll make sure all of the hardware and software is delivered, installed, and working. He'll also insure that all programs are documented, written up so all the users can run them without having to call in a consultant."

"But Marvel's got us hiring a staff of programmers to handle that."

"That's something else you want to investigate. You see, there's

---

[5] Communications controllers manage the flow of data between devices in the computer system.

a whole range of options in software purchasing. For one thing, you can get a custom turnkey system, as I explained earlier. With this option, the software and hardware are one purchase. The seller installs the whole works and makes adjustments; all you have to do is 'turn the key.' You can even add a maintenance clause to your contract. Or you can buy equipment and separately purchase software that will accept minor user adjustments. You can make these changes with practically 'zero' programming experience. Or if you hire your own programming staff, you can buy standardized software and make major modifications. Of course, once you make them, you've got to continue to support that staff. On the other hand . . ."

"Whoa, Sue, this is getting pretty complicated."

"There's a lot to consider, but it's worth the effort to be prepared when you talk with your consultants. A computer is a big investment, and good software can often cost as much as the equipment itself. You've got to clearly specify your needs."

"I'm not sure that DiGiorgio hasn't done that," you answer. "He's so convinced we need the computer, he's been keeping many of his plans to himself."

"Well, as I said before, you've got to encourage him to keep his planning open to all affected personnel. They've got to feel a part of this change, or they'll work against the computer system rather than with it."

"Well, he's started to get others involved. He and our operations VP have been planning the site for the computer center. They've got the second floor of our warehouse all blocked out."

"Second floor?" Sue remarks. "You better be careful there. Make sure there's enough structural support for the heavy equipment and that your doors are wide enough to get everything through. Have you got air conditioning?"

"Yes, Tony's seen to that."

"Good."

You check your watch and realize you've been on the phone for nearly an hour. You decide you'd better wrap things up.

"I really don't know what else to ask you now, Sue. I've got to write up my analysis of Marvel's proposal for Tony by the end of the week. Have you told me everything I need to know?"

"Well, frankly," Sue says, "I don't see how you can do an analysis of Marvel's proposal with what you have. You clearly need more information from Marvel."

"You're right," you answer. "In fact, I think we really need to work closely with a consultant—someone who's not interested in selling us equipment and software but who can help us assess our needs."

"I think it would help at least to begin by trying to assess your needs first, and then develop questions for consultants or vendors as you go along," Sue suggests. "By the way, I have scribbled out a few questions that you might want to ask Marvel about his software. I put it in the mail this morning. But I haven't covered everything there. You really ought to look at some back issues of *Computerworld*, *Datamation*, or *Computer Decisions*. You'll find some good articles on choosing hardware and software. That'll put you on the right track."

You thank Sue for all her help and after chatting a bit about old times at Star, you tell her goodbye.

You review your notes from the phone conversation and try to think this whole thing through. Sue certainly gave you a lot of information, but now you are worried that you have more problems on your hands than you had before.

You lean back in your chair and gaze absently at your bulletin board, trying to relax so you can best decide what to do first. You think to yourself that you have quite a few things to look into before you can tell Tony how to evaluate Marvel's proposal. For one thing, you will have to review Sue's questions when they come in the mail. You will use them as a guide when you go to the library for more information on choosing software.

However, you do not have Sue's information yet, and you probably will not get it before the end of the week. In addition, Tony wants you to write up something on evaluating computer proposals with copies to Cresback and Greenberg before he gets back Friday afternoon! But then again, Sue's software questions may not be relevant right now, since, as she told you, your company really has to specify its needs more clearly before you can consider software suitability. Help!

You realize that the only way to deal with this mess is to sort out the problems and handle them separately. First, you need to deal with the problem of involving all personnel in assessing the need for a computer. You decide to write a memo to Tony recommending that he call a meeting of all supervisors who may use the computer for a discussion of their needs. Your phone-call notes from Sue will help you suggest who he should ask and how they should prepare themselves for the meeting. This request will be a little tricky to make. After all, you suspect that Tony thinks he has done all the investigating he needs to do. In addition, you are not sure what he has discussed with Greenberg regarding computer needs, but you believe that he has only gone over sales projects with him. You will have to convince Tony *now* that more information on possible company uses for a computer is critical. Clearly, you cannot send copies of this request to Cresback and Greenberg; it will be between you and Tony for the moment. However, you consider that if Tony decides to call the meeting, he may choose to distribute your memo to those who will attend so that they will come prepared.

Of course, you still have another problem to deal with—how to answer Tony's request that you analyze Marvel's proposal or set up guidelines to analyze proposals from other consultants. You decide that you cannot really evaluate Marvel's proposal, but you can write a memo suggesting some questions to ask him based on what Sue said. You might also suggest to Tony that the company put off a decision until Marvel comes up with more information and perhaps even suggest hiring a disinterested consultant, someone who is not a computer or software distributor, to help the company assess Marvel's proposal.

Thinking that you have worked out a reasonable plan, you start to outline material for each memo.

ASSIGNMENT 4
Write a memo to Tony DiGiorgio, President, recommending that he call a meeting of company supervisors to assess how company personnel may need to use a computer.

ASSIGNMENT 5
Write a memo to Tony DiGiorgio, President, giving information he can use in his discussion with Marvel about the Dataterm proposal on Monday. Copies go to Julie Cresback, Senior Accountant, and Alvin Greenberg, Vice-President, Operations.

Part 3

Today, the Tuesday after Tony's meeting with Marvel, the letter from Sue Collins finally arrived (Appendix A). You notice that your company address is correct on the letter but incorrect on the envelope, so the delay seems to have been caused by a clerical error. In the meantime, Tony has spoken to you about your suggestion to call a meeting on computer usage and has distributed your memo (Assignment 4) to relevant personnel. The meeting will take place next week. However, you learn that Tony is not too keen on hiring an outside consultant to evaluate computer hardware and software proposals from Dataterm, Pavco, or anyone else he contacts. He thinks that if the meeting held next week is productive, he will have enough information to deal with Marvel and the Pavco rep without outside help.

You discussed Sue Collins's letter with Tony this morning. He asked you to look up the references Sue gave you in the library and to prepare an informational report on choosing software for those who will attend next week's meeting on assessing needs for a computer. The report should describe what software is, suggest criteria for choosing it, explain how to analyze your software needs, and perhaps include a list of questions to ask vendors. Tony realizes that you know very little about software for business applications, but he wants you to attempt this report anyway. He tells you to remember that even if *you* do not understand it very well, the other DiGiorgio employees know even less. He wants you to summarize your understanding of the software selection issue so at least you can bring other DiGiorgio employees up to speed before the meeting next week. All of you can then help Tony decide whether you need an outside consultant to help you choose software or evaluate software packages shown to you by salespeople.

ASSIGNMENT 6

Write the informational report on software selection to Tony DiGiorgio, President. Tony will handle distribution of the report to other employees. Look for articles on software selection in recent issues of computer trade journals. Use the references in Appendix A, if you wish, as a start, but investigate more current references as well.

APPENDIX A

Letter from Sue Collins

STAR FOODS INC. 400 Grosbeck Philadelphia, PA 00000

April 18, 1984

YOU
DiGiorgio Frozen Foods
800 Arbana
Kansas City, MO 00000

Dear YOU:

How nice to hear from you, though your letter reminded me of all the work it took to get that computer system installed at Star. I'd be happy to give you some tips about doing a computer changeover for DiGiorgio Frozen Foods.

I have reviewed your letter and expect to get a call from you soon. Meanwhile, I've enclosed a list with a few questions you may want to consider when you compare software packages. I found it a big help to read some articles in computer trade journals when I did the changeover for Star. You'll find attached a list citing a few sources that I used. You'll probably need to find some more recent articles for your application.

Best of luck in your work.

Sincerely,

Sue

Susan Collins
Administrative Assistant

enc

SC:jm

(continued)

APPENDIX A—*continued*

References on Selecting Software

Deschamps, Vincent. "The Turnkey Part 2: Users Must Determine Needs in Advance." Computerworld, July 25, 1977, pp. 33–34.

Frank, Werner L. "Softline: Beware of Advice from Experts About Software." Computerworld, August 24, 1981, pp. 31, 34.

Johannsen, Craig. "Software Selection Criteria Outlined." Computerworld, February 4, 1980, pp. 33, 38.

Snyders, Jan. "How to Buy Packages." Computer Decisions, June 1979, pp. 50, 51, 55, 57.

Turi, Leonard F. "Review Manual Operation Before Buying First System." Computerworld, February 5, 1979, p. 54.

APPENDIX A—*continued*

Some questions you may want to ask your consultant about
software:

1. Can the software handle size of our files, no. of
   separate data elements, table entries, and vol. of
   transactions and reports? ("Vol. of trans." = no.
   of additions and deletions made to file per day)

2. Possible to change formats, rearrange data on
   particular forms, change content of forms?

3. Can the software detect errors in data entry?

4. Adequate backup filing? How's data recovery after
   crashes?[6]

5. Log kept for every user transaction?

6. Access—how do we keep "just anyone" from entering
   data in files? how many people can use software at
   once?

7. Will vendor maintain the software? How long?

8. Warranty—is there one? what if we make changes to
   software? still good?

9. How do we get the software—lease? pay royalties?
   purchase?

10. If we buy custom software, will we own royalty
    rights (in case vendor sells it to someone else)?

11. What's the lifespan of the software?

12. Software O.K. with diff. kinds of hardware? (i.e.,
    What memory capacity, I/O device speeds, and tape or
    disk storage capacity does it require?)

---

[6] Backup filing is a method of storing data permanently (usually on tape) so that it is
not lost when the computer accidentally shuts off ("crashes").

To Burn or Not to Burn: Investigating Hazardous Waste Disposal at Cutler General Hospital[1]

Part 1

"A lot of good walking over to his office did!" you mutter upon leaving Cutler General Hospital as you brace yourself against the cold rain to head back to the Hospitals Administration Building. Next time you will call Gioberti's secretary first to make sure that he has not had to cancel for an emergency meeting or a sudden trip to Providence or whatever. So much for having a job as a *planner*. You try to laugh a bit at your unsuccessful plan to meet Gioberti. Of course, you and your colleagues often joke that *hospital* planners are something else altogether.

You quicken your step and march resolutely back to your office in the Hospitals Administration Building, keeping your umbrella aimed toward the driving rain. You check your watch and get a little wet in the process, wondering if you can get that data together for Madge Elmore in Public Relations in the next hour. She wanted to know how Cutler's expansion will contribute to the overall growth of the State Hospital Complex site in the next ten years. You think you have that information at your fingertips. By the time you get back to

---

[1] The problems presented in this case describe the ways a hospital may be affected by possible changes in an actual state public law and in federal guidelines for hospital waste disposal. The state public law referred to here is given a fictitious name: Rhode Island Public Law No. 78. Though the events in this case are based on real happenings, they do not refer to actual events that have occurred in Rhode Island. The problem of responding to changed laws and guidelines is a constant concern for public and private institutions. The situation presented here remains relevant despite the fact that some documents referenced may now be out of date.

your office, Hospital Renovation and Expansion (HRE), you have that memo for Elmore all planned. If you can avoid being interrupted, you can get it done before you have to meet with Ted LaBute at 3 P.M.

Unfortunately, you cannot keep your mind on the memo. You keep getting up, pacing the room, and thinking about that missed meeting. Of course, it was not Gioberti's fault. It is just that you were hoping you could see him before your meeting with Ted today. Then again, it was not critical that you see Gioberti first.

You stop pacing and sit down at your desk, but all you can do is stare out the window. From your office on the east side of the building you can look out at the entire State Hospital Complex: Higgins Psychiatric on the left; then the main hospital, Cutler General; and to the right, the Amanda Wesley Family Clinics Building across the street from Cutler. You squint a bit and try to imagine how the new east and west wings of Cutler will look when they are done. It is amazing how fast that steel went up. Plans to put the east and west wings on Cutler have been eight years in the making, and you have been working on them for the past three. You have learned to live with the fact that planning a large medical center is a long, complicated process that never really comes to an end. When construction finally begins on one project, plans for another are in progress. And so it goes.

You take a quick look at the familiar architect's site plan for the medical complex that is pinned to your bulletin board (Figure 1). The site plan certainly reveals the integral relationship between the medical school research facilities of Eastern Seaboard University and the State Hospital Complex. Leaning over your desk, which faces the window, you can see off to the left of Cutler two of the medical research buildings on the Eastern Seaboard University campus: the Alison Stanough and Jerome McIntyre medical buildings, or StanMed and McMed as the doctors and med students call them. The Cutler expansion is important to the medical research efforts of Eastern Seaboard University. You find yourself staring for a moment at the covered bridge between the medical research buildings and Cutler General, and you are instantly reminded that the doctors never have to walk in the rain to get back and forth from Cutler to their research offices. It is one of the percs of being a "healer," as HRE staff always say. You would like to see the day when they will build a covered bridge between the Hospitals Administration Building where you work and Cutler.

You note that time is slipping away more quickly than you thought. You put the memo project aside and turn your attention to that 3 o'clock

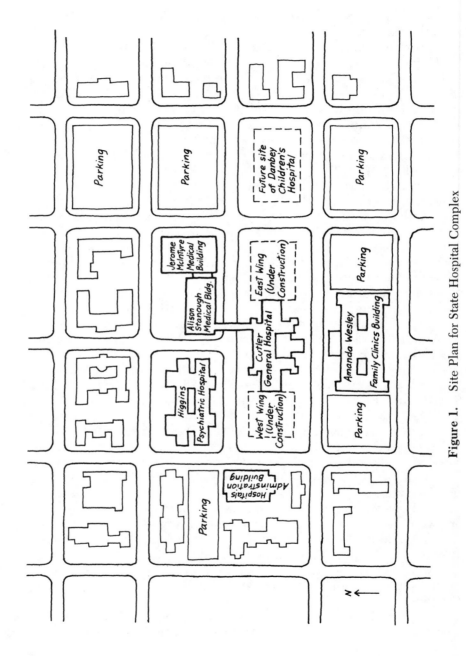

Figure 1. Site Plan for State Hospital Complex

368

meeting with Ted. He has called you in to discuss a report (Appendix A)[2] that you wrote to him last week on how wastes are classified and on what handling methods are recommended for infectious wastes. He assigned you to write the report as the first step of a larger investigation into whether Cutler General needs to include a new incinerator for handling infectious wastes in one of the two new wings under construction.

This whole investigation is a bit out of your territory. Your standard assignments as a hospital planner have included researching the state of the art in medical practices as they may affect the growth of the State Hospital Complex. You usually work for Brenda Schneider, Assistant Director, Planning; however, while Cutler is in the midst of the design and construction of two new wings, you have been "on loan," part-time, to assist Ted LaBute, Assistant Director, Design and Construction. (See Organizational Chart, Appendix B.) LaBute's section deals with the day-to-day problems of getting expansion and renovation plans through the "design" and "build" stages. And since the Cutler expansion project is following the fast-track "design-while-building" construction method,[3] new problems that demand immediate attention arise every day.

Your assignment to investigate waste disposal at Cutler went through several channels before it got to you. The waste disposal problem first came to the attention of the manager of HRE, David Knudsvig. Knudsvig received a letter from Donald Derringer, field supervisor for the Rhode Island Department of Public Health, which inquired about waste disposal facilities planned for the new Cutler wings. In particular, Derringer wanted to know whether Cutler would have a "pathological" incinerator. The health department official reminded Knudsvig that Cutler had been cited last year for not following

---

[2] Appendix A, the report which "you" wrote to Ted LaBute, is important to understanding this case. Read this appendix now.

[3] Fast-track building is a method of construction in which the design and construction stages are handled simultaneously. Construction of the supporting structure and outer surfaces of the building begins when the facility is only partially designed. As the building goes up, design of interior spaces is completed. Fast-track construction is often a hedge against inflation, since steel can be purchased, foundations can be laid, and other construction contracts can be completed without waiting until the design is finished, at a time when prices may be higher. Fast-track construction is risky, however, because later design decisions may require changes in portions of the building that are already built. This method limits design flexibility.

the code. Derringer had reported in his review of Cutler waste disposal systems that "there is no documentation on hand that a pathological incinerator is available."[4]

The current design of Cutler's new wings does not include specs for an incinerator, nor has purchase of an incinerator even been considered by the hospital's design programmers.[5] Cutler has a crematorium and also has use of incinerators in Eastern Seaboard University's StanMed and McMed research buildings. However, no office of the university or of the hospital has collected comprehensive data on how the incinerators are being used or whether new equipment is needed.

After getting Derringer's letter, Knudsvig decided to spearhead an investigation to ensure that adequate waste disposal facilities were included in the design of Cutler's new wings. He immediately went to LaBute to ask what was being done about the problem, and LaBute, having no information at hand to go on, assigned you to investigate how wastes were currently being taken care of in the hospital. However, before you started looking into that, LaBute wanted you to get a handle on how various agencies classify wastes and on what methods are recommended for disposing of pathological wastes. You finished a report on this topic for Ted last week.[6] A copy went to Frank Gioberti, Director, Environmental Health and Safety. You had hoped to meet with Gioberti today so that he could tell you how the medical complex takes care of the various kinds of wastes subject to regulation.

After thinking everything over, you conclude that despite the fact that your plans did not work out, you can at least tell Ted LaBute what you planned to do. You check your watch and find that it is 3 P.M. already. You pack up your copy of the waste report and head down to Ted's office for your meeting.

When you get there, Ted is ready to see you. Glancing at his desk, you can see that he has been busy making notes on your report and jotting down questions.

"A fine report," he says while making a few last written remarks.

---

[4] The terms "pathological" and "infectious" are used interchangeably to refer to wastes that are contaminated by disease-carrying organisms.

[5] A hospital design programmer determines what design criteria a building must meet in order to serve the needs of the people who will use it.

[6] Review Appendix A, "your" report to LaBute.

You are pleased. One thing you really like about Ted is that he always recognizes when anyone does a good job.

"So we basically have three kinds of wastes we deal with," Ted begins, summarizing your report. "Having descriptions of the materials that are classified as infectious, toxic,[7] and radioactive wastes will help us get info from Gioberti. If he knows that we know a little bit about this subject, he'll be less likely to beat around the bush."

You are curious about Ted's last remark but do not interrupt him.

"Several things interest me here," says Ted, continuing to look at your report. "First, it looks like the hospital may have to process more wastes than it does now if new regulations require that infectious wastes, in particular, must be both incinerated or sterilized *and* sent to the landfill."

"That's right," you remark. "And even if such new regulations don't materialize, the Center for Disease Control generally recommends special handling of potentially infectious materials, including incineration where possible."

"Costly," Ted mutters to himself. "I wonder if our present incinerators could handle increased capacity?"

"Well, you're asking several questions there," you answer. "First, we need to know whether our incinerators are certified for infectious waste yet. It's possible we haven't responded to Derringer's citation. Next, we've got to find out what kind of waste we're burning now and how much more waste we'd burn if we included all *potentially* infectious waste. Then we need to see if our current incinerators can handle the increase—if there will be an increase when the new wings open."

"If?" Ted asks.

"Well, as I said," you continue, "I don't know what we're burning now. Perhaps we *are* burning all potentially contaminated wastes and perhaps we *can* handle whatever we get from the new wings."

Ted smiles. "I highly doubt that we're going beyond what current regulations ask us to do now. What does Gioberti have to say about this?"

You're ready for this one. "He hasn't had time to see me yet. What I plan to do is to ask him how we're now disposing of infectious, toxic, and radioactive wastes and find out everything I can about the incin-

---

[7] The term "toxic waste" in this case refers only to hazardous *chemical* waste.

erators we use. I also plan to get some projections on weekly increases in wastes resulting from the expansion."

"Sounds good," says Ted. "When you've got all that information together, Dave Knudsvig's going to want a report with your recommendation about including a new incinerator in the design for Cutler's expansion. I can tell you right now, he isn't likely to push the State Hospital Complex board of directors for anything that will increase costs, unless we absolutely *must* have it to meet the legal requirements. We need data that will show whether we're now meeting the code for waste disposal. That info, along with reliable projections of requirements when the new wings open, should lead us to a clear recommendation."

"Well, I can't even make a safe guess now," you say. "I'll get back to you with more information as soon as I can."

"Fine," says Ted. "By the way, don't be surprised if Gioberti is closemouthed about a few things. Cutler's a pretty old facility, and I wouldn't be surprised if we hadn't cut some corners in dealing with our toxic wastes. The Health Department has been pretty low-keyed about getting existing facilities to conform to new regulations. They know how costly it is to retrofit old equipment and to institute procedures that old buildings were never meant to handle. They tend to really stick it to new facilities though, so I suspect they'll keep a close watch on this expansion project. Just be a little easy on Frank. He's got a rough job and lots of government people on his back. We don't want to make him think we're after his tail."

Ted makes a few quick notes to himself as he is talking, and then he adds, "After you talk to Frank, make an appointment with Jerry Cassidy in the State Hospital Complex Occupational Health and Safety Office. His office is down the hall from Gioberti's on Cutler's ninth level. Cassidy will be familiar with any material-handling procedures that affect employees of the complex. Tell Gioberti you'll be talking to Jerry too. Frank reports to him you know."

"Okay," you answer, thinking that Frank may be concerned that Cassidy will be checking up on him.

"The main thing to keep in mind here," Ted continues, "is that we don't want to bring old problems into the new facility. If there's a problem with our current system that needs fixing or if it's likely to be inadequate when we open the new wings, we ought to know that now."

You and Ted wrap up your meeting and you get back to your office to make appointments with Gioberti and Cassidy. Unfortunately, you suspect that Gioberti may not tell you everything you want to know. If he does not, how will you get to the bottom of things? The project promises to be a real challenge, but you are ready for it.

Part 2

You are in great spirits today. You have a meeting with Frank Gioberti in 20 minutes. You call his secretary to make sure he will definitely be there. Reassured, you only hope that Gioberti has read his copy of the waste disposal report you wrote for LaBute. From what LaBute has said about how Gioberti feels about investigations into his department's activities, you would not be surprised if Frank just put the report aside. On your way over to the hospital, you review a few diplomatic approaches to asking Gioberti about how hazardous wastes are being disposed of at Cutler. You are "up" for this meeting, and the fact that the sun is out makes you feel good too. The walk from HRE to Cutler is actually enjoyable.

When you arrive in Gioberti's office, he is full of apologies about missing your meeting last week. Frank offers you some coffee and cordially asks what he can do for you. He looks friendly and cooperative, so you open your questioning with confidence.

"As I told you on the phone last week, Frank, we need to collect some information on hazardous waste disposal at Cutler so we can determine whether we need to provide a new waste disposal system or update our old one to accommodate increased wastes when the new hospital wings open. I thought the easiest way we could talk about this is to first define how we are now taking care of the wastes that fall under federal and state regulations. Ted LaBute asked me to do a short research report [Appendix A] on how hazardous wastes are classified and regulated. I sent it to you last week. I hope it covers everything we need to be concerned about."

Gioberti ignores your remark. In the awkward silence, you stop a minute to get out your copy of the waste disposal report to LaBute. Gioberti lights a cigarette and seems to be gazing out the window without interest. You continue to look over your report and meanwhile lose a little of your enthusiasm. Maybe he has not read it, or maybe he does have something to hide, and he will try to keep it from you. Thinking about this, you change your questioning strategy. You decide it might not be a good idea to start quizzing him about the handling of infectious wastes. That subject could be too touchy. You could still get the information you want by asking generally how all biological waste is now handled.

"As, of course, you're aware," you begin, "regulations talk mainly about biological, radioactive, and chemical waste. If we could start with biological . . ."

To your surprise, Gioberti, taking a few quick puffs on his cigarette, begins to tell you how the wastes are handled. He must have been silently lining up his thoughts.

"All waste—that is, all biological waste—goes to the compactor, unless it has to be incinerated. Things like contaminated vials, paper wastes, that kind of thing, are compacted, taken to the city landfill, and covered daily."

"Are the latter, ah, pathological wastes?" you press, a bit hesitantly.

Gioberti does not respond directly.

"Pathological wastes from the ORs,[8] Pathology, the labs, and isolation rooms are generally being taken care of differently. Most of this waste falls under our 'red bag' policy; it's identified by disposing of it in red bags, and it's autoclaved[9] before it's sent to the landfill. However, it's hard to keep tabs on how closely this policy is followed. Many of our personnel who do follow it to the letter do so at great inconvenience in 'make-do' facilities during off hours. I can assure you that highly infectious wastes, such as those you designate in Section 1.1.1 of your report, are properly handled. Of course, *all* waste from isolation rooms is double-bagged before it's sent to the landfill anyway."

"And that takes care of the problem?" you suggest.

"Pretty much," Gioberti answers. "Of course, we can't guarantee that the bags don't rupture." Gioberti snuffs out his cigarette in the ashtray before he has finished smoking it. "You see, regulations covering disposal of pathological wastes are in a state of flux now. And there's quite a bit of disagreement about just how dangerous hospital wastes are—that is, compared to other wastes sent to the landfill."

You remain quiet, hoping Gioberti will explain further.

"Let me send you a couple of articles on infectious waste dis-

---

[8] Operating Rooms.

[9] A method of sterilization.

posal," he says. "They should give you a better idea of what the situation is."

"I'll be looking forward to getting them," you say.

Gioberti nods in response. "You wanted to know about radioactive waste?"

You say yes, deciding not to push more now about the pathological wastes. You suspect that you are not getting the whole story here. Gioberti's answers seemed a bit too pat.

Gioberti picks up a copy of the "Cutler Hospital Directory" and says, "You really should talk to Abe Reisman in the State Hospital Complex Radiation Control Service." He patiently reads out Reisman's office address and phone number and you write it down. "Also," he adds, flipping through the phone book, "talk to Barry Godschalk in Nuclear Medicine and Jim Fish in Radiology." Gioberti reads their phone numbers and addresses too.[10]

"All liquid or solid wastes from Nuclear Medicine go to Radiation Control," Gioberti adds, putting down the hospital directory. "They've got a storage facility there called a 'hot lab' where they hold and monitor short-lived radionuclides before they're disposed."

Somehow you feel Gioberti has given you this information straight. Nuclear waste disposal procedures are highly regulated, and you are sure that Environmental Health goes by the book on this one.

"However," Gioberti continues, "patient excreta are exempt from this process—you know, just goes into sewage."

You jot down a few notes and a reminder to check out regulations on dumping radioactive excreta.

"By the way," Gioberti adds, "you really should call Reg Fields in Pathology, and—let's see, who is it now—Marlene Bridwell in the Blood Bank and, hmm, those in charge of the Toxicology and Immunology labs to find out more about disposal of the biological wastes. But then, these labs are all under Pathology, anyway. Anything else you want to know?"

You are beginning to wonder if you might get better information from the people Gioberti recommends than from him, but you decide to ask him about the chemical wastes while you are here.

"Same problem as with the pathological wastes," Gioberti ex-

---

[10] Appendix C contains a complete list of all Cutler General and other personnel involved in your investigation.

plains, stepping toward you. "We really do no surveillance now of chemical waste disposal. There've been cutbacks, and we just don't have the staff to handle it anymore. Each unit is on its own to follow the guidelines we provide. They've been pretty well trained to do things right, but, frankly, it's highly possible that small amounts do go down the drain. Our office has a good system for collecting wastes from each department, however. We pick up the wastes and arrange disposal by an outside contractor for a fee of $6 a gallon. Now, does that cover what you need to know?" Gioberti asks, looking as if he is ready to begin working on something else.

You take your cue. "You've given me some good leads here, Frank. I'll contact these people and get back to you if I have any more questions. By the way, I'll also be talking to Jerry Cassidy over in Occupational Safety."

"Good," Gioberti says with a smile. "Glad I could be of help."

You shake hands and make a quick exit. Ted was right about Gioberti's reticence to give you detailed information. Nevertheless, he did not hesitate to tell you where to go for more data, and he did not even seem concerned that you would be in contact with Cassidy. Maybe they both have the same attitude—neither is about to give you much information. If so, you will have to do all the supersleuthing yourself.

ASSIGNMENT 1

Assume that you will make phone calls to the personnel to whom Gioberti refers you. Make a list of questions that you would use when calling to help you get the information you need.

ASSIGNMENT 2

Write a memo "for the record," documenting your conversation with Gioberti. Your letterhead will read: Memorandum, State Hospital Complex, Hospital Renovation and Expansion. The memo will be addressed to "To the Record," and copies will go to Francis Gioberti, Director, Environmental Health and Safety, and to Ted LaBute, Assistant Director, Hospital Renovation and Expansion. Your job title is Hospital Planner.

When you get back to HRE, you immediately call Fields in Pathology. Fortunately, he is in his office and gives you some hard information over the phone, which you note in your phone log (Figure 2). Fields tell you that biohazard containers for pathological materials from his area sometimes rupture before they get to the landfill. The rupturing occurs because the containers are compacted before they leave the hospital. Fields thinks this material really should be incinerated, but he does not know whether incineration is required by law.

Reg Fields, Pathology   4/24

1. Waste from Hematology, Biochemistry and Microbiology Labs – blood samples, urine containers (empty), anything like pipettes which have been in contact with blood samples, anything considered contaminated.

2. Put in 4-gallon plastic containers with gasketed lids – marked "Biohazard". Pails dist. by Glass-pack Packaging of Massachusetts.

3. Picked up daily and put in compacter. Even though pails are not pierceable by needles, etc., some do rupture in compacting. The compacted material is then taken to landfill. 2 or 2½ years ago, when it was monitored, these three lab areas put out 13 pails/day.

4. This material is not now incinerated (because of air pollution restrictions on hospital incinerators). Check this. Fields thinks it should be incinerated. Just his opinion.

Figure 2. Telephone Log of Your Conversation with Fields

He also recommends that you call those in charge of the labs under Pathology's jurisdiction, and he rattles off a list of the labs for you (Appendix D).

First, you try to call a few of the other people Gioberti mentioned and manage to get Barry Godschalk from Nuclear Medicine on the phone. From what you hear from Godschalk, it looks like radioactive wastes are handled very carefully. The procedures are pretty much as Gioberti explained them to you. Disposal is monitored well, and most wastes are handled by the State Hospital Complex Radiation Control Service. You find out that regulations do stipulate that radioactive patient excreta can be dumped down the drain. Godschalk offers to quote you the regulation, but you decide to take his word for it. When you hang up, you jot down notes of this phone conversation for the record (Figure 3).

After the call to Godschalk, you try to get Abe Reisman in Radiation Control on the phone, but you find that he has been called out of town for two weeks. His secretary refuses to make an appointment adding to his schedule. It looks like you will have to write a memo to Reisman to get the information you need. Of course, the memo will have to get him to confirm Godschalk's information and to assess the need for more hot lab storage space to accommodate wastes when Cutler expands.

In looking over the information you got today, you can see that you have not learned anything about chemical wastes yet. You hope a meeting you have scheduled with Cassidy in Occupational Safety next week will give you some information about that.

ASSIGNMENT 3
Write a memo requesting information to Abraham Reisman, Manager, Radiation Control Services. A copy will go to Ted LaBute, Assistant Director, Hospital Renovation and Expansion.

Part 3

Jerry Cassidy, as you discover when you meet him, has a very complex job. He has to keep tabs on all operations that affect employee safety on the State Hospital Complex site. This job is just one aspect

Barry Godschalk, Nuclear Medicine   4/24

1. Liquid and solid radioactive wastes are taken care of by State Hospital Complex Radiation Control. This relieves departments like Nuc. Med. of most of the burden.

2. Nuclear Medicine uses many short-lived radionuclides which, by the time they are picked up and disposed of, are no longer radioactive; the State Hospital Complex used to pay to take special precautions with materials which didn't require them. Therefore, about 6 months ago, a new procedure was started where waste with a short half-life is kept in the department until it is no longer radioactive, then disposed of as solid or liquid waste (ex. – for material with half-life of 6 hours, it's kept around for 10 half-lives or 60 hours). So, the story is: hold; monitor; dispose.

3. Storage in hot lab. Current facilities larger than nec. Don't see need for more storage area due to expansion.

4. Patient excreta are exempt from regulations and go into sewer system where they are diluted enough so that they can't be traced.

5. Exhaust hoods to outside when using volatile material – radioactive iodine; fumes filtered and monitored at hood and on roof.

Figure 3.   Log of Your Conversation with Godschalk

of managing the State Hospital Complex facilities.[11] Jerry is a sharp fellow and has a lot of the information you need at his fingertips. He is a lot less secretive than Gioberti, and you are grateful for that. When you ask him about chemical waste disposal, he outlines the State Hospital Complex disposal system succinctly:

"Waste is collected in areas—like Radiology, for instance. It's labeled and put in containers. A manifest[12] accompanies each 4-gallon carton or 55-gallon drum. Environmental Health and Safety has a routine pickup service for the departments. If the area is not on the pickup schedule, they call Environmental Health."

"What does Gioberti's office do with the waste?" you ask.

"Well, as I said, they pick it up—the State Hospital Complex supplies a special truck for this service—then they tabulate all the manifests into one, and a licensed disposer, Bateson Chemical of Providence, picks up the waste at the end of each week."

"What's all that cost?" you ask.

"The cost to each department is $6 a gallon, which includes everything from containers, packing, cartons, and forms to pickup. Last year—let's see," Cassidy says leafing through a folder on his desk, "last year Cutler got rid of 330 pounds of solid waste and 1,035 gallons of liquid waste."

You note those figures and also note that the $6-a-gallon cost figure correlates with the information Gioberti gave you earlier. "Do all personnel follow the disposal procedure?"

"There is no surveillance, but to our knowledge, most people are conscientious. In all probability, though, a little waste does go down the drain. In a place this big, a certain amount of that must go on. Radiology is the only department that uses large quantities of chemicals. You might want to check that situation out."

Cassidy is pretty straightforward with you, but, again, you suspect that people in the labs may tell you more specifically how the wastes are handled. You decide to call Jim Fish in Radiology as soon as you can. While jotting down this note to yourself, you ask Cassidy about incinerating biological wastes. Cassidy gives you names of more people to interview, including Alex Fremont in Lab Animal Medicine over at Eastern Seaboard University, Joe Scarfone of Eastern Sea-

---

[11] Facilities Management for the entire State Hospital Complex is directed by Ken Beaumont. Cassidy reports to him.

[12] A manifest is an audit slip documenting the pickup of each container.

board's Plant Department, and Leslie Compton of the Rhode Island Department of Natural Resources. Cassidy thinks Fremont may know the capacity of the incinerators in StanMed and McMed, and Compton can tell you whether they are now certified to handle pathological wastes. He is sure Cutler's crematorium is fully certified. To your surprise, he asks you about a fourth incinerator you had never heard about. It is supposedly located in the basement of Higgins Psychiatric. He thinks it is old and not being used at all now. You decide to check this out.

Upon your further questioning of Cassidy about disposal of pathological wastes, you find that he has little more to tell you than Gioberti did. As you leave Cassidy's office, you decide that since you are in Cutler anyway, you might as well drop down to Radiology and see if Jim Fish has a few minutes to talk to you. First, you check in the administrative wing where Fish, a radiological engineer, has his offices. Seeing that he is not there, you go on down to the film-processing room. There you find Fish talking with some technicians about where to put some new equipment.

"We'll sure be glad to see those new wings built," he says to you.

Looking around at the dismal and cramped surroundings that make up the film-developing area, you immediately sympathize. Every available space seems to be filled with metal shelving holding developing equipment or stored X-ray plates. The technicians barely avoid bumping into one another walking between the worktables and sinks. When you ask Fish about lab disposables, he has much to say.

"We get rid of a lot of solid junk here," he says. "Most of it is just plain trash—intubation kits, disposable catheters, film cartons, and wrappers. You can get the volume of that stuff by calling maintenance."

"Any of that toxic?" you say.

"No, it's stuff that can go directly to the landfill," Fish answers.

Looking around at all the developing chemicals, you ask Fish how the lab gets rid of chemical wastes.

"Well, that's a problem," Fish begins. "We have a lot of liquid waste that's corrosive. To have that stuff picked up and disposed of would be prohibitively expensive. Right now we dump about 250 gallons of developer down the drain every week; it's a sulfate derivative. That volume could double with the expansion of Cutler."

"Is this stuff nontoxic?" you ask.

"It contains acetic acid," Fish responds. "But all in all, it's pretty diluted when it hits the sewer. The acetic acid causes pipes to rust;

they've often got to be reamed. We've got cast-iron pipes with clean-outs every 10 feet. Now, our fixer acid is another story. We bring all the fixer solution together in one spot for silver reclamation. We get about 500 gallons a week together, and it's pretty concentrated. That goes down the drain too."

"How does the Department of Natural Resources feel about all this stuff going down the drain?"

"So far they've overlooked it; but I'm pretty sure that we're in violation of Public Law 78. I'd guess they're waiting to see if we'll clean up our act when the new wings are built."

"So what do you plan to do, have the stuff hauled away?"

"No, we couldn't afford that. I've got Gioberti over in Environmental Health working on this. We think it would be cheaper to hire a consultant who could do an analysis of the waste and tell us what we could do to dilute it to make it conform to EPA regulations before we dump it in the sewer."

"And what about the state regulations?" you ask.

"Federal and state regulations are almost identical," Fish replies. "Rhode Island, like most states, tries to copy the EPA's guidelines wherever possible."

You thank him for his information and start to go. Before you do, however, he asks you to check on what can be done about replacing the rusting cast-iron pipes as part of preparation for the expansion. You tell him that you will look into this.

You head back to HRE, and when you get there, you start phoning the people Cassidy told you to call so that you could check on the status of the incinerators in the medical complex. You start with Alex Fremont from Lab Animal Medicine at Eastern Seaboard University. Fremont tells you that two pathological incinerators belong to Eastern Seaboard. One is in StanMed, the other in McMed. They both run on a nine-to-five, five-days-a-week schedule with half a day down for cleaning and maintenance. The units are old, built in the 1950s, but they meet inspection. Ash goes to the landfill. Fremont also tells you there is a possibility they could be run on night shift. For the most part, animals from the medical research labs are disposed of here, but no waste from Cutler General or other hospitals in the complex. He believes that human cadavers and body parts from all the hospitals in the complex are disposed of in Cutler's crematorium. The Eastern Seaboard University Plant Department should have the licenses for the incinerators in StanMed and McMed. Fremont thinks that a lot of material from the hospitals should be incinerated but isn't. Contaminated disposable items and such, for instance, should be burned rather than compacted and sent to the landfill. But the StanMed and McMed incinerators cannot handle more waste. These units are operating at 75 percent of capacity now. Just as you end your conversation, Fremont asks a surprising question.

"There's a big incinerator in the Plant Maintenance Building on the Eastern Seaboard Campus. As far as I know, it's not being used for anything. How come?"

"I don't know," you tell Fremont. "I didn't even know the incinerator exists." You promise him that you will investigate it and note to yourself that this is the fifth incinerator that you have heard of in the medical complex area. You wonder if there are any more lurking about. This is just one more item you will have to investigate.

As soon as Fremont hangs up, you call Joe Scarfone in Eastern Seaboard's Plant Department to ask about the incinerator licenses. Scarfone has lots of information on the Eastern Seaboard incinerators, on the crematorium in Cutler General, *and* on the incinerator in Higgins Psychiatric which you heard about from Cassidy. According to Scarfone, the two incinerators for animal waste in McMed and StanMed need no application for a permit or operating license. They have been "grandfathered" in because they were operating prior to the 1967 state laws covering air pollution. Cutler has just reapplied for a permit for its crematorium incinerator because of modifications made to the incinerator in 1975. As far as Scarfone knows, the incinerator in Higgins Psychiatric is not now being used and probably will not be used in the future. The fifth incinerator in Eastern Seaboard's Plant Department is where the university used to burn all its refuse. It was shut down by the state or the county, he thinks, because of air pollution. The university just hauls waste to the landfill now.

You also manage to contact Leslie Compton from the Air Quality Division of the Department of Natural Resources. Her information correlates with Scarfone's pretty much, though she has a few different things to say about why the Plant Department and Higgins Psychiatric incinerators are not operating. You record this information in your phone log (Figure 4).

After your conversation with Compton, you review your day's accomplishments and decide that you really have to talk to Gioberti again. You want to see if his knowledge of the incinerator situation jibes with everyone else's, and you want his reaction to the Lab Animal Medicine man's claim that lots of hospital waste should be incinerated that now is not. You also want to know what Gioberti thinks about

Leslie Compton, Air Quality Division, Rhode Island
Department of Natural Resources   5/4

1. Her office issues both permits to install and permits
to operate incinerators. Reviews and approves air emission,
type of waste, volume.

2. Her understanding of the situation re the two incinerators
in Mc Med and Stan Med is the same as Joe Scarfone's.
One difference — she thinks that the incinerator in the
Plant Department was shut down by the University
because it was no longer efficient or cost-effective, not
by someone else because of pollution.

3. Regarding the incinerator in Eastern Seaboard
Psychiatric:
   — permit to install issued 7/31/74
   — permit to operate issued 5/26/75 #38921 in
     Eastern Seaboard's name
   — NOT a pathological waste incinerator — 50%
     rubbish, 50% garbage.

Figure 4.   Log of Your Conversation with Leslie Compton

that toxic waste disposal problem in Radiology. You call his secretary
and get an appointment with him for next week. You figure face-to-
face contact will help you get the answers you need. To make sure
Gioberti has the information you want, you will write a follow-up
memo explaining the issues you wish to discuss with him at your
meeting.

Just as you are wrapping things up, Ted LaBute stops by your
office to ask how things are going. You tell him briefly what you have

learned about the incinerators. Ted tells you that since no one has gathered info on all the incinerators systematically, it would help to have a brief status report on file. He asks you to write one and have it ready for him next week.

ASSIGNMENT 4
Write a memo "To the Record" documenting your conversation with Cassidy. Copies will go to Gerald Cassidy, Manager, Occupational Health and Safety, and to Ted LaBute, Assistant Director, Hospital Renovation and Expansion.

ASSIGNMENT 5
Write a memo to Francis Gioberti, Director, Environmental Health and Safety, explaining the issues you will want to discuss with him next week. A copy of this memo will go to Ted LaBute.

ASSIGNMENT 6
Write a short report that describes all incinerators available for Cutler's use on the medical complex site and on the Eastern Seaboard campus. The report will go to Ted LaBute, who may choose to distribute it to other personnel.

Part 4

While walking from HRE to Cutler for the meeting with Gioberti today, you try to glance over a memo you just got from Abe Reisman in Radiation Control in response to your request for information. It is raining, and you are having a bit of trouble juggling your briefcase, an umbrella, and the memo. You thought you should read Reisman's memo before you see Gioberti. Reading quickly, you see that Reisman confirms Godschalk's reports on the handling of radioactive materials. Reisman agrees that no new facilities for handling radioactive wastes are needed in Cutler General to accommodate the expansion. You are happy to learn that at least this aspect of waste disposal seems under control. You hope Gioberti has read your memo and is prepared to talk to you today about the other areas.

As you pass through Cutler General's main lobby—dripping umbrella, briefcase, and memo in hand—you spot Dave Knudsvig elbow to elbow with Ed Marsden, chairman of the State Hospital Complex board, heading toward the Cutler main exit. Knudsvig sees you too, and they both join you.

"Why didn't you take the covered bridge?" Knudsvig says drolly.

"Didn't have the toll," you say smiling. Everyone in hospital administration feels that it is an inconvenience to have to walk outside from the Hospitals Administration Building to Cutler.

Knudsvig raises an eyebrow, turns to Marsden, and briefly introduces you to him. To your surprise, he tells Marsden that you are doing the staff work investigating a possible incinerator purchase for Cutler. There are some 20 professionals working in HRE, and it continually amazes you that Dave Knudsvig seems to know what every one of them is working on.

"I was just talking to Ed about that case," Knudsvig adds, looking at you.

"Yes," Marsden remarks. "The board is never too happy to see major changes in design programming."

Fortunately, Knudsvig jumps in before you have to say anything. "We'll give them the answers they need," Dave says, changing the subject. "Of course, that's if they'll approve the change order for the covered bridge."

"That'll be a sunny day in . . . Providence," Marsden says, smiling as he and Knudsvig both move toward the exit.

You wave them on and continue on to Gioberti's office, glad that Knudsvig rescued you from a tight spot, but also wondering just what his position is on the incinerator issue.

You really like Dave, as do most of the staff who work under him. He is a manager who trusts the competency of his staff and delegates responsibility. However, he is not afraid to let his staff take the heat for decisions based on their own information either. Dave will back a recommendation any staff member makes without batting an eyelash, but if the ball ends up back in his court because a decision he supported was not well documented, he tosses it right back to the staff member who recommended the go-ahead. The incinerator issue is one of those issues that you hope Dave will take a position on. There are just too many factors that can influence the decision to purchase.

When you finally get to Gioberti's office, you find him pacing back and forth with your memo in hand. From the moment he starts talking, you can tell that he is on the defensive.

Without bothering to greet you first, Gioberti begins, "I've got the information you need on the incinerators. The Plant Department incinerator over at Eastern Seaboard isn't worth renovating. It was never for pathological wastes anyway. The information you have is correct; the state required modifications because of excessive emission of particulate matter. After analyzing the situation, the university decided it would be cheaper to haul refuse to the city landfill than to fix the incinerator, so it was shut down."

Gioberti produces some notes. "The incinerator in Higgins Psychiatric has been fixed and is in working order. It is not in use, however, and because it's not certified for Type IV disposal, it will never be used for hospital waste. Cutler's crematorium has a permit for Type IV waste; it's 13 years old, but it is equipped with thermocouple controls and scrubbers and meets all air quality standards. It's operating at about 50 percent capacity now, 5 percent of that is hospital pathological wastes from all the hospitals in the complex. The two incinerators in McMed and StanMed have scrubbers but no permits; we still have to meet emission standards when operating, however. They're operating at 75 percent of capacity, as Fremont told you. Putting anything more through them, however, might make it impossible for us to meet emission standards."

You are impressed that Gioberti has been so thorough in gathering the incinerator information for you. Of course, you will now have to amend that short report to LaBute describing the incinerators. That's okay, but you are bothered by Gioberti's deliberate tone of voice. Something is worrying him. You decide to press further and see what comes up.

"Is the crematorium sufficient to handle pathological wastes when the hospital expands?" you ask.

Gioberti sits down and looks at you directly, but he does not say anything for a moment. You suspect that he is preparing to tell you what is on his mind.

"Look," Frank begins, "we've got infectious wastes going to the landfill now that are not being processed first. Sure, we are violating Health Department guidelines for handling infectious materials, but we haven't been challenged on it." Gioberti lights a cigarette. "They're probably not bothering us for three reasons—first, we're an existing facility; second, there've been no public complaints; and third, we've addressed the concerns of all landfill employees who have raised the issue with us."

"What concerns?"

"Well, they see our red bags, and they want to know what's in them. We tell them that we haven't dumped radioactive or highly pathologic wastes. Furthermore, the Health Department is aware of our dumping procedures. They seem satisfied with that answer for the moment."

It sounds as if Gioberti is giving it to you straight here. You can see that he is clearly frustrated with the problem of balancing regulations with convenient and effective waste disposal practice. You proceed with caution.

"So what do you think will happen when we open the new wings?" you ask.

Gioberti straightens up. "It's the opinion of this office that the new wings ought to contain a pathological incinerator. We will lose our status as an existing facility, and most certainly we'll have to follow the code. There also is good indication that federal and state laws are going to get tougher, and we will have to incinerate all potentially hazardous waste. Right now that procedure is only recommended by the Center for Disease Control [CDC]. By the way," he adds, leaning across his desk to hand you a document, "here's the report I promised you. It's from the CDC, and it lists recommended procedures for handling potentially hazardous wastes. Of course, they don't go into great detail about what's potentially hazardous. That's pretty 'iffy.' Do you include all disposable bed linens, for instance? We'll be using more of those in the future."

You glance at the report (Appendix E) and recognize that this is a government report you already have, in fact, one you read to prepare your first report to LaBute (Appendix A).

"You'll note that the report recommends that potentially hazardous wastes be either incinerated or autoclaved before we send them to a landfill. Of course, they don't say too much about large-scale incineration, but that's mainly because old incinerator technology wasn't good enough for big businesses, like hospitals, to meet air quality standards. If you have a good new unit, you can burn large quantities with no trouble."

"You mean a unit equipped with a secondary pyrolitic combustion chamber and all," you say.

"Yes," Gioberti replies, "as you said in your first report."

"What about sterilizing?" you ask.

"Well, incineration costs about half of sterilization, and, in addition, it reduces volume by 90 to 98 percent; that makes the stuff cheaper to haul away."

You recall that you had noted this same advantage of volume reduction in your previous report to LaBute but had not looked into the costs.

"Well," you say, putting down the government CDC report, "if we need a new incinerator, we're going to have to document it. The board won't buy it unless it's mandatory. How much waste are we going to burn?"

Gioberti again consults his notes.

"The CDC estimates that 10 pounds of solid waste per patient per day are generated in an acute care hospital. We produce almost double—8 tons a day just for Cutler and Higgins Psychiatric. That's up about 2 tons over five years ago. You can get the figures on compacted volumes from Tom Lincoln in Housekeeping.[13] He keeps track of the solid waste that goes to our rubbish contractor. Of course, not all the solid waste we produce is infectious. But," he adds confidently, "and this is an important point, the more waste of any type we burn, the better chance we have for heat recovery. As I said before, the move is now toward using more disposables. Paper bed linens, plastic containers for single-application medicines, all sorts of paper and plastics will be purchased in greater quantities. Burning more of this stuff makes heat recovery a viable option."

You jot that point down, and then ask about the toxic chemicals being dumped in Radiology.[14] Unfortunately, Gioberti does not deal with you as directly on this one.

"The important thing there," he says, "is to make sure we have some PVC[15] or glass pipes installed in the new wings to avoid corrosion from things dumped down drains. I'm sure we can get the dilution problem under control so we can meet EPA standards. Of course, we'll meet Rhode Island regulations, too."

You decide not to question Gioberti further about this. As you get up to leave, Gioberti reaffirms his position that the new wings ought to include a new incinerator. He agreeably asks you to call on him again if you need any other information.

When you leave the Environmental Health and Safety office you immediately call Tom Lincoln in Housekeeping. He tells you that

---

[13] Housekeeping, though located in Cutler General, handles maintenance for the entire medical complex.

[14] The toxic chemicals are used to develop X rays. They are not radioactive wastes.

[15] Polyvinyl chloride (PVC) is a kind of plastic.

Garbage Unlimited has the waste disposal contract for Cutler General, Higgins Psychiatric, and the Wesley Clinics. For $40,000 a year, Cutler both rents a 42-cubic-yard container-compactor and hires the services of an outside contractor who hauls the compacted wastes to the Midtown, Rhode Island, city landfill. The annual volume is approximately 6,500 cubic yards. This is compacted volume, reduced by 60 percent. Higgins Psychiatric produces 8,000 cubic yards, and the Wesley Clinics produce 1,500 cubic yards. The waste from these two hospitals is not compacted, and the disposal is handled by Eastern Seaboard University's Plant Department by arrangement with the State Hospital Complex.

After reviewing all the data you have collected over the last week and a half, you start to organize the information you have on hand as it supports the purchase of a new incinerator. You wonder if it would help to make a few more calls to some of those supervisors in the labs under Pathology who Fields and Gioberti told you to contact. You are not confident that their data will help prove the need for an incinerator. While thinking about this problem, you get a call from Ted LaBute.

"Well, hello there," he says in his usual cheerful way. "Haven't heard from you in a while. How's that incinerator investigation going? I got your report on the incinerators and the copy of the memo you sent to Gioberti. What did he tell you?"

"He confirmed much of the information I already had, but he did tell me a few things about the incinerators I didn't learn before. I'll have to update that report to you. Also, he gave me some information that starts us on the way toward a case for putting an incinerator in one of the new wings."

"Maybe," Ted says.

You greet Ted's doubt with silence, deciding that he will tell you what is bothering him eventually.

"I talked to Dave Knudsvig this morning and he's eager to see how this is all going," Ted continues. "He told me that you bumped into him and Marsden earlier today."

"That's right," you interrupt. "When I saw them, Dave brought up the incinerator investigation. I was pretty surprised."

"Yes, he said that," Ted says. "In fact, that's really why I'm calling you. Dave thinks that Marsden and the board of directors will be particularly reluctant to approve any design changes now."

"Marsden hinted that," you reply, thinking that now you will find out what the problem is.

"Right," Ted continues. "That's why Dave thinks that we'll have to first establish, beyond a shadow of a doubt, that Cutler General has a waste disposal problem before the board will even consider looking at solutions. Dave would like a report *now* showing that we've got a problem here, including as much quantifiable data as possible. He plans to discuss it with the board next week to prepare them for the possibility of some related design changes in the new wings. Do you think you can pull one together?"

"Well," you answer, "I'm not sure. Regulations on disposal are in a state of flux. Also, it's pretty difficult to define the waste problem in quantifiable terms. We can only estimate how much pathological waste might be incinerated by the hospital in the future. Our current practice doesn't very well reflect the volumes we might expect. I could call a few more of the labs under Pathology, but I don't think their figures will help us." You pause and then lay it on the line. "Ted, the info I have strongly suggests that we have a problem and we need an incinerator, but I can't come up with exact figures to back me up overnight."

"Well, then don't try," Ted responds. "Just make sure you thoroughly explain the problem—using the data which you do have—and its implications for the Cutler expansion design. Incidentally, how did your meetings with Gioberti go? Any trouble?"

"He is a bit tight with the information, just as you said," you reply.

"True enough. What about Cassidy?"

"He was upfront; pretty much gave me what information he had," you answer.

"Well," Ted says, "this waste disposal issue isn't as touchy for him. He's more worried about how employees handle waste than how we get rid of it. Where the stuff goes in the end is really Environmental Health's concern."

You agree.

"Anything else you want to discuss before you write that report?" Ted asks.

You shuffle through your research notes. "Hmm—well, I did run into one other problem concerning the disposal of toxic chemicals that might affect the new wing construction."

"Oh, yes?"

"It seems we may need to install PVC pipes in the new Radiology Department to prevent corrosion when developer and fixer is dumped down the drain. That's the only place we need to worry about toxics going down the drain though. Everywhere else, chemicals are used in smaller quantities and are picked up by Gioberti's department for disposal by an outside contractor."

"Check with Andy Bartholomew from our outside architect's office to see what he has to say about using PVC. Might as well include that problem in your report," Ted adds. "Though it doesn't relate to the infectious waste disposal problem, it may involve a construction change order for the PVC pipes, and the board will want to hear about that eventually. Also, make sure you write about the radioactive waste situation. We've opened a Pandora's box here, and we want to show the board we've taken a look at everything."

"Will do," you say. "By the way, just what is Dave Knudsvig's position on this whole problem anyway?"

"Dave is behaving as always on this one," Ted says. "He expects us to come up with the best recommendation eventually and trusts that whatever position we recommend, we'll send him to the board well-armed. That's one reason you should do this report defining the problem and its implications *now*. Dave knows best how to approach the board, and if they need to be convinced of the problem first, that's what we'll do."

Ted tells you that he expects the report next week, and you promise to make the deadline. Of course, the report will go to him, and he will attach a cover memo and pass it on to Knudsvig. As soon as you get off the phone, you call Bartholomew at Benson and Gorlach Associates to check on the PVC pipes. Bartholomew tells you that installing the PVC pipes would be no problem; they would stand up to the corrosive. The more important issue, however, is whether that stuff should be dumped down the pipes in the first place. You tell him that the Environmental Health Department is working on that one, and thank him for his help.

With that last bit of information in hand, you start organizing materials for the report to Ted.

Note: Students need not complete Assignment 7 before doing the report for Assignment 8.

ASSIGNMENT 7
If you completed Assignment 6, revise the short report you wrote to Ted LaBute on the status of incinerators available for Cutler's use and include your new information.

ASSIGNMENT 8

Write a report to Ted LaBute, Assistant Director, Hospital Renovation and Expansion, establishing the waste disposal problem at Cutler as it may affect the design of the new wings. Remember that though the report is addressed to LaBute, it will go to Knudsvig. LaBute will attach a cover memo and send it to Knudsvig, who may choose to distribute portions or all of the report to the board of directors for the State Hospital Complex. (If your instructor required you to complete Assignments 2, 4, 6, or 7, decide now how you might use portions of what you wrote previously for the report to LaBute. Remember that none of your previous reports or memos [including the report in Appendix A] were distributed to Knudsvig.)

ASSIGNMENT 9

Assume that Ted LaBute has read and approved the report you wrote for Assignment 8. He now asks you to write a cover memo for his signature that will accompany the report when he sends it on to Knudsvig. Write the cover memo to David Knudsvig, Director, Hospital Renovation and Expansion, from Ted LaBute, Assistant Director. (Write your name on the upper-right corner of this memo to identify it for your instructor.)

ASSIGNMENT 10

Read Appendix E. Write a 250-word summary of the Center for Disease Control recommendations regarding safe disposal of infectious waste.

APPENDIX A

Your First Report to Ted LaBute

STATE HOSPITAL COMPLEX
Hospital Renovation and Expansion

MEMORANDUM

To: Ted LaBute
            Assistant Director for Design and Construction

From: YOU
            Hospital Planner

Date: April 2, 1984

Subject: Waste Disposal Investigation

Dist.: Frank Gioberti
            Director, Environmental Health and Safety

ATTACHMENT: Hospital Wastes Classification and Disposal
             Handling

    At your request, I have completed a preliminary
investigation of the kinds of wastes produced by
hospitals and the preferred methods for handling
pathological wastes.

    Further investigation is required to assess the need
for a pathological incinerator for infectious wastes.
Regulations regarding the disposal of infectious wastes
are ambiguous. Incineration or sterilization of some
kinds of infectious waste prior to disposal in a
sanitary landfill or in the sewer system is not now
required. However, federal and state regulations
requiring incineration or sterilization of these wastes
is expected in the near future.

APPENDIX A—*continued*

-2-

    I plan to meet with F. Gioberti, Director of Environmental Health and Safety, to discuss Cutler General's methods of disposing of hazardous (infectious, toxic, radioactive) and nonhazardous wastes.
    The attached report defines hospital waste classifications and describes handling methods. My sources for definitions include Rhode Island's Public Law 78 and an unpublished paper written by David Knudsvig in his former position as a hospital planner for City Hospital in Baltimore, Maryland.

(*continued*)

APPENDIX A—*continued*

ATTACHMENT

HOSPITAL WASTES CLASSIFICATION
AND DISPOSAL HANDLING

1.0 Classification of Hospital Wastes

Hospital wastes fall into two categories defined by federal and state regulations and by the waste management industry: hazardous and nonhazardous wastes. A third category of wastes, potentially hazardous waste, has been defined by the Center for Disease Control and may be subject to future regulation of wastes ordinarily considered nonhazardous.

1.1 Hazardous Waste

1.1.1 Infectious Waste

Infectious waste contains viable disease-causing agents such as those listed by the U.S. Public Health Service Center for Disease Control as Class 3, 4, and 5 etiological agents. Class 3 agents are bacterial, fungal, parasitic, viral, rickettsial, or chlamydial agents involving special hazards and requiring special conditions for containment; an example is brucella. Class 4 agents require the most stringent conditions for containment because they are extremely hazardous to laboratory personnel or may cause serious epidemic disease; an example is the encephalitis virus complex. Class 5 agents are foreign animal pathogens excluded by law from the United States or whose entry to the United States is restricted by Department of Agriculture administrative policy, such as the Asiatic strain of Newcastle disease.

APPENDIX A—*continued*

1.1.2 Toxic Waste

Toxic waste is any waste substance which contains
one part per million of a compound which
statistically can be shown to cause acutely
toxic, carcinogenic, teratogenic, hereditary
mutagenic, or severely debilitating, irrevers-
ibly adverse effects to mammals when exposed by
the oral, dermal, or inhalation route once or
repeatedly to concentrations of 100 parts per
billion or less . . .
          or
any substance which appears on the register of
the U.S. Environmental Protection Agency with
hazard codes H or T . . .
          or
any substance listed on Rhode Island's Toxic
Materials Register or Hazardous Airborne
Substances List.[16]

1.1.3 Radioactive Waste

Radioactive waste includes transuranic waste
(contaminated with more than 10 nanocuries per
gram); spent fuel from nuclear reactors; waste
directly produced in the reprocessing of spent
fuel; and paper trash, plastics, glass, clothing,
discarded equipment and tools, wet sludge, and
organic liquids which have been contaminated with
radioactivity.

1.2 Nonhazardous Waste

Waste which does not fall into the categories listed
above is nonhazardous and is classified as follows:

(continued)

[16] Waste categories and classifications named throughout Appendix A do not necessarily
reflect current federal laws or waste management research. Public Law 78, the Toxic
Materials Register, and the Hazardous Airborne Substances List are not actual Rhode
Island documents.

APPENDIX A—*continued*

Type	Name	Components	Moisture Content
0	Trash	Highly combustible paper, wood, plastic, etc.	10%
1	Rubbish	Combustible paper, cartons, floor sweepings, etc.	25%
2	Refuse	Residential rubbish and garbage	50%
3	Garbage	Animal and vegetable waste	70%

1.3 Potentially Hazardous Waste

The Center for Disease Control has outlined guidelines for the disposal of potentially hazardous waste. This includes items which might ordinarily be considered nonhazardous waste if they did not come from a source where there was potential for contamination by infectious organisms. Type 4 waste, that is, carcasses, cadavers, organs, body parts, with a moisture content of 85%, is always considered potentially infectious waste which requires incineration. Other waste which falls into this category includes disposable linens, blood specimens, scalpel blades, and needles.

2.0 Methods for Disposing of Infectious Wastes

The preferred methods for disposal of infectious waste are incineration or sterilization followed by disposal in a sanitary landfill. Incineration is a controlled process which uses combustion to convert waste to a less bulky, less toxic, less noxious material. The principal products of incineration are CO_2, H_2O, and ash. Sterilization (sometimes called autoclaving) is the use of heat (usually moist heat) or chemicals under pressure to kill all forms of life

APPENDIX A—*continued*

including spores. The objective is to eliminate all microbial life forms. Sterilization is considered a pretreatment method (like compacting) to be used prior to disposal in a landfill.

Incineration not only reduces the volume of waste by 90 to 98%, but also offers the potential for waste-heat recovery, if material rich in Btu hydrocarbons (for example, paper, plastics) is burned. An increase in combustible waste also means less fuel is required to fire the incinerator.

The problem with incineration is air pollution. If waste is not completely oxidized, particulate matter may be expelled. Other by-products that could adversely affect the environment include compounds containing nitrogen, sulfur, and halogens. However, these effluents can be reduced through proper design and operation of the incinerator. New incinerators incorporating secondary pyrolitic combustion can keep flue gases clean and can destroy almost all ash. The new technology involves two combustion chambers. In a primary combustion chamber, mechanical controls adjust the amount of air entering the chamber to reach optimum temperature. Very hot gases force material into a secondary chamber where more air is gradually added and materials are completely oxidized.

Secondary pyrolitic combustion is less expensive than older incineration technology which employed scrubbers to reduce particulate matter. However, the new technology is about 20% more expensive than traditional incineration due to the purchase and maintenance of sophisticated control systems that respond rapidly to alter air in the combustion chambers. Because secondary pyrolitic combustion involves extremely high temperatures, it offers a great opportunity for heat recovery, particularly if waste rich in hydrocarbons is burned.

Sterilization involves exposing material to saturated steam under pressure or ethylene oxide for substances which cannot tolerate sterilization by heat. Though ethylene oxide requires lower temperatures, it is

(continued)

APPENDIX A—*continued*

a dangerous substance and requires extreme precaution when used. Sterilization has none of the pollution drawbacks of incineration, but it lacks some of incineration's advantages: the volume of waste is not reduced, and there is no potential for waste-heat recovery.

3.0 Future Requirements for Infectious Waste Disposal

Rhode Island waste disposal is governed by Public Law 78, which names specific pathogenic agents that are to be designated as hazardous wastes. The act also names standards for disposal facility construction permits. Public Law 78 does not identify the "special conditions for containment" of pathogenic wastes. (See Section 1.1.1 of this report.) Rhode Island law largely reflects federal law (the Resource Conservation and Recovery Act of 1976), which also includes little specific information on the containment of pathogenic wastes. The Rhode Island Department of Public Health makes agreements with individual health institutions regarding the disposal of infectious wastes, identifying, for instance, which wastes must be incinerated or sterilized.

The Center for Disease Control, a federal agency, generally recommends that infectious wastes be incinerated or sterilized prior to landfill disposal. The center also states, however, that small amounts of contaminated material may be ground and flushed down the drain. The Environmental Protection Agency has announced that it plans to consider possibilities for regulations on the disposal of infectious wastes this year. Federal action could result in corresponding changes in Rhode Island law, possibly requiring pretreatment of more materials through incineration or autoclaving prior to landfill disposal.

APPENDIX B

Partial Organizational Chart for State Hospital Complex

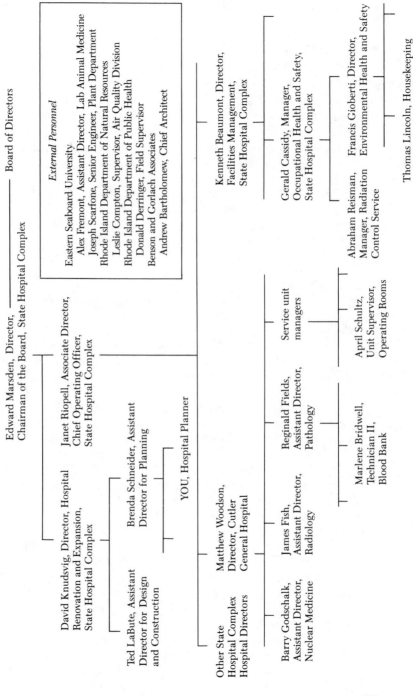

Edward Marsden, Director, Chairman of the Board, State Hospital Complex ——— Board of Directors

External Personnel

Eastern Seaboard University
Alex Fremont, Assistant Director, Lab Animal Medicine
Joseph Scarfone, Senior Engineer, Plant Department
Rhode Island Department of Natural Resources
Leslie Compton, Supervisor, Air Quality Division
Rhode Island Department of Public Health
Donald Derringer, Field Supervisor
Benson and Gorlach Associates
Andrew Bartholomew, Chief Architect

Janet Riopell, Associate Director, Chief Operating Officer, State Hospital Complex

David Knudsvig, Director, Hospital Renovation and Expansion, State Hospital Complex

Brenda Schneider, Assistant Director for Planning

Ted LaBute, Assistant Director for Design and Construction

YOU, Hospital Planner

Other State Hospital Complex Hospital Directors

Matthew Woodson, Director, Cutler General Hospital

Kenneth Beaumont, Director, Facilities Management, State Hospital Complex

Gerald Cassidy, Manager, Occupational Health and Safety, State Hospital Complex

Abraham Reisman, Manager, Radiation Control Service

Francis Gioberti, Director, Environmental Health and Safety

Thomas Lincoln, Housekeeping

Barry Godschalk, Assistant Director, Nuclear Medicine

James Fish, Assistant Director, Radiology

Reginald Fields, Assistant Director, Pathology

Service unit managers

Marlene Bridwell, Technician II, Blood Bank

April Schultz, Unit Supervisor, Operating Rooms

APPENDIX C

Alphabetical List of Personnel Involved in the Waste Disposal Investigation

Note: Each listing includes name, job title, organization or department, and office location.

Bartholomew, Andrew, Chief Architect, Benson and Gorlach Associates, 1400 Rockmorr, Providence, R.I.

Beaumont, Kenneth, Director, Facilities Management, State Hospital Complex, 750 Hospitals Administration Building.

Bridwell, Marlene, Technician II, Pathology, Blood Bank, second level, Cutler General Hospital.

Cassidy, Gerald, Manager, Occupational Health and Safety, State Hospital Complex, ninth level, Cutler General Hospital.

Compton, Leslie, Supervisor, Department of Natural Resources, Air Quality Division, 267E State Office Building II, Providence, R.I.

Derringer, Donald, Field Supervisor, Department of Public Health, R.I. Public Health Offices, 1200 Widmar, Providence, R.I.

Fields, Reginald, Assistant Director, Pathology, second level, Cutler General Hospital.

Fish, James, Assistant Director, Radiology, second level, Cutler General Hospital.

Fremont, Alex, Assistant Director, Lab Animal Medicine, Eastern Seaboard University, Alison Stanough Building.

Gioberti, Francis, Director, Environmental Health and Safety, State Hospital Complex, ninth level, Cutler General Hospital.

Godschalk, Barry, Assistant Director, Nuclear Medicine, second level, Cutler General Hospital.

Knudsvig, David, Director, Hospital Renovation and Expansion, State Hospital Complex, 640 Hospitals Administration Building.

LaBute, Ted, Assistant Director for Design and Construction, Hospital Renovation and Expansion, State Hospital Complex, 640 Hospitals Administration Building.

Lincoln, Thomas, Supervisor, Housekeeping, State Hospital Complex, first level, Cutler General Hospital.

Marsden, Edward, Director and Chairman of the Board, State Hospital Complex, 700 Hospitals Administration Building.

Reisman, Abraham, Manager, Radiation Control Service, State Hospital Complex, second level, Cutler General Hospital.

Riopell, Janet, Associate Director and Chief Operating Officer, State Hospital Complex, 700 Hospitals Administration Building.

Scarfone, Joseph, Senior Engineer, Plant Department, Eastern Seaboard University, Southeast Campus Building.

Schneider, Brenda, Assistant Director for Planning, Hospital Renovation and Expansion, State Hospital Complex, 640 Hospitals Administration Building.

Schultz, April, Service Unit Supervisor, Operating Rooms, third level, Cutler General Hospital.

Woodson, Matthew, Director, Hospital Administration, Cutler General Hospital, ninth level, Cutler General Hospital.

APPENDIX D

Labs under Supervision of Pathology Approved by Joint Commission on Accreditation of Hospitals

Biochemistry	Ligand Assay
Blood Bank	Microbiology
Hematology	Surgical Pathology
Immunology	Toxicology

APPENDIX E

Report from the Center for Disease Control on Handling Potentially Hazardous Wastes

Guidelines from the Center for Disease Control
Safe Disposal of Solid Wastes from Hospitals

At least 10 pounds of solid wastes are produced daily for each patient hospitalized in acute-care general hospitals (1). If the use of non-woven disposable fabrics—a much more expensive practice than using reusable linens (2,3)—continues, even more solid wastes may be expected since about 10 pounds of soiled, reusable linens also are generated every day for each patient (4).

Hospital solid wastes may be highly contaminated with pathogenic microorganisms. In addition, they may contain items capable of inflicting injury if not handled properly. Thus, hospitals should review their procedures for disposing of both types of potentially hazardous solid wastes. Such a review should encompass disposal of all hospital wastes since, despite attempts to segregate especially hazardous wastes from areas such as microbiology laboratories, possibly hazardous materials may be discarded from several hospital locations. This review should be directed to areas where high-risk wastes originate, to procedures that render such wastes less hazardous, to transportation of wastes within the hospital, and to methods for ultimate disposal.

A few hospital areas are obvious sources of waste materials with potentially hazardous levels of microbial contamination (hazardous chemicals or radioactive materials will not be discussed in this document). Wastes from the microbiology laboratory, all laboratories handling blood specimens or blood products, pathology services, and from patients on communicable disease isolation deserve special attention. Although handling of wastes from patients with "Class IV" virus diseases (5) requires extraordinary precautions, any item that has had contact with excreta, blood, exudates, or secretions may potentially spread disease. Therefore, there is a need to develop realistic and practical recommendations for disposal of highly contaminated solid wastes to reduce any risk of infection. In addition, the risks of either injury *or* infection from certain items, particularly syringe needles, must also be considered. Notwithstanding these hazardous wastes, however, a high proportion of hospital solid wastes are basically no more hazardous than residential solid wastes and can be handled and disposed without special precautions.

Each hospital area should have special receptacles for potentially hazardous wastes. Solid wastes from the microbiology laboratory should be placed in impervious bags or pans and should preferably be steam sterilized in the laboratory; or they may be transported in sealed double impervious bags to be steam sterilized* in another hos-

---

* About 100 to 500 ml of water should be placed in bags (or pans) used for steam autoclaving of discarded disposable or reusable laboratory plates, slides, or tubes; the water evaporates into steam and replaces residual air that if present might interfere with sterilization. Just before autoclaving, holes should be punched in the top of all plastic bags (and pan lids opened slightly) to permit steam penetration. Sterilizing cycles as long as one hour at 121°C (250°F) may be necessary, and weekly regular checking of the process with spores of *B. stearothermophilus* is recommended. After autoclaving, the residue can be safely handled and discarded with all other nonhazardous hospital solid wastes.

pital area or to be disposed of in a hospital incinerator. All slides or tubes with small amounts of blood should be packaged in double impervious bags and sent for incineration or autoclaving in the hospital; all blood specimens with more than a few ml. remaining after laboratory procedures, or bulk blood to be discarded, may be very *carefully* poured down a drain or autoclaved. Solid wastes from isolation should be double-bagged (6) for transport to a hospital autoclave or incinerator. Pathology wastes are customarily incinerated in the hospital, but they may be transported double-bagged in closed impervious containers for incineration outside the hospital.

Non-contagious wastes that are capable of producing injury, such as scalpel blades and particularly disposable syringes with needles, should be stored and handled in rigid containers. Ideally, there should be such rigid containers for disposable syringes and needles in each patient room; syringes and needles should be placed directly, unassembled to prevent injury to patient-care personnel, into the rigid containers for safe storage. When full, these containers should be securely taped shut and may be disposed with the rest of general solid wastes from the hospital.

Recommended hospital incineration of small quantities of potentially hazardous wastes (e.g., pathology and isolation wastes) is still possible in most communities, even if strict air pollution regulations are in force, since relatively small amounts of high-risk materials must be disposed of in this manner. Alternatively, however, grinding these wastes and flushing them into the sanitary sewerage system can be a practical and inexpensive method of disposal. Several Los Angeles hospitals have disposed of syringes, needles, and other hazardous items in this manner (7), and pathology wastes also can be economically disposed of using a heavy-duty "garbage" grinder that discharges directly to the sewer.

Most hospital solid wastes in patient rooms should simply be placed as generated directly into leakproof, easily cleaned containers, preferably in flameproof "waste baskets" with impervious plastic-bag liners. Items such as wound suction and urinary drainage bags and disposable dialysis membranes should be double-plastic bagged, in bags of adequate strength to prevent tearing (preferably 2-mil thickness). Bagged solid wastes should be tightly closed with "twist-ties" or heavy rubber bands prior to handling. Then, at least daily, all bags of wastes should be picked up and carried carefully (to prevent possible injury) to a large transfer cart; an impervious 2- or 4-wheel cart with a volume of about 12 cubic feet (e.g., 100 gallons) is recommended. As soon as carts are filled with bagged material, from patient rooms or other locations, this material should be taken directly to the main hospital storage container.

The great majority of hospitals centrally compact non-hazardous wastes directly into a large compacting "dumpster"-type container at the hospital loading dock; compaction greatly reduces transportation costs to disposal sites. There should be a drain to a sanitary sewer under the usual dumpster position; daily washing down the drain of any material around and under the dumpster is recommended. Keeping the dumpster and the area around it scrupulously clean will reduce odors and attraction of flies or other vermin.

Solid wastes that cannot or need not be incinerated at the hospital or disposed of in the sewerage system must be transported elsewhere for disposal. There is no evidence of hazard to public health of hauling hospital solid wastes to disposal sites in closed and leakproof dumpsters or trucks. Either municipal incineration or sanitary landfill, if operated properly to provide sufficient compaction and to prevent water pollution, is acceptable for disposal. But, unfortunately, a large number of communities in the United States do not have either satisfactory municipal incineration or sanitary landfills; many communities still use open dumps. Scavenging in open dumps that contain hospital wastes must not be permitted. Hospitals relying upon municipal or commercial systems for waste disposal should take the responsibility of confirming that the method of terminal disposal is safe. Local and State public health authorities can provide consultation regarding optimal disposal of solid wastes.

References

1. Maurer AH: A summary of waste disposal systems. Executive Housekeeper 8:16 *et seq*, April 1971
2. Bodner B: Study of a fresh look at cost of hospital laundry *vs*. disposables. Institutional Laundry 17:8 *et seq*, January 1973
3. Bodner B, *et al*: Costs of linen versus disposable O. R. packs. Hospitals 47:76 *et seq*, December 1, 1973
4. Anon: Calculation of hospital linen. Hosp Management 100:24, August 1965
5. Center for Disease Control: "Recommendation for Initial Management of Suspected or Confirmed Cases of Lassa Fever" MMWE 28: Supplement pp 1S–12S, January 4, 1980

6. Center for Disease Control: Isolation techniques for use in hospitals. HEW (CDC) Publication No. 78-8314, 104 pp, 2nd ed 1975
7. Weintraub BS, Kern HD: Wet grinding units tested for disposal of hospital solid wastes. J Env Hlth 33:338–344, 1971

From the Bacterial Diseases Division, Bureau of Epidemiology, Center for Disease Control, May 1974; revised August 1976, reprinted September 1977; second revision June 1980.

Another Burning Issue: A Follow-up Case

Note: Students should read and analyze Case 29, "To Burn or Not to Burn," before working on this follow-up case.

Part 1

Today is a catch-up day at work for you. All last week you were preparing materials for a meeting between your boss Brenda Schneider and the State Hospital Complex board of directors. Brenda was asked to outline the major reasons for including a psychiatric care facility in the new Danbey Children's Hospital planned for construction four years from now. While sorting the piles of file folders and correspondence that have accumulated on your desk, you find that you have not sorted through all the material you got together for that report you wrote to Ted LaBute on the waste disposal problem as it may affect design changes for Cutler's new wings. In reminiscing about the problem, you feel good about your report. No sooner do you start to organize materials from this project than you get a call from Ted. He has just received Knudsvig's reaction to your report.

"Apparently, Dave knew what he was doing in asking you to establish that Cutler has a waste disposal problem," Ted begins. "Dave now thinks we've begun to pave the way toward convincing the board that the Cutler expansion should include a new incinerator. But," Ted hesitates a bit, "he doesn't think the information we have so far is enough to get the board to approve a design change."

"Why not?" you say, a bit disconcerted.

"Well," Ted answers, "the board needs more quantifiable data. We haven't collected any information telling *exactly* how much waste we will have to burn and whether that quantity warrants building a new incinerator. After all, we have a crematorium that is now operating at only 50 percent of capacity."

"Okay," you concede, "but I'm not sure we can get more information from Gioberti and his crew."

"Well, I think we can get more info," Ted counters. "I've got a few ideas on how we might go about it—mainly because Knudsvig has specified what he needs."

"Okay, shoot," you respond.

"Knudsvig wants us to find out exactly what has to be burned from each lab now handling infectious or potentially infectious waste. That includes JCAH-approved labs[1] that will remain operating in the old part of Cutler and new labs that will be part of the expansion. We also should find out what wastes will be burned from splinter labs[2] or any other source."

"But I'll have to go back to Frank Gioberti for that info," you say. "It'll be like pulling teeth."

"Well, I think not," Ted counters. "Dave Knudsvig has had a heart-to-heart with Frank about all this in the last week. Gioberti's now convinced that we're out to make sure Cutler gets a new incinerator. And that is what he *wants* after all."

"True, he does," you say.

"He just needs to know that before we can get that incinerator, we've got to have more of his help. He's got to tell us specifically how he expects the federal laws regarding disposal of hazardous wastes to change. Knudsvig knows we can't get exact information now, but Frank should have a pretty good idea of what the Feds are looking into. And," Ted continues, "we will need the lowdown on how those corrosives in Radiology will be handled in the future. We have to know if the EPA is going to okay what we dump down the drain."

"O-O-Okay," you say, "I'll do my best to get that information too, but Frank will be less eager to cooperate there. He's not going to want

---

[1] Labs which perform a variety of diagnostic and research functions are certified for a period of two years by a national review board, the Joint Commission on the Accreditation of Hospitals (JCAH). (See Appendix D of Case 29 for a list of JCAH-approved labs.)

[2] Splinter labs, such as the Allergy Lab and the Hypertension Research Lab, fall under JCAH criteria for performing a limited patient function. Their test results are used in patient care evaluation and appear in the patient's hospital medical record.

us prying into any unwritten agreements he may have with the EPA." You stop to think for a minute. "You know this may take a while," you finally say. "I know Gioberti doesn't have information about lab waste quantities at hand. I ended up doing a lot of footwork for the last report. We might have to do a survey of some sort."

"You find out what he's got and get back to me," Ted tells you. "We can decide where to go from there."

You end your conversation with Ted thinking that you have a very big job ahead of you. You immediately call Gioberti's secretary, make an appointment with him, quickly type him a short memo telling what information you want and hope for the best.

ASSIGNMENT 1
Write a memo to Francis Gioberti, Director, Environmental Health and Safety, asking for information. A copy goes to Ted LaBute, Assistant Director, Hospital Renovation and Expansion. Your letterhead should read MEMORANDUM, State Hospital Complex, Hospital Renovation and Expansion.

Part 2

It has been a week since you wrote the memo to Frank Gioberti. Today when you enter his office, you can see that he has already gathered some data for you. You start to cheer up a bit.

"So we have to start a campaign for that incinerator," he remarks while sorting through some reports. "I've put together a list to help you get started."

"Started on what?" you say, a bit puzzled.

"Well, we don't have a survey of wastes produced by our various labs, so we're going to have to contact them all ourselves. I've got a list of all the labs under our jurisdiction; there are 8 main labs[3] and about 20 splinter labs."

"Twenty splinter labs!" you say. "This is going to take a long time."

---

[3] These are the eight labs under the jurisdiction of Pathology listed in Appendix D of Case 29.

"Maybe not," Gioberti answers. "If you call Pathology, for instance, I'm sure Fields over there can give you the info you need for the Microbiology labs and the Blood Bank. Most of the labs handling infectious wastes work under a central unit. Just ask Fields how much waste is 'red-bagged' or put in biohazard containers from the labs under Pathology. That should do it. If you call as many units as you can this week and check with me next week, I'll see if I can get some of my staff here to do more of the calling. This week we're a little tight and can't schedule it in."

You decide not to take Frank's offer lightly, and you agree to do some calling this week. You then ask him what he knows about how laws on waste disposal might change in the future.

"Afraid I can't predict much about what the EPA will do," he says. "But I can tell you this: Grinding and flushing infectious waste down the sanitary sewer is acceptable now, but it probably won't be for long. Also, you can expect the clean water rules will become tougher. No doubt the water purification plants and sewage treatment plants will start looking upstream—if they can't meet standards—to see who is supplying them with what. In short, the inevitable is coming—we're going to have to dispose of the infectious wastes in other ways."

"What about the toxic wastes being dumped down the drain in Radiology?" you ask.

"I'm confident that we can neutralize those before they're dumped," Gioberti answers. "They shouldn't be part of your consideration here."

You jot that information down.

"When you call those lab supervisors," Gioberti adds, "make sure you get quantities for wastes that *must* be burned—just the infectious stuff which falls under our 'red bag' policy. And ask them to give you quantities in cubic yards. That's what we'll need to figure out the incineration needs. I don't have many weight-to-volume conversion figures for solid wastes. If they give you the measurement in gallons, though, you can figure about 202 gallons per cubic yard."

You do not say anything for a bit as you try to plan how you will go about getting the waste data. Finally, you decide that you will start with Pathology, see what you get, then come back to Frank to check your progress with him. You tell him so, and then you decide to hint that you might solicit more help from him directly.

"You know, Frank," you point out, "if I can't get the information we need by calling, we may have to do a formal survey. Do you think that could be handled through your office?"

"Well," Frank says reluctantly, "we could issue some kind of form and have it circulate through Housekeeping to our maintenance employees. They could count bags of trash and identify the kind of waste thrown out from every unit, say, over a period of seven days." For a moment Frank gives this idea some support saying, "We could estimate moisture content from identifying the waste's source and even estimate the weight by considering the volume and type of waste. There are formulas for that. The moisture content and weight will tell us what kind of efficiency or heat recovery we could get, given what we have to burn." But then Frank quickly adds, "However, a full-scale survey's a lot of work, and I don't think it's really necessary. We should get sufficient information from the lab supervisors."

You decide not to push your suggestion any further, thank Frank for his time, and promise that you will get back to him.

As there is no point in delaying your unpleasant job, you decide to get on the phone right away and call Pathology. Fields gives you some data for the Blood Bank and Microbiology Laboratory, but every figure he gives is an estimate, with the exception of some data from back in 1975 when the lab did extensive bookkeeping. On top of that, he tells you that his estimates should be increased by 40 percent to account for volumes over the next five to ten years. Another guess. You should have figured on this; Fields really did not have any information to give you the last time you talked to him. Fields does, however, bring up something you had not considered before: Labs are not the only areas where infectious waste accumulates. Patient treatment areas also are a source for pathologic waste. Fields gives you some estimates of waste from the Hemodialysis Treatment Unit under his supervision and then ends your conversation by referring you to April Schultz, service supervisor for Cutler General's operating rooms. You record his information in your phone log (Figure 1).

Upon calling April Schultz, you get some sketchy estimates of what must be burned, again, guesses about volumes and materials based on her experience. After recording this data in your phone log (Figure 1), you can see right away that the problem of collecting data on waste disposal is more complicated than even *you* thought. Some of the waste comes from labs, other comes from hospital service units, still more comes from patient rooms. Even if you could call personnel in all these units, you might only get more guesses. You are coming to the conclusion that an extensive survey of all waste produced by the hospital must be done. Ironically, Frank Gioberti himself described the obvious way to do this—through Housekeeping, under *his* au-

Reg Fields, Pathology   5/24

Three labs (Micro, Blood Bank, Hemodialysis) — in 1975, put out 18 4-gal pails/day = 72 gal.

Estimates of waste per week now:

1. Microbiology Laboratory: 3/4 cu yd of plastic and glass daily (7-day week). (152 gal.)

2. Blood Bank: 2¼ cu yd of glass, plastic, needles and paper per day (7-day week). (60 cu ft.)

3. Hemodialysis Unit: 2¼ cu yd of paper, plastic and needles/day (needles = 1 gal). Work on a 6-day week. (60 cu ft and 1 gal needles.)

4. These materials are not processed at all before disposal.

5. Recommends increasing whatever estimates we get by 40% to account for the next 5-10 years.

April Schultz, Operating Rooms   5/24

Blood goes down drain. All other waste is contaminated: disposables (drapes, linens, gowns, sheet covers, etc.). Clots from suction machines. Tissue goes to Pathology.
Volume 2-5 bags/room/day: 13 rooms (35-40 cases every 24 hours).
Bag = 4 ft x 1 ft x 2 ft
= (about) 16 cu yd/day of infectious waste.

Figure 1.   Log of Your Conversations with Fields and Schultz

thority. The maintenance people have to make an actual count of how many red bags are thrown out and characterize the other trash produced everywhere in the hospital. You think that he will be the last one to applaud this idea, since it will mean a lot of work for his own staff. In the end, however, creating and distributing a survey, though time-consuming, will be far more productive than calling the lab supervisors—and Gioberti has already volunteered his staff to do that. Of course, you are not sure how much of the calling he had counted on you to do.

You decide to call on Ted LaBute and ask him where to go from here. After you explain the situation to him, he agrees with you completely about the need for a survey. However, the request for a survey cannot come from him to Gioberti. Dave Knudsvig must make the request, and he must be convinced of the need. While you and Ted are meeting to discuss this problem, you both review the main reasons for instituting a survey.

"The most important thing," Ted argues, "is to give Knudsvig a clear idea of why the survey is needed and to convince him that the information we want really can't be obtained any other way."

"Well, it can't," you say. "The unit supervisors can only give estimates, and the only way we can be sure we've covered every room of the hospital that produces infectious wastes is to have Housekeeping look for the red-bagged items coming from every area of the hospital. Of course, we could continue to survey the lab supervisors and get their opinion of how wastes are likely to increase over the next five to ten years. Their estimates, coupled with the specific data on current waste disposal from Housekeeping, will give us about the best data we can get. I think the survey is the only way we can go."

"You're right," says Ted.

Both of you are silent for a minute.

"You know, I've just had a scary thought," you begin. "We've really got to survey the wastes produced by Higgins Psychiatric and the Wesley Clinics as well as Cutler General."

"Afraid you're right," Ted says. "What they potentially could burn could make or break our argument for a new incinerator."

You get up and start pacing a bit.

"Look, Ted," you say, "are we really going to get Gioberti to go for this? He said he'd have his staff do some phone calling, but to compile and distribute a survey . . ."

"We have to get him to do it," Ted interrupts. "He's the only authority we can count on to get support for that incinerator purchase. The problem is that Frank's pretty accustomed to the operations personnel in the medical complex staying out of his business. He knows the score and knows just what to do to keep our labs and patient service areas in good shape with the Health Department. Because of this, the hospital administration has pretty much let him do things his own way. I wouldn't be surprised if he thinks his mere request for an incinerator amounts to 'the word.' He'll support our efforts, but he probably believes that whatever help *he decides* to give us should be enough. He doesn't understand the board's need for proof before they'll spend the money. To the board this will look like a straight dollar and cents issue. Burning more will cost us more, and they have got to have proof that we need the incinerator. Frank simply must agree to the survey."

"So what now?" you say.

"I want you to write a proposal to Dave Knudsvig. We want him to ask Environmental Health to design and conduct through Housekeeping a survey of the disposal of infectious wastes throughout the State Hospital Complex."

"Good," you answer. "We really need to put this whole problem in Gioberti's court. Plus, I think his group is the only one that can come up with a suitable survey. Frank already knows what kind of information will help us evaluate the advantage of incinerating more waste."

"Well," Ted says encouragingly, "the sooner you write that proposal, the sooner this will be out of our hair. Of course, I'm sure after Knudsvig approves our plan, he will want you to consult with Gioberti to make sure the survey his group draws up meets our needs."

"I'm counting on it," you say.

"Good," Ted answers. "Then write it up, and I'll see that Knudsvig gets it before the end of the week."

Feeling better about everything, you go back to your office to work on your draft. The survey you are going to request will help ensure that Cutler is equipped to meet all waste disposal regulations and help the board of directors make an informed decision about including an incinerator in Cutler's new wings. It may even help Gioberti get a better handle on how departments are responding to directives from his and Cassidy's office regarding waste disposal. As you begin writing, you realize that you should aim to make Knudsvig's job of requesting the survey from Gioberti a little easier. If you can write the proposal positively, adopting Dave Knudsvig's perspective, he may be able to send it directly to Gioberti with a short cover memo. You work out the details of your draft with that strategy in mind.

ASSIGNMENT 2

Write a proposal that HRE request a survey from Environmental Health. Your office address is State Hospital Complex, Hospital Renovation and Expansion. The proposal will go to David Knudsvig, Director, and be from Ted LaBute, Assistant Director. You will be designated as writer, with the title Hospital Planner. Assume that Knudsvig may choose to send the proposal on to Gioberti with a short cover memo.

The Motown Motors Case: Improving Wire Connections in Alternators

Day 1

You are an engineer working for Motown Motors, Inc. (a major American automaker) in the Research and Development Office, a division of Motown's Central Staff Services. Your division does research on new ways to increase manufacturing efficiency and quality, providing a service for other arms of the company that are directly involved in producing and marketing Motown Motors' products.

Your division must produce solutions that save money and time, cause no manufacturing problems, and can be quickly implemented. Since Research and Development has no single focus, its engineers may be working on several diverse projects in their efforts to answer the requests of Motown's production divisions. For instance, your division may be asked by Motown's Marketing Division to develop tests to evaluate the quality of an auto repair product, manufactured by an outside vendor, which Motown would like to purchase and sell under its own name. Or your division might be asked by the Body and Frame Assembly Division to automate a device that will reduce the need for extensive handwelding operations.

This morning you met briefly with Harold Simak, your supervisor, to discuss a new assignment. Simak has asked you to work on improving a manufacturing process that has led to the failure of alternators produced by Motown Motors. The problem was identified by Motown's Customer Service Division, which notified Product Engineering in the Engine, Transmission, and Parts Group. Thomas Pierson, manager of Product Engineering (PE), in turn has requested the services of Research and Development (R & D), your unit. (See Appendix A, Organizational Chart.)

417

Apparently, Customer Service has recently received several complaints about alternators failing; many are even failing during the 24-month warranty period. The lead wires from stator windings frequently become disconnected from their soldered connections to terminal lugs.[1] The problem is particularly severe in Motown's 40-, 57-, and 70-ampere alternators. (See Appendix B for a summary description of the Motown alternator.)

Pierson's department, Product Engineering (PE), has already analyzed the cause of the soldered-connection failures. Alternator stators are wound with high-thermal-rated magnet wire with a tough insulation coating. The insulation must be removed from the lead ends of this magnet wire so that they can be soldered to terminal lugs. The insulation is currently being removed from leads by a wire-brush tinning operation which both removes the insulation and tins the wire preparatory to soldering. Unfortunately, the insulation removal process is not 100 percent effective, and tinned wires have spots where no solder adheres. If wires are insufficiently tinned, the soldered joints will eventually fail. Pierson is asking Research and Development to come up with a method for removing insulation and tinning stator lead wires that would allow for an adequate solder connection.

You decide to spend some time this morning digging up information on methods that have been used to remove insulation from high-thermal-rated magnet wire. You also make an appointment with Simak so that you can discuss the problem in greater detail.

Day 2

Today you are reviewing the information you have collected on removal of insulation from magnet wires. Insulation on many magnet wires is meltable. As soon as the wire is dipped in hot solder, the insulation comes off and the wire tins easily. Insulation on high-thermal-rated magnet wires, however, is designed to resist high temperatures and abrasion. This insulation prevents wound wires, which become hot and vibrate when current flows, from making contact with one another.

You have discovered that Motown has tried several methods of removing the insulation in the past, including grit blasting and scrap-

---

[1] The failure of the soldered connections has grave consequences. The alternator is the power source for regenerating the car battery while the engine is running.

ing. Grit blasting removed the insulation well enough, but it removed too much copper along with it. The mechanical scrape method was too inefficient. The wire-brush tinning operation in use now works more efficiently, but it does not always remove all of the insulation. You are wondering if you could remove the insulation chemically; a molten caustic might do it. While you are scanning Motown's technical bulletin on alternators (Appendix B), you decide to call Bill Starsky, a fellow engineer in PE. You are going to need a few alternator assemblies to look at firsthand. Your timing is good; Starsky is in when you call. He is in a chatty mood though, and you find it hard to get him down to business, but finally you do.

"Ah, look, Bill, I'm reviewing our technical bulletin on Motown's alternators and trying to come up with something for that stator lead wire problem you sent us. It looks like I'm going to need a few alternators to look at. The drawings here don't show enough detail."

"Sure enough, I'll send over one each of the 40-, 57-, and 70-amp models. Anything else?"

"Maybe you ought to send the 65- and 117-amp assemblies too."

"Okay, but it's the other ones we've been having the most trouble with."

"Why's that Bill? I can see that the 40-, 57-, and 70-amp models are wye wound from the pictures in the alternator bulletin. What's coming loose, the single-wire connections or the triple-wire neutral joint?"[2]

"The worst trouble is with the triple-wire joint."

"Well, I can see why that might happen; here we are trying to solder three wires that still have insulation residue on them."

Bill says nothing in reply.

"You know, from those drawings in the bulletin," you continue, "you can't even tell for sure how the stator wire leads are soldered to the posts on the rectifier assembly. Some look like they have lugs on 'em, but some look like they're just hooked around the posts and soldered directly."

"Well, you're right," Bill interrupts. "On the 40- and 57-amp models, the single-wire connections are simply made with bare wires. The lead wire is curved like a shepherd's hook around the terminal post on the rectifier assembly and soldered in place. We use a lug for

---

[2] Appendix B clarifies the technical issues raised in this dialogue about the alternator problem.

40-57 AMP   70 AMP

Figure 1.   Single-Wire Connections

the single-wire connection on the 70-amp alternators though. The lug's got a C-shaped end that slips over the post. We also use lugs on the triple-wire connections for all three models."

You make a few quick sketches while Bill is talking (Figure 1).

"Does the triple-wire lug have a C-shaped end?"

"No, that's got a square-shaped end, sort of like a flat, square nut, that can be bolted to a neutral ground."

You sketch an approximation (Figure 2).

Suddenly you get a bright idea.

"Say, Bill, why are we using lugs on the single-wire connections on the 70-amp alternators? After all, we're just hooking the wire around the terminal post on the 40- and 57-amp models."

"Don't know. Probably because we've got more vibration on the high-amp model. The lug is bare metal and makes a better connection to the post. There's more stress at the post than where the wire connects to the lug. That bare wire on the 40- and 57-amp lead-wire-to-post connections isn't exactly bare—still got spots of insulation on it." Bill chuckles. "That's all part of the problem we've got you working on, whiz kid."

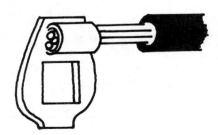

Figure 2.   Triple-Wire Connection

You take this in and then ask, "If we could strip that wire bare, do you think we'd even need a lug on the ends of the 70-amp leads, Bill?"

"Don't know. Perhaps not."

Hmm, you think to yourself. If a molten caustic will strip all of the insulation off, that could save the company money. Soldered connections made with clean wires would be less likely to fail. But, as a bonus, if you could determine that good bare wire connections do the job as well as the lug-to-post connections, that could save even more money, because fewer parts would be used.

"Look, Bill," you finally say, "you've been a great help. Send those alternators along, okay?"

"Of course."

You get off the phone and check your watch. It is 4:45 P.M. already. You are pretty excited about this project now. It looks as if there is a clear money-saving angle you can work on. You decide to quit for the day, but before you go, you glance at your calendar to see what is scheduled for tomorrow. It looks as though you will be talking this over with Simak at 9:30. Well, you are ready for him.

Day 3

It is 9:15 A.M., and you are waiting outside Simak's office, sipping a cup of coffee while reviewing your questions about the alternator project. Your appointment with Simak is stuck between two big department meetings he must attend, and you will have to hurry to make sure you get all the pertinent information from him. At 9:20 A.M., Simak asks you in. You decide to start right off.

"Got your note on the alternator project. I've already been over a few details with Starsky from PE. Just wanted to ask you a few questions."

"Fire away," Simak says, glancing at his watch.

"Well, it seems pretty clear what PE wants us to do here; come up with a quick and simple way to get all the insulation off the leads of the magnet wires so they can be tinned the way they're supposed to be. I'm just curious why this problem has just surfaced now. According to a couple of our technical bulletins, we've been using high-thermal-rated magnet wires since 1965. I don't think the insulation has changed much. I see we tried grit blasting and mechanical scraping a few years back."

Simak interrupts. "Yeah, I know. Motown's been working on this

one as long as I can remember. Failing connections have been crop-
ping up during the warranty period and after for several years, but
now there seems to be an epidemic. I suspect that more alternators
fail now than in the past simply because we put on lots more electronic
gadgets than we used to. That puts more drain on the battery and
makes more demands of the alternator—more heat, more wire pul-
sation. So it goes."

Simak again looks at his watch and seems preoccupied. You decide
to risk finding out what he is *really* thinking about this project.

"You don't seem overly concerned about this job for PE."

Simak gets up and paces a bit. "To tell the truth, I'm not sure what
PE wants from us anymore. Lately, they've taken to working out solutions themselves or getting outside vendors to redesign products. If
a vendor comes up with something they like, they buy it. If they keep
that pattern up, there's not going to be much left for our research
division to do."

"So, the outside vendors are getting the projects, and we're not."

"You got it, and that doesn't look good for us. PE doesn't really
want us to go under. We're useful to have around. Lots of times it's
cost-effective in the long run to solve the problem using our own
resources."

"Well, this alternator problem seems to be a chance to make that
point, doesn't it?"

Simak stops short. "Well, it all looks pretty straightforward, but,
as you just said, the insulation-removal problem has been with us a
long time. I wouldn't be surprised if PE has got some vendors working
on it too."

"Maybe they don't."

"Maybe," he replies doubtfully.

"Well," you ask anxiously, "where do I start?"

"You'll have to get a list of types we now use from PE and have
them get our vendors to send samples." Simak again glances at his
watch. "Look, ah, keep me posted on this thing. I've got a department
meeting that started five minutes ago." Simak starts to shuffle through
some folders as you get up to leave. "Wait," he says, grabbing your
coat sleeve. "I've got something for you." He holds up a 20-foot coil
of 17-gauge magnet wire that he's just found buried under the mass
of stuff on his desk. "Pierson stopped by yesterday to tell me PE is
thinking of switching the kind of magnet wires they're using in alternators to one with an even higher thermal rating. They're now using
Tough Polycoat, rated at 200 centigrade. They may switch to this."

Simak tosses the coil to you. "It's called Heavy Guard—got a 220 centigrade rating. Comes in several gauges. You could start your tests with this sample." Simak leaves you examining the coil and rushes off.

When Simak goes, you start thinking over what he said. You are not sure that you like the idea of working on what may be a dead-end project. You prefer to work things through, from start to finish, from finding the solution to specifying the production particulars. However, you have little choice in the matter; you must give it a whirl. First, you have to get more wire samples. You call Bill Starsky and ask him for the product names and insulation types of all magnet wires that Motown has used or has contemplated using in its alternators. Bill spouts off the names of four products, together with the type of insulation and the manufacturer. You scribble down this list (Figure 3).

Bill tells you that Haywire's Heavy Guard has the highest thermal rating of all these wires, 220°C. Motown is now using Tough Polycoat, which is rated at 200°C, in all alternators that are produced in high volume (40-amp, 57-amp, 65-amp, 70-amp, and 117-amp). The gauges range from $14\frac{1}{2}$ to 16. The higher-thermal-rated Heavy Guard is being used on a limited basis in heavy-duty trucks. This wire is 17-gauge, but Heavy Guard is also available in gauges $14\frac{1}{2}$ to 16. As Simak said, the Heavy Guard variety is being considered for mass use, so a method

"NYLOCOAT" — POLYURETHANE   MANUFCT. by HAYWIRE
    WITH NYLON OVERCOAT

"SOLDERITE" - SOLDERABLE   "   WHIPPLE
    POLYESTER w/ NYLON OVERCOAT

"TOUGH POLYCOAT" - POLYAMIDE-IMIDE   "   HAYWIRE

"HEAVY GUARD" - POLYIMIDE   "   "

Figure 3.   Your List of Wire Types

of stripping quickly should be investigated now. Since the truck alternators are produced in smaller quantities, a speedy method for removal of the insulation has not been developed; use of a manual wire stripper has proved sufficient. The other wires Bill lists are magnet wires with lower thermal ratings which have been used by Motown in the past but are not in use now. After reviewing the list with Bill, you decide to make arrangements to order all of these wires through PE; you will decide later which wires you will test with a molten caustic.

ASSIGNMENT 1
Write a memo to T. Pierson, Manager, Product Engineering, from H. Simak, Section Supervisor, Research and Development. Your letterhead will read: Motown Motors, Inc., Research and Development. Your name and title, Staff Engineer, will be listed next to "Prepared by." Ask Pierson to order 20-foot coils of each of the wires you will need. (Pierson, the manager who requested service from R & D, must initiate and approve your purchases from outside vendors.)

Day 4

Today you decide to give a molten caustic dip a try. In designing the lab test of the dip process, you want the quickest and cheapest way to do both the caustic dip and subsequent solder operation. You figure that it would save space and money if the caustic bath and solder are heated to the same temperature in one dipping pot. You rig up a device to melt the solder in a cup placed within the molten caustic bath. You make the small solder pot of 1-inch pipe by welding a $\frac{1}{4}$-by-$1\frac{1}{2}$-by-$1\frac{1}{2}$-inch plate to one end of a 3-inch length of pipe. Extension arms $\frac{3}{8}$-inch rod 12 inches long welded to the top of the pot allow you to suspend it within the caustic salt bath. You heat the caustic salt in an electrically heated 2-quart Accumelt pot rated at 1,000 watts, 110 volts alternating current. You connect a Hedges 0–2500 pyrometer to an Alumochrome thermocouple to read bath temperatures.

The caustic salt (NaOH)[3] you try first is a commercial product

---

[3] The term "salt" is often used for NaOH even though it is technically a base.

called DGS salt which is stocked by Motown's chemical store. You have no choice but to start testing with the Heavy Guard that Simak gave you as the other wires requested from Pierson have not arrived yet. However, you are fairly certain that whatever removes the insulation on this high-thermal-rated wire will remove it on the other wires with lower ratings. You cut several 6-inch lengths of the Heavy Guard wire and prepare a bath of molten DGS. You dip several samples in the molten DGS bath and vary the bath temperature several times. After processing these samples, you find the Heavy Guard sample strippable at 720°F if left immersed in the DGS solution for 40 seconds. Although the wire strips easily, you note that an oxide deposit is formed on the exposed copper surface, and the wire cannot be tinned.

Reflecting on this test, you realize that you have made a big blunder. DGS salt contains an additive which retards decomposition of sodium hydroxide (NaOH) by controlling its conversion to sodium carbonate (NaCO) from air-absorbed carbon monoxide (CO). This additive caused the oxide deposit to form on the wire. You now realize that both higher temperatures and a pure caustic solution, free of oxidizing agents, will be needed if you are to cut the strip time down and effectively tin the wire. Nevertheless, you are encouraged by your progress thus far. You decide to check out the current wire-brush process as soon as possible to see what kind of production time your solution must beat. You record your day's work in your logbook and then call Starsky in PE and set up a date to bat around a few ideas and get details on the wire-brush process. You then drop a note to Frank Harris at the company's chemical store to send you about 50 pounds of pure sodium hydroxide (NaOH). You will set up the strip trials using the pure NaOH tomorrow.

On your way out at 5:00 P.M., you find a brief note from Simak in your in box reminding you that you must write a 300-word summary of your progress on your most recent project for *In Development*, a monthly newsletter which keeps engineers informed about current investigations at R & D.[4] Of course, Simak wants you to summarize your work on the caustic dip project.

Though you are busy with dozens of other things, you will have to put your best foot forward for this effort. The newsletter item is

---

[4] The newsletter helps engineers to exchange ideas and gives management a good handle on who is doing what.

your chance to show management that you have the caustic dip project under control and to pique the interest of engineers who may give you some suggestions and help your investigation along.

ASSIGNMENT 2
Write a 300-word summary of your progress on the caustic dip project for *In Development*.

Day 5

Just before lunch today, you review your progress on the alternator project. Earlier this morning you met with Starsky, and he explained how the line workers are doing the strip and solder operation down at the Pleasantville Parts Plant. You filed away a few notes from Starsky's comments (Appendix C). The process, you learned, takes about 40 to 50 seconds and involves two wire-brush operations and two solder dips. To save money on equipment, only one set of brushes is employed; this arrangement requires that the operator process each assembly twice. A single solder and brush treatment would only partially remove the insulation and would not tin the wire; the double-dip, double-brush process removes most of the insulation and tins most of the wire.

Thinking back over your discussion with Starsky, you start making some plans. You know that you can get the caustic dip process to leave the wire entirely free of insulation. To really sell PE, though, you need to show that the process can also save time and money.

Well, you can see right away that the process would eliminate the need for a wire-brushing machine. The caustic dip could be placed right next to the solder pot. If you can get the caustic dipping time down to about 5 seconds, the whole process should take under 20 seconds—5 seconds in the caustic, 10 seconds for tinning, a few seconds for transfer time. Pretty slick.

You catch yourself in this pleasant reverie and remember that you have a lunch meeting at Manufacturing Engineering (ME) on that heater core project you started two years ago. Your solution is finally going into production!

You check your mail before you leave, and lo and behold, there is a memo from Simak. Looks like Pierson is pressing your department to submit a solution fast. He has gone ahead and scheduled an interdepartmental meeting for Thursday, next week. He says that he will bring along a couple of engineers so they can start thinking about production-line details. (Boy, you sure didn't think things would get rolling so fast!) You stop by Simak's office to see if you can get any particulars, but he is not there. You know you do not have enough to go on now, so you decide to resume caustic dip testing this afternoon to see if you can cut down the strip time on the Heavy Guard. Of course, you wish you could get started on testing the other wire types, but the samples still have not arrived.

When you return from the lunch meeting at ME, you get right down to testing the Heavy Guard. You prepare a NaOH bath for dipping at 670°F. This temperature is slightly above the melting point of sodium hydroxide, which is 604°F. You slowly dip 6-inch lengths of wire at varying temperatures and decide to define stripping as "adequate" if a 100% coating of solder can be applied following the strip.

In your first trials, you achieve an average strip time of 45 seconds when the bath is maintained at 670–700°F. A temperature of 760°F brings the time down to 30 seconds, 800°F to 15 seconds. When the bath temperature is kept between 850° and 920°F, strip time is 10 seconds. The caustic dip process leaves the Heavy Guard bright and shiny, not a shred of insulation left. You have been a bit concerned that the copper might be adversely affected by the caustic, so you leave one sample immersed in caustic for 30 minutes at 930°F. The wire is unaffected by the molten salt and accepts tinning readily.

You are relieved that the tests with the pure sodium hydroxide have come out so well, and you feel more confident about going to next Thursday's meeting with Pierson. You hastily set up a few tables illustrating your results and drop them off with Simak's secretary, who will type them up for the meeting. Tomorrow, you will prepare a summary report on your progress to date to go with the tables. It will have to be upbeat. You have to sell your idea to Pierson and assure him that your investigation will conclude successfully.

Just before you leave for the day, the alternator assemblies that Bill promised arrive. You do some preliminary inspection of them, separating the stators from the housings. You do not note anything too revealing, except that on the 70-amp alternator the triple-wire connection is almost inaccessible. You wonder what implications this has for production. You will have to ask Bill.

ASSIGNMENT 3
Construct the tables you will distribute as handouts at the meeting with Pierson. Your name, title, department, and today's date should appear on the handouts.

ASSIGNMENT 4
Prepare a short report of your progress to date with the caustic dip to be distributed prior to the interdepartmental meeting. The report will go to H. Simak, Section Supervisor, Research and Development. Copies will go to T. Pierson, Manager, and W. Starsky, Staff Engineer, Product Engineering. Study Appendix A and determine who else might get this report.

Day 6

At 3 P.M. today you have a meeting scheduled with Seymour Franklin from the Whipple Wire Company. It seems Franklin insisted on bringing the Whipple magnet wire samples to you personally. Pierson has sent him to talk to you. You do not understand why, especially since the one Whipple wire you might test is not used in Motown alternators any longer. You suspect that Franklin wants to show you the whole Whipple line, just in case you might want to specify a Whipple wire for some other application. At 3 P.M. on the dot, Franklin arrives at your desk, loaded down with sample cases. You are tempted to say, "Mr. Franklin, I presume," but think better of it. The salesman sticks out his hand.

"Seymour Franklin here."

You introduce yourself.

"Glad you were able to take the time to see me. I'm very interested in this project with the magnet wires. Down at Whipple, we're real enthusiastic that PE is thinking about switching from Haywire's tough-poly[5] to our Double XX." Seymour keeps chattering while opening his sample cases. "You know, of course, the Double XX is rated at 215 centigrade; that's 15 centigrade higher than the tough-poly. And we can give it to you for lots less than Haywire's high-thermal-rated Heavy Guard."

You smother your surprise at PE's plans to switch to Double XX and quietly ask Franklin for details.

"Well," he continues, "Pierson over here in PE tells me that with your average car owner's new love for electronic doodads, you guys've got to beef up your alternators, protect them against overheating and short circuits. You know as well as I do that that means a tougher insulated wire in your stator."

---

[5] Motown staff and outside vendors often refer to Tough Polycoat as "tough-poly."

"So, you think I ought to test your Double XX?" you say, figuring that Franklin must have found out from Pierson which wires you were testing—and that your list did not include the Double XX variety.

"Well, no, I don't think you need to test it, matter of fact," Franklin grins. "We've got a better answer. Haven't you heard the good news?"

You lift an eyebrow. "Well, not exactly."

"We've got your insulation problem solved."

"Your Double XX wire has a solder-meltable coating? But that's impossible."

"Hey, you know better than that. No, ah—let's see—it's a polyamide-imide," Franklin says, checking his data books.

You note to yourself that tough-poly has the same kind of insulation.

"No, I'm telling you that you don't need to worry about melting the insulation off," Franklin continues, "because it doesn't have to come off *at all*. Get the picture? Ever heard of what they call a terminal piercing lug, a tpl?"[6]

"Yea, I've heard of it." And, you think to yourself, you have heard nothing good about it.

"Well," Franklin prattles on, "we've come up with a tpl that you can use for making lead-wire connections in your stator assemblies."

"A tpl!" you exclaim. "You mean *three* tpl's. We've got three different kinds of connections to make with those lead wires—single-wire, double-wire, and triple-wire links to terminals. One lug can't handle them all."

"Our lug is for single-wire connections to terminals. Here, this is what it looks like." Franklin draws you a crude sketch (Figure 4).

"We've done vibration tests on the device," Franklin continues. "No problem. We're forwarding Pierson the results this week."

"Pierson?"

"Yeah, he's had us working on this for the last six months."

You examine the sketch of the device and try to act cool. "What's the extension sleeve for?"

"Oh, that's our special feature. The sleeve takes stress off the wire

---

[6] A terminal piercing lug is a metal device with a flat plate at one end and a housing at the other. The interior of the housing is lined with sharp teeth. The housing is clamped onto a wire, the teeth piercing through all layers of insulation to make contact with bare wire. The flat plate provides a metal surface for making a solder connection to a terminal. Tpl's are not very reliable. If applied with too much pressure, they can snap a wire; if applied with too little pressure, the lug teeth do not maintain contact.

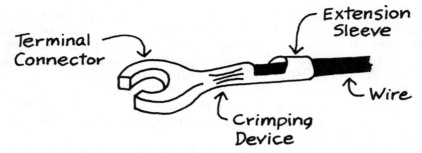

Figure 4.   Franklin's Sketch

so pressure isn't exerted at the joint where the teeth clamp it. The sleeve eliminates the risk of the wire snapping at its weakest point."

You continue to examine the tpl. You can see that the upper extension sleeve merely holds the copper wire, while the lower lug crimps and pierces the insulation, making contact with bare copper. Contact appears sufficient for a nonfailing electrical connection between lug and wire. You are still skeptical though about the reliability of a terminal piercing lug as opposed to a terminal lug that is soldered to a lead wire.

Franklin fidgets. "Of course we're going to have you guys run dynamometer tests on it and fleet test it."[7]

You nod.

"Look, I'm going to leave you a 20-foot coil of our 16-gauge Double XX; it comes in all the sizes that tough-poly does. Do whatever you want with the sample. I've got to stop by and see the people in PE. Just wanted you to know you can set your mind to more important things. We've got this sticky insulation problem under control."

You are speechless. You give Franklin a brief handshake as he breezes out. You wonder how much of what he has told you is the straight story. Even if only some of it is true, it seems that PE is string-

---

[7] A dynamometer test is conducted by setting up a car engine assembly on a test stand and running the engine. The test allows engineers to simulate automobile operating conditions and to test the efficiency and wear of individual engine components. If a newly developed component passes efficiency and wear standards in a dynamometer test, it is then fleet tested. In a pilot assembly line, the new component is introduced into the engine assembly of a fleet of cars (usually taxicabs or police cars). If the component passes efficiency and wear tests after one year of operation in a fleet, mass adoption of the component is recommended.

ing your division along. Your mind starts racing ahead. Pierson will come along any day now and say that he is having vibration tests done on the tpl. You can hear him already. You begin to get angry, when you suddenly realize that you better tell Simak right away about what PE is up to. You stop by his office, but again find that he is not there. His secretary is busy typing away, but you interrupt.

"Do you know exactly when Simak will be back this afternoon?"

"Oh, he's out of town, at the national SAE[8] convention in Minnesota."

The SAE convention, you think to yourself. You have been so busy you forgot all about it.

"When will he be back?" you ask.

"The convention ends Saturday, but he leaves again early Monday morning for a three-day trip to Toronto. Has a big presentation to deliver to the brass in the International Division. I'm sending the data via Federal Express." She flicks the page in the typewriter.

"He won't be back 'til Thursday?"

"'Fraid not," she answers.

"But he's got a meeting scheduled Thursday afternoon with PE," you mutter.

She checks Simak's calendar. "Well, he's got it marked, so he should be there," she replies.

"I'd like to give him a call," you say.

"Well, he told me he didn't want to be bothered with anything unless it had to do with the Toronto presentation," she says, resuming her typing.

You begin pacing the floor, mulling this whole thing over. You decide not to bother Simak, though he has to find out soon that Pierson has some outside people working on this project. You cannot understand why Pierson just gave the alternator problem to R & D a few weeks ago when he has had Whipple working on the solution for some time. Maybe he had reason to believe Whipple could come up with their three lugs within a couple of months. Maybe he just got tired of waiting. Maybe now the whole tpl solution looks less attractive; too much time was spent developing something that does not have a reputation for reliability. Abruptly you stop wondering; there is no use guessing why Pierson did not bring in R & D until so late in the game.

---

[8] Society of Automotive Engineers.

The best thing to do now is to prepare your presentation for Thursday's meeting and try to fill Simak in on the tpl just before he arrives.

ASSIGNMENT 5
Prepare a five-minute informal oral presentation for Thursday's meeting to accompany your written progress report on the caustic dip (Assignment 4) which will be distributed at the meeting.

ASSIGNMENT 6
Prepare an informal oral briefing on the tpl for Simak to be given before the meeting.

Day 7

The meeting with Pierson and the PE engineers assigned to the alternator failure case is set for this afternoon. All morning you try to get in touch with Simak, but you have no luck. Just before lunch you make one more stop by his office before picking up your mail and heading for the staff lounge. Simak still has not arrived.

The morning mail is most interesting. You get a package from R. Sabo, a Haywire sales rep, containing the magnet wires samples that Pierson ordered and technical bulletins describing the properties of the wires. At last you can begin testing the other wires! You note that the technical bulletins on Heavy Guard and Nylocoat (a nylon-coated wire rated at 155°C that was used in alternators prior to 1965) include stripping and tinning data. The Heavy Guard bulletin notes: "The polyimide insulation on Heavy Guard can be removed by a molten caustic or molten salt bath; or by burning, and then sanding or brushing; or by mechanical stripping tools." You are a bit red-faced upon finding out that the molten salt procedure is hardly a new notion. Making the procedure suitable for production, however, will require your creative ingenuity. The Nylocoat bulletin indicates that this wire can be "stripped and tinned in a five-second solder dip." Nothing is mentioned regarding insulation removal in the tough-poly (Tough Polycoat) bulletin.

The information in the Haywire technical bulletins has made you a little uneasy about discussing the parameters of the caustic dip procedure this afternoon. If Haywire knows that the Heavy Guard insulation can be removed in molten salt, why haven't they recommended this procedure for stripping insulation from tough-poly? Anything that removes a polyimide coating should strip the polyamide-imide coating that is used on the tough-poly. You regret that you could not begin testing the tough-poly wire before this. If only the samples had arrived earlier!

You decide to try to get Sabo, the Haywire rep, on the phone. Fortunately he is in. You tick off your questions, asking him first whether he has seen anyone use the caustic dip in an assembly-line setup. Sabo tells you that he has not. He says most corporations would be hesitant to implement a production process involving molten salts, because of worker safety problems, for one thing. He reminds you the Heavy Guard is not used for high-volume applications; mechanical stripping methods, though slow, are adequate for most buyers. As he is talking, you think to yourself that molten caustic is no more dangerous than molten solder; workers are exposed to that now. You interrupt Sabo, who has lapsed into a sales pitch for Heavy Guard.

"Have you guys run into trouble with the caustic dip? Is that why you don't recommend it for large applications?"

"No," Sabo says. "We know it will take the insulation off Heavy Guard clean as a whistle."

"And off the Tough Polycoat too?"

"What's it say in the technical bulletin?" Sabo asks.

"It doesn't say anything. That's what puzzles me. Your Heavy Guard bulletin recommends the use of molten caustic to remove insulation, the tough-poly bulletin says nothing. What do you guys recommend to take the coating on the tough-poly off?"

"I'm not sure," Sabo says evasively.

"Can you find out from your research people right away? I'd like to know this morning." You briefly explain the focus of your investigation to Sabo, and he agrees to call you back as soon as he can find out whatever data Haywire has on removal of polyamide-imide insulation.

You spend the next couple of hours preparing for the big powwow this afternoon. Intermittently you call Simak's secretary to see if he is back, but without success. It seems that he might not be back until after lunch. Just five minutes before the meeting you remember Sabo. He has not telephoned you, and there is no time to get him now.

At meeting time, Pierson, Starsky, and Linda Harbrooke, another PE engineer assigned just this week to monitor the progress of the alternator project, all arrive together in Simak's conference room. A bit later, Al Jakubek, plant manager for Pleasantville Parts, arrives.

You had not expected to see Jakubek here, but you are happy to see that Pierson invited him. It is likely that a final production solution to the wire-stripping problem would be tested at Pleasantville. Simak himself breezes in five minutes late.

Just before the meeting begins, Pierson appoints you to take the minutes of the meeting. You suppress your annoyance. Those present at project meetings take turns with the minutes. Pierson must have decided to start with you.

From the beginning, things appear quite congenial. After your presentation, all at the meeting generally agree that, based on your preliminary investigations, it seems feasible to strip the stator lead wires using molten caustic. Pierson does raise some objections, however. Though pleased that your preliminary tests worked well with the Heavy Guard, he notes that this wire is currently in limited use. He admits that the Heavy Guard wire has chances of being adopted, but presses you on how well the process will work on tough-poly. You tell him that you just received the tough-poly samples today, but that you know that any product that removes the polyimide coating on the Heavy Guard will certainly remove the polyamide-imide coating on the tough-poly. Pierson seems satisfied by your answer.

Bill Starsky and Linda Harbrooke, who have been assigned to detail specifications for a production-line setup if the caustic process is adopted, suggest that you begin trial tests on actual stator assemblies. They also believe there may be some unanticipated problems connected with dipping wires after they have been wound on the stators. Linda Harbrooke adds that you should send the stripped wire samples you just processed over to Fred Troester in PE, who handles product testing. He will check to see if any unusual conditions persist as a result of the strip process.

At this point in the meeting, everyone starts chatting. Simak's secretary drops in with an urgent note for him, and he looks anxious to leave. You are afraid that things are going to break up before you have a chance to question Pierson about the Whipple terminal-lug project. You decide to jump in now.

"Ah, before we break up here, I'd like to hear a little about some of the other solutions you fellows in PE have been investigating . . . that is, ah, to get rid of failing lead-wire connections in the stators."

Simak looks surprised and Pierson pauses, waiting for you to say more.

You take a deep breath and say, "I just heard about Whipple Wire's work on the terminal piercing lug."

Pierson mumbles something under his breath, then turns to address you. "Yes, yes," he begins, "they seem to be coming along with it. Fact is, I just got a report on vibration tests. These were for single-wire lug connections made on stators with wye windings. [See Appendix B.] They look pretty good. Ah, I've got Fred Troester in our lab verifying the results. When he does, I think you fellows over at R & D ought to take a look at them."

Pierson stops for a moment. Simak eyes you closely. You can tell that he is irked because you did not tell him about the tpl stuff before now. There just wasn't a chance to see him. You decide to risk things and push Pierson a bit.

"Do you have Whipple Wire working on tpl's for our double-wire and triple-wire-to-terminal connections?"

Pierson leans over to ask Starsky something. Whatever info Starsky gives him does not please him. "Oh, they've been working on the triple-wire connection; looks like they'll have a device perfected soon." Pierson throws a glance at Starsky, who shrugs his shoulders.

Simak has been listening to all this, up to now stoic as a sphynx. At this point he breaks in, speaking very deliberately. "We think the caustic process is a good prospect, but we don't want to be spinning our wheels on it if you fellows at PE have got something else in mind."

Pierson bristles a bit, and then launches into one of his sermons: "This problem has been with us a long time, but now the boys upstairs are pushing us to solve it. Warranty claims cost the company money, and we don't want lots of alternators failing in the first couple of years after the warranties expire either. I think the dip process looks good. Let's go ahead and try it out on the stator assemblies. As for the tpl, it's a possibility we still have to check out. When the Whipple reps first showed me what they were thinking of putting together, I was very skeptical. I reminded them that tpl's don't have a reputation for reliability and that the cost of tooling up to produce three custom-made tpl's may be prohibitive. They were still eager to go ahead and develop them. At the time, the lead-wire connection problem was not a top priority item here. I decided it wouldn't hurt to have someone working on it, for free at that. So I encouraged Whipple to continue research. Now things have gone into high gear. We've got to have an answer in the shortest possible time, but we've got to have a good answer; we simply can't afford to shut the door on any possibility."

Pierson makes motions to leave, as do the others. As the meeting breaks up, Simak corners you. He does not look pleased.

"You sure pulled a fast one today," he starts out. Then he looks at his watch, muttering, "I've got to hurry to catch a flight back to Toronto. They've really got troubles up there." Simak stares off into space for a minute, before saying impatiently, "Look, I need to see you the moment I get back into town. Make an appointment with my secretary before you leave today. We've got to have a long talk about what's going on here."

Simak strides out. You check times with the secretary and set up an appointment for the day when he is due to return. You are a bit anxious about his terse remarks at the end of the meeting. He certainly was not too happy to hear about the tpl for the first time when he was face-to-face with Pierson. Since you did not get to brief him orally before the meeting as you had planned, you decide to write him a memo explaining all you heard about the tpl from Franklin and Starsky so he understands why you thought it was a good idea to bring the issue out into the open at the interdepartmental meeting. He will have the memo before you meet with him when he returns from Toronto.

When you return to your desk, you dash Sabo a note requesting more information on insulation removal and drop it in the mail. Then you get to work putting together minutes of the meeting.

ASSIGNMENT 7
Write up minutes for the interdepartmental meeting. At Motown, meeting minutes are written in memo form. The heading of your memo should identify the date and subject of the meeting and those present. The body should cover the "meeting purpose," "points discussed," and "meeting conclusions."

ASSIGNMENT 8
Write a memo to H. Simak, Section Supervisor, telling what you have heard about the tpl from Seymour Franklin and Bill Starsky.

Day 8

This morning you get a call from Linda Harbrooke over in PE. She reports that laboratory phenolphthalein tests show considerable amounts of caustic on the tinned wire specimens you sent over to PE for testing. Troester from PE, who did the lab work, suggests that when you start writing up a production procedure, you should include a hot water rinse as part of the production setup. The rinse would add to the life of the stators.

You are a bit upset by this call. The amount of NaOH left on the wires had to be a trace at most. However, to be on the safe side, if PE wants a water rinse, they will get it.

Meanwhile, you resume experimentation to reduce immersion time in caustic before you develop the procedure to be tested on the 200 wound stator assemblies due to arrive from PE. You continue testing with the 17-gauge Heavy Guard. This time you add samples of all gauges of the tough-poly wire ($14\frac{1}{2}$, 15, and 16) and, for good measure, the sample of Whipple's 16-gauge Double XX you got from Franklin. If Pierson's unit is looking at the Double XX, as Franklin says, you might as well do some preliminary tests on it. You have to reduce the strip and tin operations to 5 seconds each and also determine the relationship between stripping efficiency and tinning efficiency.

You decide to dip 6-inch lengths of each wire in molten caustic for 5 seconds at a range of temperatures starting at 900°F and follow each dip with a fiberglass wipe so you can clearly see the surface of the processed wires. In a second test, you dip each wire sample in molten caustic for 5 seconds, then immediately dip each sample in hot solder at the same temperature for 5 seconds, and follow the solder dip with a fiberglass wipe to remove excess solder and solder dross. This second test is also conducted over a range of temperatures beginning at 900°F. You note that all gauges of the tough-poly wire behaved the same in your tests. You quickly summarize the results of both tests in a chart (Table 1).

You also noted while testing that on stripped and tinned samples, charring of insulation above the stripped portion occurred at less than $\frac{1}{32}$ inch, and the stripped surface was 100% tinned in every case where it was 100% stripped. You are particularly happy to see that all the tough-poly samples stripped with no trouble. You take another look at your table of results, redesign it, and then write up an entry for your engineer's logbook which will record today's work clearly. You then ask two of your colleagues in the lab to witness your entry.

When you have finished writing the logbook entry, you run a Xerox copy of it for Simak and add a brief note announcing that you are ready to begin testing on wound stators.

ASSIGNMENT 9

Write up your record of the progress you made on Day 8 as it would appear in your engineer's logbook. At Motown, you *must record* in your logbook all ideas, events, informal meetings, or tests that relate

Table 1.   Caustic Dip Test Summary

WIRE TYPE	CAUSTIC TEMP. (DEGREES F)	5-SEC CAUSTIC DIP, WIPE HOT (PERCENT STRIPPED)	5-SEC CAUSTIC DIP, 5-SEC SOLDER DIP, WIPE HOT (PERCENT TINNED)
TOUGH-POLY (ALL GAUGES)	900	100	100
DOUBLE XX	"	100	100
HEAVY GUARD	"	5	5
TOUGH-POLY (ALL GAUGES)	920	100	100
DOUBLE XX	"	100	100
HEAVY GUARD	"	10	10
TOUGH-POLY (ALL GAUGES)	1000	100	100
DOUBLE XX	"	100	100
HEAVY GUARD	"	30	30
TOUGH-POLY (ALL GAUGES)	1050	100	100
DOUBLE XX	"	100	100
HEAVY GUARD	"	80	80
TOUGH-POLY (ALL GAUGES)	1080	100	100
DOUBLE XX	"	100	100
HEAVY GUARD	"	100	100

to a problem you are working on. Entries are handwritten, and the date and your signature appear on every logbook page. No pages are left blank. For patent purposes, the ideas you record which are noteworthy often are witnessed by two other persons whose signatures appear below yours in the logbook. The logbook serves as your personal history of the investigation. While it may follow any format you choose, it must be understandable and thorough. All test data which you include in formal or informal reports must come from your logbook. For this exercise, use the logbook format illustrated in Appendix D. Get two of your classmates to "witness" the entry.

Day 9

Today you meet with Starsky and Harbrooke to discuss how you will arrange equipment for the trial run of the caustic dip on wound stators. You give them copies of your last logbook entry.

They both have helpful suggestions for setting up the trial runs. Bill tells you how stators are currently assembled. When the stators first reach the assembly station where the leads are soldered, the leads are all bundled together. As a step preparatory to tinning, all leads have to be combed out to lie in a plane. Bill notes that since you will be doing trials on stators with wye-type windings, three of the leads will have to be cut long ($4\frac{1}{8} \pm \frac{1}{8}$ inches) and three short ($2\frac{3}{4} \pm \frac{1}{8}$ inches). After discussing your test results with you, Linda suggests that the leads be dipped into molten NaOH flake (maintained at 1100°F) to a minimum of $1\frac{1}{2}$ inches. She thinks that you should use a separate solder pot for the 50–50 lead-tin solder (maintained at 1000°F), instead of heating the solder in a small cup placed in the NaOH bath. The separate solder pot would allow for easier cleaning and maintenance of the receptacles containing solder and salt. After dipping the stator in NaOH, you could position the stator over the solder pot, and dip leads in the solder to a minimum of 1 inch.

Having specified the particulars of the operation, the three of you start examining how the caustic dip process might operate on a production line. Bill and Linda immediately start firing questions that you are not prepared to answer.

"What are you going to use to lower the stators into the dip?" Linda asks.

"Well, I thought they could be lowered by hand," you answer. "I thought that in the current wire-brush tinning operation the stators were dipped by hand into the solder."

"Well, that's true," Linda replies. "The man on the line simply puts the stator on the lip of the solder pot. The solder is maintained at a consistent level to insure that leads are tinned at the right depth."

You look puzzled.

"Here, it looks like this." Linda draw a rough sketch (Figure 5).

"You see," she continues, "that stator just sits on the lip and the leads hang down into the pot."

"Can't we just use a separate pot for the caustic and handle the dipping the same way?" you ask.

"Well, I don't know," Linda says. "I think you're taking a risk doing that. What if the caustic splashes as the man places the stator on the edge? He's got his hands right over the pot."

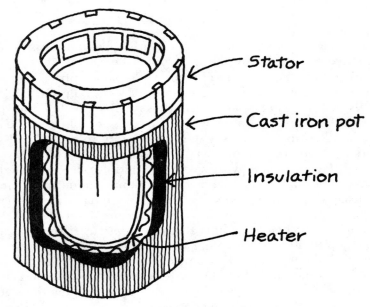

Stator

Cast iron pot

Insulation

Heater

Figure 5.   Solder Pot and Stator

"Come now," you reply, "the solder could splash, too. And yet we're now handling it this way with the solder."

"Well," Linda answers, "when you start talking about using caustics, our plant operations division gets very ticklish about worker safety . . . OSHA[9] and all that. We've got to avoid all possibility of worker contact with any caustic."

"I've got it!" you interrupt. "How about making a steel holder with a long arm? The guy on the line can put the stator in the device and then he can use it to dip the leads in the caustic, transfer the stator to the solder bath, and dip the leads in the solder."

After a moment, Bill says, "Sounds okay to me."

You draw a sketch (Figure 6).

"See, the man on the line can lower the stator onto the pot using the extension arm on this device," you explain, pointing to your drawing. "Here's how it will work." You draw another sketch as you explain the procedure (Figure 7).

---

[9] OSHA stands for Occupational Safety and Health Administration.

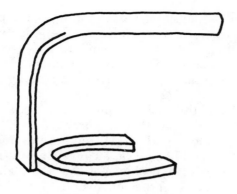

Figure 6.   Steel Holder

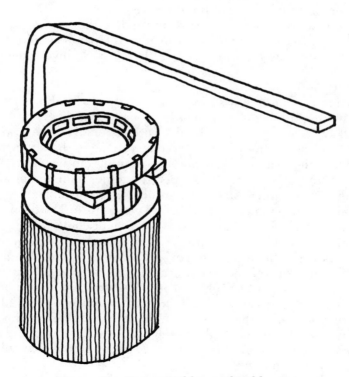

Figure 7.   Stator, Holder, and Solder Pot

"You see the 'holder' just rests on the lip of the pot. The worker can just leave it there for 5 seconds, and the ledge will support the stator. The operation won't be tiring, and it will leave the worker free to ready another stator for the dipping operation."

Linda and Bill examine your drawing. Suddenly Linda brightens up.

"You know, I like this 'holder' concept," she says, "but why don't you incorporate it with a small conveyor?"

"I get it," you add eagerly. "Our guy on the line could put the stator on the holder and hang it on a conveyor belt running over the caustic pot . . . and over the solder pot, too! Let's see . . . a series of microswitches could control the conveyor to lower the stator onto the pots and then raise it. The worker would never have to come near the caustic!"

"Sounds possible," says Linda. "You probably should call in some people from Pleasantville to work the conveyor angle out . . ."

"We might even save a person on the line," you interrupt, "if the conveyor could take care of the dipping . . ."

"Well, we still need a worker to remove the excess solder from the leads," Bill reminds you, peering over the pages copied from your logbook. "And this guy can't use the fiberglass cloth you suggest here in your log."

"Why not?"

"Same reason . . . possible worker contact with the caustic. How about wiping the leads with asbestos-faced tongs?"

"Okay," you say. "That should work to remove excess solder."

After some discussion, the three of you agree that after the leads are wiped, they should be dipped in running tap water at 140°F for 5 seconds to wash off excess caustic. Altogether then, the process will include a 5-second caustic dip, a 5-second solder dip, a 3-second asbestos-faced tong wipe, and a 5-second water rinse. The dipping could be handled by a worker or perhaps by a small conveyor.

You ask Starsky and Harbrooke to double-check your notes while you drop over to the lounge to get you all some coffee. When you get back, the three of you get to jawing about the company. You have been around long enough to know that it is best to keep your mouth shut about some things; Bill is a little green though. Before long he starts quizzing you about what was really going on at last Thursday's meeting. He notes that things looked pretty tense at the end of the session.

"Why were you jumping all over Pierson about that tpl project Whipple's working on?" Bill asks.

You shrug your shoulders and say nothing. You remember that

Bill and Pierson were discussing something on the side when the tpl issue was raised at the meeting.

"You guys are pretty touchy over nothing," Bill starts in. "There are lots of bugs to be worked out of that tpl."

You try to look only mildly interested. "Oh, yeah?"

"Yeah, that single-wire model looks okay, but we're having a heck of a time with the double-wire and triple-wire models they sent us."

"They've sent you the double- and triple-wire tpl's?" you ask, trying to suppress your surprise.

"Just a few. We tried 'em out in production. The double-wire jobs didn't make sufficient contact with the wire. We had to mechanically strip the wires first, then clamp the tpl's on. They seemed to stay put once we got them on though."

"What about the triple-wire tpl?"

"Couldn't get that to last through the assembly procedure."

"Why?" you ask.

"Well, that triple-wire connection has to be tucked back into the alternator housing after the wires are attached to the lug. The only way to tuck it in is to hammer it so it fits snug. In our production tests, every time our man gave one of those tpl's a slug, it split apart. The old soldered lugs at least held up through that," he adds disdainfully.

Now you are beginning to see why Motown has had so much trouble with the soldered connections on the wye-wound stators.

Harbrooke starts looking a little uneasy and gives Starsky a nudge. "It's getting late, Bill. I think I'll head on back to PE. Got to tie up a few things before I go."

Starsky gets the hint and grabs his briefcase. "Ah, I think we got a lot done this afternoon."

You nod. "We sure did. Thanks for your help, Bill." You give him your hand. "Thanks, Linda." Harbrooke smiles and the two of them leave.

After recording the proceedings of this conference in your logbook, you decide that there is not much more you can do with anything today. Bill surely shed new light on the tpl affair, but then you do not know if he has the whole story. You are anxious to get home and reflect a bit.

ASSIGNMENT 10

Write up the decisions made in your conference with Starsky and Harbrooke as a logbook entry. (See Assignment 9 for logbook instructions.)

Day 10

Today you are at work bright and early trying to pull together your thoughts on the trial run as you discussed it with Starsky and Harbrooke. The meeting you set up with Simak before he left for Toronto is for 9 o'clock this morning. At 8:45 A.M. you are busily gathering notes and getting ready to head down to Simak's office when you get a call from his secretary. You just know what she is going to say, and she does: Simak has canceled your appointment; he is stuck in Toronto again. Oh well, you will just have more time to work out the trial caustic dip runs which you planned to start today.

You spend the day doing runs with about 30 stators, all wound with 15-gauge tough-poly wires currently used in many wye-wound alternators. While you are doing the tests, you note a few peculiarities. These are on your mind at the end of the day as you summarize your work in your logbook, trying to think things through.

You managed to strip and tin all stator lead wires at 100% efficiency. However, you still are not convinced that the water rinse is needed, so you processed half of the stators with the 5-second rinse and half of the stators without it. You estimate that stripping and tinning and rinse can be accomplished in about 20 to 25 seconds, allowing for transfer time between baths. If the caustic dip process were adopted, the wire-brushing machine at the Pleasantville plant could be eliminated, and a caustic pot could be put in its place. That should be less costly. The caustic pot is easier to maintain than a machine with a motor and parts, like brushes, that need to be periodically replaced. Of course, if you decided to go with a conveyor, you would be replacing a machine with a machine. The conveyor-dip system might cost a little more than the wire-brush machine, but it would do a better and faster job of stripping the wires.

You are most concerned about what happened when you first dipped stator leads in the caustic. Unlike the former situation, you found yourself lowering the leads somewhat quickly into the dip, probably because of the weight of the stator. When these tough-poly leads were plunged quickly into the NaOH bath, there was extensive flaring and fuming. When this happened, you immediately recalled Haywire's bulletin on the tough-poly and recollected that you still had no word from the Haywire rep about tests they may have conducted to remove the polyester insulation. Perhaps Haywire researchers were aware of the flaring problem, and that is why they did not recommend a caustic for removing polyester insulation. However, in your tests, flaring did not occur when wires were dipped slowly as they were in your previous tests. Reflecting on this, you reason that slow dipping allows the gases formed when heat destroys the insulation to escape freely and thus prevents spattering of the caustic. You decide that if leads were dipped slowly, that should take care of the problem. You then review the process once more and finally make a few more notes for your logbook (Figure 8).

You send the 30 stators to Troester over in PE. He will test whether the rinse process is really needed to get rid of excess NaOH. Before heading home, you set up another appointment with Simak for the day he is due to return.

Day 11

Today you decide to work on some of the other pending projects you have been assigned. There is no sense in fussing any more with the caustic dip project before Simak's return. Just as you start reviewing the progress reports on project A3456, "Sintered-vinyl battery separators," you get a call from Seymour Franklin, the Whipple Wire

1. CAUSTIC <u>MUST</u> BE MAINTAINED AT 1100°F, BUT SOLDER OK AT 670°F. WIRES TINNED AT THIS TEMP IN EARLY TRIALS.

2. WATER TEMP COULD BE RAISED FROM 140°F TO 180-200°F FOR MORE RAPID CAUSTIC DISSOLVING AND DRYING OF WET LEADS.

3. NEED FACILITIES FOR DUMPING SPENT CAUSTIC AND RESIDUE.

4. CHEMICAL COATING ON CAUSTIC BATH MIGHT REDUCE FLARING.

Figure 8. Your Logbook Notes

salesman. Apparently Starsky let loose what he told you about Whipple's tpl. Franklin is coming on like "supersalesman" on the phone. He says that Starsky has only half of the story on the tpl. You are puzzled and decide to quiz him.

"Are you trying to tell me Whipple's refined the double- and triple-wire units?"

"We sure have," Franklin says enthusiastically. "We've got a new triple-wire tpl that clamps three wires separately instead of bunching them together. You can pound the heck out of that item and it won't come apart."

"Hmm," you murmur skeptically.

"Look. I've sent you a sketch of the thing already; you should get it today."

You do not say anything.

"The point is," Franklin continues, "we have this problem solved now. In fact, I'm sure our research division has already forwarded a report to Pierson on our latest unit."

"Oh, when do you think the report was sent?" you ask.

"Well, I know one is planned, anyway," Franklin says, hedging a bit. "Look, this new device is really A-okay."

"What about the double-wire tpl's?"

"Just a matter of time," Franklin says, and then he changes the subject.

You figure that things are not quite as marvelous as he claims. You thank him for calling and tell him you have to go.

Sure enough, just when you get off the phone and check the morning mail, there is Franklin's sketch (Figure 9). Franklin's drawing is

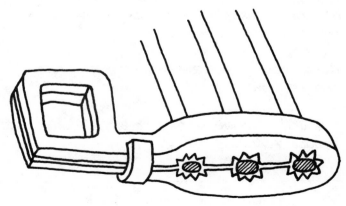

Figure 9.   Franklin's Sketch

crude, but it looks as if Whipple's new tpl functions much like a tongue-and-groove joint. The three wires are clamped into three separate grooves surrounded by a piercing edge. A tab wraps the terminal connector, holding the clamped joint and securing the connection between the bare wire and the lug connection.

You wonder if this device really holds up as Franklin says, but you decide that there is no point in fretting about it. You just have to see how Pierson reacts to the Whipple report—if he got it, that is. You spend the rest of the day continuing with your work on the battery project.

Day 12

Today at 10 A.M. you are finally supposed to meet with Simak. You sent him a copy of the logbook entry which details your testing of the caustic dip process on the leads of the 30 stators you sent to Troester in PE. Meanwhile, Troester has confirmed that caustic *does* remain on stator lead wires that are not rinsed. In fact, Troester found some caustic on the bodies of several of the processed stators. In trying to account for this, you figure that the flaring that occurred when you dipped the leads too quickly probably caused molten salt to splash on the stator bodies. Slow dipping should take care of that problem.

At 9:30 A.M. you are getting together some notes at your workstation when Simak shows up with the copy of your log entry in hand.

"About time we got together on this."

"I've been trying to get an appointment with you. You've been out of town a lot."

"Objection noted. Nevertheless, I need more communication. I was caught off guard at that meeting with Pierson. How come you didn't tell me they were testing a tpl?"

"I tried to when I first heard it, but you were in Minnesota, and then Toronto, and I didn't get to see you again 'til you know when. I just had to get the goods from Pierson while I had the chance. Sorry, I couldn't brief you ahead of time. I've heard some more news since then . . ."

"Well, I've got a few things to say to you, too," Simak interrupts. "I've read this log entry. What's this about a flaring problem? How come it didn't crop up before?"

"Well, when I tested the wires in the lab, I always dipped them slowly. Hadn't anticipated what would happen if they were dipped quickly. I didn't discover the flaring until I actually worked with the stators."

"Pierson's not going to like this flaring thing," Simak continues. "I got a call from him this morning. He's getting more pressure from above to get a production-ready solution fast. He wants a progress report on the feasibility of our caustic process. I'll bet he's thinking about going with Whipple's tpl."

"Well," you chime in, "things might not be so bad. It's true the tpl may have some advantages; it does eliminate a soldering operation from the stator assembly process. But Whipple is a long way from proving the tpl will work. Pierson wants a fast solution. I think we can solve the flaring problem in the caustic dip process and set up a pilot line. A slow dip or perhaps a chemical coating on the top of the caustic bath should take care of the problem."

"Pilot line? Do you think you have enough to go on here?" Simak asks.

"Well, we've got a process that removes the insulation and allows tinning within about 20 seconds. It won't take up much space on the line, just a place for another solder pot, and it won't take much new equipment. In fact, it eliminates the need for a wire-brush machine. All we need is a device to hold the stators when they're dipped, a pot to melt the caustic, a sink with running hot water, and asbestos-faced tongs."

"Yes, but the tpl probably could be applied in under 20 seconds. Clamping the fixture to the wire is a one-step operation. That's got to be simpler than removing insulation from the wire, tinning the leads, and then soldering them to lugs as we're doing now."

"Look," you say, "if Motown goes for the tpl, we've got to purchase three new products—a single-wire, a double-wire, and a triple-wire lug—and we have to add that cost to our expenses. Sure we're using lugs now, but we get them for about ten per penny. The tpl is a fancy device. It has to require more precision tooling—there are those teeth in the crimping device, and don't forget the extension sleeve on the single-wire model. The price we pay per piece has got to run at least a penny. Plus, we'll probably need new equipment to do the crimping operation. Who knows how they're doing it over at Whipple right now. The device they've got is so new they're probably applying it manually." You stop for a second or two to catch your breath.

"Besides," you raise your voice a bit, "it's likely the tpl won't work for the double- and triple-wire connections."

"So you've got the inside story?" Simak asks skeptically.

"Well, sort of," you smile. You tell Simak about Whipple's fiasco with their first attempt to make a triple-wire tpl and tell him they haven't even begun to work on a double-wire model that will work. You then show him Franklin's sketch of Whipple's new triple-wire model.

"Now, I don't know if they've sent Pierson a report on this," you say tapping the sketch.

"I'm sure they haven't," Simak says. "He would have told me about that if he'd gotten it."

"Well," you say, "even if Whipple sends a report along and the device looks good, it could cause production problems."

"How so?"

"Well, this triple-wire thing works differently from the single-wire model. The single-wire device is crimped on. This triple-wire model can't be crimped. The parts have to fit like a glove; a crimping action for application won't do. This could even require another machine."

"Hmmm . . . ." Simak seems to be listening to you seriously now.

"Now, if you consider what we'd have to put out for the caustic dip, things look better. About two dollars worth of sodium hydroxide will strip thousands of lead wires. It'll probably cost us 30 cents an hour to heat the bath."

You smile and are pretty pleased with yourself.

"What you say sounds good," Simak muses. "But we don't have all the bugs out of this caustic dip thing yet. What about the caustic flaring and what about possibly spattering the stator body?"

"I did not *see* the caustic spray the assembly in my tests," you say. "However, Troester over in PE told me today that caustic was detected on the bodies of stators that I processed in my trial runs. I think the caustic sprayed and the flaring occurred because I dipped the wires too quickly. The flaring and fuming isn't going to happen if the dipping process is controlled. Again, we need to set up a pilot line here in R & D to show that we can do it. I think we can work out the optimum dipping time with experimentation over the next couple of weeks."

"What kind of a line? One with a worker processing the stators or one with a conveyor system handling the dipping? You talk about both in your log."

"Well," you say, "the conveyor's just an open issue. Once we control the flaring, we can decide whether we want to introduce a conveyor. And there are other open issues to be resolved with a pilot line."

"What else?" Simak asks.

You step back to think a minute before you answer.

"Processing hundreds of stators may leave a scum on the surface of the caustic or make it otherwise ineffective over time," you say. "Also over time the sodium hydroxide could convert to sodium carbonate and leave residue on the wire. And then, too, we don't know whether we can add sodium hydroxide flake to the bath when it's low and get good results. Only a pilot line will resolve these questions."

Simak takes a seat at your desk, grabs a pad, and scribbles a few notes. "I guess you *are* ready to write up a progress report on this project for Pierson. I'm going to call Al Jakubek at Pleasantville and tell him that we'll process some of his stators in return for his help in setting up a caustic dip pilot here. I think he'll go for the deal. It should save him some operation costs."

Simak gets up and starts pacing. You are about to tell him that you also thought it was a good idea to get Jakubek involved when he adds another remark.

"I think that when you discuss the advantages of this dip process in your report, you should say something about how it compares to a mechanical solution, like the tpl. I'm convinced your caustic dip will take the insulation off clean and fast. What else can you say to recommend it?"

"Well," you counter, "we're ready to move to the pilot stage with this project. Even if tpl testing continues favorably, that project is far from the pilot-line stage. Because the tpl introduces a new device into our product, it has to undergo dynamometer testing and fleet testing. You have to figure a couple of months for the dynamometer tests and at least a year for the fleet tests. Our caustic dip doesn't change the components of the alternator—no dynamometer tests, no fleet tests. Simple."

Simak is still not convinced. He starts pacing up and down the office again.

"I agree that our solution is simple," Simak concludes, "but there may be another angle to this tpl thing. The point at which the tpl connects with the post on the rectifier is stable; the flat-plate end of the tpl fits snugly over the post. A bare wire is flexible; its shape can change. It's possible that sometime in the future Motown may want to use lugs for all their wire-to-post connections from the stator assembly to the rectifier. We may even put lugs on the single-wire connection in the 40- to 57-amp alternators. We've got lugs on the 70-amp alternators now—not piercing lugs, but lugs just the same."

"Why switch to lugs?" you wonder.

"Because they may prove more stable than the bare wire connections."

"Look, the main reason those bare wire connections don't hold is because the wire is not insulation free. The caustic dip insures a good connection for all soldered joints involving high-thermal-rated magnet wires, whether we're soldering the wire to a lug or directly to the post."

You flash Simak a smile. Once again he is pacing. You hope that he is thinking about this proposal the same way you are, and you cross your fingers. Finally he stops and puts his hand on your shoulder.

"Okay, I think we've got a good case. Write up that report showing your progress on the caustic dip investigation to date. Recommend the project be continued and move toward development of a pilot line here in R & D. Make sure you discuss the advantages of this dip process as well as the open issues. You'll also need to explain what further action we've got to take to get that pilot operating."

"Fine," you say with relief. "I can get started on it this afternoon."

"You'll have to give a brief assessment of the tpl," Simak adds, "and of course you'll have to show the caustic dip will meet PE's criteria for technical feasibility, manufacturing ease, and quick implementation."

"We can do that," you say, assuring Simak.

Simak then leaves, and you begin gathering all your data on the dip process. Later in the day, Simak lets you know that he reached Jakubek. The Pleasantville plant manager is willing to support your recommendation for the pilot line and help you with specs for a conveyor. You think Jakubek's support is just the edge you need to sell the caustic dip to Pierson.

You are very pleased with the day's events and ready to start planning that progress report. This may get you across that first bridge toward seeing an idea through to production.

ASSIGNMENT 11

Write a progress report to T. Pierson, Manager, Product Engineering, from H. Simak, Section Supervisor, Research and Development. You will be listed after the heading "Prepared by." Study Appendix A and determine who should be on the report distribution list and how to set up your report heading.

ASSIGNMENT 12
Assume that you have completed a draft of the report for Assignment 11. You decide to ask a fellow engineer in your unit to review it and make suggestions for revision. Ask one of your classmates to assume this role and critique your report.

ASSIGNMENT 13
Assume that trouble in Toronto has cropped up for Simak again. This time he cannot take care of it by himself. You are to start working on the Toronto problem with him and will leave in three days. Your current projects will be reassigned to others. Simak wants you to get Lou Davis, a junior engineer, to work on the flaring problem while you are gone. Apparently you have no say in the matter. You have no time to speak to Davis before you leave, so you will have to give her a written description of the flaring problem and suggest directions she might take to eliminate it. Fortunately, Davis is somewhat familiar with your investigation and has witnessed some of your logbook entries. Write Davis a memo (a copy goes to Simak) which explains the particular tasks you want her to complete while you are gone. Address the memo to Louise Davis, Staff Engineer.

ASSIGNMENT 14
Assume that Pierson has responded positively to your report. Simak now asks you to prepare a ten-minute oral presentation for Al Jakubek at the Pleasantville Parts Plant that describes the particulars of the caustic dip process so Jakubek can provide specs for a conveyor. You should produce visual aids (charts) as needed to accompany your presentation.

APPENDIX A

Organizational Chart

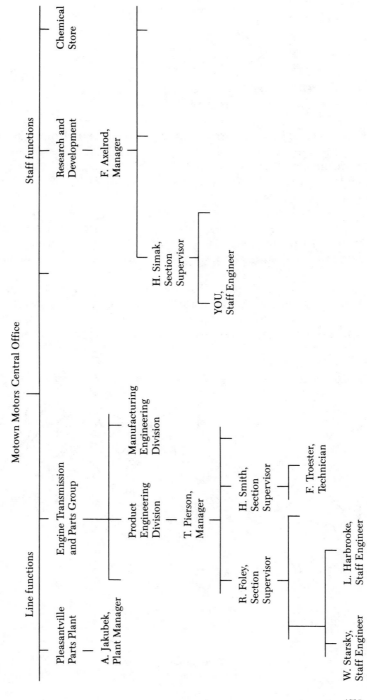

APPENDIX B

Background Information: The Motown Alternator[10]

The Motown alternator makes use of electromagnetic induction to produce a current which regenerates a car battery while the engine is running. The alternator has three main parts: a rotor assembly, a stator assembly, and a rectifier assembly (Figure 1). These parts are enclosed in front and rear metal shields or housings.

When the alternator is engaged, the rotor assembly develops a magnetic force which is translated into an alternating current in the wires of the stator assembly. The rectifier transforms this alternating current into a direct current, which is necessary to recharge the battery.

The rotor assembly (Figure 2) rotates within the inside walls of the stator assembly. The rotor assembly consists of a metal shaft, a coil assembly, and two rotor halves. The coil assembly consists of a nylon spool coiled with magnet wire. This assembly is encased by two rotor

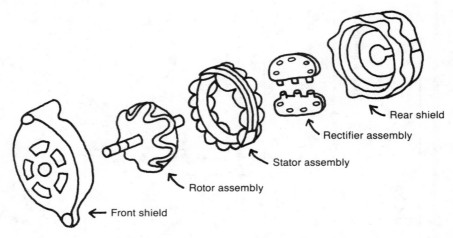

Figure 1.   Main Parts of Alternator

---

[10] This appendix provides a generic description of an alternator, explaining only its basic functions. It does not show all the components of an actual device.

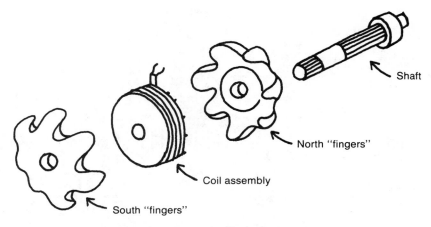

Figure 2.   Rotor Assembly

halves called north and south "fingers." The fingers protruding from each rotor half slip between one another but do not touch.

The stator assembly (Figures 3 and 4) remains stationary and surrounds the rotor assembly but does not touch it. The stator assembly consists of a metal cylinder with several grooves. Three lengths of magnet wire are wrapped in and out of the grooves. In Motown alternators, the lead wires of these three magnet wire lengths are connected to a rectifier assembly in one of two ways. Delta-wound stators are used in Motown's 65- and 117-amp alternators, whereas wye-wound stators are used in Motown's 40-, 57-, and 70-amp alternators. In the delta connection, lead wires are paired and each pair of wires is connected to a diode in the rectifier assembly (Figure 3). In the wye connection, one lead from each of the magnet wire lengths is soldered to one of the posts on the rectifier assembly. The remaining leads of each of the three magnet wires are connected together to form a neutral junction (Figure 4).[11]

The rectifier assembly consists of diodes encased in heat sinks and a circuit board to connect the diodes to the stator leads. The diodes

---

[11] Lead-wire connections on most models are made with terminal lugs. One end of the lug is a cylinder which is soldered to one or more lead wires. The other end of the lug is an O-shaped or C-shaped plate which slips over a post on the rectifier and is soldered in place.

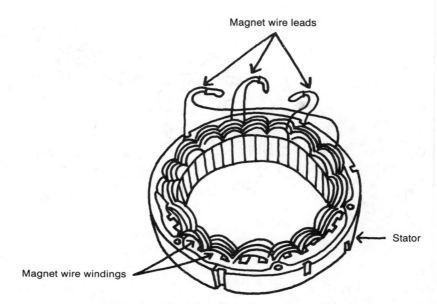

Figure 3.   Delta-Wound Stator Assembly

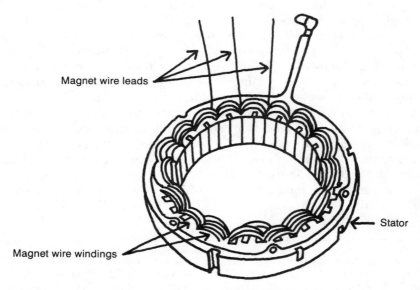

Figure 4.   Wye-Wound Stator Assembly

convert alternating current to direct current. This process generates heat, and the heat sinks serve to carry away the heat from the diodes as quickly as possible to prevent damage.

When the alternator is in operation, a current from the battery is sent through the rotor assembly as it is rotating within the stator. The current in the rotor core coil increases the magnetic forces in the north and south fingers surrounding the coil. The wires wound around the stator assembly are alternately exposed to a building up and falling off of magnetic force caused by the gaps between the north and south fingers surrounding the rotor core. This exposure results in the production of an alternating current in the stator windings.[12] The alternating current flows from the stator windings to the rectifier assembly, where it is transformed into direct current which can be used to re-generate the battery.

---

[12] As current builds up in the stator wires, the wires heat up, pulsate, and rub against one another. Alternators must contain high-thermal-rated wires—wires with a tough insulation that will not melt when the wires heat up or abrade when they pulsate. If insulation should fail, the alternator would short out.

APPENDIX C

Wire-Brush Tinning Operation
(Notes from meeting with Starsky)

```
1 solder pot
1 wire-brushing machine

Process (simultaneous operations are bracketed)
     1) Stator #1 is placed, leads down, in solder pot
        (10 seconds)
   ⌈ 2) Stator #1 is removed from solder pot and placed
   |    in machine which directs leads through a set of
   |    rotating wire brushes (10 seconds)
   ⌊ 3) Stator #2 is placed, leads down, in solder pot
        and leads dipped (10 seconds)
   ⌈ 4) Stator #1 is removed from brushing machine
   | 5) Stator #2 is placed in wire-brushing machine (10
   |    seconds)
   ⌊ 6) Stator #1 is placed in solder pot (10 seconds)
   ⌈ 7) Stator #2 is removed from brushing machine
   | 8) Stator #1 is placed back in brushing machine to
   |    remove insulation and excess solder dross (10
   |    seconds)
   ⌊ 9) Stator #2 is placed in solder dip (10 seconds)
    10) Stator #1 moves to next assembly operation;
        stator #2 is placed in wire-brushing machine for
        final brush (10 seconds)

-First solder dip melts and chars insulation; second
dip tins. First brush removes insulation; second brush
removes insulation and excess solder dross.

-Process time per stator varies 40-50 seconds depending
on handling time.
```

APPENDIX D

Logbook Format

DATE

Reported by: Date:

I have read and understand
the entries on this page.

Witness: Date:

Instructor's Guide to the Cases

Here are some highlights about the cases to help you use this book. For a detailed description of all the cases and assignments see the *Instructor's Manual*.

Case 1. Customer Complaint at Beta Corporation

Student role: Sales trainee in marketing at regional headquarters of large manufacturer of office equipment.

Assignments: Standard forms; summary; memos.

Features:
- Accommodating standard formats to meet contextual requirements.
- Summarizing and selecting relevant details.
- Writing to get attention and immediate action.

Case 2. Poor Service at Big-1 Car Rental

Student role: Assistant director of human resources in automobile assembly plant.

Assignment: Letter to upper management for company distribution.

Features:
- Writing for plant manager's signature to major corporate account.
- Stating negative message for quick action while preserving long-term business relationship.
- Determining necessary detail for wide array of audiences.

Case 3. The Agricultural Institute Mystery

Student role: Laboratory technician in agricultural testing laboratory of government institute.

Assignment: Memo to laboratory director.

Features:
- Shifting from writer-based narrative to reader-centered report.
- Documenting sufficiently for reader action but as briefly as possible.
- Deciding on a perspective and presenting a professional image in a difficult situation.

Case 4. Muddy Waters at Mariners Museum

Student role: Administrative assistant to curator of museum.

Assignment: Letter to project architect.

Features:
- Documenting action; clarifying agreements between internal and external parties.
- Presenting information that contradicts reader expectations.

Case 5. Enzyme Testing for Morton-Hayes Drug Corporation

Student role: Research technician in biological laboratory of drug manufacturer.

Assignment: Laboratory report in memo format to management.

Features:
- Presenting credible professional image under unfavorable circumstances.
- Conveying negative results for which no cause is apparent.
- Interpreting lab test data for management.

Case 6. Treadwell Developers, Inc., Gets Caught in the Middle

Student role: Assistant project manager for development firm.

Assignments: Telephone call plan; letter to outside architect.

Features:
- Describing procedures and standards for quality control.
- Documenting oral agreement.

- Facilitating working relationships among company, city, and consulting firm personnel.

Case 7. The Telemarketing Campaign

Student role: Cooperative trainee in marketing at large manufacturer of business machines.

Assignments: Team reports; construction of form; outline for interview script.

Features:
- Writing in collaboration with peers; individual writing to represent group view.
- Accepting responsibility to initiate upward communication; deciding whether to make recommendations.
- Presenting data effectively.

Case 8. Information and Communications Systems Planning at Pure-Pac

Student role: Communications systems planner for expansion project at packing company.

Assignments: Several memos to middle and upper management.

Features:
- Assuming authority of upper management; communicating on one's own initiative.
- Resolving delicate situation with implications for writer's future working relationships.
- Representing management position that may conflict with personal view; persuading management of alternative plan.
- Adjusting style for brief but critical communication.

Case 9. The Stockroom Case

Student role: Administrative assistant in university chemistry department.

Assignments: Departmental memo suitable for public posting; revision of job description composed by committee.

Features:

- Preparing introduction to document designed for different audience.
- Summarizing relevant information from long document and changing perspective for new audience.
- Editing and formatting job description.

Case 10. Trouble for County Extension Agents

Student role: Extension agent in "family living" at County Extension Service.

Assignments: Progress report; standard form; guidelines and procedures; cover memos; newsletter article.

Features:

- Selecting, grouping, and transforming fragmented information.
- Designing effective progress reports to highlight accomplishments and meet documentation requirements.
- Preparing guidelines based on official policy and writer's experience.

Case 11. Quality Control at Standard Steel, Inc.

Student role: Co-op trainee in metallurgical engineering at steel mill.

Assignments: Quality control report on manufacturing process; technical instructions; persuasive letter describing writer's technical experience.

Features:

- Gaining control of technical information and determining what audience needs to know.
- Interpreting technical data for management.
- Preparing complex instructions for novices; providing adequate detail for reference.

Case 12. Representing Accounts for Adler Advertising

Student role: Account representative for small advertising agency.

Assignments: Information organizing exercise; letter explaining designs to client.

Features:
- Describing and interpreting graphics.
- Selecting and developing appropriate information to initiate decision-making process.
- Introducing professional self to establish working relationship.

Case 13. Design of the Phototherapy Room

Student role: Nurse working as health facilities consultant for architectural firm.

Assignment: Memo to supervisor for use in preparing long report to health department official.

Features:
- Combining rhetorical patterns in one document; narrating procedures and making recommendations.
- Formatting material so reader can easily find answers to questions.
- Assuming authority of supervisor; persuading health department official that design requirements have been met and changes to plan are warranted.

Case 14. The Vacuum Freeze Dryer Problem

Student role: Junior scientist at large research foundation.

Assignments: Letter and report in letter format to vendor; two persuasive memos to laboratory management.

Features:
- Outlining advantages of new equipment to secure approval to purchase.
- Maintaining strong business relations while registering complaints.
- Admitting error while maintaining professional stance.
- Prioritizing problems to get effective response without narrating the writer's whole experience.

Case 15. The Farnsworth Paper Works Case

Student role: Environmental engineer at paper manufacturing plant.

Assignments: Proposal to government official; memo to manager reporting results of telephone survey.

Features:

- Convincing government official to reverse position; providing documentation for company proposal.
- Drafting proposal for manager's signature; representing company stance that may conflict with personal view.
- Applying organizational patterns, such as problem-solution and cause-effect.

Case 16. The Industrial Relations Cases

Student role: Administrative assistant in industrial relations at manufacturing plant.

Assignments: Letters to public officials, union officers, and vendors; memos to management, staff, and hourly workers; short memos.

Features:

- Writing for manager's signature; constructing sensitive messages for wide distribution.
- Maintaining goodwill while conveying negative messages.
- Describing new procedures and physical layout; presenting benefits and plans.
- Adapting information for widely divergent audiences, including those with limited reading skills.

Case 17. A Missing Deposit Verification

Student role: Management trainee in credit department of large, regional bank.

Assignments: Letter handling customer complaint; standard complaint report form; report documenting complaint.

Features:

- Determining facts from inferences; deciding on a position from conflicting information without supervisory direction.
- Determining writer's ethical responsibility to customer and professional responsibility to employer.
- Documenting for audits and legal purposes.

Case 18. Specifying Materials for the Fire Marshal

Student role: Interior designer in design firm serving office and residential buildings.

Assignments: Letter describing graphic brochure; letter to sales representative; customer complaint letter.

Features:
- Interpreting technical graphics for lay audience; describing product advantages to users.
- Requesting technical information from sales representative.
- Detailing dissatisfaction with vendor to secure improved product specifications.

Case 19. Evaluating Polyglop

Student role: Engineer in process development at auto company.

Assignments: Product evaluation for technical manager and marketing executive; description of technical procedures for quality control; memos requesting tests.

Features:
- Producing two documents covering same data using parts of one for the other.
- Developing positive conclusions from less than ideal results.
- Determining limits of professional role in reporting.
- Combining organizational patterns in single report to satisfy reader needs.
- Formulating data in tables to support report purpose.

Case 20. Cashing in a Bright Idea

Student role: Quality assurance representative for the federal government.

Assignment: Report on employee suggestion form.

Features:
- Describing complex problem and defining it tactfully for audiences associated with it.
- Explaining proposed changes in detail.

- Adopting appropriate tone for low-level employee to persuade management to change procedures.

Case 21. Wastewater Treatment Planning

Student role: Field engineer for consulting firm on municipal project.

Assignments: Report in letter format to city officials; report to project manager according to federal guidelines.

Features:
- Reporting for larger, official document authored by others; making recommendations based on investigation.
- Presenting confusing and conflicting data for municipal officials and general public.
- Detailing physical changes to system for maintenance staff.
- Disclosing negative conditions and potentially embarrassing information without offending audiences involved.

Case 22. Facilities Planning for Southfork Public Schools

Student role: Facilities planner assigned to school building project by consulting firm.

Assignments: Request for information to computer center administrators; progress report to supervisor.

Features:
- Reconciling and interpreting data for comparison.
- Obtaining information from resistant audience; persuading audiences to modify positions.
- Summarizing project activity for progress report.
- Establishing professional credibility with new client.

Case 23. The Staff Development Case

Student role: Staff development nurse in training unit of large hospital.

Assignments: Policy and procedures; report; memo; communication strategy and oral report.

Features:
- Developing appropriate strategies for antagonistic audience; supporting contested claims adequately.
- Documenting procedures; formalizing policies.
- Revising documents written by others; using pieces of documents to prepare writing; following guidelines and document specifications.

Case 24. Evaluating a Cost Proposal for EMI Suppression

Student role: Engineer in systems engineering at federal contracts administration office.

Assignments: Report on contract costs to be used at negotiating session; memo requesting information; oral briefing.

Features:
- Questioning contract costs without adequate support; attempting to secure back-up information from contractor.
- Providing background orally at negotiating session; outlining complaints while securing cooperative atmosphere.
- Conforming to government reporting standards.

Case 25. Controlling Pollution

Student role: Associate refining engineer in technical services at oil refinery.

Assignments: Report in memo format to change plant procedures and set policy; memo summarizing meeting decisions; report with graphics describing maintenance improvements.

Features:
- Designing communications to deal with highly aggressive and antagonistic manager.
- Developing persuasive supporting material out of technical data.
- Describing mechanical changes for maintenance staff.

Case 26. The Absence-Reporting Case

Student role: Personnel compensation analyst for manufacturer of optical products.

Assignments: Graphics and oral presentation; reports and memos to superiors and subordinates; letters requesting information.

Features:

- Converting detailed tabular data for graphic display to support communication purpose.
- Proposing, defending, and explaining a change in procedure; securing cooperation of management and staff.
- Providing written and oral instructions accompanied by graphics.
- Analyzing conflicting and inadequate statistical data; selecting relevant information and developing an interpretation.

Case 27. The Model Plant at Clarkstone

Student role: Entry-level technical writer in precision parts manufacturing firm.

Assignments: Nine assignments including newsletter article, long report in letter format, cover memos, press releases, and speeches.

Features:

- Determining facts from contradictory documents and presenting a clear position; developing new document from other written materials.
- Creating a perspective on company activities acceptable to management, employees, and the writer.
- Translating technical information for general readers.
- Revising in response to critiques.

Case 28. The Computer Center Proposal

Student role: Administrative assistant to owner-operator of frozen foods company.

Assignments: Written summary of proposal presented in case dialogue; memo on own initiative to company owner; informational report on software selection; memos and letters evaluating and requesting information.

Features:

- Organizing unwieldy information about topic unfamiliar to writer for uninformed audiences.
- Conducting library research and relating it to information from telephone interview; integrating disparate information in report.

- Deriving and proposing written criteria for company evaluation of computer software and hardware.
- Securing co-workers' cooperation in planning for potentially threatening computer changeover.

Case 29. To Burn or Not to Burn

Student role: Hospital planner on special investigative assignment in state hospital complex.

Assignments: Long report defining problem for upper management; memos for the record and requesting information; short descriptive report; report revision; summary of government document.

Features:
- Sorting and interpreting conflicting data to define a complex internal problem.
- Incorporating technical descriptions and patterns such as cause-effect and problem-solution in a long, complex report.
- Meeting the needs of diverse personnel with varying interests and stakes in the report information.
- Dealing with masses of information obtained in interviews, some of which is missing, inaccurate, or contradictory.
- Reporting on activities with political consequences for staff and chief executives.

Case 30. Another Burning Issue

Student role: Hospital planner. (See Case 29.)

Assignments: Proposal for extensive hospital operations survey; memo requesting information.

Features:
- Explaining and defending proposed survey to reluctant administrator who must develop and carry it out.
- Writing with authority of upper management.

Case 31. The Motown Motors Case

Student role: Engineer in research and development at auto company.

Assignments: Long investigative report with recommendations; numerous internal communications including informal oral reports accompanied by graphics, memos, newsletter item, progress reports, log-book entries, minutes, and critique of draft.

Features:

- Reporting technical results in the context of interdepartmental politics; writing for powerful audiences with diverse and competing interests.
- Combining several organizational patterns, including problem-solution, comparison-contrast, technical description, and process in long, complex report.
- Detailing procedures for different audiences and purposes.
- Addressing multiple issues, such as technical feasibility, production ease, worker safety, and costs.
- Defending writer's technical solution against competing solution possibly favored by audience.